Imperial Islands

Perspectives on the Global Past

Anand A. Yang and Kieko Matteson
SERIES EDITORS

Imperial Islands

Art, Architecture, and Visual Experience in the US Insular Empire after 1898

Edited by Joseph R. Hartman

University of Hawai'i Press
Honolulu

Paperback edition 2022

Printed in the United States of America

Library of Congress Cataloging-in-Publication Data

Names: Hartman, Joseph R., editor.
Title: Imperial islands : art, architecture, and visual experience in the US insular empire after 1898 / edited by Joseph R. Hartman.
Other titles: Perspectives on the global past.
Description: Honolulu : University of Hawai'i Press, [2022] | Series: Perspectives on the global past | Includes bibliographical references and index.
Identifiers: LCCN 2021038694 | ISBN 9780824889203 (cloth) | ISBN 9780824890391 (pdf) | ISBN 9780824890407 (epub) | ISBN 9780824890414 (kindle edition)
Subjects: LCSH: Imperialism and architecture—United States. | Imperialism in art. | United States—Insular possessions.
Classification: LCC F970 .I66 2022 | DDC 720.9171/27309041—dc23
LC record available at https://lccn.loc.gov/2021038694

ISBN: 9780824890421 (paperback)

Cover art: "Well, I hardly know which to take first!" From the May 28, 1898, issue of the *Boston Globe.*

University of Hawai'i Press books are printed on acid-free paper and meet the guidelines for permanence and durability of the Council on Library Resources.

To those made invisible by empire,
and to all those who have yet to be seen

Contents

Acknowledgments

This volume is the result of an ongoing dialogue, begun in earnest over the past five years. The research presented here would have been impossible without vigorous discussions between colleagues, presentations of new research, and debates on the cultural and political stakes of US imperialism today. That dialogue, whether relaxed conversations over drinks or more formal presentations and writings, is interwoven into the arguments and research collected herein. To approach visual histories and geographies as vast and different as the islands of the Pacific and the Caribbean, as well as the imperial legacy of the United States, requires active listening, humility, and rigor. We would thus like to acknowledge the participants in various conferences and discussions held on these topics. These include the College Art Association in Los Angeles; the Latin American Studies Association in Barcelona; the International Planning History Society in Yokohama; the Humanities Department of the Universidad de Puerto Rico–Río Piedras; and the John F. Kennedy Institute of American Studies at the Freie Universität Berlin.

This project has also benefited from the financial support of various institutions and foundations, both in the process of producing the book and in the research and conferences leading up to the book's conception. These include the Art Research Institute at the University of California, Santa Cruz; the Bernice Pauahi Bishop Museum; Bonhams Fine Art Auctioneers and Valuers; the College of Arts and Sciences at Vanderbilt University; the College of Arts and Sciences at the University of Missouri–Kansas City; Frazer Fine Arts; the Graham Foundation for Advanced Studies in Fine Arts; the Hawaiian Historical Society; Pratt Institute; the Office of the City Historian of Havana; the Instituto de Historia de Cuba; Kamehameha Schools; the Smithsonian American Art Museum; and the Terra Foundation for American Art.

The editor and authors would also like to thank Masako Ikeda, Grace Wen, Ivo Fravashi, and the editorial staff of the University of Hawai'i Press for their support, as well the external readers whose critical and encouraging comments helped to strengthen the book manuscript. Any remaining mistakes in grammar, spelling, or fact are our own. The reader may notice that while spellings are generally consistent throughout the volume, there are a few cases where individual chapters handle terms differently (as exemplified by the many variations for the Cuban War of Independence, Spanish-American War, or War of 1898). These variances are a result of the interdisciplinary nature of this project, drawing from multiple backgrounds and knowledge communities. Particular individuals who have contributed insights and support to this project include Paulo Alcazaren, David Brody, Taína Caragol, John Milton Cooper Jr., Jorge Duany, Amanda Guzmán, Adam Herring, Mabiel Hidalgo, Kris Juncker, Laura Katzman, Kate Lemay, Gerard Lico, Eusebio Leal Spengler, Jorge Lizardi-Pollock, Craig McCormack, Rebecca Tinio Mckenna, Francisco Morán, Jorge Oller Oller, Louis Pérez, Jr., Cameron Seglias, Pamela Scott, Lisa Schrenk, Roberto Tejada, Eduardo Tejeira-Davis, and Augusto Villalon, among many others. Thank you.

Introduction

How to See an Empire

Joseph R. Hartman

The US Imperium's "Big Bang"

The horizons of the US empire expanded to a global scale with the "big bang" of the USS *Maine* in Havana's Bay on February 15, 1898. The US Navy's lightly armored battleship was then docked in Havana's harbor to protect American interests in war-torn Cuba. The ship exploded under mysterious circumstances. Over two-thirds of the 355 crew members died. Some perished in the blast. Others drowned. Late twentieth-century studies by US naval investigators revealed that an accidental fire likely caused the ship's ammunition stocks to explode. But in 1898, Americans largely believed Spanish saboteurs were to blame. The nation's "yellow journalists," well known for sensationalism and dubious sources, led the charge to unleash the dogs of war. "Remember the *Maine!* To Hell with Spain!" So went the popular slogan. Nineteenth-century news reports provided an eerie prelude to current debates over digital media, politically biased news, and the indiscernibility of fact from fiction. Images of "torpedo holes" (actually shots of the eclipse of 1896) were stirred in with all too real and disturbing photos of Cuban concentration camps.[1]

War seemed inevitable. Media pressure created a powder keg in 1898, which blended with the nation's mid-nineteenth century philosophy of "manifest destiny." That is to say, the project of US imperialism actually began nearly a century before the *Maine* exploded in Havana's harbor. In a letter penned to James Madison in 1809, Thomas Jefferson already envisioned Cuba as a part of the American Union. This was just six years after the continental borders of the United States expanded dramatically with the Louisiana Purchase of 1803.[2] By the 1830s, the US government had come to believe it had an inevitable role as the master nation of the Western Hemisphere. The government sanctioned the mass murder, cultural genocide, and displacement of hundreds of thousands of Indigenous peoples on the western "frontier," culminating with the infamous Trail of Tears. The US empire expanded further with the annexation of Texas from Mexico, ensuring the practice of slavery there in 1836. The United States' territorial aggressions reached an apogee when president James K. Polk instigated a border war with neighboring Mexico, resulting in the Treaty of Guadalupe Hidalgo in 1848.[3] Mexico not only officially recognized US rule in Texas but also agreed to sell California and other territories north of the Rio Grande (previously Río Bravo). Even as the United States' conquest of native and neighboring lands slowed, the socioracial hierarchies undergirding the young nation's growth persisted. Racist displays of peoples from the Americas, Africa, and Asia, which were a common part of the World's Fairs of the late nineteenth century, served to amplify those earlier colonialist philosophies of land acquisition and empire in the United States.[4]

That same school of thought led president William McKinley as he deployed the US Army to Cuba on April 25, 1898. US troops, including Theodore Roosevelt and his famously eclectic team of Rough Riders, were to join rebel forces to "liberate" Cuba and to avenge the victims of the *Maine.* "Cuba Libre! Free Cuba!" was their battle cry. It soon rang hallow. Already, by the start of the New Year in 1899, the US flag (not that of Cuba) officially replaced that of Spain atop Havana's Morro Castle. Cubans soon found themselves under the power of a new American imperium. Though the United States claimed to enter Cuba's revolutionary war as a liberator, it ultimately joined Spain in signing the Treaty of Paris with no Cuban representatives in attendance on December 10, 1898. By the end of the "Splendid Little War," the United States took possession of the remaining Spanish colonial holdings of the Caribbean and Pacific, including Cuba, Puerto Rico, Guam, and the Philippines. Spurred by military successes and dreams of a global empire, the United States annexed Hawai'i that same year. The United States expanded its island empire in the coming decades, establishing colonies in the US Virgin Islands, American Sāmoa, the Marshall Islands, and the Northern Mariana Islands in the twentieth century.[5] Subsequent wars and revolutions would create a very different set of historic relationships in each island's case, ranging from nationhood to statehood to thinly veiled colonialism.

Throughout the process, from 1898 into the present, visual objects and built environments shaped the US empire and the island cultures affected by it. New art, architecture, monuments, and infrastructure joined a new governmental order from the United States, redefining the ex-colonies of Spain and the island cultures of the Caribbean and Pacific now suddenly caught in the strategic scope of a growing imperial power. In asserting that argument, the essays in this volume contribute an important art historical, visual-cultural, architectural, and materialist voice to a growing body of scholarship on the US empire and the long-lasting effects of the War of 1898. There are many excellent histories written on these topics, including a few key studies focused on visual materials, most notably by contributors to this volume Bonnie Miller and Lanny Thompson.[6] In the broader field of history and American studies, there are also edited works, such as *The Colonial Crucible: Empire in the Making of the Modern American State* and *Archipelagic American Studies,* which trace the formations of the US empire before and after 1898.[7] Still other monographs, well pronounced in the Cuban histories of Louis Pérez Jr., excavate nationalist agendas in relationship to the US imperial project of 1898.[8] No study, however, has yet considered how art, architecture, and visual culture affected the new environments of US imperialism (and what arose from those changes) in the Caribbean and Pacific, both in the immediate aftermath of 1898 and well into the twentieth- and twenty-first centuries. Our volume thus offers a fresh look at the history of the US empire and the islands affected by it, one that asserts the agency of visual and spatial cultures in the development of insular identities through and against US colonial rule.

The built environments and visual documents produced in the new island territories of the United States created a visible confrontation between local Indigenous, African, Asian, Spanish and US imperial expressions. Yet, those material and visual histories often go unacknowledged in the scholarly discourse. If noted at all, objects of art, architecture, and visual culture tend to serve as uncomplicated "proof," rather than active and constituent agents, of imperial and local histories. This is especially so following the historiographic context of the empiricist archival tradition that came to dominate American studies in the Cold War era. Donald Pease and Amy Kaplan's edited volume *Cultures of United States Imperialism* helped spawn an important subfield in American studies by analyzing imperial politics and the politics of war through cultural media, resulting in a number of important monographs and anthologies in the last twenty years.[9] Our volume, however, engages equally with the nuanced discourses of visuality, materiality, space, and cultural conquest that have evolved in studies of imperialism and visual culture and material culture during the twenty-first century—and to which literary and historic models have traditionally not accorded much importance, taking visual objects as epiphenomena of ulterior intellectual, social, and economic prime movers.[10] That distance also helps explain the importance of our collection, as we look to test and inflect so many focal postcolonial and decolonial arguments (arising during the 1990s and at Columbus' quincentennial) in an arena that social criticism so far has been remarkably unable to penetrate, including the disciplines of art history and architectural history.

The authors of this volume propose to take new directions, using histories of visual culture and spatial experience as a rich and nuanced terrain for writing, envisioning, and revising US-American, Caribbean, and Pacific histories. Drawing from multiple disciplines, we join a recent movement to challenge the "culture of national amnesia around imperialism" in American art history, in particular.[11] As the Smithsonian's National Portrait Gallery prepares a groundbreaking exhibition in 2023 to mark the anniversary of the War of 1898 and the foundations of the American imperium, our book likewise suggests ways to *see* an empire that are all too often occluded in US visual studies and cultural histories.[12] Put otherwise, our essays offer a visual critique with more recent social histories, as in Daniel Immerwahr's widely acclaimed book *How to Hide an Empire,* which focus on retelling stories of insular communities largely erased from popular memory in the United States.[13] This volume therefore brings together scholars from around the globe whose works focus on individual case studies of visual and material history in the US insular empire. In weaving these art, architectural, and visual cultural essays from both sides of the United States' global empire together, we gain a much better understanding of the US imperial project, its far reaches, and ultimately its limits. Equally important, we advance our knowledge regarding the formations of national and local identities in the Caribbean and Pacific that emerged, in one form or another, from the "big bang" of 1898.

Those encounters between empire and local island cultures were many and widespread. In the realm of art, architecture, and visual culture, they could be subtle and bureaucratic. At other times, they were outwardly violent. Photographs and postcards of hanged bodies in the Philippines, as well as in Cuba and Puerto Rico, circulated widely at the turn of the century. They accompanied equally disturbing photos of grinning white male US soldiers, posed with a skull in each hand, and standing over the bone piles of conquered Spanish cemeteries.[14] Such scenes reiterated what Puerto Rican philosopher Nelson Maldonado-Torres later called the "non-ethics of war,"[15] or, as Mark Twain dubbed it at the time, "the taste of Christian butchers."[16] They testify to the employment of racist and sexist paradigms to justify the US insular empire. Ironically, those same "Christian" philosophies supported the Spanish colonial enterprise from 1492 until 1898. Nineteenth- and early twentieth-century discourses of race, racism, and eugenics haunted those scenes, too, which were created just thirty-three years after the US Civil War and the end of slavery.[17] And those images continue to reiterate a long and still significant history of racism in the United States today, witnessed in episodes of police and military violence against Black and Brown bodies at home and abroad.

More often found on the pages of eBay, and thus divorced from the coordinates of US imperial histories, those same images suggest both an ethical and a political impetus for rewriting the history of America's global empire in visual terms. That also includes visual and spatial histories of Indigenous resistance to empire, which deserve amplification. A distinctive sense of cultural identity emerged in the islands affected by the US empire after 1898. Public artists and architects of Cuba, Puerto Rico, and the Philippines in the 1920s, for example, strategically employed neoclassicism to assert local autonomy, while simultaneously navigating shared histories of Spanish colonialism and US imperialism. Designers of the Caribbean and Pacific drew not only from US models but also from Indigenous traditions as well as localized cultural inheritances from Africa, Asia, and Europe. After World War II, modernist styles took on similar valences in the civic monuments of Hawai'i and Guam. There, buildings echoed the United States' style known as federal modernism but also articulated local histories of Indigenous culture and political resistance. In the Hawaiian case, this included a legacy of sovereign rule, resulting in multiple rebellions against US imperial presence prior to and after 1898. Native Hawaiian artists such as Joseph Nāwahī were actively involved in those struggles at the turn of the century, alongside notable politicians and revolutionaries such as Robert Wilcox and the last Hawaiian queen, Lili'uokalani. Still today, in Guam, local Chamorro artists and artisans employ native signs and symbols, too, as they assert an Indigenous sense of space within the seemingly imperialist context of US military parades.[18] In all these cases, we find that visual and material objects are more than passive facts. They are instead active and dialogic agents, expressing not only US cultural ideals but also local resistance and assertions of indigeneity. Above all, those insular buildings, artistic objects, and visual performances tell stories that are often left unacknowledged in broader US histories. They suggest narratives that need to be *seen* as much as heard.

The essays collected in this volume aim to reveal those visual narratives, with the understanding that the issues raised here are ongoing and much farther-reaching than any one study could encapsulate. Our quest nonetheless is determined and ambitious. We seek to reconsider how the United States and the island cultures of the greater Caribbean and Pacific were transformed (for insular, domestic, and international audiences) through histories of visual, spatial, and material culture after 1898. That is, not only how the transition between Spanish, other European, Japanese, and US empires took shape but also the lasting aesthetic legacy of the US empire in the formation of national and regional identities in the Caribbean and Pacific, from 1898 to the present. Art, architecture, urban design, and visual culture are fundamental to that history. The relationship between the United States and the island cultures affected by its empire took physical and visual forms, ranging from maps to legislative buildings to photographs, easel paintings, and art leagues. The studies herein examine an equally wide range of geographies, temporalities, and material objects. Of the latter, these include cartography, photography, print culture, popular media, performance, urbanism, fine arts, and architecture.

A set of fundamental questions unites these essays. How does empire define vision and experience (and how do the shaping of vision and experience constitute empire)? How might images, materials, and built objects serve as a form of resistance to and negotiation of empire? Do images and built environments reflect, countersign, or challenge ideals of local or imperial cultures? And how do these images and constructed spaces respond to the cultural geography of the islands themselves? These original essays address, among other topics, the role of art and architecture in expressions of state power; forms of resistance and negotiation to US cultural presence; visual regimes of race and racism; and gendered representations of the United States and its "foreign" holdings in the Pacific and Caribbean. Some papers examine the consumption and production of art in support of US imperialism at the turn of the century and the proceeding decades. While others glance back to the nineteenth century prewar context and look forward, thinking of the ongoing significance of vision and experience in the US empire for Caribbean, Latinx, Pilipinx, and Pacific Island communities today.

The histories contained in this volume, moreover, remain obviously and sadly relevant. These case studies resonate with contemporary debates over racial injustice, the criminalization of immigration, climate change, global health, and the US empire today. The manifestations and consequences of the War of 1898 are manifold and still unfolding. We need list only a few: the United States' ongoing embargo of Cuba, which prevented the island most recently from receiving aid during the outbreak of the coronavirus, known as COVID-19, in 2020; the Puerto Rican debt crisis, and the US government's fumbling response after hurricane Maria in 2017, which made clear the unjust colonial relationship between the island and the mainland still today; ongoing debates around birthright citizenship and the preservation of Indigenous culture in the "unincorporated territories" of the United States, from American Sāmoa to the US Virgin Islands; the US imperial project's dehumanization of the nonwhite "Other," which sought to justify violence against Black and Brown bodies, at home and abroad, resulting most recently in massive public protests against racism and police brutality; and, finally, the history of migration that stemmed from US imperialism and that has come to redefine the nation. Still today, significant communities of Cubans, Puerto Ricans, Pilipinxs, and peoples of the Caribbean and Pacific Islands come to the United States' shores, symbolically guided by the visual icon of Lady Liberty's light, to escape political and economic strife, very often caused by the US government. The histories in this volume cannot pretend to predict the future of those conflicts, or the fate of insular communities affected by them. Nonetheless, these essays provide important and necessary insights into the role of visual culture, art, and architecture in our political and cultural present, telescoping back to the War of 1898 and expanding forward into the interwoven global and visual economies of today.

Imperial Islands and Visual Histories

The essays in this volume engage a wide-ranging set of nuanced visual, material, and architectural histories relating to particular case studies in the United States' insular empire, from 1898 to the present. The volume is arranged in four thematic groups, which also generally progress geographically and temporally. We begin with the outbreak of the War of 1898 and end with the ongoing consequences of US colonialism and imperialism today. Each section will attend to larger cultural themes in the US empire of the Caribbean and Pacific, from photography, vernacular architecture, and cultural heritage to environmentalism, tourism, and military interventions.

The first part, "Bone Machine: Mapping and Murder in America's Insular Empire," examines the overlay of visual culture, mapping, and representations of death and dying during and just after the War of 1898. The first two essays look at how mapping helped to construct public opinion around the United States' newly acquired global empire. The last two essays reveal how photography similarly economized and degraded the bodies of insular inhabitants, as a means of justifying state-sponsored violence deployed to expand that seemingly benign cartographic image of an American imperium.

Bonnie M. Miller's chapter "Map-Mindedness in the Age of Empire: The Role of Maps in Shaping US Imperial Interests in Cuba, Puerto Rico, and the Philippines, 1898–1904" opens our discussion through the special imperialist function of cartography, already evident in maps of Cuba, Puerto Rico, and the Philippines circulating in the US marketplace at the turn of the century. She argues that mapping offered a tool for justifying war and empire, allowing Americans to reconceive of US power in broader geographic terms. Lanny Thompson's "Military Cartography and the Terrains of Visibility: The Field Books of Lt. William H. Armstrong, Puerto Rico, 1908–1912" builds on the previous chapter's discussion of mapping and empire. His essay presents the illustrated works of lieutenant William H. Armstrong, produced for the Puerto Rico Regiment of Infantry. Armstrong's cartographic survey included not only topographic maps but also photographs, illustrations, postcards, and visual materials that documented the peoples, resources, and environments of Puerto Rico. Those works suggested terrains of visibility that mediated the landscape, its resources, and its people within the US colonial regime.

The next chapters turn from representing island geographies to the visual commodification and dehumanization of island inhabitants. In particular, the essays examine photographic representations of death and dying in Cuba,

Puerto Rico, and the Philippines, recorded during and just after the War of 1898. Krystle Stricklin's "With a Skull in Each Hand: Boneyard Photography in the American Empire after 1898" uncovers a widespread economy of death among US soldiers stationed in Manila, Havana, and San Juan after the War of 1898. As young, white, male soldiers hold the skulls of exhumed Cuban, Philippine, and Puerto Rican bodies in postcards and photographs, Stricklin too unearths deeper narratives of empire, subtle tactics of resistance, and the desensitizing strategies of the state. In "Sustained Constraint: Locating Corporeal Control through Archived Images of the Breath," Alejandro T. Acierto expands on this discussion. His essay excavates how the US colonial project was sustained through photographs of US colonizers in control of Black and Brown bodies, specifically their breath. Drawing on an archive of photographs and postcards of smoke inhalation, torture, and hangings during and after the Philippine-American-Spanish War of 1898, Acierto argues that US colonialists sought to contain Pilipinx bodies by controlling how or when they could breathe. That history continues to haunt the cultural politics of the Philippines and the Pilipinx diaspora, and it has corollaries with the United States' violent treatment of Black and Brown bodies today. Together, the four essays in this part show us how visual media engaged narratives of empire to justify state-sponsored violence and military expansions, from maps and field reports to photographs and popular media.

The second part, "Making Our Empire Beautiful: Archipelagos of Whiteness after 1898," shifts from military maps and war crimes to turn-of-the-century representations of built environments, landscapes, and people in the newly acquired territories of the US insular empire. The first two essays expose how painting, photography, and architecture served to reimagine the islands of the Caribbean and Pacific through white settler paradigms. The final two essays demonstrate how US city planners themselves responded to and transformed island landscapes, employing urbanism and architecture as political tools to articulate US power on a global scale.

In "Architecture, Domestic Space, and the Imperial Gaze in the Puerto Rico Chapters of *Our Islands and Their People* (1899)" Paul B. Niell analyzes the visual language of vernacular and local architecture in Puerto Rico. Niell argues that photographs (particularly those published in *Our Islands and Their People as Seen with Camera and Pencil* of 1899) served as a critique of colonial subjects through an interrelated critique of domestic architecture and spaces. Photos of dilapidated hovels and condescending captions conditioned the gaze of a US domestic readership to justify US architectural and military interventions. Stacy L. Kamehiro's essay "The Kilohana Art League: The Aesthetics of Annexation, 1894–1913" shows us how the genre of landscape painting was similarly employed to affect US politics. Her essay looks, in particular, at the

Kilohana Art League in Hawai'i, a largely white male organization founded by US annexationists in 1894 and active until 1913. The landscape paintings of the league excluded representations of local native communities, so as to recast the Hawaiian landscape as a white American one. The work of the Kilohana Art League, she argues, was essential in the political transformation of the Hawaiian Islands at the turn of the century from an independent, Native Hawaiian kingdom to a US territory.

Ian Morley's and Christopher Vernon's essays examine similar strategies of whitening and "Americanization" through urbanization. Both consider, among other sources, the plans drafted by famed US architect Daniel Burnham, aimed at transforming the urban and, by extension, moral character of the Philippines. In "The 1905 *Report on Proposed Improvements at Manila* by Daniel Burnham: The American Imperium in Textual and Urban Design Form," Morley takes Burnham's 1905 proposal to improve the city of Manila as a text to be analyzed in itself. Using Frankfurt school scholars such as Theodore Adorno, he reveals how Burnham bolstered US imperial agendas through the aesthetic concept of cultural evolution. Vernon's essay "Manufacturing American Imperial Landscapes in the Tropics: Baguio and Balboa" shifts our focus to examine how tropicality and topography transformed US City Beautiful plans into American imperial ones. His essay looks at the 1904 plans Daniel Burnham drafted of Baguio, a proposed US summer capital in the mountains of the Philippines. He then reveals how Burnham's plans informed those of Austin Lord for the American town of Balboa (1913) in the Panama Canal Zone, an isthmus region crucial to the maintenance of United States' insular empire in the Pacific and Caribbean. With these four essays taken together, we see that the discourse of "beauty," whether envisioned in the form of architecture, photography, paintings, urban plans, or texts, operates within combined logics of territorial expansion predicated on the dehumanization of imperial subjects.

The third part, "Negotiating Paradise: Design, Environment, and Identity in the Modern Era," continues our discussion on the aesthetic stakes of US imperial art, architecture, and urbanism. These three essays examine how political, commercial, and environmentalist agendas dovetailed with both US imperialism and emergent national identities during the early twentieth century. Erica Morawski's essay "Havana's Early Modern Hotels: Accommodating Colonialism, Independence, and Imperialism" focuses on the broader themes of nationalism and imperialism through two Cuban hotels—the Hotel Inglaterra and the Sevilla Biltmore Hotel. The design history of the hotels, she argues, participated in constructing images and experiences of Cuba during the US occupation and the early years of the Cuban republic under the United States' economic influence. Chris Balaschak's essay "Forest Formats:

Photography, Puerto Rico, and the *Caribbean Forester*" then takes us back to Puerto Rico to discuss the interweaving of forest preservation, industrial agriculture, and US colonialism in the 1930s and 1940s. He tells a story of a US forester and photographer, Frank Wadsworth, whose goal was to protect and revive Puerto Rican forests but whose troubling worldview ultimately conflated the island's citizens with their vulnerable environments. Joseph R. Hartman's essay "Making Islands Beautiful (Again?): Rhetorics of Neoclassicism in the US Insular Empire" broadens our scope further to look at the nuanced operations of neoclassical monuments in Cuba, Puerto Rico, and the Philippines. His essay argues against reading those civic monuments as mere mimicry of the US federal style but rather as expressions of "dreams of dreams," as designers simultaneously identified their works with universal symbols of democracy and with their specific Cuban, Philippine, and Puerto Rican cultures and geographies. These three essays thus ultimately show us how visual regimes of the United States inserted themselves subtly in the local political, commercial, and environmental contexts of the Caribbean and Pacific after 1898 and well into the twentieth century.

Those same military, political, and commercial interests of the United States visually transformed the greater Pacific region long after 1898, too, especially during and just after World War II. The fourth and final part, "War, Resistance, and Spatial Experience in the Pacific," focuses on two case studies of US military presence, visual culture, native space, and Indigenous resistance in the Pacific Islands. As the United States expanded its military foothold in the region after the War of 1898, the government invested heavily in infrastructural projects in imperial holdings such as Guam, American Sāmoa, the Northern Mariana Islands, and, with the start of the atomic age, the Marshall Islands. Brenda S. Gardenour Walter's essay "Colonial Concrete: American Architectures of Containment and Marshallese Reinscription of Space as Resistance" calls attention to the cultural politics of containment in the colonial constructions of the Marshall Islands, beginning in the 1940s. The concrete forms of the Kwajalein Atoll spoke to various discourses, including the official view of the Pacific Islands as "empty" space for US atomic tests, as well as the transculturation of native Marshallese cosmologies (views on health and the body) that resulted from and served to resist US imperial presence. Sylvia C. Frain's "Images of Empire and Visualizing Resistance in Guam (Guåhan)" builds on the previous chapter's discussion of US military presence in the Pacific by looking especially at military performance and resistance to it in Guam from the 1940s into the present. The visual and performative actions of young Indigenous troops during parades in honor of World War II serve to annually reassert US military and cultural dominance. Yet, even today, local Chamorro communities offer a subtle challenge to the US militarized empire through digital images of native space, especially seen in popular photos of the limestone *lattes,* which formed the foundation of ancient Indigenous homes. Frain thereby closes our volume with an important contemporary case of Indigenous resistance to the US military agenda, which speaks to the ongoing tensions between local cultural identity and the US imperial project still today.

All told, *Imperial Islands* seeks to review and reimagine the history and cultural politics of art, architecture, and visual experience in the post-1898 US empire. Our studies examine overlapping aspects of the United States' colonial project: the history of mapping and representing islands and their inhabitants in the US empire after 1898; the role of photography in degrading human subjects while also documenting and attempting to justify state-sponsored violence and war; the use of various media, from photography and architecture to landscape and easel painting, as a means to classify, contain, and reform colonial territories and subjects; the "beautification" and urbanization of island landscapes themselves as an imperial tool; the built and natural environments of desire and disaster that informed emergent national identities within and beyond the US island territories of the twentieth century; and, finally, how local cultural geographies were transformed by, and employed to resist, US military presence throughout the twentieth century and into the current era. Each of these essays offers a case study in the rhetorics of power, vision, and resistance in the United States' insular empire, looking back to the tragedy of 1898 and projecting forward to reveal new insights into our globally complex present.

Notes

1. For period discussion of faux torpedo holes, see Willis Fletcher Johnson, *America's Foreign Relations* (New York: Century, 1921), 250. Many thanks to Jorge Oller Oller for sharing this "fake news" history with me. During Cuba's War of Independence (1895–1898), the infamous Spanish governor Valeriano Weyler rounded up prisoners of war and civilian sympathizers into *campos de reconcentración*. These were, arguably, the first known examples of a concentration camp in the modern world, predating Nazi Germany by over thirty years. For more on this and the cultural politics of incarceration, generally, see Giorgio Agamben, *Homo Sacer* (Stanford, CA: Stanford University Press, 1998), 95.

2. Thomas Jefferson, "Thomas Jefferson to James Madison," April 27, 1809, accessed August 3, 2015, http://www.loc.gov.

3. On the connection between "frontier," empire, and Americanization worldwide, see Frederick Jackson Turner's 1893 speech, reprinted in *The Significance of the Frontier in American History* (Mansfield Centre, CT: Martino, 2014). For more recent discussion of territorial expansion and the long process of European and US colonialism as well as ongoing Indigenous efforts at decolonization, see Andrew Herscher and Ana María León, "At the Border of Decolonization," *E-Flux,* May 6, 2020, accessed May 21, 2020, https://www.e-flux.com. For

further discussion, see also Reginald Horsman, *Race and Manifest Destiny* (Cambridge, MA: Harvard University Press, 1981); Walter L. Williams, "United States Indian Policy and the Debate over Philippine Annexation: Implications for the Origins of American Imperialism," *Journal of American History* 66, no. 4 (1980): 810–831; and Paul Foos, *A Short, Offhand, Killing Affair: Soldiers and Social Conflict during the Mexican-American War* (Chapel Hill: University of North Carolina Press, 2002).

4. The World's Fair of 1893, commemorating the four-hundredth anniversary of Columbus' infamous voyage, may have had a particular resonance within white supremacist narratives. See, for example, Barbara J. Ballard, "African-American Protest and the Role of the Haitian Pavilion at the 1893 Chicago World's Fair," *Multiculturalism: Roots and Realities* (2002): 108–124; Robert W. Rydell, *All the World's a Fair: Visions of Empire at American International Expositions, 1876–1916* (Chicago, IL: University of Chicago Press, 2013); and Robert W. Rydell, "The World's Columbian Exposition of 1893: Racist Underpinnings of a Utopian Artifact," *Journal of American Culture* 1, no. 2 (1978): 253–275.

5. There are fourteen "unincorporated" island territories of the United States still today. Two additional islands, Nuevo Bank and Serranilla, are disputed between the United States and Colombia.

6. Bonnie M. Miller, *From Liberation to Conquest: The Visual and Popular Cultures of the Spanish-American War of 1898* (Amherst: University of Massachusetts Press, 2011); and Lanny Thompson, *Imperial Archipelago: Representation and Rule in the Insular Territories under US Dominion after 1898*. (Honolulu: University of Hawai'i Press, 2010).

7. Alfred W. McCoy and Francisco A. Scarano, eds., *The Colonial Crucible: Empire in the Making of the Modern American State* (Madison: University of Wisconsin Press, 2009); and Brian Russell Roberts and Michelle Ann Stephens, eds. *Archipelagic American Studies*. (Durham, NC: Duke University Press, 2017).

8. Louis A. Pérez Jr., *The War of 1898: The United States and Cuba in History and Historiography* (Chapel Hill: University of North Carolina Press, 2000). Louis A. Pérez Jr., *On Becoming Cuban: Identity, Nationality, and Culture* (Chapel Hill: University of North Carolina Press, 2008; and Louis A. Pérez Jr., *Cuba in the American Imagination: Metaphor and the Imperial Ethos* (Chapel Hill: University of North Carolina Press, 2008).

9. Amy Kaplan and Donald E. Pease, *Cultures of United States Imperialism* (Durham, NC: Duke University Press, 1999); of the authors influenced by that works, see the writings of Melani McAlister, Rebecca Adelman, David Lubin, and Roger Stahl, among others.

10. See especially Martin Jay and Sumathi Ramaswamy, eds., *Empires of Vision: A Reader* (Durham, NC: Duke University Press, 2014).

11. Maggie M. Cao, "What Is the Place of Empire in the History of American Art?," Bully Pulpit, *Panorama: Journal of the Association of Historians of American Art* 6, no. 1 (Spring 2020), doi.org/10.24926/24716839.9804; see also the writings of Anna Arabindan-Kesson, Shana Klein, Florina H. Capistrano-Baker, Stacy L. Kamehiro, J. M. Mancini, Taína Caragol, and Kate Lemay in the same issue; and the monographs of David Brody, *Visualizing American Empire: Orientalism and Imperialism in the Philippines* (Chicago, IL: University of Chicago Press, 2010); and J. M. Mancini, *Art and War in the Pacific World: Making, Breaking, and Taking from Anson's Voyage to the Philippine-American War* (Berkeley: University of California Press, 2018). For a recent conference dealing with similar themes, see Laura Katzman and Cameron Seglias, "1898: Imag(in)ing the Caribbean in the Age of the Spanish-American War," June 25, 2019, H-Soz-Kult: Kommunikation und Fachinformation für die Geschichtswissenschaftenin, accessed June 17, 2020, www.hsozkult.de.

12. See Taína Caragol and Kate Clarke Lemay, "Imperial Visions and Revisions," Bully

Pulpit, *Panorama: Journal of the Association of Historians of American Art* 6, no. 1 (Spring 2020), doi.org/10.24926/24716839.10096.

13. Daniel Immerwahr, *How to Hide an Empire: A History of the Greater United States* (New York: Farrar, Straus and Giroux, 2019).

14. See chapters 3 and 4 of this volume; for parallel examples of commodifying death along the Mexican-US border, see Claudia E. Zapata, "Walter Horne's 'Triple Execution' Postcards: Death on the Border," *Panhandle-Plains Historical Review* 88 (Fall 2017): 49–63.

15. Nelson Maldonado-Torres, "On the Coloniality of Being," *Cultural Studies* 21, no. 2 (2007): 247–260.

16. A transcript of Twain's speech appeared in the *Boston Herald* in 1900. For a gathering of Twain's writings on imperialism, see the Hispanic Division of the Library of Congress' presentation "The World of 1898: The Spanish-American War," accessed May 21, 2020, http://www.loc.gov.

17. Laura Briggs, *Reproducing Empire: Race, Sex, Science, and US Imperialism in Puerto Rico* (Berkeley: University of California Press, 2003), 60–95; and Paul A. Kramer, "Race-Making and Colonial Violence in the US Empire: The Philippine-American War as Race War," *Diplomatic History* 30, no. 2 (2006): 169–210.

18. See chapters 6, 11, 12, and 13 of this volume. For more on the history of the Hawaiian Kingdom and its resonance for native resistance efforts, see D. Māhealani Dudoit, "Against Extinction: A Legacy of Native Hawaiian Resistance Literature," in *Voices of Social Justice and Diversity in a Hawai'i Context* (Leiden: Brill, 2019), 45–62; and David Forbes, ed. *The Diary of Queen Liliuokalani of Hawaii, 1885–1900* (Honolulu, HI: Hui Hanai, 2020).

Part I

Bone Machine

Mapping and Murder in America's Insular Empire

One

Map-Mindedness in the Age of Empire

The Role of Maps in Shaping US Imperial Interests in Cuba, Puerto Rico, and the Philippines, 1898–1904

Bonnie M. Miller

After going to war against Spain in 1898 to secure Cuba's independence, president William McKinley resolved in the peace negotiations to acquire all of Spain's remaining colonial holdings: Cuba, Puerto Rico, the Philippines, and Guam. McKinley's personal narrative of how he came to this decision, particularly with regard to the Philippines, centered on the optics of the map. When speaking with a group of clergymen, he recounted the decision-making process as one of great emotional turmoil: "I walked the floor of the White House night after night until midnight; and I am not ashamed to tell you, gentlemen, that I went down on my knees and prayed Almighty God for light and guidance more than one night. And one night late it came to me this way—I don't know how it was, but it came." He said the decision to acquire the Philippines at last became clear and then he "slept soundly"; he woke the next morning and his first action was to call upon the chief engineer of the war department (the mapmaker) to put the Philippines on the map of the United States. Presaging Glinda the Good Witch's famous words from the 1939 film in reference to the ruby slippers,[1] McKinley told the mapmaker, "There they are, and there they will stay," and then concluded, "while I am president!"[2] It matters little whether or not his personal account was true; his broadly circulated story stipulated the map as the instrument to signal finality. Once the map changed to indicate US dominion, the deed was done. As cartography expert John Rennie Short has argued, "Maps of a nation-state are not just depictions of surface area or even representations; they also embody the nation-state. Maps do not simply reflect or represent: they are."[3] Maps were more than tools for visualizing space; they were symbols of American power that represented the permanence of shifting imperial domains across the globe.

The reality was that at the start of the Spanish-American War, most

Americans had little to no knowledge of the geography or history of the Philippines. This isn't surprising given that prior to the war, neither the press nor the McKinley administration had set the expectation that this war would be fought in or involve the Philippines. Rather, for all intents and purposes, all discussions of war prior to the official declaration centered on liberating Cuba.[4] Based on ongoing reports of the humanitarian crisis in Cuba and the US naval board's findings that an external cause (probably a mine) was responsible for sinking the USS *Maine* in Havana Harbor in February 1898, killing 266 Americans on board, McKinley resolved to intervene militarily in Cuba's struggle for independence from Spain. The press gave consideration to the Philippines only after war was already declared, with the unexpected announcement that admiral George Dewey was in Manila Bay engaging the Spanish fleet in the first days of May. One month after the war had begun, *Gunton's Magazine* observed, "So far as the western hemisphere is concerned the Philippine Islands are practically an unknown empire.... Many, indeed, would have had difficulty in locating the islands correctly until the war maps began to appear in the daily press. It is this unknown region that has, for all practical purposes, suddenly become a possession of the United States."[5] The United States was at war in unfamiliar territory, and this kicked into gear a demand for cartographic information to help Americans understand where the action was taking place, spurring an interest in maps that bordered on popular obsession.

During and after the Spanish-American War, there was a growing expectation that for the nation to govern colonies successfully, informed citizens needed to have intimate knowledge of their locations and relative distances to US coastlines and other world powers. One could express this new imperial identity through gaining a sense of geographic or spatial consciousness by viewing maps, developing what some have called "map-mindedness." Psychologist David Uttal describes this mindset as "the internalization of a map-like view of the world," which enables viewers to "think about space in map-like ways, even if they are not looking at a map at the time."[6] Demonstrating map-mindedness did not necessarily require one to achieve actual geographic mastery. We see evidence of this phenomenon in the vast production and consumption of maps of America's newest possessions that filtered through American popular culture in this period. As Camilo Arturo Leslie has shown, maps functioned to collapse the distance between the abstraction of territories far away and the everyday lived experience of viewers, making them feel part of the political community.[7]

For readers, the means to claim geographic knowledge was not just to view maps and to think in geographically minded terms but also to purchase them and display them: to perform map-mindedness as a consumer. As Diane

Dillon's study of map consumption contends, "Maps have often been sold and used to embellish the interiors of homes, offices, and public buildings, where they could project the social ambitions, local and national pride, and artistic tastes of individuals and communities."[8] In the late 1890s, many newspapers, railroads, and retailers capitalized on popular interest in maps to sell their goods and services by commissioning maps that they could offer to customers with purchase or subscription. It has been well argued that maps help create and legitimize forms of knowledge in order to facilitate a sense of imperial belonging; I posit here that this cartographic sensibility was closely linked to consumer practices, such that performing the role of an imperial citizen was as much about evincing interest in war and empire as it was about becoming a newspaper reader, a traveler, and a consumer of books, atlases, and other goods. As an editorialist of the *Hawaiian Star* observed, "A Chicago map publisher states in a recent interview that his firm could scarcely print enough maps of Porto Rico, Hawaii, and the Philippines, while of Cuba there have been more maps sold in the last twelve months, than in twelve years before. Bankers and merchants are also buying fine atlases and high priced maps which were formerly only supplied to large universities."[9] The editorialist was making an important observation about how the consumer base for purchasing maps was changing, extending beyond more specialized audiences. What is more, the repeated refrain that maps were in high demand became a self-fulfilling prophecy; as editors told their readers that maps were highly sought-after commodities, it boosted the cultural capital of map consumption.

Many historians point to the powerful influence of the press in shaping American foreign policy in this period, but the role of maps has not been adequately explored. Mark Monmonier's study of newspaper maps in this period demonstrates that the press acted as society's "cartographic gatekeeper and its most influential geographic educator."[10] As *Century Illustrated Magazine* noted in 1902, "Whether trade follows the flag, certainly knowledge does. What the geography is doing for the school-boy, the newspapers and magazines are doing for the adult. . . . In short, geography has advanced in dignity to a place of first importance in the more-or-less-exact sciences."[11]

Cartography enjoyed an epistemological cachet and scientific aura that masked the biases and selectivity contained within its making, thus allowing maps to be particularly effective visual forms of propaganda. Maps were less conspicuous as propagandistic texts because readers saw them at best as scientific and objective, or at the very least, straightforward and unmediated, because their techniques of representation were not explicit. Although some maps, like published atlases, made attempts to utilize methods of scale and measurement, all maps could become political instruments, for the process of transforming three-dimensional space into a two-dimensional representation inevitably involved simplification, distortion, and selectivity.[12] Newspaper maps, in particular, were often grossly inaccurate, though the cultural perceptions of maps as scientific tools may have primed viewers to read them without skepticism. This chapter looks at how maps were produced, distributed, and consumed in order to explore the cultivation of this ethos of map-mindedness in the print culture of the Spanish-American War and its aftermath. It will examine the printed maps of America's new acquisitions as well as how maps figured into iconography and advertising of the period.

Maps: Nineteenth-Century Cartographic Culture

Most maps that circulated prior to the American Revolution had been imported, but with independence came the rise of a domestic cartographic industry that gave visual shape to the nation's territorial growth and political development. Over the course of the nineteenth century, the professionalization of disciplines such as geography and history lent greater legitimacy and credibility to maps as critical scientific tools.

Westward expansion coupled with advancements in printing and transportation fueled public demand for maps. One of the greatest cartographic achievements of the early nineteenth century was William Clark's map made during his expeditions with Meriwether Lewis between 1806 and 1810, charting unknown areas of the Missouri and Columbia Rivers as well as the Northern Rockies. By the 1820s, lithography replaced older methods of engraving and etching, facilitating a wider dissemination of maps. Such innovations created a thriving market for Mexican-American War prints, which offered topographical views of varying degrees of accuracy of Mexico and the new lands seized by the Treaty of Guadalupe Hidalgo. Maps gained visibility in the mid-nineteenth century for specific purposes: to map routes for the transcontinental railroad, to chart the extension of slavery, and to map out the topography of the territories newly acquired from Mexico. Newspaper maps were rare prior to the Civil War, but innovations in printing illustrations, such as the use of steam-powered rotary printing presses and wood engraving, led some printers, particularly in the North, to publish maps during the war. It was during the Civil War, then, that many American readers became acquainted with seeing printed maps of battlefields in the news pages, though these were less frequent as the war drew on.[13] Commercial publishers in the North also satisfied popular interest in maps by selling maps produced by lithographers, some of which were hand-colored. Topographical engineers supported both the Union and Confederate Armies to provide generals with reliable maps, but the South lacked adequate personnel and supplies, and both sides had a limited capacity to reproduce the maps that were made. While it is difficult to quantify the influence that maps had on Abraham Lincoln's presidency, he clearly valued maps as a strategic asset during the civil conflict. Artist Francis Bicknell Carpenter, who stayed in the White House for six months, claimed to have repeatedly observed Lincoln perusing maps. This prompted Carpenter to depict a map as a background detail in his famous painting *First Reading of the Emancipation Proclamation of President Lincoln* (1864). Similarly, John Sartain's mezzotint *Abraham Lincoln* (1864) pictured the president seated at his desk, with two large wall maps beside him (rolled up on the floor).[14]

While continental expansion helped to inspire popular interest in maps earlier in the nineteenth century, it was the prospect of overseas expansion that drove interest in the late 1890s. The Spanish-American War was certainly not the origin of America's fascination with maps, but the overseas context of the war intensified their appeal in unprecedented ways. The importance of maps registered in both military practice and popular culture: its military necessity was paramount given the mandate to defeat Spain and suppress ongoing insurgency; likewise, newspaper and other popular accounts utilized geographical knowledge as a means of bringing Americans into the military and civil projects of empire. Mapping was not merely a visual aid; it promoted a way of thinking, of conceiving war and empire within both a global and a geographic framework. As Martin Brückner has shown, "thinking cartographically" was a skill that had to be learned and habituated, and over the course of the nineteenth century, many Americans gained greater facility and access to maps as a medium of communication.[15] During the war with Spain and its aftermath, the combination of maps produced for popular consumption and by the government for military purposes fostered a cartographic culture that was integral to shaping public conceptions of America's new colonial acquisitions.

The nation's imperial venture followed a period of great transformation in the printing industry that made the mass production of maps more efficient and affordable. William Rand, a Boston-trained printer who opened a printing shop in Chicago, later partnered with an Irish immigrant printer, Andrew McNally. They innovated cost-saving map-making techniques to replace the more cumbersome method of using copper-engraved plates. Rand McNally and Company used wax engraving and electrotyping, or relief line engraving, in a method called "cerography" that gave it a distinct advantage over its competitors. Cerography allowed for map plates to be easily updated and for both type and graphics to be produced on the same plate. This significantly reduced production costs, allowing for cheaper retail prices and transforming maps from what had been an elite craft to a mass-produced commodity.[16]

At the turn of the twentieth century, Rand McNally—along with competitors George F. Cram, Caleb Hammond, and the National Geographic Society—dominated the market for public map consumption as well as government use, which had no formal mapping agencies of its own until World War II. The distribution networks of Rand McNally and its competitors consisted primarily of booksellers, railway agents selling at train stations, and the popular press.[17] By the last quarter of the nineteenth century, owning an atlas became fairly commonplace. Many consumers may have opted to purchase a new atlas after the Spanish-American War in order to possess one with additional maps and material on the colonies. Rand McNally published a number of new atlases immediately following the war, including *Rand McNally & Co.'s New Imperial Atlas of the World* (1899) and *Rand McNally & Co.'s Universal Atlas of the World* (1899). Although commercial atlases did not take an overt stance on the imperial question, they supplemented maps of the colonies with descriptions of the natural resources of the islands and demographic information that reinforced economic rationales for acquisition.

Newspaper maps were qualitatively different from the ones printed in commercial atlases: the former were not drawn to scale and typically had much less detail than atlas maps. Some appeared improvised, as if drawn by a correspondent on the scene. As David Brody's study of Philippine-American War map consumption has shown, "simplified representations of the islands were far more desirable in the pages of the popular press [compared to published atlases], where readers did not want to be taxed with details."[18] At the turn of the twentieth century, the technology had just become available for editors to share maps and hand-drawn illustrations with other papers, resulting in widespread reprinting of the same maps in different newspapers. German immigrant Ernest Hummel developed the telediograph in the late 1890s, allowing for the exchange of line drawings over the wire via a varnish-coated foil scribed with a stylus. By 1899, a syndicate of five newspapers—the *Boston Herald*, the *Chicago Herald-Times*, the *New York Herald*, the *Philadelphia Inquirer*, and the *St. Louis Republic*—had already purchased rights to Hummel's instrument, and interest grew quickly.[19] Now reproducible and without the need for spatial accuracy or minute specificity, newspaper maps could easily be deployed for ideological purposes.

The project of empire building and the demand for maps went hand in hand. Public fixation with maps was growing in Europe as well. For Americans, what differentiated the map craze at the turn of the twentieth century from earlier interest were the technological advances that enabled mapmakers to reproduce maps cheaply, so that maps could be obtained at little cost. Henceforth, maps became highly desired household consumables. This is the same period that Kristin Hoganson noted for its swell of "cosmopolitan domesticity," a rise in "bourgeois householders' enthusiasm for imported goods and styles perceived to be foreign, in large part because of their foreignness."[20] Although produced domestically, map books of the colonies exuded themes of far-off places, exploration, and conquest; as household commodities, they could be used for personal reference, patriotic decoration, or conversation starters. Displaying maps in the home was a cultural performance that valorized the social currency of geographic knowledge as a way to signal investment in the nation's rise to global power. Tourism was also on the rise, and maps promoted travel via the nation's expanding rail lines. The mission of mapmakers would change significantly with the mass-production of automobiles and the establishment of a nationwide highway system later in the twentieth century, as mobility needs changed. But at the turn of the twentieth century, maps gained stature in both public and private settings and were commodities that enabled consumers to fashion themselves as politically informed, cosmopolitan, and cultivated at a remarkably accessible price point.

Maps: Doing the Work of Empire

The semantics of empire were of critical importance to President McKinley's expansionist foreign policy, as he contended with anti-imperialist dissent at home and ongoing insurgent resistance abroad. Historians have shown that his administration preferred to classify the new possessions as "territories" rather than "colonies," invoking the metaphor of expansion rather than colonialism in order to justify the exceptionalism of American imperialism in contrast to other empires. Government maps, which newspaper maps often reproduced, facilitated this ideological understanding.[21] The general land officer of the Department of the Interior announced in October 1899 the creation of a new national map that included the colonial additions. In order to fit all the colonies on the two-dimensional map, it showed them detached. Mapmakers found space by removing Mexico and placing the Philippine archipelago, Hawai'i, and Guam in the Gulf of Mexico.[22] Viewers could see the United States and its new territories in one visual frame, making it appear as if these new territories were extensions of the continental United States rather than entities located at a great distance.

The press regarded McKinley's commissioning of land surveys and maps as evidence of the nation's readiness to govern overseas territories. An editorialist for the *Arizona Republican* wrote about Cuba, "When a man gets so far along as to want a photograph of his girl, she is justified in expecting a proposal. Now that the United States is preparing to make a map of Cuba for our own use the Cubans are warranted in supposing our intentions must be growing serious."[23] In other words, committing to the work of map making was seen as engaging in the "serious" work of governing colonies; as Short emphasized, "By mapping a territory, the state reinforces its claim to power and dominance. Its claim to sovereignty is partly vindicated by its ability to map and represent the territory."[24] Conversely, Spain's paucity of accurate, detailed maps became another indicator of its ineptitude. "This lack of maps and charts [of Cuba] shows the quality of Spanish rule as clearly as do the murders of non-combatants or the wholesale misappropriation of public funds about which every correspondent has so much to say," claimed an editorialist of a Texas newspaper.[25] Editorialists blamed Spain's inability to suppress Cuban insurgency on its "unfamiliarity with trails," such that they "ventured into obscure trails" and "were often surprised by the lurking rebels." According to one editorialist, the US government would be better equipped to maintain local control because it prioritized cartographic knowledge, a key element of successful occupation. The editorialist responded to critics concerned with an escalation of US military commitment abroad by saying that American-made maps of the colonies would be "a better guaranty of peace" than "a reinforcement of many thousands of men would be."[26]

The work of military leadership, moreover, was largely conceived of as map driven. After Congress declared war against Spain in April 1898, newspapers reported of the new "war chamber" created for President McKinley, a special room fit with maps of Cuba and the West Indies along with telegraphic instruments by which the president might receive updates from abroad. Frances Benjamin Johnston took a photograph of the room in 1898, foregrounding the presence of the map (figure 1.1). In 1901, the war room underwent a critical transformation, with the addition of a new map twenty feet long by eight feet wide containing movable representations of the world's armies and fleets in miniature form. Nationwide press described the visual space of McKinley's "war room" in great detail, enabling readers to picture the commander-in-chief at work, with maps as his critical tools indicating topography, cable lines, coaling stations, and commercial routes. The same month that newspapers reported on the creation of this war room, the *Boston Globe* published a multipage map of the Atlantic coast alongside images of the nation's major naval vessels. Next to the map, it directed, "Any reader cutting them [pictures of the naval vessels] out and saving this page will be enabled to pin each vessel in its proper place on the map and follow all the future movements of the fleets intelligently."[27] The *Globe* essentially provided readers with the tools to create their own interactive maps, prioritizing geographic thinking in how readers processed war news.

McKinley's official "war room" map was color-coded by empire for the major world powers, with the US empire in blue. McKinley had the ability to use different color pins to track movements and mark out key places. According to the *Washington Evening Star,* "The great map will be absolutely up to

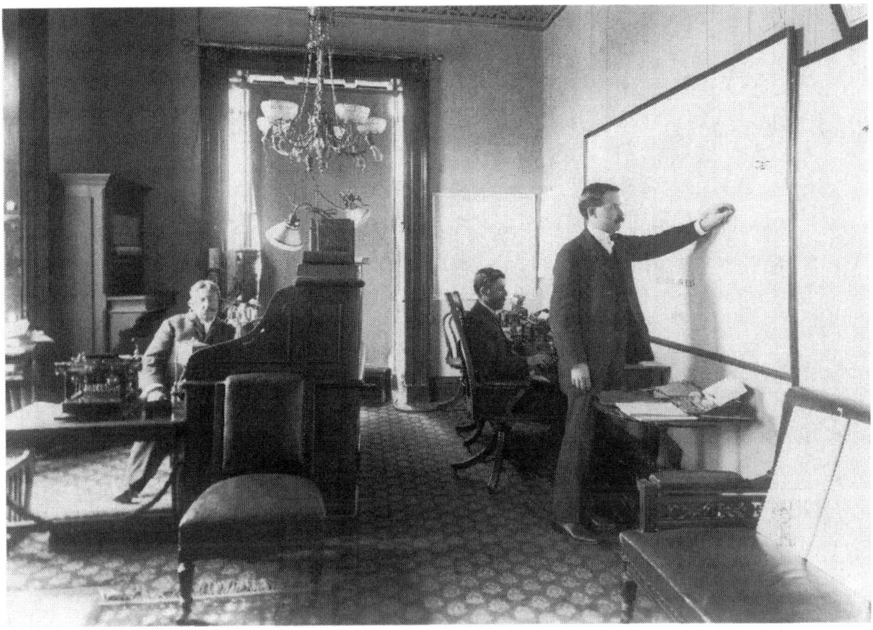

Figure 1.1. Frances Benjamin Johnston, *Temporary Spanish-American War Room, Second Floor White House Office, Washington, DC, 1898.* Courtesy of the Library of Congress, LC-USZ62–105703.

date, geographically, to the hour when it is put in place. It is believed to be the only map in the world, large or small, which today shows in exactness and completeness of detail all of the political sub-divisions of the newly reorganized world." The *Indianapolis Journal* wrote, "Over the face [of the map], as though it were a great chess board, miniature representations of the armies and fleets of the world will be moved, while skilled geographers and cartographers will continually alter it to represent changes of boundaries, new cable lines, interoceanic canals and whatsoever may alter the political complexion of mother earth."[28] The press described the significance of the map, which covered the western side of the room, as visualizing the world into a set of imperial configurations, impressing upon readers that the work of empire positioned cartographic knowledge at its center.

Wartime press coverage placed great value on cartography to defeat Spain and ensure a successful and peaceful transition to US occupation. Numerous press reports conveyed to readers the necessity for new government cartographic projects, such as the US Coast and Geodetic Survey, to map out the coasts, harbors, and interiors of the islands to aid in pacification; the construction of railroads, bridges, and telegraphs; and the promotion of commercial enterprises in agriculture and mining.[29] In so doing, news media framed cartographic knowledge as critical for the nation to achieve its foreign policy objectives, which in turn added to the aura of maps as essential commodities for readers to stay informed.

Maps: Informing the Citizenry during Wartime

Advertisements and editorials pitched the critical importance of map literacy in order for readers to stay abreast of war news. An advertisement for the *Advocate and News Standard Atlas* stated, "Every reader is recommended to procure one at once, and thus be able to watch the strategic movements of our army and navy from the vantage point of knowledge." For one to stay informed, a spatial and geographic understanding of the theaters of war was deemed requisite for participation in the political community. Not seeking out that literacy was a mark of social failure. An advertisement for the new *Century Atlas,* which featured maps of Cuba and the Philippines, printed a letter written to the editor of the *New York Tribune* asking when the exact date of the Battle of Manila Bay was since admiral George Dewey's fleet crossed the "international day line [*sic*]" as it sailed from Hong Kong to Manila. The editor in response chastised the reader: "If the writer of the above letter had owned the new CENTURY ATLAS he would not have needed to write to a newspaper for such information."[30]

Driving such advertisements was the pervasive belief that Americans were geographically ignorant. According to the *Anaconda Standard,* "No doubt that the [war] department is kept busy in its study of geography: so utterly foreign to us is all this business that the American people have next to no idea where their countrymen are fighting. We believe it to be true that if to-day the census could be taken, it would be found that not two per cent of the intelligent, newspaper-reading public in this country has any clearer view of the localities in which our soldiers have been fighting than they have of the whereabouts of the mountains on the moon—if the moon has mountains."[31] Geographic awareness of territories such as the Philippines or Puerto Rico had been of little consequence to most Americans before the war; recognizing their place on the map became essential knowledge only when the United States began thinking of itself as a global power in competition with other empires.

The war spurred the popular consumption of maps and study of geography. In 1903, the Department of the Interior, under the direction of the commissioner of the General Land Office, issued for sale a map of the country with its new acquisitions, using the latest information obtained through military, naval, and commercial channels. It was specifically intended for sale to schools and other civic institutions. The *Washington Times* noted that the

Spanish-American War "has given an impetus to the study of geography in all the schools, and maps of Cuba and the other scenes of action are suspended on the walls of the rooms" and "have been closely studied daily by the pupils."[32] The War of 1812 had also been a catalyst for maps to become a regular fixture in American schoolrooms, and over the course of the nineteenth century, geography curricula trickled down from universities to secondary schools throughout the country. As the nation expanded westward, school maps changed accordingly. Once again, mapmakers responded quickly following the US victory in 1898 to create new maps to highlight the nation's overseas territorial gains. Prisons, too, were institutions in which maps could serve educational functions. At Leavenworth prison in Kansas, the warden honored the nation's victories in the Spanish-American War by lecturing the prisoners on governing the nation's new colonies using maps of Cuba, Manila, and Puerto Rico.[33]

Map literacy was not only a growing expectation for educating Americans but was also a requisite for proficient journalism. In July 1898 a *Washington Times* editorial scolded the Associated Press for a mistake in its coverage of the US military landing into Puerto Rico, in which reporters confused Bahía Honda in Cuba with the city of Ponce in Puerto Rico. The *Times* praised those editors who had "been wise enough to preserve the maps of Cuba and Porto Rico published in *The Times*" and had "escaped many of the blunders which the less provident and foresighted war editors allow to go through." Similarly, the savvy readers of the *Times,* with their maps in hand, would "be amazed by such a ludicrous and exasperating mistake" as they had seen in the report. In a period of "yellow" journalism when newspapers closely scrutinized their competitors for sensationalism and bias, maps were one factor that differentiated the "wise" editors and informed readers from those whose cartographic ignorance allowed inaccurate reports to seem credible. Rival newspapers pitched cartographic knowledge as a sign of journalistic superiority, and it became popular practice for editors to point out the geographic errata in reports of their competitors. In its coverage of military developments in Cuba, the *Daily Kentuckian* praised its maps for providing "the first correct representation of the scene of war that has been given to the readers of any local paper in this section."[34]

Nonetheless, newspapers and periodicals published (and reprinted) a whole slew of maps that were fundamentally inaccurate. One of the most common maps printed in the popular press conveyed a sense of spatial distance between the territories and coastlines of the United States and other world powers such as Japan or China. Figure 1.2, a map reprinted in many papers, was crudely drawn without attention to scale and offered little detail of the countries or territories. Instead, the map collapsed distance between geographic entities so that they could all exist within a two-dimensional plane. The perspective of distance was significantly distorted; the distance from the eastern coastline to Puerto Rico appeared greater than the distance between the Pacific coastline and Hawai'i. If the map's nationalistic sentiments were not blatant enough, the American flag further framed it in patriotic trappings.

In a map drawn and engraved for the *Ohio Farmer* magazine (figure 1.3), the illustrator similarly distorted the reality of relative sizes, depicting Cuba at three times its actual size and shrinking the size of the Pacific Ocean, making the West Coast of the United States appear close to Hawai'i and the Philippine Islands. While Hawai'i wasn't acquired directly from Spain, the Senate successfully passed its annexation during the Spanish-American War, despite earlier repeated failures, on the justification that its location was valuable militarily. The dashed lines denoting mileage on the map made certain trade and military routes appear natural and inevitable, as straight shots across the ocean or connecting certain ports. Such distortions could convey potential arguments for both colonial acquisition and Hawaiian annexation by establishing proximity as it relates to matters of trade or foreign affairs. An illustrated article in the *Richmond Times* (figure 1.4) depicts a businessman, with his back toward the viewer, studying a map of this type, as these maps appeared with slight variation in many publications. Captioned "Choosing His Future," the article stated, "To the soldier of commercial fortune who is ever on the watch for new fields to conquer, the three new island possessions of the United States present an attractive prospect." Emboldened by the text, the maps conveyed the new business opportunities that acquisition could afford. To this end, insurance firms advertised in the press that they would offer patrons free maps of Cuba and the surrounding islands to help assess financial risk and spur foreign investment.[35]

Though few and far between, there were some voices that took issue with these cartographic inaccuracies. The periodical the *Watchman* on multiple occasions sought to call readers' attention to how maps were being manipulated for propagandistic purposes, expressing its deep concern that the maps were giving readers the "radically false impression" that, as one editorial put it, "Manila is a natural stepping-stone from our Pacific coast ports to the Chinese Empire." It quipped that the maps "almost make you believe that the shortest route from New York to Boston is by the way of Manila."[36] The *Watchman* feared that most readers did not have the geographic expertise or skeptical eye to even think to question the information they received in these maps.

While one cannot generalize how all readers interpreted and consumed maps, the evidence suggests that the proliferation of maps encouraged readers to think geographically in conceptualizing the nation's imperial project. Henry Martyn Field, clergyman and editor of the New York periodical the *Evangelist*,

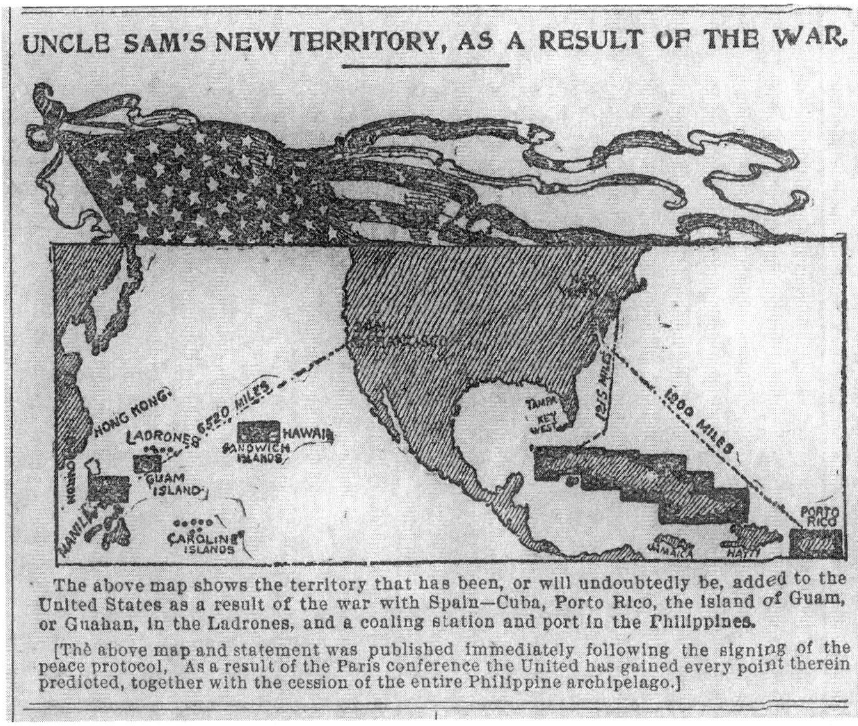

UNCLE SAM'S NEW TERRITORY, AS A RESULT OF THE WAR.

The above map shows the territory that has been, or will undoubtedly be, added to the United States as a result of the war with Spain—Cuba, Porto Rico, the island of Guam, or Guahan, in the Ladrones, and a coaling station and port in the Philippines.

[The above map and statement was published immediately following the signing of the peace protocol. As a result of the Paris conference the United has gained every point therein predicted, together with the cession of the entire Philippine archipelago.]

Figure 1.2. *San Juan Islander,* December 8, 1898, 1. Courtesy of the San Juan Historical Museum (Friday Harbor, WA). Many other newspapers published this same map; for example, see the *Atlanta Constitution,* August 1, 1898, 1.

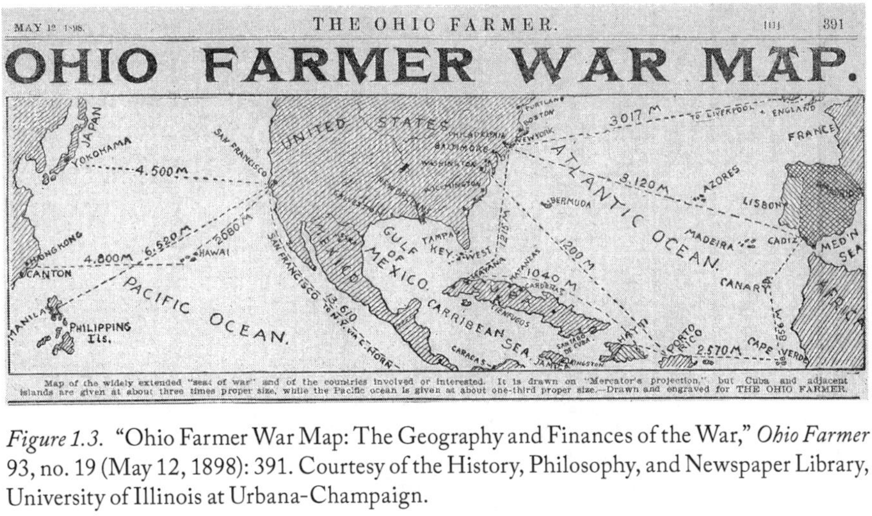

MAY 12 1898. THE OHIO FARMER. 391

OHIO FARMER WAR MAP.

Map of the widely extended "seat of war" and of the countries involved or interested. It is drawn on "Mercator's projection," but Cuba and adjacent islands are given at about three times proper size, while the Pacific ocean is given at about one-third proper size.—Drawn and engraved for THE OHIO FARMER.

Figure 1.3. "Ohio Farmer War Map: The Geography and Finances of the War," *Ohio Farmer* 93, no. 19 (May 12, 1898): 391. Courtesy of the History, Philosophy, and Newspaper Library, University of Illinois at Urbana-Champaign.

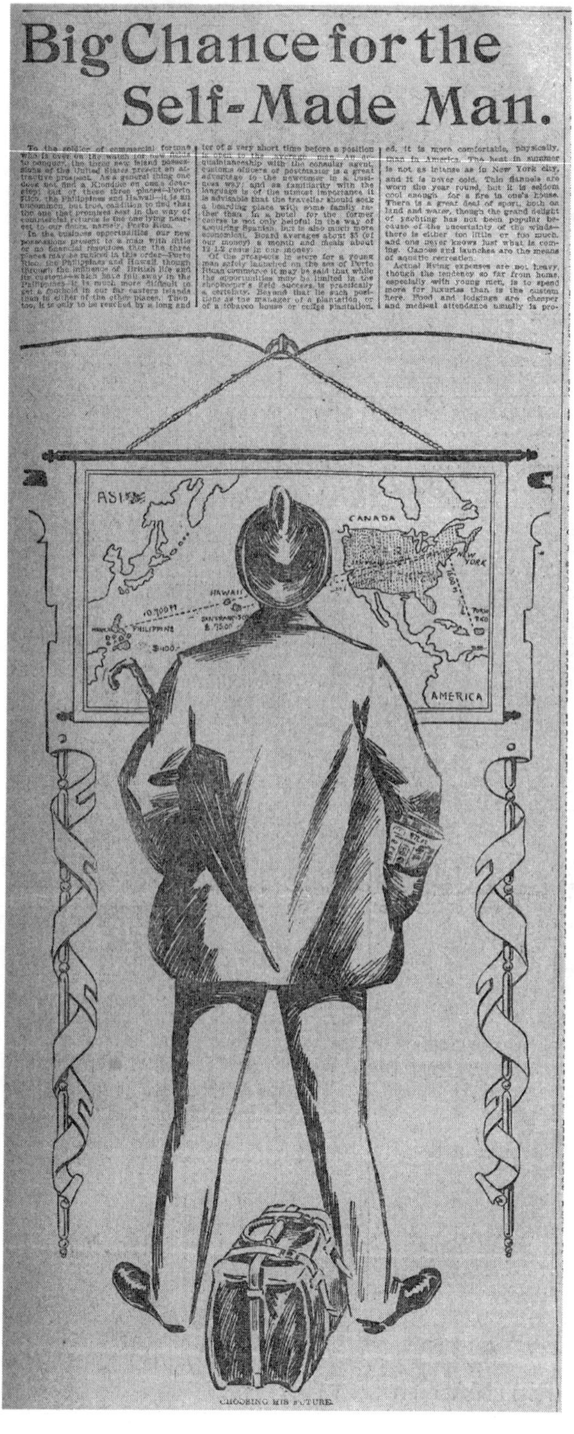

Big Chance for the Self-Made Man.

To the soldier of commercial fortune who is ever on the watch for new fields to conquer, the three new island possessions of the United States present an attractive prospect. As a general thing one does not find a Klondike on one's doorstep; but of these three places—Porto Rico, the Philippines and Hawaii—it is an uncommon, but true, condition to find that the one that promises best in the way of commercial returns is the one lying nearest to our doors, namely, Porto Rico.

In the business opportunities our new possessions present to a man with little or no financial resources then the three places may be ranked in this order—Porto Rico, the Philippines and Hawaii, though through the influence of British life and its customs—which have fallen away in the Philippines—it is much more difficult to get a foothold in our far eastern islands than in either of the other places. Then, too, it is only to be reached by a long and [illegible]

[illegible] of a very short time before a position is open to the stranger. An acquaintanceship with the consular agent, customs officers or postmaster is a great advantage to the newcomer in a business way, and as familiarity with the language is of the utmost importance it is advisable that the traveller should seek a boarding place with some family rather than in a hotel, for the former course is not only helpful in the way of acquiring Spanish, but is also much more economical. Board averages about $5 (of our money) a month and meals about 12 1-2 cents in our money.

Of the prospects in store for a young man safely launched on the sea of Porto Rican commerce it may be said that while the opportunities may be limited in the shopkeeper's field success is practically a certainty. Beyond that lie such positions as the manager of a plantation, or of a tobacco house or coffee plantation.

ed, it is more comfortable, physically, than in America. The heat in summer is not as intense as in New York city, and it is never cold. Thin flannels are worn the year round, but it is seldom cool enough for a fire in one's house. There is a great deal of sport, both on land and water, though the grand delight of yachting has not been popular because of the uncertainty of the winds—there is either too little or too much, and one never knows just what is coming. Canoes and launches are the means of aquatic recreation.

Actual living expenses are not heavy, though the tendency so far from home, especially with young men, is to spend more for luxuries than is the custom here. Food and lodgings are cheaper and medical attendance usually is pro-

CHOOSING HIS FUTURE.

Figure 1.4. "Big Chance for the Self-Made Man." *Richmond Times,* November 6, 1898, 12. Courtesy of the Library of Virginia.

wrote letters to his readers expressing his thoughts on contemporary events. When coming to terms with the nation's stake in Cuba's future, he told his readers that he turned to the map. "The more I study the map the more Cuba seems to me an island of immense possibilities. This harbor is a part of the Caribbean Sea, which lies between the two Americas, North America and South America; and as soon as a canal is cut through Nicaragua, or across the Isthmus of Panama, it will be in almost a direct line between the Atlantic and the Pacific Oceans, and in the very track along which will pass back and forth the vast commerce between Western Europe and Eastern Asia." Field's perceptions on Cuba's value to the United States directly reflected his absorption of the cartographic narrative that collapsed global distances and positioned the new colonies at vital junctures to connect trading routes from east to west and north to south. Given Field's belief in maps as critical informational tools, it makes sense that he offered Rand McNally's *New Atlas of the World* at the reduced cost of three dollars to new subscribers of the *Evangelist,* to ensure, as he put it, that they can "read intelligently."[37] In a cultural moment when cartographic knowledge was highly prized, maps had great efficacy as propaganda because they could tell selective stories and naturalize geographic connections through a representational apparatus that appeared technical and unmediated.

Maps: Creating a Heightened Cartographic Consciousness

Just as nineteenth-century Americans, particularly those in the eastern states, came to envision the "American West" through prints, maps, and other images, American readers in and after 1898 learned about and engaged in a new relationship with the colonies through map consumption. As Matthew Edney has argued, "The mapping by one polity, within its own spatial discourses, of the territory of another establishes a geography of the mind, within which empire can be conceptualized and advocated, and a geography of power, within which empire can be physically constructed."[38] Consequently, newspaper editors and illustrators seeking to express support or denounce the nation's policies often turned to cartographic narratives to do it, making maps an integral part of the national conversation over empire.

One way for newspaper editors and illustrators to add their voice to the imperial debate was by integrating graphic imagery or text into maps in order to create concise, visual arguments for expansion. A map published in the *Arizona Republican* in August 1898 exemplifies this strategy, as it incorporated image and text into the map to justify acquiring Puerto Rico, described in the map's caption as a "rich little island" with "the most prosperous aborigines in the world" that would provide America with "some new sugar and coffee kings."[39] Rather than depict the island's major geographical landmarks, the map contained demographic information and aboriginal imagery that specifically connected geographic space to the extraction of resources and to land use, promoting the island as an arena for economic opportunity. It also selectively positioned the island in relative distance to New York and no other locations.

Even when not incorporated directly, textual matter accompanying maps often provided ethnological information about the native peoples and economic resources, making it seem "factual," linked to geography rather than political argument. Some illustrated articles of the Philippines, for example, differentiated the archipelago by island groupings, categorizing the native population into demographic categories: Luzon, Mindanao, Panay, and so on. The supplemental text directed viewers to see in the map evidence of demographic divergence rather than unity. In one article reprinted broadly, the text in juxtaposition with the map stated, "The Moros of the south are warlike, active, intelligent, with a civilization as advanced as Turkey's. The Negritos are a diseased and dying pigmy [*sic*] tribe, absolutely animal in their existence, less advanced than any known people. The term 'Filipino' embraces Manila rabble and secluded islanders, mountaineers and seamen, priests and the cannibals. It is necessary, therefore, to use only the broadest terms in describing the group collectively."[40] The text directed viewers of the map to imagine the islands as racially, culturally, and politically disparate, in need of a unifying presence and lacking any central nationalist core. It was this type of map that senator Jonathan Dolliver of Iowa had in mind when he defended McKinley's imperial policies in the Senate and urged the placement of a map of the Philippines in every school and newspaper office across the country because he thought that the key to persuade Americans that Philippine nationalism was limited to only a few provinces was through geographic awareness.[41]

Maps also figured into the political cartoon commentary on the imperial question. Political cartoonists often chose to represent imperial acquisition through the visual motif of seizing entities on the globe or world map. Two political cartoons represent this iconographic strategy: a *New York Herald* cartoon "Staking a New Claim" depicting Uncle Sam straddling a globe, as he sets a stake into the Philippine Islands, and a *Philadelphia Press* cartoon of the bald eagle gathering up his new island acquisitions under his global wingspan. The effect of such cartoons was to represent empire physically as a geographical grab, with symbols of American power and nation taking dominion over new spaces on the map.[42] Figure 1.5, in the *Chicago Tribune,* follows a similar pattern. At first glance it might appear as an actual map, but it was actually a work of geographic caricature. The illustrator reconstituted the map of Luzon, and specifically Manila Bay harbor, into the shape of Admiral Dewey's

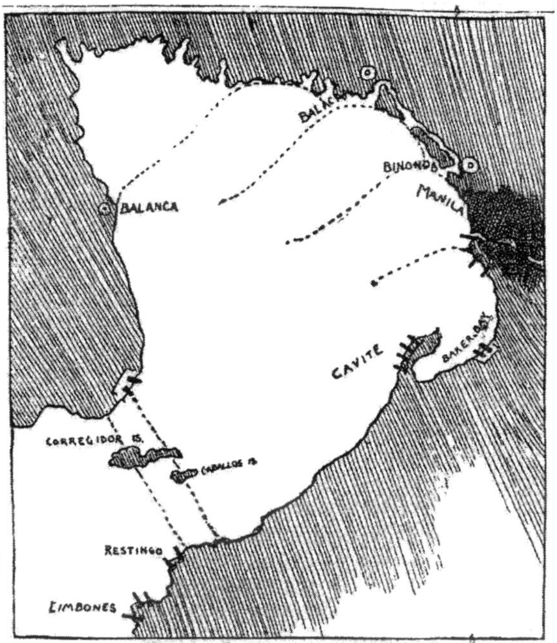

A STUDY OF ADMIRAL DEWEY'S FIST.

Figure 1.5. *Chicago Tribune*, May 15, 1898, 5. Courtesy of the David M. Rubenstein Rare Book and Manuscript Library, Duke University.

clenched fist: a symbol of strength to mark Dewey's victory. The corporeal reimaginings of American figures and symbols into maps shows the cartographic liberties that newspapers took to express political and military agendas. The recurring cartoon representation of Uncle Sam as himself globular in shape or with his clothes or face redrawn into a map manifests imperial acquisition in both corporeal and cartographic narratives.[43] Uncle Sam physically embodied the nation's expanding political borders: now no longer continental but global.

The use of cutouts was another recurring trope in cartographic discourse that provides insight into the practice of map-mindedness. Many cartoons represented President McKinley or Uncle Sam engaged in the work of empire by cutting out the colonies from the map for the purpose of rearranging imperial configurations. Exemplifying this trend (figure 1.6), a *Chicago Tribune* cartoon published in June 1898 depicted a hand called "Destiny" holding a pair of scissors with one tine labeled "Uncle Sam" and the other "John Bull"; the caption read, "Is This the Implement with Which a New Map of the World

Is to Be Cut Out?" Using map cutting as a metaphor for acquisition, cartoonists represented imperial competition between different world powers as the exchange of literal cutouts of geographic space on the map, as if colonies were in and of themselves printed commodities that could be held and traded.

Cartoonist Charles Nelan of the proimperialist *New York Herald* borrowed this trope to convey the politics of overseas expansion (figure 1.7). In his cartoon, the figure of Europe looks on as Uncle Sam cuts out the new colonies from the world map as a symbolic act of appropriation adherent to the negotiated peace conditions. The caption read, "Europe: my goodness, how he is mutilating that beautiful map!" Despite the *Herald*'s editorial stance in favor of the acquisition of the Philippines, Nelan's use of the term "mutilating" captures his own apprehension toward the consequences of empire. Europe, depicted as a domestic servant, is left to clean up Uncle Sam's mess. Nelan's reputation as a cartoonist allowed him a rare degree of editorial independence in his work, even if subtly executed, that most cartoonists of that period did not enjoy.[44] He guards the inviolability of the American polity by seeking to preserve the physical incarnation of its space—the map—claiming it best left untouched.

This map-cutting theme filtered into the public consciousness in striking ways. Many editors directed readers to cut out portions of their newspaper maps to use as reference when reading the war news. Alice Carlotta Wheeler published her suggestion for a Fourth of July picnic game in the *Woman's Home Companion;* she recommended pasting cutouts of maps of the thirteen original states along with the new colony of Cuba on wooden plates. The map literacy game required guests to guess the identity of the maps, which, intended or not, made the annexation of Cuba seem like a foregone conclusion. Her idea must have had social currency, as newspapers around the country reprinted it.[45]

Amusing anecdotal reports published in the press, some bordering on bizarre, confirmed not only a popular fascination with maps of the new colonies but also a near obsession with them. "The grammar school boy who drew a chalk map of Cuba on a Portland sidewalk the other day drew almost as big a crowd as a bulletin board does," claimed the *Lewiston Journal* (this report appeared in multiple papers of that region). A farmer in Jackson County, Mississippi, claimed that the community was stirred by the birth of a calf with a white spot on his forehead that resembled the map of Cuba. A "curious phenomenon" was reported in Florida in which the clouds in the southern sky were said to have appeared in the shape of the island of Cuba. Described a witness from Mississippi: "There was the bay of Havana, the bay of Santiago, and the various inlets that are to be found on the map. It was as perfect as could be found in the geographies and as plain as if printed in ink on fine paper."[46] What makes these printed tidbits revealing is that these were newsworthy

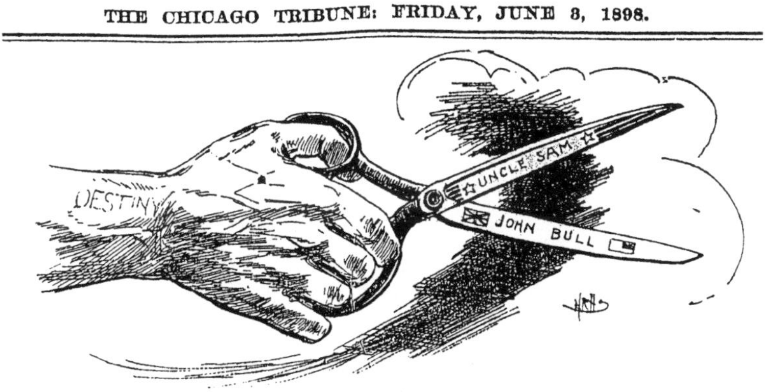

"Is This the Implement with Which a New Map of the World Is to Be Cut Out?"

Figure 1.6. *Chicago Tribune,* June 3, 1898, 3. Courtesy of the David M. Rubenstein Rare Book and Manuscript Library, Duke University.

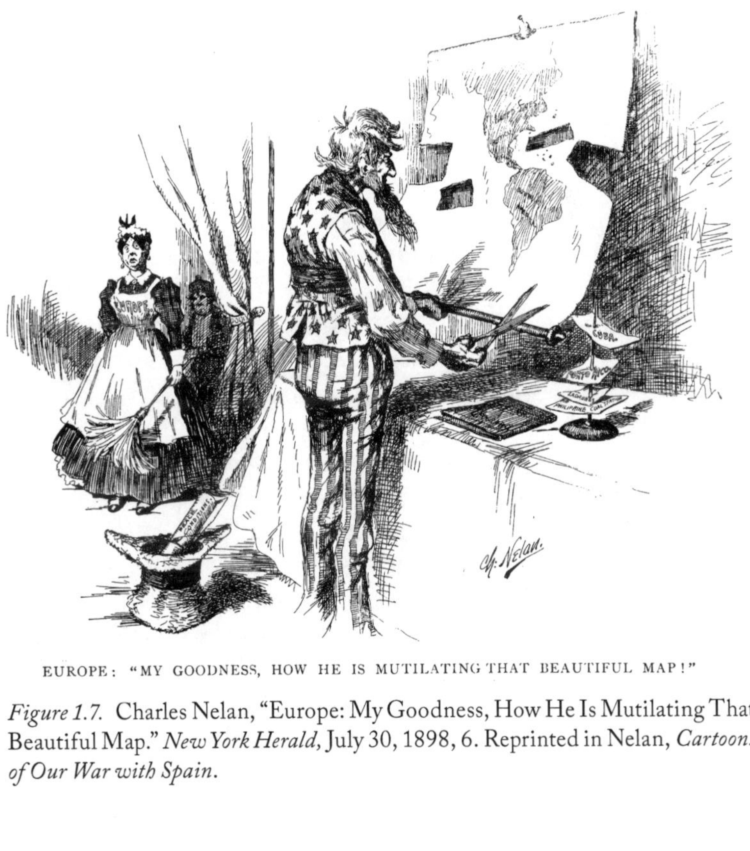

EUROPE: "MY GOODNESS, HOW HE IS MUTILATING THAT BEAUTIFUL MAP!"

Figure 1.7. Charles Nelan, "Europe: My Goodness, How He Is Mutilating That Beautiful Map." *New York Herald,* July 30, 1898, 6. Reprinted in Nelan, *Cartoons of Our War with Spain.*

stories, important enough to be widely reprinted. They speak to how everyday Americans had maps on their minds, a phenomenon that reflects the pervasiveness of cartographic thinking in American print, popular, and commercial culture at this moment.

Maps: Advertising, Purchase, and Display

While newspaper editors, advertisers, and illustrators may have helped to create a citizenry invested in the projects of empire, their impact went beyond the political realm; they leveraged map-mindedness to promote commercial consumption. The imperial project abroad was closely tied to the spread of consumerism at home, and not just because of interest in selling to foreign markets or acquiring foreign goods. Maps were desirable commodities that could serve as a decorative prop in addition to fulfilling a nationalistic or imperialistic function.[47] As a result, map offers became an important advertising incentive for many companies, railroads, and even for the press, all seeking to take advantage of the spike in cartographic interest at a moment when the nation was engaged in military and imperial affairs abroad. Private industry sought to mobilize the social importance of being an informed citizen by ascribing value to owning and reading maps as a means of boosting consumption of a wide array of products and services.

Purchasing a map or photographic album became a way for Americans to express and perform patriotism to their social networks. In turn, mapmaking companies thrived, hardly keeping up with demand, and maps of the new colonies flooded American popular culture. A *Washington Evening Star* editorialist noting how "the demand [for maps of Cuba and the Philippines] seems to be increasing instead of diminishing," observed, "The public don't seem to care for accuracy as much as they do for anything that looks like a map." This is a revealing commentary on consumer expectations; the content of the maps may have been largely immaterial. Maps were commodities that were not meant simply for edification but also to be acquired as keepsakes or put on display in one's parlor. Nationwide newspapers offered beautiful portfolio albums of photographs depicting naval cruisers, maps, and views of the colonies at reduced rates. Many papers kept these albums affordable by selling them in installments, which also functioned to retain consumer loyalty. The *Kansas City Journal* called its portfolios a "work of art." A rival paper, the *Kansas Advocate and News,* advertised its albums as "bound in paper cover," "printed on heavy calendared paper," with "maps clear and handsomely colored." The *Nebraska Valentine Democrat* praised its pictorial portfolio for its "high grade enameled stock" with "presswork and binding first-class." The ad read, "This book sells on sight. It is just what everybody wants now. Remember, it is not cheaply put together…but well made in every way and handsomely and durably bound in blue and red silk cloth."[48] Such descriptions suggest that the fine quality of maps and photographic reproductions were meant to be preserved, valued, and shared.

Newspapers, especially, made use of the growing interest in maps to boost circulation and subscription. Many editors obtained contracts with mapmaking firms to produce free or reduced-cost atlases and map books for their subscribers. This promotional strategy grew out of the nineteenth-century shop-keeping tradition of soliciting customers by handing out collectible trade cards. Rand McNally had contracts with newspapers such as the *Richmond Times*, the *Boston Journal*, and the *Omaha Bee*, and with periodicals such as the *Cosmopolitan: A Monthly Illustrated Magazine*, the *Southern Cultivator*, *Life Magazine*, *Literary Digest*, and the *Christian Observer*. The *San Francisco Call* paid for exclusive rights to provide *Cram's Superior Atlas* (one of Rand McNally's major competitors) on the Pacific coast at a significantly reduced price to encourage new subscribers. Its advertisement suggests the audience and purpose of such a commodity. The ad called out to "Teachers, Pupils, Mechanics, Business Men, [and] Professional Men" as potential buyers. Bound in silk cloth and "printed on fine Atlas paper," the atlas was clearly intended for display.[49]

Railroad companies followed a similar pattern. They dispensed maps in order to stimulate corporate investment, promote land sales along their routes, and facilitate shipping. The Atlantic Coast Line Railway, which ran up and down the East Coast, gifted a large wall map of "Cuba, Porto Rico, Hayti, Jamaica, and other West India islands" to eastern city papers in 1899. Even though their rail lines went only as far south as Florida, it made steamship connections to the islands from Miami, Tampa, and Key West. The map, printed and paid for by the railway company, was given to newspapers as a means of self-promotion.[50] Commercial agents for the major railroads also offered travelers free or low-cost wall maps at train depots across the country. Newspapers directed readers to where railway agents could be found to obtain such maps. A South Dakota newspaper, for example, printed an editorial letting readers know that an agent of the Chicago, Milwaukee, and St. Paul Railway would be stationed at the railroad depot selling Rand McNally map books for twenty-five cents that featured "sixteen pages of colored maps in one book, containing new and correct maps of Cuba, the Philippine Islands, the West Indies, North America, Europe, etc." The fact that this advertisement was written as an editorial rather than placed on the borders of the page with the other advertisements lent it a special sense of legitimacy, of being newsworthy.[51]

Many companies whose products had no direct ties to cartography used the lure of the map to entice customers. John Friedel and Company, a wallpaper store in Wheeling, West Virginia, promised in its newspaper advertisement a free map of the Philippine Islands with each inquiry. W. A. Washburn and Company, a clothing company based in Hancock, Michigan, distributed maps of Cuba to its patrons. F. L. Hitchcock of Watertown, Connecticut, a seller of garden implements, seeds, and fertilizers, offered a map of Cuba free with purchase. Its ad read, "Like Dewey we are prepared to conquer with our new designs and low prices." The E. C. Stearns Bicycle Company offered a free Rand McNally atlas with postage paid: "Ride to the Front on a Stearns Bicycle" became their slogan. Libby, McNeill and Libby, a Chicago-based food manufacturer and caterer, published a world atlas with "new maps of China, South Africa, the Philippines, Cuba, [and] Porto Rico."[52] This business practice clearly spanned different retail types and regions of the country, demonstrating a national link between imperial cartography and domestic commerce.

Likewise, some companies opted to make special gifts of atlases and wall maps to local newspapers. The Parry Manufacturing Company of Indianapolis gifted a set of large maps of the Philippines, Cuba, Puerto Rico, and Hawai'i to Idaho's *Solver Messenger* in 1899, enabling the paper to provide them to subscribers at a minimal fee. Sutton and Bowen, a banking and brokerage firm, gifted a map of Cuba and the West Indies to their local Vermont newspaper. The Nicholas Kuhuen Company of Davenport, Iowa, a cigar manufacturing company, gave Montana's *Philipsburg Mail* a map of Cuba.[53] Newspapers, in turn, thanked them in print for their generosity and patriotism.

The quantity of these different types of advertisements suggests that wall maps and map portfolios were pitched as desired commodities not only for schools and civic institutions but also for private homes. Retailers, railway agents, and the press worked together to entice readers' interest in imperial cartography as a means of selling a broad array of goods and services. This had a circular effect: as more maps of the colonies were put into circulation, map consciousness likely increased; as more consumers sought maps for purposes of self-edification or to increase their social capital, demand for maps continued to rise, thus making them effective advertising incentives for any commercial outlet.

During and after the Spanish-American War, maps of the nation's new acquisitions became ubiquitous in American print and popular culture. They appeared in schools, prisons, and other civic institutions. They were the subject of museum displays; for example, the new library building in Washington, DC, put on a special exhibit in 1898 that displayed early Spanish maps of Cuba and the Philippines. Maps were posted on store windows and in store advertisements; the *New York Sun,* reporting on the "harvest" of map selling, observed, "A crowd can be secured in front of any window if that window contains a map of Cuba or a map of Spain." And maps became featured components of world's fair exhibits; in the Government Building of the 1904

Louisiana Purchase Exposition in St. Louis, a great map was put on display that received national attention. Elliptical in shape and 110 feet long by 75 feet wide, the relief map was the centerpiece of the Philippine exhibit, with a circular plank walkway around it. Inside the exhibit were eighteen additional relief maps, showing the mines, hot and cold springs, forests, agriculture, and other physical features of the Philippines.[54]

As a central part of the media ecosystem of war and empire, maps helped to shape the popular imagination of how the colonies could serve as strategic military and economic assets. "The map and atlas makers are profiting by the war boom.... It seems as if everybody in the country must have taken to studying geography. The presses are working night and day, but it is simply impossible to supply the demand," observed an editorialist of the *Houston Post*.[55] In this moment, the press, mapmaking firms, and private industry constituted a loud consensus in favor of pushing the purchase and consumption of maps in order for readers to stay informed and support the nation's interests abroad. In this way, fostering a culture of map-mindedness was as integral to facilitating the projects of war and empire in this historical moment as it was to promoting domestic consumption of all types of goods, especially commodities of print culture.

Notes

1. Many have speculated that L. Frank Baum's book *The Wonderful Wizard of Oz* offers a parable about 1890's populism. Even if that is true, this line from the movie version of the book does not appear in the original text. So, delicious as it would be, there doesn't appear to be a connection between Baum and McKinley's words here. I mention it only in jest.

2. This account was reprinted broadly. One such report is James Rusling, "Interview with President McKinley," *Christian Advocate* 78, no. 4 (January 22, 1903): 137. David Brody analyzes this media spin in *Visualizing American Empire: Orientalism and Imperialism in the Philippines* (Chicago, IL: University of Chicago Press, 2010), 89–112.

3. John Rennie Short, *Representing the Republic: Mapping the United States, 1600–1900* (London: Reaktion Books, 2001), 20.

4. See my argument in Bonnie M. Miller, *From Liberation to Conquest: The Visual and Popular Cultures of the Spanish-American War of 1898* (Amherst: University of Massachusetts Press, 2011): 87–95.

5. "The Philippines—An Unknown Empire," *Gunton's Magazine* 14, no. 6 (June 1898): 384.

6. David Uttal cited in Camilo Arturo Leslie, "Territoriality, Map-Mindedness, and the Politics of Place," *Theory and Society: Renewal and Critique in Social Theory* 45, no. 2 (April 2016): 178. See also David Uttal, "Seeing the Big Picture: Map Use and the Development of Spatial Cognition," *Developmental Science* 3 (2000): 247–286; Denis Wood, "Maps and Mapmaking," *Cartographica* 30, no. 1 (Spring 1993): 1–9.

7. Leslie, "Territoriality," 178–179. See also Matthew H. Edney, "The Irony of Imperial

Mapping," in *The Imperial Map: Cartography and the Mastery of Empire,* edited by James R. Akerman (Chicago, IL: University of Chicago Press, 2009), 11–45.

8. Diane Dillon, "Consuming Maps," in *Maps: Finding Our Place in the World*, edited by James Akerman and Robert Karrow, Jr. (Chicago, IL: University of Chicago Press / Field Museum of National History and the Newberry Library, 2007), 290.

9. Untitled, *Hawaiian Star*, December 28, 1898, 4.

10. Mark Monmonier, *Maps with the News: The Development of American Journalistic Cartography* (Chicago, IL: University of Chicago Press, 1989), 19.

11. "The Whole World in the Geography Class," *Century Illustrated Magazine* 64, no. 5 (September 1902): 805.

12. There is a wealth of sources that link the historical practice of cartography with expectations of objectivity, veracity, and science. See Leslie, "Territoriality," 172; Short, *Representing the Republic*; John Pickles, "Texts, Hermeneutics and Propaganda Maps," in *Writing Worlds: Discourse, Text, and Metaphor in the Representation of Landscape*, edited by Trevor Barnes and James Duncan (London: Routledge, 2011): 193–230; Christine Leuenberger and Izhak Schnell, "The Politics of Maps: Constructing National Territories in Israel," *Social Studies of Science* 40, no. 6 (2010): 804–805; Kitchin Rob and Martin Dodge, "Rethinking Maps," *Progress in Human Geography* 31, no. 3 (2007): 331–344. The seminal texts that transformed the field into conceptualizing maps as socially constructed texts that interpret rather than neutrally convey data are John B. Harley, "Maps, Knowledge and Power," in *The Iconography of Landscape: Essays on the Symbolic Representation, Design, and Use of Past Environments*, edited by Denis Cosgrove and Stephen Daniels (Cambridge: Cambridge University Press, 1989): 277–312; and John B. Harley, "Deconstructing the Map," *Cartographica* 26, no. 2 (Summer 1989): 1–20.

13. David Bosse, *A Historical Atlas: Civil War Newspaper Maps* (Baltimore, MD: Johns Hopkins University Press, 1993), 3–56; David Woodward, *The All-American Map: Wax Engraving and Its Influence on Cartography* (Chicago, IL: University of Chicago Press, 1977).

14. Susan Schulten, "The Cartography of Slavery and the Authority of Statistics," *Civil War History* 56, no. 1 (2010): 5–32; Susan Shulten, *Mapping the Nation: History and Cartography in Nineteenth-Century America* (Chicago, IL: University of Chicago Press, 2012); Susan Schulten, "Mapping American History," in *Maps: Finding Our Place in the World*, edited by James R. Akerman and Robert W. Karrow, Jr. (Chicago, IL: University of Chicago Press, 2007), 159–205; Martin Brückner, *The Social Life of Maps in America, 1750–1860* (Chapel Hill: University of North Carolina Press / Omohundro Institute of Early American History and Culture, 2017), 239; Earl B. McElfresh, *Maps and Mapmakers of the Civil War* (New York: Harry N. Abrams, 1999); Christopher Nelson, *Mapping the Civil War: Featuring Rare Maps from the Library of Congress* (Colorado: Fulcrum, 1992).

15. Brückner, *Social Life of Maps*, 3.

16. Walter Ristow, *American Maps and Mapmakers: Commercial Cartography in the Nineteenth Century* (Detroit, MI: Wayne University Press, 1985), 303, 467–472, 479; Short, *Representing the Republic*, 224–225.

17. Susan Schulten, *The Geographical Imagination in America, 1880–1950* (Chicago, IL: University of Chicago Press, 2001), 222.

18. Brody, *Visualizing American Empire,* 94.

19. "Pictures by Wire," *Newspaper Maker* 9, no. 214 (April 27, 1899): 5. Cited in Monmonier, *Maps with the News*, 91, 262.

20. Kristin Hoganson, "Cosmopolitan Domesticity: Importing the American Dream, 1865–1920," *American Historical Review* 107, no. 1 (February 2002): 57.

21. Scott Kirsch, "Insular Territories: US Colonial Science, Geopolitics, and the (Re)Mapping of the Philippines," *Geographical Journal* 182, no. 1 (March 2016): 3; Richard Drinnon, *Facing West: The Metaphysics of Indian-Hating and Empire-Building* (Norman: University of Oklahoma Press, 1997), 295.

22. "New United States Map," *Bolivar (TN) Bulletin*, October 13, 1899. See published map in Schulten, *Geographical Imagination in America*, 42.

23. Untitled, *Arizona Republican*, January 23, 1907, section 1, 2.

24. Short, *Representing the Republic*, 19.

25. "No Good Map of Cuba," *Brenham (TX) Weekly Banner*, December 23, 1897.

26. "The American Map of Cuba," *New York Sun*, May 22, 1907, 6.

27. "President McKinley Has Charts, Maps, and Telegraph Wires," *Las Vegas Daily Optic*, April 27, 1898; "The *Boston Globe*'s Map of the Atlantic Coast and Scenes of the Naval Manoeuvres," *Boston Globe*, April 4, 1898, 5.

28. "A Wonderful Map," *Washington (DC) Evening Star*, June 29, 1901, 10; "M'Kinley's War Map," *Indianapolis Journal*, June 30, 1901, part 2, 16.

29. "Maps of Philippines Are Seriously Needed," *Washington (DC) Times*, November 8, 1903, 4.

30. "Popularity of the Advocate and News Standard Atlas," *Advocate and News* (Kansas), June 29, 1898, 13. The advertisement referred to the original letter of the reader, who mistakenly referred to the International Date Line as the "day" line. The International Date Line was decided at the International Meridian Conference in Washington, DC, in 1884. Advertisement, *New York Tribune*, May 17, 1898, 4.

31. "After Calumpit," *Anaconda (MO) Standard*, April 28, 1899, 6.

32. "Department of the Interior," *Socorro (NM) Chieftain*, August 29, 1903; "Flag Day," *Washington (DC) Times*, June 14, 1898, 8.

33. "Peace Services in a Prison," *Red Cloud Chief* (Nebraska), August 19, 1898, 6; Brückner, *Social Life of Maps*, 141, 277–286.

34. "A Delicious Blunder," *Washington (DC) Evening Times*, July 26, 1898, 4; untitled, *Daily Kentuckian*, May 1, 1898.

35. For examples, see the *Greenville (MO) Times*, April 30, 1898; "Insurance Men's Maps," *Washington (DC) Times*, October 15, 1899, part 2, 3.

36. Untitled editorial, *Watchman* 81, no. 5 (February 1, 1900): 5.

37. "Dr. Field's Letters: A Rusty Old Town Like Nantucket Waking from the Sleep of Centuries," *New York Evangelist* 70, no. 17 (April 27, 1899): 4; advertisement, *New York Evangelist* 69, no. 28 (July 14, 1898): 31.

38. Edney, "Irony of Imperial Mapping," 44–45.

39. "An Illustrated Map of Puerto Rico," *Arizona Republican*, August 12, 1898.

40. "Comprehensive Map of the Philippine Islands" embedded in the article "Facts about the Philippines," *Western News-Democrat* (Nebraska), June 8, 1899.

41. "Senator Dolliver on the Philippines," *Washington (DC) Times*, May 20, 1902, 2.

42. Charles Nelan, *New York Herald*, May 12, 1898; *Iowa Plain Dealer*, August 23, 1898 (originally printed in the *Philadelphia Press*).

43. Schulten, *Geographical Imagination*, 176.

44. Charles Nelan, "Europe: My Goodness, How He Is Mutilating That Beautiful Map," *New York Herald*, July 30, 1898, 6. Cited in Schulten, *Geographical Imagination*, 43. In my book I describe another Nelan cartoon that evokes a similar imperial ambivalence by representing Uncle Sam in globular form, with cartographic imagery of the new colonies represented on his attire. See Miller, *From Liberation to Conquest*, 175–177.

45. "An Independence Day Frolic," *Denison (IA) Review,* July 02, 1901.

46. "Firing Off the Coast," *Wheeling (WV) Daily Intelligencer,* May 26, 1898, 4; "Personal and General," *Pascagoula (MI) Democrat-Star,* May 27, 1898; "At the White House," *Washington (DC) Evening Star,* June 7, 1901.

47. Brückner, *Social Life of Maps,* 161–199.

48. "Things Heard and Seen," *Washington (DC) Evening Star,* June 11, 1898, 14; "The Portfolio Series," *Kansas City Journal,* June 3, 1898, 8; Advertisement, *Advocate and News* (Kansas), November 16, 1898, 13; "The American Navy Illustrated," *Valentine (NE) Democrat,* May 26, 1898.

49. "The Superior Atlas," *San Francisco Call,* March 10, 1901, 27; Dillon, "Consuming Maps," 327.

50. Dillon, "Consuming Maps," 321; "From the North to Tropics," *Semi-Weekly Messenger* (North Carolina), February 17, 1899, 1; spellings match the original source.

51. "A War Atlas," *Dakota Farmers' Leader* (South Dakota), June 3, 1898.

52. Advertisement, *Wheeling (WV) Daily Intelligencer,* March 29, 1899, 5; untitled, *Copper Country Evening News* (Michigan), May 5, 1898; advertisement, *Waterbury (CT) Evening Democrat,* May 20, 1898; advertisement, *Literary World: A Monthly Review of Current Literature* 29, no. 15 (July 23, 1898): 240; advertisement, *Starkville (MS) News,* May 1, 1903.

53. Untitled, *Silver Messenger* (Idaho), September 19, 1899; untitled, *St. Johnsbury (VT) Caledonian,* May 4, 1898; untitled, *Philipsburg (MT) Mail,* January 29, 1897.

54. "Old and Rare Books," *Washington (DC) Evening Star,* August 13, 1898, 10; "Harvest for Map Sellers Up State," *New York Sun*, April 17, 1898, 3; "Constructing Relief Map of Philippine Islands," *St. Louis Republic*, November 1, 1903, part 1, 7; John Bancroft Devins, "Four Days at the World's Fair in St. Louis—IV: The Philippines Seen without an Ocean Journey," *New York Observer and Chronicle* 82, no. 37 (September 15, 1904): 349.

55. Untitled, *Houston Post*, May 16, 1898, 8.

Two

Military Cartography and the Terrains of Visibility

The Field Books of Lt. William H. Armstrong, Puerto Rico, 1908–1912

Lanny Thompson

In 1908, the Puerto Rico Regiment of Infantry assigned lieutenant William H. Armstrong the task of producing ten segments of a topographical map known as the "Progressive Military Map of Puerto Rico," printed by the Army War College in 1914.[1] While surveying the terrain from 1908 to 1912, Armstrong created a dozen field books complete with descriptions of the transportation networks of primary and secondary roads, local trails, and railroads, including sketches of local topography, bridges, and culverts. He also offered detailed maps and descriptions of thirty towns and their agricultural environs. He profusely illustrated the field books with annotated photographs and postcards.[2] These cartographic materials are of particular interest because they show a layering of scales and perspectives that correspond to varied operations in the deployment of power. As Christian Jacob has argued, "A map can always conceal another map, and that geography is only one of the effects of meaning that the cartographical mechanism brings forth. . . . More than an object, a map is a function and a mediation."[3] I will argue, moreover, that underlying Armstrong's topographical map are several maps of different types with distinct functions, levels of scale, and deployments. Armstrong used these other maps—itineraries, photomaps, town sketches, and panoramas—to document his work in the field and add high-resolution detail. The field books revealed processes and objectives of the topographic map that were not evident in the map itself, including the deployment of security forces (police or troops), an assessment of the loyalty and military capacity of the local population, the modernization of transportation by road and rail, and the facilitation of the agricultural export economy.

The overall effect of these cartographic materials was to produce knowledge that mediated the landscape—its resources and people—and the colonial regime. This analysis will demonstrate how the military cartography coincided with the overall interests of the colonial regime: the maintenance of social order with limited military intervention and the modernization—known as "Americanization"—of the society and economy. Armstrong's four-year cartographic journey revealed his unique capacity for integration of distinct kinds of maps with the interweaving of commentary that reflected a profound lack of respect for the people of the towns and the countryside. Indeed, as the lieutenant distanced himself from the San Juan barracks and the military chain of command, his work became more creative and, at the same time, more intolerant of the local populations, institutions, and social practices. As we shall see, the descriptions of his travels along the coast and his incursions into the mountainous interior often resonated with the character of Kurtz in Joseph Conrad's *The Heart of Darkness.*

Matthew Edney has argued that the cartographical methods in the colonial possessions are virtually indistinguishable from those deployed in national territories. The difference between national and imperial mapping consists in the deployment of similar techniques for diverse ends, namely, nation building versus empire building. In the first instance, maps symbolize the nation and create a geographic and demographic administrative unit. Maps create a certain unity among national elites, common citizens, and information about the nation. In the second instance, maps were but another method to claim territory and produce knowledge allowing imperial administrators to subjugate and govern colonial subjects. Cartographers, as agents of the colonial state, produce knowledge that delimit, define, and control territories and subjects.[4] From this follows that a map does not always designate a colony, but there can be no colony without a map.

Edney's argument, however, has certain limitations. First, he assumes the uniformity of cartographic techniques regardless of their diverse functions or ends in different contexts. In contrast, this chapter will focus upon the overlapping of diverse techniques and varied functions. Second, he overlooks those instances in which nation building and empire building coincide. As Bonnie Miller has shown in this volume, maps of the United States and its newly acquired overseas territories were essential tools for embodying the nation while consolidating its recent geographic expansion. Through the inclusion of the nation and its colonies in a single cartographic frame, maps did much of the work of empire building while strengthening the nation's resolve: claiming dominion, producing practical knowledge, projecting ideological justifications, and creating consensus among leaders and the public. In contrast to these openly ideological, low-resolution imperial maps, this chapter will focus on the practical mediations of the close-grained military cartography in a specific colony.

As in all mapping, military cartography is performative geography, a description of terrains that has the effect of producing the defining elements of those very terrains.[5] These maps achieve their performative effect through a "gaze," through the establishment of fields of visibility and modes of enunciation. This cartographic gaze is a way of viewing, describing, and acting upon territories, their resources, and populations. In particular, military cartography configures terrains that consist of descriptions of areas with regard to tactical advantages, troop movement, provisioning, and the characteristics of the population. These terrains of visibility constitute ways of acting and of preparation for possible future action.[6] In the colonies, cartography supports military, political, and economic dominion over territories and their inhabitants.[7] On this view, colonial cartography in Puerto Rico was specifically an instrumental process of appropriation (by an imperial state), reconfiguration (under a new security apparatus), and modification of colonial spaces (the Americanization of transportation, political economy, and education).[8] This chapter will examine the specific instrumentalities and particular mediations of Armstrong's field books and their variegated cartographical techniques that underlay his topographic military map of Puerto Rico.

Maps within Maps: Itineraries, Photomaps, and Town Sketches

Created in 1901, the Puerto Rican Regiment of Infantry did not have police functions, except to serve as possible back-up for the insular police. This meant that American soldiers were not required to intervene directly in the maintenance of law and order among the local population. The regiment was not the principal means of internal control, and only two cities were garrisoned: San Juan and Cayey. Regular and volunteer troops of the US Army, no longer needed after the Spanish-American War was over, were retired from Puerto Rico, and many went on to serve in the Philippines, where an anticolonial war was raging. Meanwhile, the insular police was organized under the centralized command of high-ranking officers appointed by the colonial government. Its command structure was parallel to that of the regiment. Its principal function was to keep order in the towns and countryside. In this way, the local police force could exercise control and vigilance of the population, while at the same time policemen and lower-ranking officers were subject to the supervision of their superior US officers. This model was a variant of the Spanish system of municipal and rural guards, and was adapted with great success by the United States in Cuba and the Philippines, as well as in Puerto Rico previously.[9]

The topographic military map was a function of the reduced responsibilities of the regiment and the increased centralization of the insular police.

The topographical map and the field books provided the means of troop movement if the Insular Police required additional forces to control unrest or in the unlikely case that foreign invaders threatened the island. For these reasons, they paid attention to the elements essential to troop movements, provisioning, and strategic deployment.[10] The field books offered high-resolution itineraries that corresponded directly to the possible routes of the regiment from one town to another. Itineraries are a kind of map in that they instruct a traveler on how to get from place to place in relation to local conditions, obstacles, and landmarks from a linear, horizontal perspective. The information regarding transportation infrastructure provided more local details than a topographical map. Armstrong noted the quality of the roads and trails, the size and construction of bridges and culverts, the provisioning of water and grass along the way, and any strategic or dangerous points. For example, there were photographs or sketches of all bridges and culverts, including their measurements and construction materials. He also provided the same detailed information for the railways (figure 2.1). This was all valuable logistic information for the regiment.

These itineraries often included topographic sketches and annotated photographs, which added visual complexity and high-resolution detail. In one difficult section of the railway and military road along the north coast, Armstrong included a sketch of the topography and transportation features of the valley of Guajataca on the way to Isabela (figure 2.2). For this same section, he included several photomaps, that is, annotated photographs from either a horizontal or a panoramic perspective, that served as maps. Figure 2.3 shows a horizontal photomap of the bridge in the valley, while figure 2.4 shows a panoramic photomap with indications regarding the location of the town of Isabela and the positions of the bridges and one tunnel, all within the context of the same topographic contours of the sketch and the itinerary.

Upon arrival in a town, Armstrong provided a map and description of the strategic and tactical information of the locality. The field books explained where horses could be pastured and watered, identified campsites and provisions for troops, provided details on buildings that might be used for lodging or defense, evaluated sanitary and health conditions, identified hospitals and medical supplies, noted who in the town might provide reliable information, estimated the local munitions and the number of persons in town who could bear arms, and evaluated whether the town residents were hostile or receptive to the US government. The field books also located commanding strategic positions, observation points, lines of telegraphic and telephonic communication, and bridges, roads, and railways. Figure 2.1 shows the small town of Camuy, which had very little military importance except that it was the entry point from the military road along the coast to several towns in the interior.

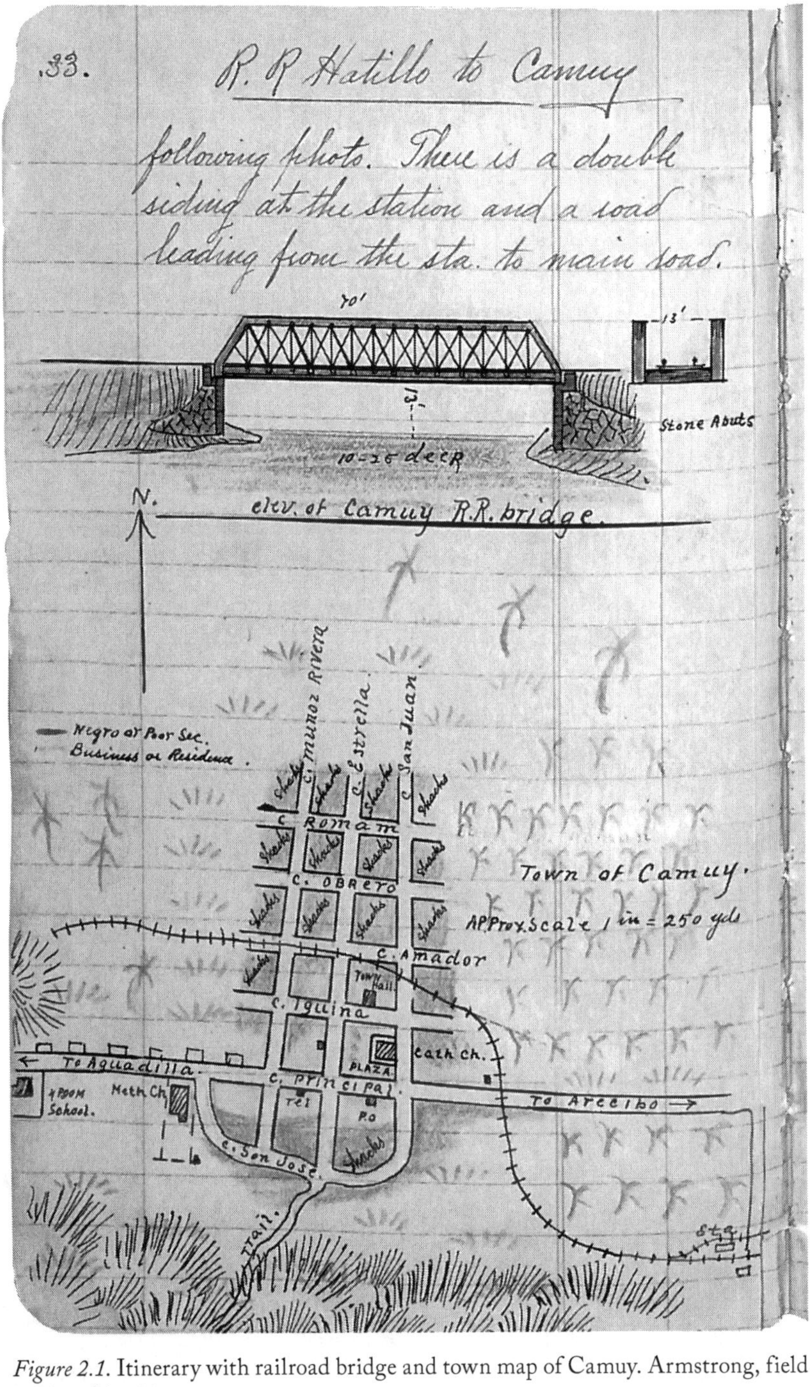

Figure 2.1. Itinerary with railroad bridge and town map of Camuy. Armstrong, field book 4, folio 33.

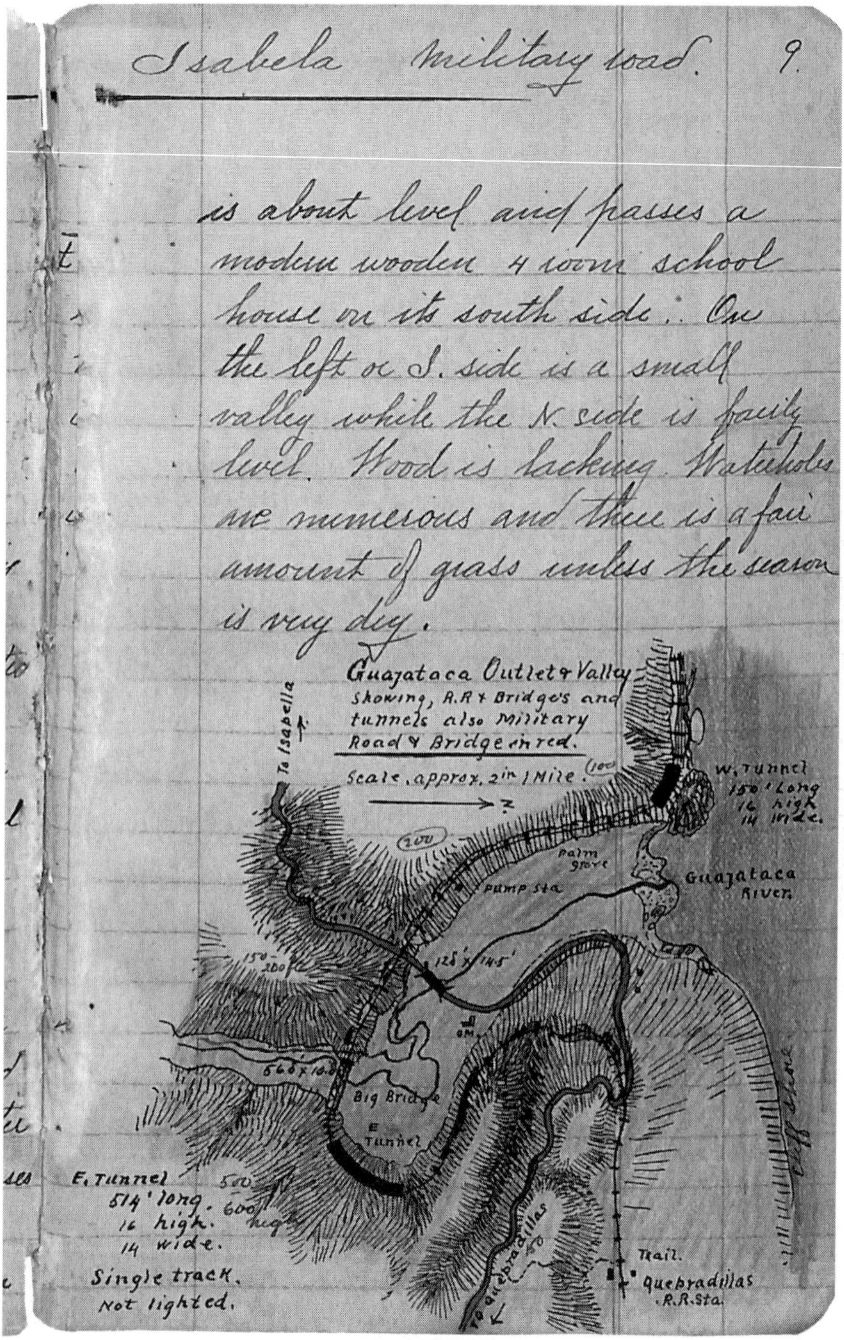

Figure 2.2. Itinerary (fragment) with topography, road, and railway, Guajataca. Armstrong, field book 5, folio 9.

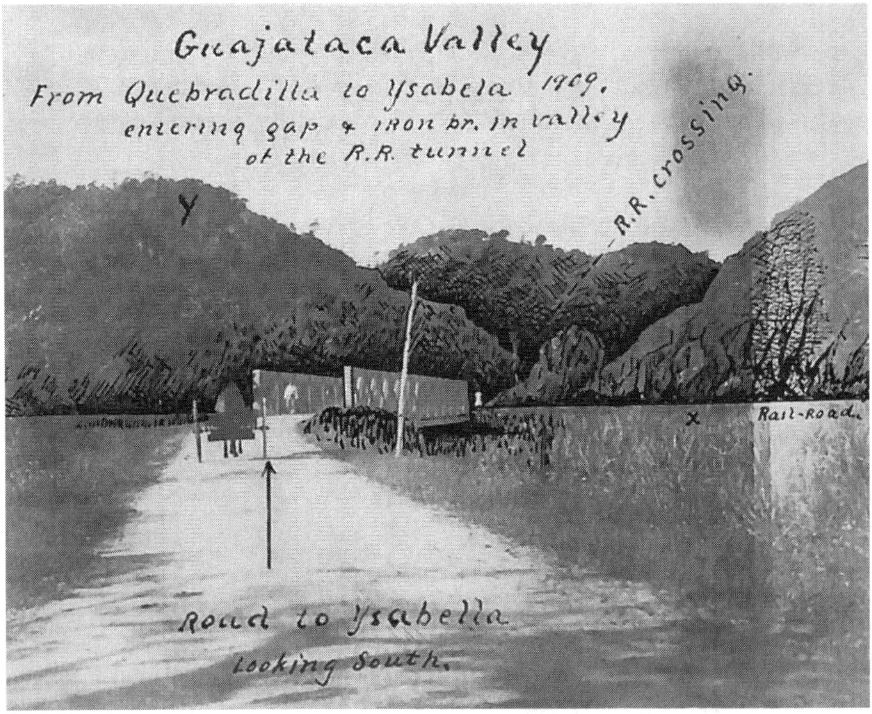

Figure 2.3. Photomap of road and bridge in Guajataca valley. Armstrong, field book 5, folio 5.

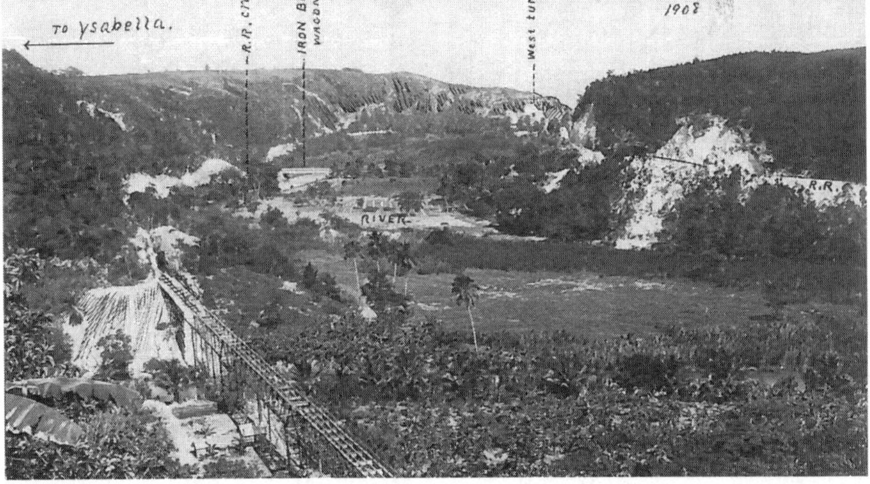

Figure 2.4. Panoramic photomap of Guajataca valley. Armstrong, field book 5, folio 15.

The town sketch indicated transportation (railway and military road), communications (telegraph and post office), important buildings (churches, schools, town hall), and social structure (business and poor sections). The field books also included annotated photographs of the towns that in many cases also served as photomaps.

The regiment was a disciplinary regime dedicated to the training of the hearts, minds, and bodies of officers and enlisted men. Writing in 1905, governor Beekman Winthrop justified the continuation of the Puerto Rico Regiment of Infantry not on military grounds but rather for its positive effect on the soldiers and officers by means of basic training and an officers' school. The governor argued that the regiment was a "school of mental and physical development," a disciplinary regime that trained subjects for both military service and later civilian life. Much like the public school system, the regiment appeared in the report as an instrument of Americanization: the men learned English and were trained for civil service positions and jobs in the expanding plantations and commercial concerns. They both learned and inspired in others a respect for and loyalty to the colonial state.[11]

Similar to the regiment, the insular police was a coercive apparatus that functioned simultaneously as a disciplinary regime. The insular police was organized along military lines, with a centralized chain of command, under the direction of an American officer. The governor considered the police an "impartial, model, and well-disciplined force." Discipline was achieved through various techniques, including constant evaluation and renewable one-year appointments. Other disciplinary techniques were the drill, the concentration, and the police academy. Officers and guardsmen worked long hours and undertook a wide variety of tasks, including supervising elections and strikebreaking.[12]

Armstrong was not particularly impressed with the disciplinary effects of the regiment and the insular police on the general population. Above all, however, he was disturbed by the character of the "native" police. He described them as a "more or less useless set," although he added that there were exceptions. The work of the three departmental detectives was very good, but the privates were, as a whole, "simple minded, timid, easily excited, and little versed in fistics [fist fighting]." His evaluation of their character addressed the issues of their on- and off-duty appearance, hygiene, and morality, all of which he associated with their urban, low-class origin: "The police coming mostly from the lower class (not the peon) are as low minded, immoral and as dirty as any other native. Their dress appears neat and most of them use a shower bath here but their homes are, in many cases, only shacks. . . . Their habits are dirty and they are content to live in dirt."[13] Regarding the policemen who were dispatched out of Arecibo to Hatillo, he wrote, "They are professionals in the use of hair oil, face powder, perfumery and in coquetry with the female population but they will use a respectable water closet as an American dog uses a curb stone."[14] Armstrong seemed most concerned about the discipline of the male body as evidenced by physical appearances and hygienic practices. For him, the undisciplined male body was an indicator of the institutional disorder of the insular police.

His description of the former army barracks in Mayagüez, now under control of the insular police, painted an image of civilian institutional disorder. The barracks were filthy and in disrepair; the roof leaked. On the denuded parade grounds, papers from both the office and the water closets blew about, where they intermingled with syphilitic cotton used to treat the infected policemen. The water closets contained stopped-up toilets, paper-strewn floors, and shit-smeared walls. The flagpole, which should have proudly flown the symbol of the new regime, was almost falling down. Although Armstrong reported the police force to be operative, he found that the discipline instilled by that institution did not fundamentally alter the character of the common police: he described them as vain, effeminate, uneducated, dirty, immoral, and diseased. This disconcerting portrait of the transition from military to civil government certainly ran counter to the accounts of progress and optimism that filled the official reports of the day. The discussion of prostitution raised similar issues regarding discipline of the masculine body, and introduced concerns regarding the health of the police, the army (in the case of troop mobilization), and public health in general.

In addition, the field books expressed concern over two elements that were not evident in the topographical map: the military capacities of the population and its loyalty to the colonial state. Armstrong continuously addressed the following questions: Is the town pro- or anti-American? Is the police force reliable? How many local men can effectively bear arms? Are they willing to fight for the United States? Armstrong was not optimistic about the capacity of the local police forces or the towns' population to defend the island from foreign invasion. The inhabitants of the towns seemed to be "indifferent" at best, and "decidedly anti-American" at worst. In addition, he found very few men capable of bearing arms, and even fewer able to shoot well. He concluded that the working classes were neither ready nor willing to fight for any cause. Among the educated and propertied classes he also found poor military character and very little loyalty. In general, the population seemed to be of no military importance; few could effectively handle firearms, and even fewer were inclined to take up arms for any cause. Armstrong did not find pro-American sentiment in the towns and countryside, although with few exceptions he found the population friendly and courteous. Likewise, he noted that local politicians were paradoxically courteous to him and fond of stirring speeches about independence.

A close reading of Armstrong's evaluations of the various towns suggests that loyalty, in part, related to recent economic turns of fortune. In his travels through the coffee regions, he found much opposition to the change of colonial regime because of the subsequent collapse of the coffee market. The depressed coffee areas were "anti-American," even though the more isolated, backward areas were sometimes desperate for government assistance in education and agriculture. The booming sugar areas were somewhat positive with respect to the American economic regime, but at best indifferent toward the colonial government. Yet, even in the sugar regions, the wealthy attributed their good fortune to the new political economy but still sought more political autonomy or independence. He considered them to be misguided but not a military threat.

At the local level, the field books evidenced only a low intensity resistance to the colonial regime. However, open opposition was developing in the political sphere. Formed in 1904, the Partido Unión was the most powerful political party at the time of Armstrong's cartographic journey. From the lower house of the legislature, it was devoted to combating the very structure of the colonial government, namely the appointed governor and the appointed executive council, which functioned also as the upper house of the legislature. Much of the political discussion focused on the issue of colonial status. Although the Partido Unión included many annexationists, in the face of government indifference to the widespread aspirations for self-government, the party began to lean toward autonomy and independence. In 1912, just after Armstrong finished his field work, the Partido de la Independencia, Puerto Rico's first independence party, was formed.[15]

At the same time, militancy was growing among the working classes, especially artisans and sugar workers. Most important was the formation, in 1899, of the labor union Federación Libre de Trabajadores de Puerto Rico and its political wing, the Partido Obrero Socialista. The local labor union soon affiliated with the American Federation of Labor to struggle for the workers' rights and better conditions. There were important strikes by sugarcane workers in 1905 and 1906 and again in 1915. Tobacco workers organized only a handful of strikes between 1906 and 1910, although they became more militant from 1911 to 1913. Despite the rather conservative, reformist nature of the federation, the local union found many advantages of the affiliation, including the organizational assistance it received and the possible extension of US labor standards to Puerto Rico. Not surprisingly, then, the labor movement was predominantly assimilationist, seeking the eventual annexation of Puerto Rico.[16]

Armstrong was unmindful of the details of the formation of the new political parties and of the growing organization and militancy of the working classes during the first two decades of the twentieth century. His cartography reflected his confidence in the colonial regime and of its strategy of modernization through capital investment and the government's development of transportation infrastructure and education.

Panoramas of Modernization

Armstrong witnessed the transformation of the landscapes of Puerto Rico under the new colonial government. His field books documented the material expansion and improvement of transportation, urban services, and agricultural production. First, the field books captured the processes of improving old trails and roads and creating new macadam roads. Armstrong commented that his map would soon be obsolete since the government was building "good macadam roads in all sections of the island and before many years trails now found on the map will be roads. . . . The roads and trails should be corrected every year on the map so long as road construction continues."[17] He included photographs of roads and bridges under construction. Second, the field books documented the improvement of urban infrastructure, in particular water works and electrification, in various towns throughout the island, but especially in the sugar regions. In addition, Armstrong recorded the establishment of hospitals, clinics, anemia stations, and public schools. Third, the decline of coffee and the advent of sugar were evident in the reconfiguration of the landscape: the panoramic views and the topographical map illustrate the geographic distribution of cultivation, and the location of coffee haciendas, old sugar mills, and modern *centrales* (massive, highly mechanized sugar mills).

Armstrong's cartographic work graphically documented a new phase of expansion of the sugar industry in which the highly mechanized sugar mills now dominated the coastal landscape. The panoramic photographs and topographical map illustrated the transformation of the landscape under the impetus of large-scale capital investment in sugar; they showed the wide distribution of cane cultivation and modern *centrales.* The topographical map is littered with dozens of "old mills," many designated as mere "ruins" in the field books. Armstrong portrayed the sugar regions with expansive panoramic views of the sugar lands, crisscrossed with new lines of transportation and modern technology (figure 2.5). His panoramic landscapes appear as if they were natural spaces for capital investment in sugar.

From 1901 to 1912, the area in cane cultivation tripled, raw sugar output quadrupled, and land values rose 600 percent. This was due to improved methods of cultivation, the use of fertilizers, the installation of irrigation systems, and the introduction of *centrales.* By 1910, the year that Armstrong visited the

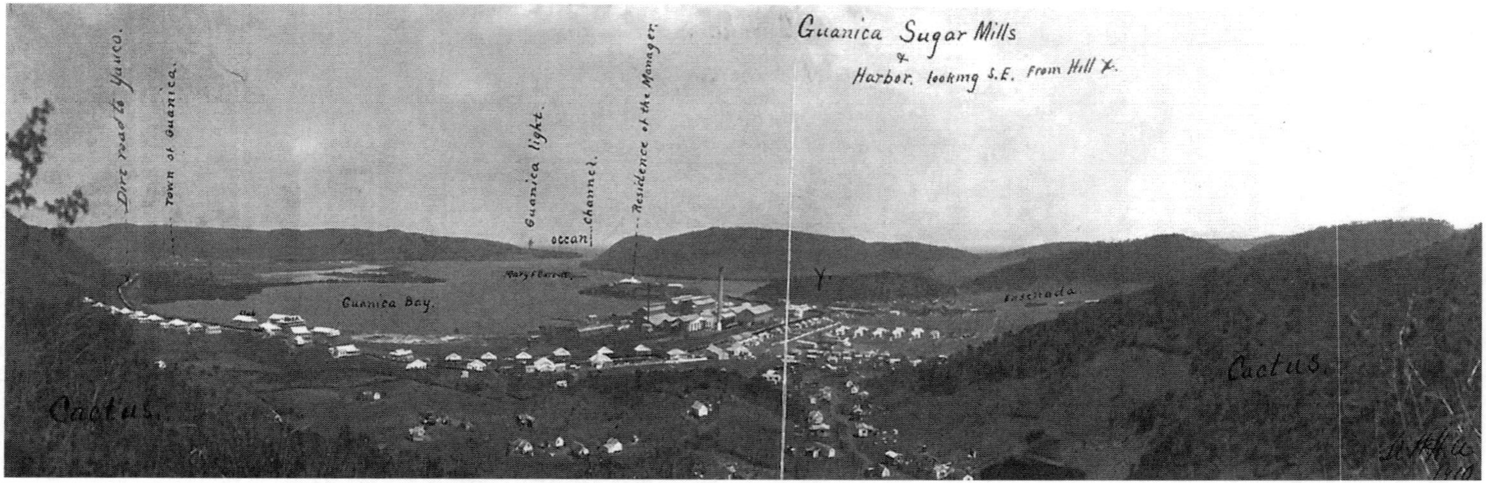

Figure 2.5. Guánica Sugar Mill. Armstrong, field book 11, folio 33.

southern cane areas, forty-one modern mills were in operation in Puerto Rico. Puerto Rican capital still financed about three-fourths of these mills, although often in consortium with US capital. The rest, including the largest mills (Guánica, Aguirre, and Fajardo), were financed principally by US capital, although some foreign investment also found its way into the modern mills, especially in the northern areas of the island. The central sugar mills required considerable investment in machinery, and many were capable of grinding more sugar cane than their own land base could grow. In 1905, for example, the Guánica Central, owned by the South Puerto Rico Sugar Company, was the largest sugar mill in the world. The large mills made obsolete the small mills quickly converted their owners into *colonos,* capitalist farmers who hired wage labor to grow and harvest sugar cane and who would deliver their cane to the central mills, often by railway.[18]

Armstrong introduced many spatial perspectives into the field books. The photomaps and panoramic views complemented the descriptions of the road reports and the perpendicular view of the topographical map. While the bridge and building sketches provided close-up, horizontal orientations, the topographical and town maps provided detached, vertical orientations. In contrast, the landscapes provided panoramic unobstructed views of regions from an oblique angle, neither the vertical view of topography nor the linear, horizontal perspective of itineraries. Armstrong's physical presence in the field for almost four years underscored colonial dominion over Puerto Rico, while his panoramic gaze helped create the knowledge that made it possible. While his assistant took photographs in 1910, Armstrong stood at the summit overlooking the valley of Guayanilla and figuratively dominated the landscape by sweeping his arms over the mountains. He repeated the pose in a series of photographs and created a panorama by pasting adjacent views together. Later he inscribed relevant cartographical information onto this photographic image. He repeated this pose in another segment of the panorama (cropped due to space) as well in other panoramas (figure 2.6). He thus multiplied his gaze indefinitely.

A Kurtzian Moment

Armstrong was in the field continuously for roughly four years under little direct supervision. His first field book was a simple road report, but as he distanced himself from his commanding officer in San Juan he began to introduce more detailed descriptions and varied cartographic techniques, as we have seen. He also began to make observations regarding life in the towns and the character of the inhabitants, especially regarding their military capacity and loyalty, and their discipline and hygiene. The more removed from the

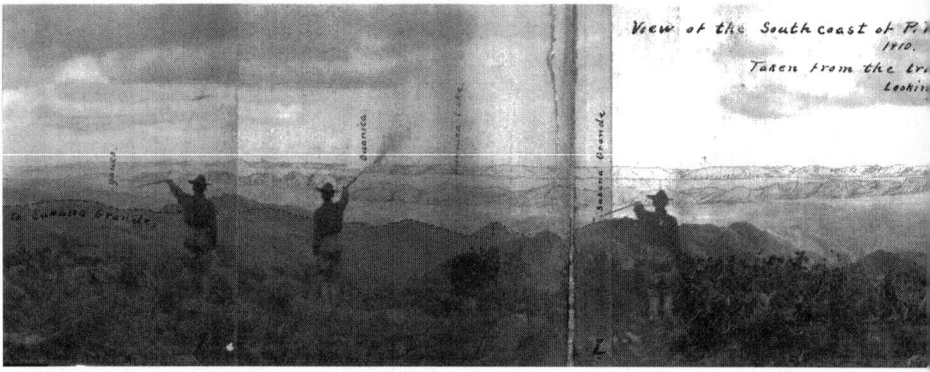

Figure 2.6. View South of Guayanilla. Armstrong, field book 10, folio 55 (one figure cropped).

chain of command, the more Armstrong expressed his intolerance and contempt for the population. The descriptions of his travels along the coast and his incursions into the mountainous interior began to resonate with the fictional character of Kurtz in Joseph Conrad's *The Heart of Darkness* (1902). In Conrad's novel, the main character, Marlowe, is sent upriver into a remote area of Africa to investigate reports of the erratic behavior of a colonial trading agent, Kurtz, who was in charge of ivory extraction and the civilization of the natives. Kurtz was considered a brilliant man, a knowledgeable colonial agent, and an efficient business manager. However, recent information had suggested that Kurtz had resorted to extreme cruelty in the management of the upriver trading stations, and that in the interior, the enterprise was in disarray. In addition to supervising the company's ivory trade, Kurtz had agreed to produce a report for the "International Society for the Suppression of Savage Customs." Marlowe had the opportunity to peruse Kurtz's personal copy of the report and was impressed by its content and its lofty intentions. However, he was a little taken aback by some of the measures it seemed to recommend. Marlowe, our narrator, described the report in the following manner:

> It gave me the notion of an exotic Immensity ruled by an august Benevolence. It made me tingle with enthusiasm. This was the unbounded power of eloquence—of words—of burning noble words. There were no practical hints to interrupt the magic current of phrases, unless a kind of note at the foot of the last page, scrawled evidently much later, in an unsteady hand, may be regarded as the exposition of a method. It was very simple, and at the end of that moving appeal to every altruistic sentiment it blazed at you, luminous and terrifying, like a flash of lightning in a serene sky: "Exterminate all the brutes!"[19]

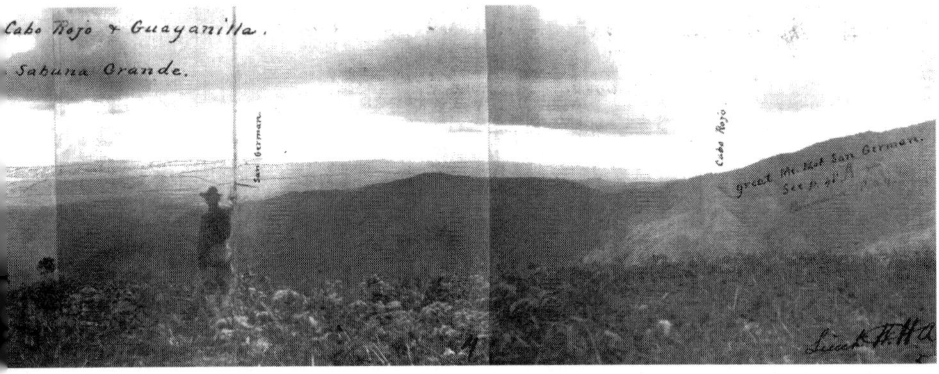

The reader of Armstrong's field books might perceive an uncanny affinity between him and the fictitious Kurtz and find a correspondence between the field books and the novel on colonial Africa. The field books (1908–1912) and Conrad's *Heart of Darkness* (1902) are roughly contemporaneous, although the first were military reports and the latter was a work of fiction. Like Kurtz's fictitious report, Armstrong's field books were indeed an incredible effort, eloquent in their meticulous documentation and careful assembly. His landscapes and panoramic views suggested a certain immensity that was coming under the control of a benevolent colonial power, and he included glowing remarks about the progress in the development of the transportation infrastructure and sugar production under the guidance of the colonial regime.

Like Kurtz, after a masterful and detailed pictorial, cartographic, and descriptive presentation of the city of Mayagüez and neighboring towns, Armstrong felt compelled to add a portentous note to the end of the field book: "Note. In this book an attempt has been made to describe everything as accurately as is possible under existing conditions at the present time. American ideas and progress will cause great changes in the future. New roads will be laid from year to year and old trails will disappear. Means of communication and transportation will improve as more Americans come in and more natives die off. To make an American out of a native Porto Rican is a hopeless and thankless task."[20]

The mix of the objective style of the field books with the complete deprecation of the "natives" in this final note is shocking. Here, Armstrong suggested that the local population would disappear along with the old mountain trails, that the Puerto Ricans would die off and be replaced by American settlers. Armstrong included a photograph of a dying man in his home in the presence of an unidentified observer (figure 2.7). This sick man suffered from

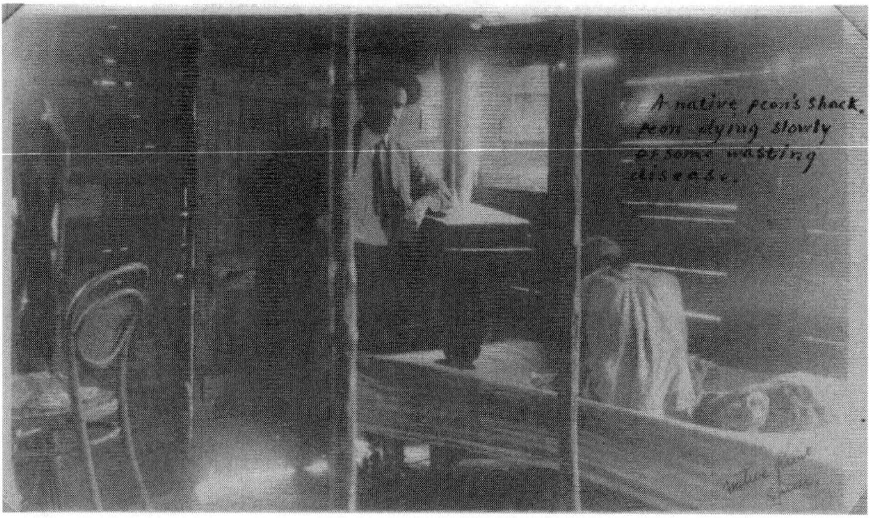

Figure 2.7. "A native peon's shack." Armstrong, field book 8, folio 168.

a "wasting disease," most likely anemia caused by hookworm, which continued in the countryside even after the discoveries of Dr. Bailey Ashford. An effective clinical treatment became available in 1904.[21] This photograph suggested the continuing misery of rural workers, and yet the observer appears detached from and indifferent to the suffering of the hunched, dying man. Armstrong's ominous field book note was not a policy recommendation, nor did he explicitly suggest genocide. Rather, it seemed to him that most of the local population was "unfit," in the evolutionary sense, and unable to adapt to the social changes underway. The changes would be brought about by capital investment and the transformation of the landscape, but not by white settlers, as Armstrong vaguely suggested.

In this brief note, Armstrong shifted literary registers. His document was about troop movement, provisioning, sanitary conditions, and strategic positions. His description of the population related to military concerns of loyalty and the capacity and willingness of locals to bear arms. His observations regarding progress stressed the rapid improvement of roads and urban infrastructure, the construction of new schools, and the expansion of modern sugar mills. In general, he wrote the field books in an objective, denotative mode: the straightforward description of a population and a territory. Suddenly in this concluding note, however, the objective style and the optimistic sentiments give way to deep-felt deprecation of the native. It was a Kurztian moment, if you will, a rupture, an unveiling. It reads as an outburst of a frustrated colonizer who has lost confidence in the project. The hope of the colonizer suddenly vanished and he recognized that all expectations for betterment of the native were a project doomed to failure. Of course, consistent with colonial discourse, the native was to blame. The native was seen as an abject, reprehensible being, an unappreciative brute who would die out. The Kurztian moment was the crisis of the colonizer; he saw the colonized as a faceless, indomitable force of nature, even more intractable than the terrain itself. The landscape was being transformed, but not the population.

Terrains of Visibility

Lieutenant William H. Armstrong's field books give us an inside look at the process of making a topographical military map of Puerto Rico during the early years of the twentieth century. He introduced different spatial perspectives into the field books that revealed the deployment of power not immediately evident in the topographical map he produced for the regiment of infantry. The field books provided itineraries to guide the regiment along the routes from town to town, and included photomaps and panoramic views that complemented the road reports and the perpendicular view of the topographical sketches. While bridge and building drawings provided close-up, horizontal orientations, the topographical and town maps provided detached, vertical orientations. In contrast, the landscapes provided an unobstructed view of regions from an oblique angle, different from vertical view of topography and from the linear, horizontal perspective of itineraries. The integration of these diverse perspectives resulted in the multiplication of terrains of visibility, from the closely observed patterns of the town, its resources, and its people to the most distant panoramas of agricultural land the transportation networks that joined them. These terrains of visibility underlay the principal topographic map printed by the Army War College.

Together these cartographic materials deployed power by means of diverse resolutions, scales, and functions. First, the field books provided detailed information essential to troop movement and provisioning at the local level, while the topographic map presented a strategic overview of the different towns and regions of the island in relation to one another. Together, these cartographic materials made functional the division between the policing of the local population, undertaken by the insular police, and the suppression of any possible internal disturbance or foreign threat, which was the responsibility of the regiment of infantry. Second, the field books showed a commitment to material progress in agriculture and transportation throughout the towns, cities, and countryside of Puerto Rico that went beyond a strictly military perspective. They charted spaces of agricultural production and their connections through the increasingly dense networks of transportation. In particular, they documented the rise of the sugar industry and its transformation of rural landscapes and horizons. The material process of "Americanization" was evident also in the towns and landscapes, in new schools, churches, urban services, roads, and railways.

Finally, Armstrong mapped a crucial moment in the transformation of the island's landscapes under a new regime, at once modern and colonial. His attention to detail, commentary, and recommendations suggested an attempt to capture graphically and thus master these ongoing changes. The field books were an enthusiastic endorsement of the modernization of transportation and agriculture throughout Puerto Rico. Although Armstrong witnessed the material transformation of the landscape, he was not convinced that a modification of the hearts and minds of the population was proceeding at the same pace. Indeed, he conveyed the idea that the colonial subjects were unwilling and unfit for these changes. The lieutenant voiced doubts regarding the loyalty, military character, and capabilities of the population. The desire to discipline subjects and shape landscapes, meticulously channeled into cartography, met with low-intensity resistance on the part of the population. Moreover, throughout Puerto Rico, new political parties increasingly opposed the colonial regime, while labor unions organized to improve conditions.

Notes

1. Another team, composed of lieutenants Teófilo Marxuach and Louis Emmanuelli, produced two additional segments. *Progressive Military Map of the United States Eastern Division: Porto Rico,* William H. Armstrong, 1st Lt., PRRI Authority for Topography and Teófilo Marxuach, 1st Lt., PRRI, Authority for Topography; F. B. Essex, draftsman; surveyed 1908, drawn 1914; Washington, DC, Library of Congress, Madison LMB01 (Geography and Map Reading Room).

2. The research, conservation, and translation into Spanish of these materials was a joint effort of the University of Puerto Rico, Río Piedras (UPR-RP) and the Fundación Puertorriqueña de las Humanidades, an affiliate of the National Endowment for the Humanities. For the bilingual, facsimile edition of these cartographic materials, see Lanny Thompson and María Dolores Luque, *El viaje cartográphico del teniente William H. Armstrong: Puerto Rico, 1908–1912 / The Cartographic Journey of William H. Armstrong: Puerto Rico, 1908–1912,* 2 vols. (San Juan, Puerto Rico: Centro de Investigaciones Históricas and Fundación Puertorriqueña de Humanidades, 2020). This chapter draws on the content of this book. Most of the original field books may be found online in the digital library of the Colección Puertorriqueña, Universidad de Puerto Rico, Río Piedras. In this chapter, endnote references refer to the number of the field book (FB) and the folio.

3. Christian Jacob, *The Sovereign Map: Theoretical Approaches in Cartography throughout History* (Chicago, IL: University of Chicago Press, 2006), 361–362.

4. Matthew Edney, "The Irony of Imperial Mapping," in *The Imperial Map: Cartography and the Mastery of Empire,* ed. James Akerman, 11–45 (Chicago, IL: University of Chicago Press, 2009), 11–19.

5. Lisa Fletcher, "'Some Distance to Go': A Critical Survey of Island Studies," *New Literatures Review* 47 (2011): 17–34.

6. According to the *Oxford English Dictionary*, a terrain is "a tract of country considered with regard to its natural features, configuration, etc.; in military use esp. as affecting its tactical advantages, fitness for maneuvering, etc.; also, an extent of ground, region, district, territory."

7. Tiara Na'puti, "Archipelagic Rhetoric: Remapping the Marianas and Challenging Militarization from 'A Stirring Place.'" *Communication and Critical/Cultural Studies* 16, no. 1 (2019): 4–25.

8. Cf. Edney, "Imperial Mapping," 19.

9. The Puerto Rico Regiment of Infantry was created in 1901 as a provisional regiment and in 1908 became a regular regiment of the US Army. Héctor Marín Román, *¡Llego la gringada!: El contexto socio-militar estadounidense en Puerto Rico y otros lugares del Caribe hasta 1919* (San Juan: Academia Puertorriqueña de la Historia, 2009); Héctor Andrés Negroni, *Historia militar de Puerto Rico* (San Juan: Comisión Puertorriqueña para la Celebración del Quinto Centenario del Descubrimiento de América y Puerto Rico, 1991).

10. The first to describe the strategic functions of these field books was Aníbal Sepúlveda Rivera, "La mirada de William Armstrong," in *Puerto Rico urbano: Atlas histórico de la ciudad puertorriqueña*, vol. 3, *Entresiglos, 1880s–1910s*, 45-55 (San Juan: Carimar, 2004).

11. Beekman Winthrop, *Fifth Annual Report of the Governor of Porto Rico Covering the Period from July 1, 1904, to June 30, 1905* (Washington, DC: Government Printing Office, 1905), 33–34.

12. Ibid., 145.

13. FB 8, 162–163.

14. FB 4, 17–18.

15. Francisco Scarano, *Puerto Rico: Cinco siglos de historia*, 2nd ed. (Mexico: McGraw-Hill, 2000), 719–729.

16. Ibid., 729–736; Gervasio García and A. G. Quintero Rivera, *Desafío y solidaridad: Breve historia del movimiento obrero puertorriqueño* (Río Piedras, Puerto Rico: Ediciones Huracán, 1982).

17. FB 1, summary, n.p.

18. Humberto García Muñiz, *Sugar and Power in the Caribbean* (San Juan: Editorial de la Universidad de Puerto Rico and Ian Randle Publishers, 2010).

19. Joseph Conrad, *Heart of Darkness* (New York: Penguin, 2017), 57.

20. FB 8, 179.

21. For more on Ashford and hookworm eradication, see José Amador, *Medicine and Nation Building in the Americas, 1890–1940* (Nashville, TN: Vanderbilt University Press, 2015); and José Amador, "The Pursuit of Health: Colonialism and Hookworm Eradication in Puerto Rico," *Southern Spaces*, March 30, 2017, https://southernspaces.org.

THREE

With a Skull in Each Hand

Boneyard Photography in the American Empire after 1898

Krystle Stricklin

With a skull in each hand, a man dressed in white sits atop a pile of human bones. In a morbid balancing act, he squats awkwardly with a skull resting on top of his head, two more tucked under each arm, and his right foot perched upon yet another skull. A jumble of sun-bleached bones and even more skulls are scattered at his feet in a grassy field, with fenced enclosures on each side in the background (figure 3.1). The man's name is Frank M. Rainey, an American soldier who served as a private in the 1st Ohio Volunteer Cavalry during the War of 1898, or the so-called Spanish-American War.[1] The bones he has disturbed are of dead Filipinos who were laid to rest in a graveyard near the port city of Cavite on the island of Luzon in the Philippines. However, that rest would not last for those souls or for many other deceased persons in the Philippines, Puerto Rico, and Cuba as a result of the US colonial occupation of the islands after the war. Posed in a Filipino graveyard as a conqueror, Rainey embodies a macabre photographic practice that emerged in the aftermath of 1898, in which American soldiers and tourists desecrated island cemeteries by plundering and photographing the boneyards located within, where thousands of skeletal remains were deposited into large heaps after removal from their original graves. As I demonstrate in this chapter, this morbid photographic activity was normalized and perpetuated through personal snapshots taken and collected as souvenirs or "trophies" and by the extensive commercialization of boneyard images through books, popular magazines, and newspapers, as well as stereographs and postcards. Moreover, I examine the ways in which they functioned to satisfy mainland-American desires for lurid pictures of the new empire, and also how they shaped the enforcement of new US policies regarding the business of death and burial on the islands. As well, I aim to show the inherent violence of such images and how their making involved the disturbing of persons—both living and dead.

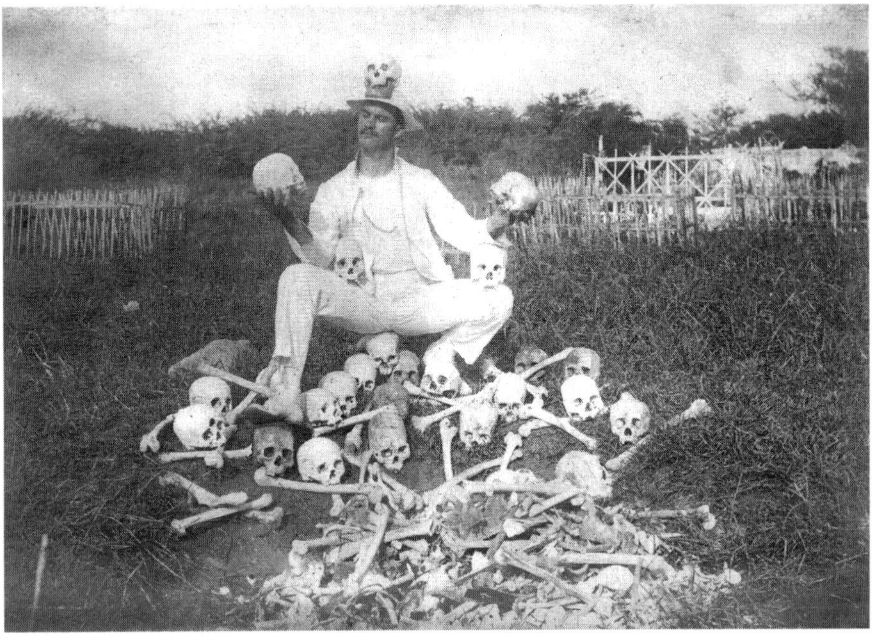

Figure 3.1. Frank Rainey with Human Skulls at Cavite Cemetery, c. 1900s. Photograph. Naval History and Heritage Command, Washington, DC, Elizabeth Davis Price Collection.

A sight that would have appeared strange and shocking to most, boneyards were fairly commonplace in the Pacific and Caribbean island territories of Spain, and then in the United States after the war. They were a matter of both cultural and natural geography. That is, what do you do when you have more bodies to bury than land to bury them in? Sometimes referred to as "bone piles," "bone pits," or even "bone valleys," these were designated spaces within or near cemeteries where disarticulated human skeletons were piled en masse without identification, either above ground or in an open pit. The bone piles amassed throughout Cuba, Puerto Rico, and the Philippines varied in size and formation, and were typically located in the corners of a cemetery. By definition, they are secondary graves, as the standard custom was for a deceased person's family to "rent" a grave space, often in an above-ground crypt, for a fixed time that varied anywhere from two to ten years, with a yearly fee.[2] Once the burial "lease" had expired or if the grave rent was not paid or renewed, the skeletal remains were removed from their crypt and transferred to the bone piles. Many families could not afford a burial, and so their loved one's remains were sent straight to the pile. The bodies were covered with quicklime to aid in the decomposition process before being transferred to the bone pile. In the

United States, where land is abundant, there is little concern about burying people in the ground in individual plots; however, for island nations, land space is limited and large burial yards are simply impractical.

In large part, the boneyards and burial practices of America's new empire attained notoriety through countless sensationalized stories that appeared in the press. Many Americans who traveled to the islands and first encountered the boneyards expressed horror and shock at what was perceived to be a callous treatment of the dead. Writing home to their families, American soldiers and sailors repeatedly described the bone piles as "ghastly," "strange," "gruesome," and "horrific" sights, and many journalists likened the "eviction" of bodies from their graves to poorly managed tenement houses.[3] On April 18, 1898, three days before the official declaration of war with Spain, the *Washington Post* published a story written by Fannie Brigham Ward, a well-known journalist and traveler, in which she described her first sighting of a Cuban boneyard in Havana's Colon Cemetery.[4] Working as a special correspondent for the *Post*, Ward stumbled upon the boneyard while visiting the graves of the American sailors who died onboard the USS *Maine* when it exploded in Havana Harbor on February 15, an event that precipitated the war. At the cemetery, Ward visited the "Dead-House" where many corpses were taken to be covered in quicklime, and in her article, she described the large bone pit as "a place which few who visit the cemetery ever hear of."[5] This fact changed quickly as a result of the war with Spain and the subsequent Philippine-American War (1899–1902), and as more boneyard stories and photographs emerged, they continued to be a topic of American debate well into the new century.

In October 1898, leading papers such as the *Boston Journal* and the *Evening Times* in Washington, DC, published their first stories about boneyards found in cemeteries throughout Puerto Rico, and by early December, more newspapers and magazines featured similar reports from the Philippines and Cuba, with ever-increasing frequency.[6] The most detailed accounts came from soldier's letters published regularly in regional and hometown papers. In these letters, soldiers wrote of their many new experiences abroad, the challenges of war, and their local regiment's activities. For many Americans at home, these letters provided the first knowledge of places and peoples largely unknown to a mainland-US audience, and sightings of boneyards were described often and with great attention. In May 1899, when describing a boneyard in the Philippines, private Rob C. Blakely from Kansas wrote, "One can see here bodies in all stages of decomposition, some with skin dried up and some the bones merely hang together. There are thousands of bodies in these bone piles."[7] Another solider wrote to his niece in June 1900, "I was down to a Filipino cemetery not long ago and saw them bury a few natives. There is a pile of human bones and skulls where they dump them out to make room for more. I climbed up on the pile and there must have been a thousand person's skulls in the pile . . . once seen never to be forgotten. I can see them yet when I shut my eyes."[8] These letters are illustrative of a growing public interest in the new empire's cemeteries, and the coinciding craze for boneyard pictures that arose during the early years of US colonialism.

Together with firsthand descriptions, boneyard photographs served as important proof for a broader audience back in the United States, and were quickly reproduced as stereoviews and postcards, printed in books and magazines, and displayed in public venues, all of which amounted to a vast constellation of visual objects. Dramatic scenes of tangled human bones stacked in mounds high and wide enough to stand upon made for morbid yet altogether engrossing photographs. Stereoviews sold by Stroymeyer and Wyman, the Kilburn Brothers, and the Keystone View Company allowed armchair tourists the opportunity to observe the bone piles in the safety of their homes (figure 3.2). Group portraits and personal snapshots taken at the bone piles functioned both as war mementos and travel souvenirs, and were shared in intimate settings among family and friends, often preserved in travel albums and scrapbooks. With the recent development of affordable personal cameras, Americans traveling to the new territories generated an untold number of photographs of every subject imaginable. Pictures of the boneyards often received special attention in the press with reports of photos mailed home and announcements of their display, clearly indicating their desirability as objects. In one case, a

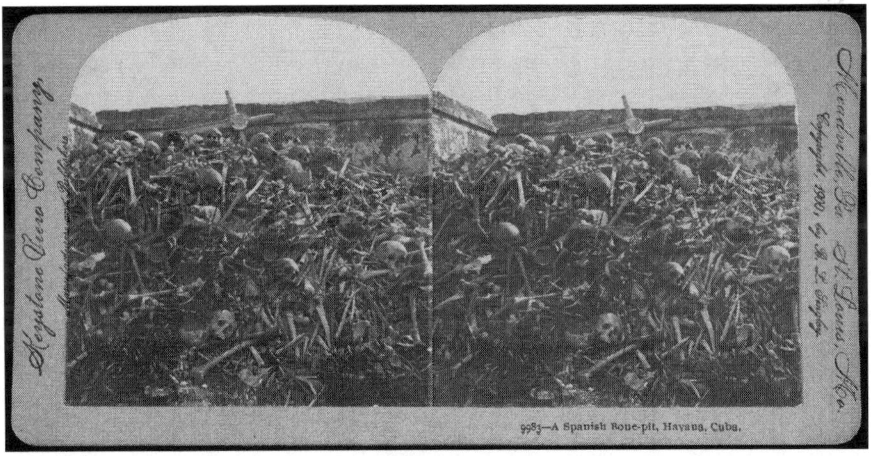

Figure 3.2. B. L. Singley, Keystone View Company, *A Spanish Bone-Pit, Havana, Cuba,* 1900. Stereograph. Stereo Foreign Geog. File—Cuba—Havana. Library of Congress, Prints and Photographs Division.

furniture store in Iowa advertised a display of war "curios" brought back from Cuba belonging to a young American bugler who had recently returned home from his station in Havana.[9] A local newspaper article provided a detailed list of items on display, many of which were objects taken or stolen from significant sites around Havana, and highlighted on the list was a photograph taken of the famous bone pile at the Cristóbal Colón Cemetery.

In the northeast corner of the Cristóbal Colón Cemetery, so-named for Christopher Columbus, existed the largest boneyard in Cuba and the most notorious for camera-wielding Americans in Havana. In an 1899 article for the *New York Times,* one such visitor, a lieutenant colonel Oliver Ellsworth Wood, described his first sighting of the Colón boneyard as follows: "On the right of the main entrance and inside the grounds, about two hundred yards from the gate, are to be seen the high stone walls of an enclosure of some sort with no apparent opening. Being on horseback, I was enabled from my height to look over the wall, and there before my very eyes were skeletons complete and in fragments, numberless skulls with the hair still growing on them, and the various bones of the human form—all heaped up and thrown promiscuously into one huge pile!"[10] Constructed in the 1870s, Colón Cemetery served as Havana's primary burial ground after city officials recognized a need for a larger burial space, due in part to a devastating cholera outbreak in 1868 and a growing population.[11] Prior to that, the Espada Cemetery, founded in 1806 by Spanish bishop Juan José Díaz de Espada y Landa, was the first public burial ground in Havana and the place where the city's first boneyard took shape. An American journalist, who visited the Espada Cemetery in 1843, wrote that "in each of the four corners of the cemetery there is raised a pyramid-like pile of human bones bleached to snowy whiteness."[12] The Espada Cemetery was abandoned soon after the opening of the larger Colón Cemetery, which covered an area of roughly 504,400 square meters located east of the Rio Almendares and southwest of the city center.[13]

A visit to the Colón Cemetery boneyard was all but mandatory for newcomers to Havana in 1898. Described by one newspaper as a "resort for sightseers," the graveyard was perhaps the most talked about site in all of Havana, and a first stop for many curious onlookers. "The first place we visited was the boneyard in the Cristobal Colon cemetery," wrote John Nolan, a private in the 160th Indiana Volunteer Infantry, to his parents in 1899.[14] "There are said to be 860,000 skeletons in the pit," Nolan claimed. Similarly, US Navy machinist Louis P. Lipps wrote to the editor of his hometown paper, "The Cristobal Colon cemetery is about as interesting as Havana itself. About the first question one asks of an acquaintance is 'Have you seen the bone pile?' The bone pile is in an enclosure about fifty feet square, walled about seven feet about the ground and excavated about fifteen feet. . . . The enclosure presents a ghastly sight."[15] Newspapers in the United States published countless stories and descriptions of the bone pile at Colón Cemetery, often noting the many photographers at the site. Many popular images depicted groups of soldiers standing on top of the pile, posing with skulls or crossed bones in their hands (figure 3.3). One visitor to Colón reported seeing soldiers playing ball "with a skull and a thigh bone" while being photographed.[16] The general frivolity displayed by American visitors to the boneyard affirms that such callous acts of desecration were viewed by many as a normal leisure activity, as well as unique photographic opportunity.

The Detroit Photographic Company produced a series of photographs from Colón Cemetery that reveal the boneyard's post-1898 paradox as both functional burial ground for Havana's many inhabitants and tantalizing tourist destination for US visitors. Founded by Detroit entrepreneur William A. Livingston, Jr., and photographer Edwin H. Husher, the Detroit Photographic Company was a leading publisher of postcards and photographic views in the late 1900s, and one of the largest producers of images related to the war and new territories.[17] In their photographs at Colón, the two photographers wander about the graveyard and bone pile, one dressed in all black and the other in a stark white jacket and hat, sometimes with a lit cigar hanging from his mouth. Treating the cemetery as their photographic playground, the two men alternate turns with the camera, capturing one another in several clichéd poses, for example, each standing perched atop the pile while gazing contemplatively at a skull in his hands. In many images, the cameraman's shadow appears as a ghoulish black silhouette cast onto a tangled white web of sun-bleached bones. As if deliberate, one of the photographers positioned himself so that his shadowy figure appears headless, cut-off, in contrast to his associate, who holds his seemingly "missing" head in his hands (figure 3.4). In such images, the man's severed shadow cast over a sea of anonymous death seems an inadvertent allusion to the long shadow of empire that loomed over Cuba, as well as the violence it brought about, first with Spain and then with the United States.

In addition to ominous arrangements of shadows and bone, the Detroit photograph series unveils how the practice of boneyard photography disturbed the grueling labor of death and the cemetery's occupants, both living and dead. The straw baskets featured in multiple images served as advantageous props for the photographers, but more importantly as valuable tools used in the transportation of bones from one location to another within the cemetery. As mentioned previously, skeletal remains were often removed from their shallow graves and deposited at the bone pile, a process that required great physical labor as well as means of transport. The photographers documented this work, with images of two Cuban workmen using large straw baskets to load and unload an oxcart full of bones (figure 3.5). In one photograph, a workman

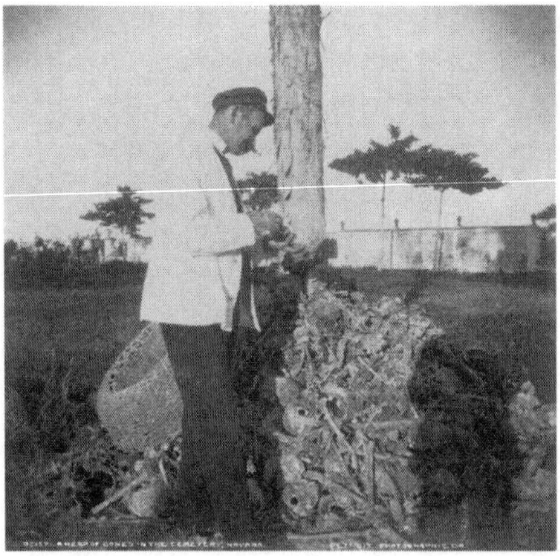

Figure 3.4. Detroit Publishing Company, *A Heap of Bones in the Cemetery [Necropolis Cristobal Colon], Havana,* c. 1898–1902. Photograph. LC-D4-21573. Library of Congress, Prints and Photographs Division, Detroit Publishing Company Photograph Collection.

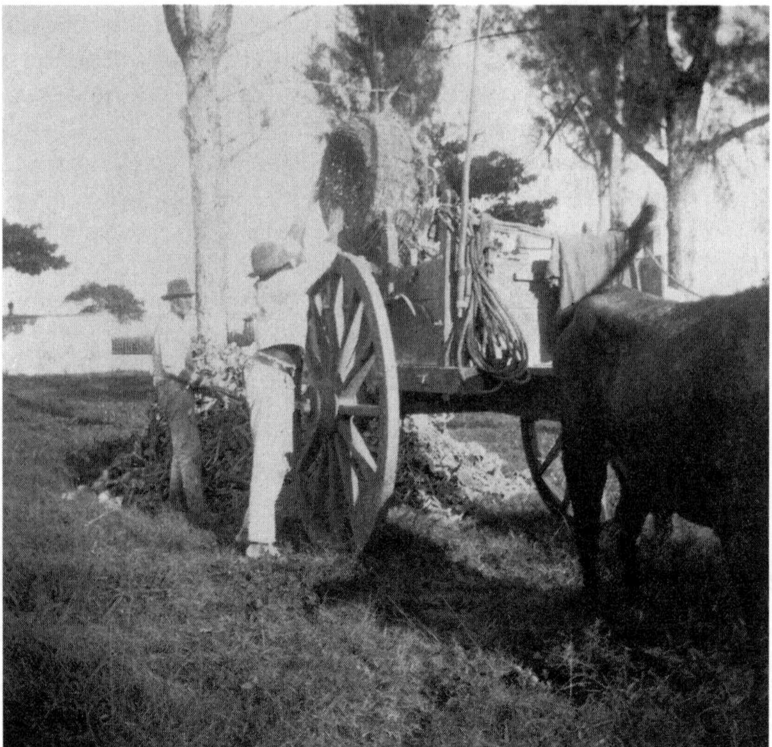

Figure 3.5. Detroit Publishing Company, *Workmen in the Cemetery [Necropolis Cristobal Colon], Havana,* c. 1898–1902. Photograph. LC-D4-21567. Library of Congress, Prints and Photographs Division, Detroit Publishing Company Photograph Collection.

throws a large basket of bones over his head and into the oxcart, with wheels as tall as the man, while another worker stands beside him, holding the cart's next occupants. Once the cart was full, the workmen would have wheeled it to the top of the bone pile to unload the remains. In 1899, a journalist from South Carolina observed, "There is a narrow opening in the wall, through which the newest arrivals are wheeled up on the sea of skulls and there dumped,"[18] and, as Fannie Ward described in her story for the *Washington Post*, "The tracks of wheels over crumbled bones show where horses and carts are driven in over the heap to deposit fresh loads."[19] In other images, the Cuban workers vigorously empty baskets and hunch over piles of bones, all the while exposing the backbreaking nature of cemetery work. It is unclear how many, if any, of these photographs were reproduced for the public; however, for a contemporary audience they underscore the intense physical labor that was required to maintain the bone piles.

Despite their appeal to photographers and tourists, many people in the United States regarded the boneyards as paradigms of Spanish "barbarism" and beheld them with admonishment, directed mainly at the Catholic Church. After the war with Spain, the United States was quick to establish a provisional military government in Cuba, and relations were openly hostile between the newly appointed US administrators and the Spanish-run Catholic Church. During the Spanish-colonial period, Catholicism became the dominant religion across the island, and the church wielded considerable power over all aspects of Cuban life, from birth and marriage to death and burial.[20] The US government sought to diminish that power with new laws and regulations that promised broad political, economic, and social reform. John R. Brooke, the first military governor of Cuba, under advisement from then Secretary of State John Hay, vigorously led the early occupation efforts to safeguard American political and economic interests on the island. On April 12, 1899, Brooke issued the publication of a nine-part decree, or military order, concerning the management of Cuban cemeteries.[21] The aim of the new law, in sum, was to shift control of the highly lucrative burial business away from the church, following the belief that the United States' model of separation of church and state should be adapted to Cuba as well. This was a politically and economically strategic move, which aligned with the prevailing American distrust of Cuba's lingering ties to Catholicism, a religion that was perceived by many as distinctly Spanish and undemocratic.[22] This distrust was conveyed often in the American press, with scathing reports of the church's "for rent" burial system as corrupt and the bone piles themselves as unhygienic and amoral. As such, boneyard photographs, in addition to their value as souvenirs and war mementos, were treated as evidence of the perceived need for such vast overhauls of civic and religious institutions on the island.

Similarly, across the Philippine archipelago, the Catholic Church exerted considerable power over daily life and social customs, particularly in the northern island of Luzon, including control over funerals and cemeteries. At the time of the Philippine-American War and subsequent occupation of the islands, the foremost Catholic orders and friars were among the richest and most influential segments of Filipino society, and ongoing tensions mounted between those friars who maintained loyalty to the Spanish government and Filipino friars who supported the nationalist movement and Filipino independence.[23] This situation posed a number of problems for the United States when, as in Cuba, the military government imposed new laws adhering to the strict separation of church and state, including an overhaul of the lucrative grave rental business. From 1898 to 1902, while the Philippine-American War was fought between US troops and the revolutionary forces of the nascent First Philippine Republic, a series of military governors were appointed to rule the islands, as well as devise and enforce the new policies. Thus abruptly, many Filipinos faced the new colonial regime's aggressive regulations concerning the burial of their dead.[24]

During the war and early years of occupation, public discourse in the United States on boneyards intensified in the press, and notably, Filipino boneyards aroused more condemnation than those in Cuba or Puerto Rico. The push to abolish the boneyards was largely influenced by a US-imperialist agenda that hinged on the belief that Filipinos were incapable of self-government and a growing hostility toward the Catholic Church. In the American press, Protestant missionaries working in the Philippines voiced their indignation at the sight of the bone pits, and some even attempted to end the practice by buying land for in-ground burials that would be kept beyond the reach of the Catholic clergy. For example, in June 1899, American chaplain Charles C. Pierce wrote from the Philippines to his friend back home in Lincoln, Nebraska, "The first great necessity is a cemetery where these people can be buried. . . . We must have one!"[25] While proselytizing in villages and towns near Manila, Pierce conveyed his horror at the sight of a boneyard, and in his letter published in the *Lincoln Nebraska State Journal,* he outlined a plan to raise money for a public cemetery, which he would eventually transfer to the Protestant church that he hoped to establish there. The chaplain's concerns aligned with a large segment of non-Catholic religious communities in the United States that strongly supported the government's efforts to weaken the influence and power of Catholic clergymen in the Philippines.

To be sure, photographs played a decisive role in America's efforts to upend the Catholic Church's authority in the new empire. Art historian J. M. Mancini has written in depth on the visual and material culture of the Philippine-American War, and deftly argues that photographs showcasing the destruction of Catholic sites and symbols during the war, including churches, architectural ornaments, and sacred religious objects, triumphantly celebrated the US use of force to control the changing political landscape in the Philippines.[26] The success of the new US regime required a literal and visual collapsing of the former Spanish regime, which, as Mancini suggests, was "sold" in part through images of destruction and the aggressive enforcement of American ideals. Further, the United States had a vested interest in normalizing the size, scope, and ambition of its emergent empire. Rather than hiding that fact, photographs were used to make US imperial agendas highly visible. In so doing, they helped shape a plain-to-see narrative that might convince citizens of the value in the United States' rapid and violent territorial projections toward empire on a global scale. In this context, certain photographs can be read as reinforcing the government's attempt to regulate the burial practices of foreign peoples as part of a larger agenda designed to subjugate and control the bodies (both living and dead) of colonial inhabitants.

This is evident in a photograph of a Filipino funeral from José de Olivares and William Smith Bryan's influential two-volume book *Our Islands and Their People as Seen with Camera and Pencil* (1899). Appearing in the second volume, the photograph titled *A Filipino Funeral under American Auspices* (figure 3.6) includes the following caption: "The Spanish style of depositing

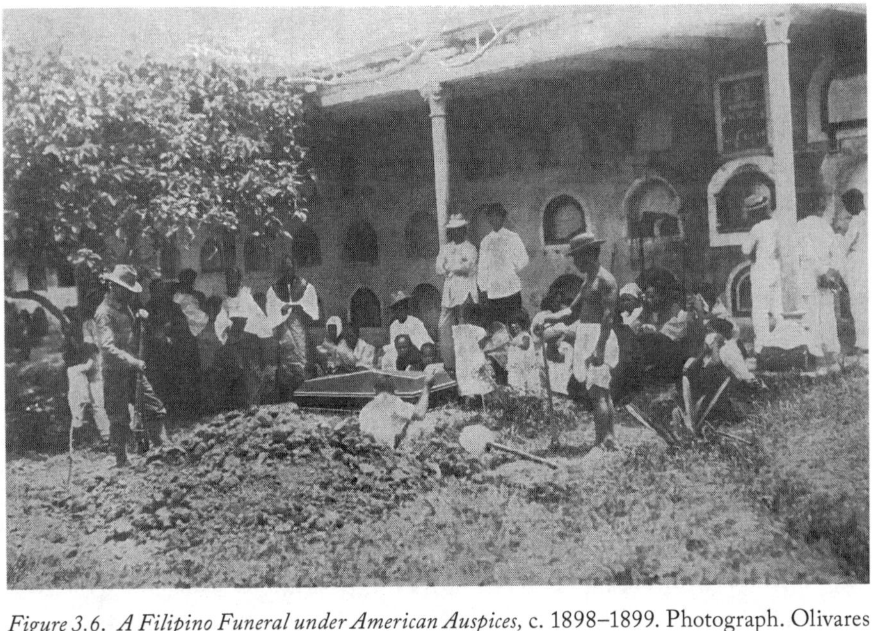

Figure 3.6. A Filipino Funeral under American Auspices, c. 1898–1899. Photograph. Olivares and Bryan, *Our Islands and Their People*, 2: 719. From the library of the author.

corpses temporarily in a vault, and after a few months or years throwing the bones in a common heap[,] has been discontinued under American influences. But the prejudices of the people were so firmly fixed that in some instances it was necessary to send an armed guard to enforce the rules of the authorities."[27]

On the far left in the photograph, an American guard stands with his head bowed and both hands placed firmly on a rifle poised between his legs. With a crowd of somber mourners behind him, the armed guard gazes down at the work of a gravedigger who is shoveling dirt from inside a grave. This scene reveals the armed intrusion of US imperialism into Filipino cemeteries, and also highlights how Filipino burial and mourning practices were openly exposed to American eyes—and cameras. The purpose here is twofold—to offer viewers both a denunciation of the barbaric "Spanish style" of boneyard burials and to show how Filipinos were resisting American "civilizing" efforts. Yet, a closer look at the photograph tells a different story. None of the funeral attendees appear in any way defiant or in protest of the burial. Instead and contrary to the caption's claim, the women seated around the edge of the grave look appropriately grief-stricken, some with handkerchiefs held up to their faces, quietly mourning for the unnamed deceased. Resistance here is not necessarily to the "civilizing" efforts of the United States, but rather, in this case, the mournful scene embodies the new realities of death and dying in the aftermath of war and a changing colonial regime.

During the Philippine-American War, cemeteries and boneyards were not only sights of fascination and horror but actively used spaces of war. Many Filipino churches and graveyards were utilized by American troops as strategic hideouts, for places to rest on long marches, and for the burial of their own dead. For one example, in July 1899, private Frank S. Brown of the 4th US Infantry wrote of a night he spent camped on top of a bone pile while on his march to fight in northern Luzon. In his letter, published in the *Daily Times New Brunswick,* Brown described "an old Filipino graveyard" located about eight miles north of Manila, where he and his compatriots "put up our shelter tents and slept on top of bones in the grave yard."[28] He further surmised that "many victims of Spanish crimes and murders lie buried in the graveyard."[29] Whether truthful or not, the language of his letter and the assignment of Spanish blame for the bone piles' many occupants is indicative of an oft-repeated sentiment expressed in many such letters sent home by soldiers. Without any proof of how the bones he slept on came to the pile, perhaps it was merely an attempt to assuage his mind as to why he was fighting in a war eight thousand miles from home.

The most photographed boneyard in the Philippines was at Paco Cemetery in the capital city of Manila, just south of the Pasig River and adjacent to two of the city's most important historical sites, the Intramuros and Luneta

Park. Originally built by Spanish colonizers for the burial of their dead, Paco Cemetery was by the end of the twentieth century a place of great significance to the Philippine independence movement as the initial burial spot of José Rizal, the beloved revolutionary politician and poet whom the Spanish had executed in 1896. The protonationalist writings of Rizal inspired the Philippine Revolution against Spain that same year, which concluded with a tense resolution of nonaggression, the Pact of Biak-na-Bato, in 1897. When the United States declared war against Spain in 1898, pronationalist rebels in the Philippines first sided with American forces. However, after American soldiers opened fire on Filipino insurgents in what would be called the Battle of Manila in February 1899, the revolutionaries would declare war against the American government, thus beginning the Philippine-American War.

Coincidently, on February 4, 1899, the same day as the start of the war, *Harper's Weekly* published an article written by their most prominent correspondent in the Philippines, John F. Bass, telling of a nighttime visit to the Paco Cemetery boneyard, including a conversation Bass heard between a Filipino man and an American who desired a souvenir skull. For some Americans, trips to the boneyard meant leaving not only with a token photograph but also with stolen skulls and other bones as trophy souvenirs. Accompanied by a small group of friends and with his camera in tow, Bass toured the entire cemetery to provide a detailed report for the readers of *Harper's Weekly* on the "curious" burial customs of the Filipino people, a topic that endlessly captivated the American public. Upon reaching the bone pit, he writes,

> A rather pretty Filipino girl, nonchalantly smoking a cigarette at the edge of the pit, gave a light to one of our party. Her escort climbed down into the bone-yard, and picking up a skull, muttered something in Tagalog. The relic-hunter among us asked the man, in Spanish, to give him the skull to take home as a memento. "Oh, señor," answered the Tagalo, "if you take it home, it will jump about at night, and give you no rest until you either break it or bring it back here!"[30]

Upon hearing the Filipino's response, the unnamed "relic hunter" in Bass' party suggested that a "splash of holy water" on the skull might keep it from "jumping about at night." The story was featured along with Bass' own photograph of the Paco Cemetery bone pit, captioned "A Valley of Dry Bones," and this particular excerpt was reprinted and circulated widely in newspapers across the country.

The encounter certainly raises a few interesting questions. The first regards the identity of the Filipina girl or woman and her Tagalog-speaking "escort." Who were they, and why were they at the cemetery near the bone pile that night? While the "who" remains impossible to verify, one clue as to "why" might be found in the precise date of Bass' visit, which was during the middle of Allhallowtide, specifically on the night of November 1st, or All Saint's Day.[31] As Bass described for his readers, the following day, All Soul's Day (November 2), "is the only day in the year when souls in purgatory have a chance to get out."[32] The cemetery that night would have been full of people visiting the graves of loved ones to light candles and say prayers, and it was one of the few nights of the year when women were allowed to enter the cemetery. It may also explain the warning of the haunted skull. Bass' story goes on to tell that the suggestion of holy water was scoffed at by the Filipino man, who insisted that it would do no good. One can only speculate whether this warning was based on a sincere belief that removing skulls from the pit would incur such a haunting or if the man was merely trying to scare off the would-be American relic hunter. In any case, his story demonstrates the popular desire for such gruesome tales, as well as stolen relics, from the new territories.

In Cuba and Puerto Rico, similar social restrictions barred women from attending funerals and visiting cemeteries, and, as in the Philippines, those restrictions were lifted during the observance of Allhallowtide, which to this day remains an important time for remembering the dead. Historian Luis Martínez-Fernández has argued that women in nineteenth-century Havana faced harsh social restrictions and segregation due in part to societal issues of class and race, wherein the Cuban elite desired to "protect" elite white women—and their whiteness—from the predominantly black and mixed-race populations of Havana.[33] These gender restrictions, however, did not keep some intrepid American women from visiting the boneyards. In addition to Fannie Ward's account from 1898, journalist Dorothy Stanhope visited and wrote about the boneyard at Colón. While working for the *New York Times*, Stanhope made at least two trips to the Colón Cemetery—one in February 1899, and again in November 1902.[34] Like Frank Bass in the Philippines, Stanhope visited the cemetery during Allhallowtide on All Saint's Day or All Soul's Day, otherwise known as Decoration Days in Cuba. Writing in 1902, she recalls, "I well remember that on my first visit to Colon in February of 1899, I saw many little heaps of human bones all about, waiting for the cart to carry them to the others in the far corner. Today nothing of the kind is to be seen, and the osario is no longer open to the public."[35] In fact, Stanhope's first visit to Colón would have coincided with the mounting pressure on US military officials to restrict access to the boneyard and stop soldiers from stealing the remains.

The widespread theft of skulls and bones from the piles was a topic of great concern in the United States, with such reports stating that "soldiers returning to this country have brought with them a skull or two, or a tibia, or a grilled rib."[36] In Havana it was such a problem that in late January major general Fitzhugh Lee, who commanded the volunteer army in Cuba, issued an order to all soldiers that they were no longer permitted to keep human skulls or bones in their tents, with one paper even proclaiming, "American Soldiers Had Too Many Bones about Their Tents."[37] In addition, guards were placed at Colón Cemetery and at a nearby boneyard in Quemados.[38] Eventually the Colón boneyard was covered over to prevent the further addition or removal of human remains. By September 1899, it was reported that the government "has at last filled over the ghastly 'bone pit' and the days of 'luncheon on skulls' are past."[39] This act was widely praised in the US press, and seen by many Americans as a symbol of the positive effects of the US colonial administration in Cuba; however, it arguably did nothing to lessen public interest in boneyard photographs, many of which were already in circulation by this time, or the desire to obtain skulls and bones as souvenirs.

In fact, as late as 1907, US tourists were still visiting, photographing, and robbing skulls from Cuban boneyards. Early that year, Mrs. Charles R. Miller, a prominent Baltimore photojournalist, traveled to Cuba on a mission to dispel the numerous and vague rumors circulating in the United States that it was unsafe for Americans, particularly women, to travel outside of Cuba's larger cities.[40] Miller quickly disproved this notion, reporting back of the ease with which she traveled alone from Havana to Santiago de Cuba, declaring it "absolutely safe" for any American man or woman. That June, *Leslie's Weekly*, whom Miller had worked for since 1898, published her story on Cuban funerals and cemeteries, along with four of her photographs.[41] In the article, Miller described the funeral and burial practices she saw at Colón Cemetery, as well as a trip she took to Camagüey to see the boneyard of "Cristo Cemetery."[42] Her visit to Camagüey was made on the recommendation of an American man, who approached her in a café one afternoon. Hearing that she was in Cuba working for *Leslie's*, the man suggested that she travel to Camagüey. Of the conversation, she writes, "'Well,' he continued, "if your nerve is good go out to the cemetery and get some pictures of the bones. See, I've been there," and he drew from his pocket a human skull and several teeth, which he laid on the table before me. Then he added, "I think I'll have an inkstand made of the skull, and the teeth I'll just keep for souvenirs."[43] Upon seeing the relics, Miller writes of her disgust and disbelief that a "civilized American" could be "such a degenerate." Yet, despite her apparent revulsion, the very next morning she set out for Camagüey, a nearly seven-hour trip, to see the boneyard for herself. When she got to the boneyard, she described seeing bones "scattered about like leaves in autumn," as she was guided around by a man described only as "the old care-taker," presumably a Cuban cemetery worker, who is pictured in one of the four photographs chosen for the article. Miller does not admit to taking any photographs of the boneyard, though it seems likely that she would have done so, given the opportunity. However, her story does demonstrate that the closure of the Colón Cemetery boneyard in 1899 did not, in fact, put an end to the American practice of trophy taking, as it had been widely reported in the United States. As well, Miller's story provides another example of boneyards as spaces where American visitors encountered, or more accurately interrupted, the laborious work of death in island cemeteries, such as the case with the Detroit Photographic series.

In addition to personal souvenirs and wartime trophies, many Americans stole remains under the guise of "scientific" study and tutelage. In his 1903 book *History and Geography of the Philippine Islands,* Oscar William Coursey, a US Army major who served in the Philippines, wrote of the bone piles he visited and how "being a teacher, [he] selected a well-shaped Filipino skull from one of these piles and brought it home."[44] Back home, Coursey used the skull as a visual aid in his public lectures titled "The Philippines and Filipinos," and for what he called "concrete instruction in Physiology."[45] These types of lectures were common from self-proclaimed "experts" who had returned from fighting or touring in the new territories, and were often extensively illustrated with photographs and stolen objects. Likewise, in 1901, soldier Leslie N. Collins wrote in a letter published in the *Christian-Evangelist,* "I have a little Filipino skull which was taken from one of these bone-piles, which I purpose to keep as a relic, and when I get home I shall exhibit it as proof of the truthfulness of the statements contained in this letter."[46] For Collins, it would seem, photographs and words alone were unsatisfactory "proof" of what he described as the "inhumane practice" of a "Catholic burial in the Philippines."[47]

This brings us, at last, back to the photograph of Frank Rainey sitting in a boneyard surrounded by Filipino skulls, one of which he kept for his own souvenir. Rainey took many photographs at the cemetery in Cavite, posing with his friends in all manner of disregard for the human remains they disturbed (figure 3.7), and he kept his photographs in albums and displayed them in his home along with his skull. His photographs, and the many others discussed in this chapter, exemplify the dehumanization of foreign remains that occurred in the making, taking, and circulating of boneyard images and relics during this period of US colonialism. Boneyard photographs depict the visual progression of imperial violence, in which the overt physical violence of colonialism is transformed into a kind of playful sociality or, put otherwise, wartime tourism. Rainey's posed photographs taken atop the bones of deceased Filipinos speaks to the soldier's participation, whether wittingly or not, in US imperial agendas. His photographs convert a space resonant with Spanish colonialism, US violence, and Filipino national history into a site of amuse-

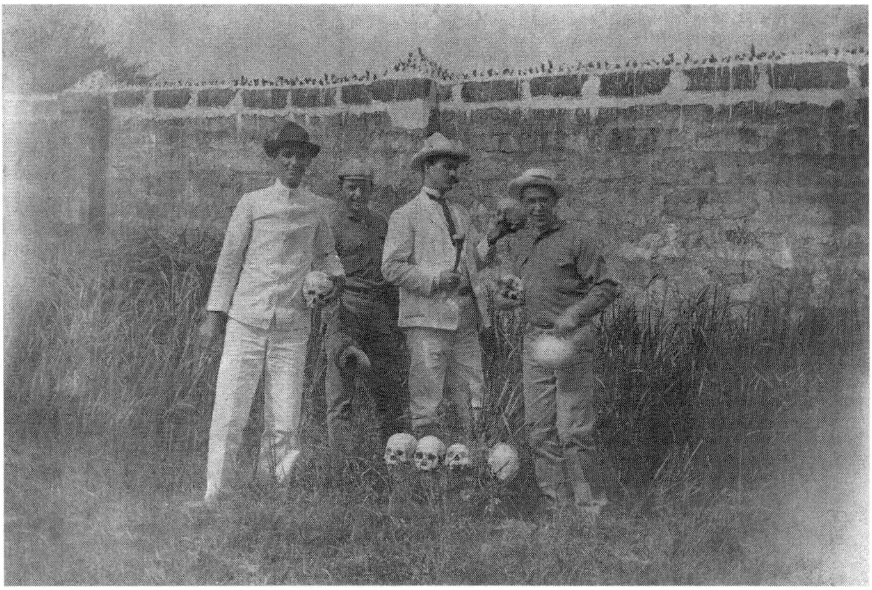

Figure 3.7. Frank Rainey and Friends at Cavite Cemetery, c. 1900s. Photograph. Naval History and Heritage Command, Washington, DC, Elizabeth Davis Price Collection.

ment for American soldiers. Such a gesture is far from inconsequential. The photographs offer a means of devaluing the nationalist discourse of the Philippines and also defanging the history of violence that undergirded the United States' global empire.

At large, the bones found in Cuba, Puerto Rico, and the Philippines were seen as objects of display for the American soldier and tourist, as grisly comic props divorced from their original human origins. This use of the deceased human body as a source of amusement is thereby a violent gesture that is not uncommon in the United States history of war or in the nation's treatment of Black, Brown, Indigenous, and nonwhite bodies. Following the writings of Puerto Rican philosopher Nelson Maldonado-Torres on the coloniality of being and the concept of the Imperial Man, we might thus view Rainey's photographs and the commercialized boneyard images discussed above as products of a social body oriented by the nonethics of war.[48] That is, these photographs constitute visual objects that attempted to construct a narrative of justified warfare and Anglo-Saxon supremacy in the aftermath of 1898. When considered today within the lens of history, these images ultimately reveal their underpinnings as artifacts of state-sponsored violence, dependent on the dehumanization of a wartime enemy and, as in many cases in the history of the United States, foreign peoples.

Moving into the present, there are important questions that loom over this material and the history of boneyard photography in the United States. For instance, what do we *do* with these photographs today? Many still exist in circulation, available through eBay and other online auction sites, and others remain dormant, but still accessible, in archives and libraries across the United States. There are questions of ethics and responsible viewing that must be discussed when looking at images of past, as well as present, colonial violence, especially when that violence manifests in subtle, obscured, or hidden ways. As Filipino-American media artist, educator, and curator Angel Velasco Shaw writes in the introduction of her coedited anthology *Vestiges of War,* "The subtle violence of war haunted me more than I ever imagined it would."[49] In 1995, Shaw visited the National Archives in Washington, DC, to conduct research for a documentary film on Filipinos in America. It was there that she came across thousands of photographs of the Philippine-American War, including one of American soldiers "standing on human bones." In her 1998 documentary video *Umbilical Cord,* Shaw presents a montage of archival images from the Philippine Revolution and Philippine-American War, on-the-spot interviews conducted around Manila, and personal family photographs. In one section of the film, while quick cuts of images from the war play on the screen, Shaw narrates, "A war written in indelible ink. Not in American history books, only as paragraphs here and there in Philippine history books, yet there are images of American soldiers standing on mounds of skulls and bones piled up in mass graves... evidence of betrayal... 250,000 Filipinos dead... the official count."[50] In the same scene, Shaw speaks of her personal history, sharing that her grandmother was five years old when José Rizal was executed by the Spanish, and eight when the Philippine-American War broke out. Her work importantly addresses the cultural amnesia about the legacies of war and the half century of US colonial occupation of the Philippines.

Boneyard photographs are troubling objects from our country's violent colonial past. They were created in a different, albeit all too familiar, era when US politics, economics, and social practices were shaped by paternalistic ideologies, colonial desires, and xenophobic mentalities toward peoples of differing races, religions, and geographies. However, these images are not so far removed from our nation's collective memory or the history of colonial photography. Nor is the practice of human trophy collecting during wartime, particularly by American soldiers in the Pacific, as we saw during World War II in Japan and during the Vietnam War. These objects and photographs persist today, serving as ever-present reminders of our country's violent past.

Notes

1. Historically known as the Spanish-American War, this name negates Cuba's struggle for their own independence, thus some historians prefer to use the term War of 1898 or the Spanish-Cuban-American War. For more see, Jorge Duany, *The Puerto Rican Nation on the Move: Identities on the Island and in the United States* (Chapel Hill: University of North Carolina Press, 2002), 1–11. A collection of Frank Rainey's photographs is located in the Elizabeth Davis Price Collection at the Naval History and Heritage Command in Washington, DC.

2. The exact amount owed for a grave space varied by country, city, and cemetery, as did the process of collecting burial "rent." While unpaid graves were often quickly emptied of their remains, in some situations, attempts were made to locate the deceased's family and renew the grave lease. One method used in the Philippines was to display an "unpaid" casket with remains on the side of the road along with the deceased's name and see if someone would claim them. If not, then the remains would go to the bone pile.

3. George Kennan, "The Regeneration of Cuba," *Outlook* 62 (June 10, 1899): 336.

4. Fannie B. Ward, "Our Sailors' Graves: Visit to the Havana Cemetery Where They Are Buried," *Washington Post,* April 18, 1898, 9. The same account was published in the *Los Angeles Sunday Times,* April 24, 1898, 6. For more on Fannie B. Ward and other female correspondents who reported on the war, see Carolyn M. Edy, *The Woman War Correspondent, the U.S. Military, and the Press: 1846–1947* (Lanham, MD: Lexington Books, 2017), 15–32.

5. Ward, "Our Sailor's Graves," 9.

6. "Strange Porto Rico," *Evening Times,* October 12, 1898, 4.

7. Rob C. Blakely, "Letter," *Burr Oak Herald,* May 4, 1899, 1.

8. "To Miss Ora Carpenter, Another Niece," *Pleasanton (KS) Observer-Enterprise,* June 16, 1900, 1.

9. "An Excellent Collection," *Carroll (IA) Sentinel,* May 25, 1899, 5.

10. Oliver Ellsworth Wood, "Cristobal Colon Cemetery and Its Occupants," *New York Times—Illustrated Magazine,* August 12, 1899, 4.

11. In 1987, the Colon Cemetery was declared a National Monument of the Cuban Republic and remains one of the most important funerary sites in the Americas. For a concise history, see Lohania Aruca, Narciso G. Menocal, and Edward Shaw, "The Cristóbal Colón Cemetery in Havana," Cuba-themed issue, *Journal of Decorative and Propaganda Arts* 22 (1996): 36–55.

12. *The Daily Picayune,* as cited in Peter B. Dedek, *The Cemeteries of New Orleans: A Cultural History* (Baton Rouge: Louisiana State University, 2017), 31.

13. Aruca, Menocal, and Shaw, "Cristóbal Colón Cemetery."

14. From a letter published in the *Steuben Republican,* March 22, 1899, 4.

15. "The Maine Dead—Their Graves Decorated in the Cemetery in Havana," *Massillon (OH) Independent,* February 28, 1899, 3.

16. F. S. Pursell, "From the Pearl of the Antilles Comes an Interesting Letter," *Ohio Democrat,* February 16, 1899, 1.

17. For more on the Detroit Photographic Company, see Cynthia Read-Miller, *Main Street U.S.A., in Early Photographs: 113 Detroit Publishing Co. Views* (New York: Dover, 1988). The Colón Cemetery photographs are in the Detroit Publishing Company collection at the Library of Congress.

18. "Havana's Golgotha," *Yorkville (SC) Enquirer,* February 4, 1899, 1.

19. Fannie B. Ward, "Our Sailors' Graves," 9.

20. See Enid Lynette Logan, "The 1899 Cuban Marriage Law Controversy: Church, State and Empire in the Crucible of Nation," *Journal of Social History* 42, no. 2 (2008): 469–494.

21. For a full text of the decree, see *Civil Report of Major-General John R. Brooke, U. S. Army, Military Governor, Island of Cuba* (Cuba: US Government Printing Office, 1900), 33.

22. For more on Catholicism and photography in the Philippines after the war, see J. M. Mancini's essay "The Pacific World and American Art History," in *A Companion to American Art,* by John Davis, Jennifer A. Greenhill, and Jason David LaFountain (Malden, MA: Wiley-Blackwell, 2015), 228–245; and Katherine D. Moran, "Catholicism and the Making of the U.S. Pacific," *Journal of the Gilded Age and Progressive Era* 12, no. 4 (2013): 434–474.

23. For more on Catholicism in the Philippines, see Steven Shirley, *Guided by God: The Legacy of the Catholic Church in Philippine Politics* (Singapore: Marshall Cavendish Academic, 2004).

24. For a history of the military operations of the Philippine-American War, see Brian McAllister Linn, *The Philippine War, 1899–1902* (Lawrence: University of Kansas Press, 2000).

25. "Missionary Work—Former Lincoln Pastor Finds Plenty to Do," *Lincoln Nebraska State Journal,* June 12, 1899, 6.

26. For more on this, see J. M. Mancini, *Art and War in the Pacific World: Making, Breaking, and Taking from Anson's Voyage to the Philippine-American War* (Berkeley: University of California Press, 2018), 147–211. For more on photography and visual culture in the Philippines generally, see Enrique B. De la Cruz and Pearlie Rose Baluyut, eds., *Confrontations, Crossings, and Convergence: Photographs of the Philippines and the United States, 1898–1998* (Los Angeles: UCLA Asian American Studies Center, 1998); and Benito M. Vergara, *Displaying Filipinos: Photography and Colonialism in Early 20th Century Philippines* (Quezon City: University of the Philippines Press, 1995).

27. José de Olivares and William Smith Bryan, *Our Islands and Their People as Seen with Camera and Pencil* (St. Louis, MO: N. D. Thompson, 1899), 719.

28. Frank S. Brown, "A Soldier's Views," *Daily Times New Brunswick,* August 29, 1899, 5.

29. Ibid.

30. John F. Bass, "Our New Possessions—The Philippines," *Harper's Weekly,* February 4, 1899, 119–121.

31. *Allhallowtide* referred to the three-day religious observance of All Saints' Eve (October 31), All Saints' Day (November 1), and All Souls' Day (November 2).

32. Bass, "Our New Possessions—The Philippines," 119–121.

33. Luis Martínez-Fernández, "Life in a 'Male City': Native and Foreign Elite Women in Nineteenth-Century Havana," *Cuban Studies* 25 (1995): 27–49.

34. Dorothy Stanhope, "Cuba's Decoration Day in Winter," *New York Times,* November 16, 1902, 35.

35. Ibid.

36. "Havana's Golgotha—Skeletons of Cuba's Dead at Last Covered Over by Americans," *Marion County (FL) News,* September 28, 1899, 7.

37. "Must Let Skulls Alone," *St. Joseph (MI) Herald,* January 24, 1899, 1.

38. "Guarding the Cemeteries," *Buffalo (NY) Evening News,* January 24, 1899, 5.

39. "Havana's Golgotha," *Daily Herald,* September 27, 1899, 7.

40. Miller wrote of her ability to travel alone throughout the interior of the island

without any harm, and even when she went looking for trouble, found none. See "Women Safe in Cuba," *Salina (KS) Daily Union,* April 26, 1907, 3; and *Evening-Times Republican* (Iowa), July 2, 1907, 5.

41. Miller published stories as "Mrs. C. R. Miller," seeing her husband's name as her protection. For more, see "Perilous Camera Trips of Woman Photographer," *Baltimore Sun,* December 22, 1907, 14. For her article on Cuba, see Mrs. C. R. Miller, "Cuba's Queer Funeral Customs," *Leslie's Illustrated Weekly,* June 6, 1907, 10.

42. Although unclear in the article, it is likely that the "Cristo Cemetery" Miller visited is the Necropolis de Camagüey located beside the Iglesia de San Cristo del Buen Viaje.

43. Miller, "Cuba's Queer Funeral Customs," 10.

44. Oscar William Coursey, *History and Geography of the Philippine Islands, for General Reading and Use in Our Public Schools* (Mitchell, SD: Educator School Supply, 1903): 137.

45. Ibid.

46. Leslie N. Collins, "Letter from the Philippines," *Christian-Evangelist,* April 25, 1901, 523.

47. Ibid.

48. Nelson Maldonado-Torres, "On the Coloniality of Being," *Cultural Studies* 21, no. 2 (2007): 247–260.

49. Angel Velasco Shaw, "Introduction: Exquisite Betrayal," in *Vestiges of War: The Philippine-American War and the Aftermath of An Imperial Dream: 1899–1999* (New York: New York University Press, 2002), x.

50. Ibid., 413.

Four

Sustained Constraint

Locating Corporeal Control through Archived Images of the Breath in the Philippines after 1898

Alejandro T. Acierto

> But all our phrasing—race relations, racial chasm, racial justice, racial profiling, white privilege, even white supremacy—serves to obscure that racism is a visceral experience, that it dislodges brains, blocks airways, rips muscle, extracts organs, cracks bones, breaks teeth.
>
> —Ta-Nehisi Coates, from *Letter to My Son*

> The pacified Filipinos are those who have been laid beneath the sod of the Philippine Islands. The pacified Filipino is the dead Filipino.
>
> —Edward W. Carmack,
> from US Senate *Congressional Record*, 1902

In a harrowing three-minute video that took social media by storm, Ramsey Orta managed to capture the horrific death of his friend Eric Garner on July 17, 2014. The video shows police surrounding Garner, as New York Police Department officer Daniel Pantaleo restrains the asthmatic four-hundred-pound man in a choke hold, bringing them both to the ground. Pantaleo strangled his captive after Garner moved his arms away from the officer during an attempted arrest. Pantaleo was seeking to arrest Garner on suspicion of selling untaxed or "loose" cigarettes. Orta's video of Pantaleo choking Garner quickly circulated across multiple social media platforms, putting Pantaleo (and the NYPD) under intense scrutiny. While Pantaleo would continue to work for the NYPD on "desk duty" through June 2019—five years after the incident—the moments captured on Orta's cell phone were integral to the #BlackLivesMatter movement (BLM), which ultimately propelled a widespread public response for more stringent police accountability.[1] Not only did the video function as filmic evidence of the legacy of racialized violence against Black bodies across the United States, specifically at the hands of police and law enforcement officials, but Garner's traumatic exclamations of "I can't breathe!"—shouted eleven times preceding his death—embodied a new kind of urgency and metaphoric resonance that seeped into a broader public consciousness.

For scholar Shermaine M. Jones, Garner's last phrase captured a "sense of a psychic chokehold" that signified a "condition of affective asphyxia" among Black bodies, highlighting "the precarious state between life and death."[2] Proposing a framework of analysis through Claudia Rankine's largely influential lyrical poem *Citizen,* she writes that "the ways that black emotional expression is heavily policed" end up "producing a sense of emotional suffocation, whether self-imposed or externally inflicted."[3] That is, "affective asphyxia results from the expectation that black people must choke down the rage, fear, grief, and other emotions that arise when confronted with racism and racial microaggressions."[4] Writing between the physiological and metaphoric, wherein Black breath is tethered to expressions of exhaustion, Jones' writings position the breath as a theoretical space through which we can begin to understand larger legacies of abjection, dispossession, and restriction as related to histories of racism.

In much of the ways that Garner's death illustrated the power dynamic between Black bodies and the State, it also highlighted the persistence of the Black criminal body as a trope subject to its own critiques. Quoting the writing of bell hooks, Safiya Umoja Noble notes that spectacles of Black death mediated through television and social media platforms articulate an "eating of the other" that "speaks to the uncontrolled fetishizing of the Black body that results in consumption of 'the other' in white imaginaries through cultural and physical appropriations."[5] Thus, while the circulation of Orta's video ultimately jolted the BLM movement, becoming what Sandra Y. Govan and Sandra G. Shannon call "a kind of tipping point . . . where technology emerges as public testimony and the deep history of victimization of Black men and [to a lesser extent] women,"[6] it should be noted that it further perpetuated the racialized image of Black bodies as depositories of white supremacist and state-sanctioned violence. As an image that offered a different yet consistent iteration of a Black man suffering at the hands of law enforcement officials, the viral video enabled the recurrence of a trope that situated Black men as incapable of standing up to systems of power, particularly systems born from white supremacist settler colonial power structures.

The viral video of Garner's death by strangulation articulates a broader history of imperialism, colonialism, and white supremacy. Shifting to a series of photographic images taken in the Philippines during the US colonial era, nearly one hundred years before Orta's video, I hope to invoke the mediation of Garner's death in part to locate the *breath* specifically as a strategy for militarized systems of power. By examining photographic documents of the US military restricting Pilipinx bodies through control of the breath at the turn of the twentieth century, we also encounter a history of maintaining and managing corporeal control of criminalized and racialized bodies that resonates with issues of race and racism today. With the image of the chokehold rebroadcast to highlight the ways institutionalized racism affects Black and Brown bodies, we witness a different formation of what racialized populations have historically witnessed as lynchings, the ultimate signifiers for the assertion of white power though the restriction of the breath. Though lynchings and hangings were not the invention of white supremacy, situated within a US context, the symbol of the noose regardless of application has become a signifier for racist aggression toward Black and Brown bodies, as well as other historically marginalized communities. While the armatures of suffocation differ in the cases of Pantaleo's chokehold and the ropes used for the deaths of countless Black, Indigenous, and other dispossessed peoples across the US historical territorial trajectory, the affective register of these kinds of images remain similar. Power continues to be held by white supremacist systems of control, which are sustained in part through images of the erasure of a body's ability to breathe. Within this affective turn, Ulla D. Berg and Ana Y. Ramos-Zayas remind us of how the recognition of affect can be productive as part of an examination of the ways that racial hierarchies continue to be sustained. For them,

> this recognition allows us to begin to comprehend the deeply felt and visceral sociality of race and how racialized populations of color in the Americas situate their individual history in national and international histories of slavery, colonialism, and imperialism that are not only comprehended intellectually but also are profoundly felt, experiential, and actively embodied conceptions of a social reality and historical reference. Being a racial subject is thus a highly historically conscious way of existing at multiple scales—as an individual, as part of a community, as part of a nation, and transnationally—that are expressed, knowable, and manifested in ways that require intense, ongoing intellectual and emotional work.[7]

Comparing a group of picture postcards produced and distributed during the US military occupation of the Philippines after the Spanish-American War and the prevalence of lynching postcards during the same era, we can begin to see and feel the complexity of racialization among and between Black and Brown bodies in relation to the breath. As part of this study, I am interested in locating how images of breath control within the US image archives of the Philippines helped to sustain various articulations of constraint within the so-called American Tropics. As the images discussed reveal a pattern of relationships tethered to breath, I should note that I am proposing an analysis that is distinct from processes of stereotyping. While the stereotype relies on the recurrence of visual and textual tropes that lead to formations of an essentialization, or a single trope that is meant to represent a particular group of people,[8] I offer the phrase "sustained constraint" as a distinct process that seeks to articulate the broader legacies of racialized violence apart from the specificities of identification. Within this theorization, sustained constraint thus becomes a way to identify legacies of racialization bound by technologies of corporeal control, whether located within the specificities of the breath or not. While I draw on Jasbir K. Puar, following Lauren Berlant, in her description of slow death as "the debilitating ongoingness of structural inequality and suffering," I offer the notion of sustained constraint as a localized articulation that describes the body in relation to power, control, and embodiment.[9] Puar's concept of debility highlights the legibility of power on dispossessed bodies, particularly as an affective register by which we can understand legacies of corporeal control historically. Sustained constraint goes further to interject the notion that constraint can also be sustained as an embodied form of subjectivity. Put another way, while debility and slow death highlight ongoing formations of constraint toward the eradication of the Other, sustained constraint focuses on speculating ways colonialism has been internalized and has sustained itself within the bodies of those affected by it.

Specifically, the larger project of benevolent assimilation initiated by the desire for "American exceptionalism" sought to "civilize" Pilipinxs as it aimed to refashion Indigenous peoples into a white American ideal. Tied to fantasies of manifest destiny and westward expansion that was cultivated during the annexation of Indigenous lands in the continental United States, the Philippines became a critical opportunity for the United States to develop a rhetoric of "civilizing" rather than replicating tropes of extraction and tyranny that marked European colonialism.[10] Philippine-American scholar Sharon Delmendo describes this project as "the renegotiation of American national identity through dramatized confrontations with and pacification of the savage aboriginal other."[11] In establishing credibility for this project, the United States thus relied on the racialized identificatory matrix that calibrated Pilipinxs in relation to both African and Native Americans, and thus landed on the descriptor of "savage" as a rhetorical marker in between the two. While benevolent assimilation utilized various technologies to imbue Pilipinxs with "Anglo-Saxon values," Pilipinxs were still designated as colonial subjects with limited rights. Following a ruling in 1901 by the US Supreme Court in what are known as the Insular Cases, the Philippines were designated as an "unincorporated territory" that marked the archipelago, in the words of justice

Edward Douglass White, "foreign in a domestic sense." As Vicente L. Rafael indicates, Pilipinxs were "consigned to a racial state of exception" where "they were subject to US laws but, by virtue of their racial difference, not entitled to the same rights."[12] Thus, entangled within the fabrics of benevolent assimilation was the necessity to racialize Pilipinxs that could essentially prolong US colonial presence so long as they continued to be marked as savage.

Such was the case in the work of David Folkmar, an anthropologist hired to help prepare the anthropological exhibitions for the 1904 St. Louis World's Fair Philippine Reservation. Assigned to the Bilibid Prison prior to the World's Fair, Folkmar was tasked with taking physiognomic and craniometric measurements of its diverse pool of inmates that would be published as his *Album of Philippine Types*. With photographs of eighty inmates that produced 160 mug shots containing detailed anthropometric information, Folkmar's images, as Oscar V. Campomanes discusses, were meant "to break down the physical features of its subjects—to archive the other's body, as it were—and isolate them as measurable parts."[13] As measurable parts, Pilipinxs could be codified through various metrics that would enable them to be calibrated against the already existing racial matrix.

Such was also the case in Dean C. Worcester's lengthy article in *National Geographic* that included not only physical and phenotypical descriptions of "non-Christian peoples" but also dozens of color and black-and-white photographs that enabled the magazine's readership to see in more detail the differences in racial types. Compounding social and cultural differences that were also included within the descriptions, Worcester's account of the Philippines in the November 1913 issue of *National Geographic* remained an important source that not only continued a justification for US military presence in the Philippines but also perpetrated the need for the colonial imaginary to categorize different peoples throughout the American Tropics. In a caption of a photograph of Bagobo warriors, he writes, "The Bagobos have curious religious beliefs which incite them to certain bloodthirsty and repulsive deeds."[14] Alluding to perceived cannibalistic desires that Bagobos were supposedly practicing, Worcester and other imperialists employed a rhetorical and visual conflation of representation wherein the logics of racialization within and beyond the government chambers of the United States developed a rationale for formations of constraint that further justified US colonial presence in the Philippines. While the image of the Bagobos alone does not specifically imply any violent tendencies, Worcester's use of text helps bridge the gap for his viewers to adequately mark these Indigenous peoples as savage.

The frontispiece of one of Worcester's last published works, volume 2 of the *Philippines Past and Present,* presents two photographs of an Indigenous subject taken over a span of nine years. The photographs are meant to show the civilizing impact of US colonialism on the "savage" body. The photographic diptych is captioned: "THE METAMORPHOSIS OF A BONTOC IGOROT." The photograph on the left shows a boy wearing only a sash around the waist of his bare body. In the photograph on the right, he is depicted as a fully grown man, dressed in a white suit and holding a fine hat.[15] Images of this type, in which Indigenous people are completely dressed and groomed to the standards of American white masculinity, helped to continually validate US imperial presence even beyond the ends of US occupation. In this example, Worcester's use of the caption not only helps to inform the viewers of who the subjects are but also shapes how the viewer comes to understand the content of the photographs. Importantly, the use of the word "METAMORPHOSIS," presented in capitalized type denoting its significance, thus functions as a tagline for the impact of colonialism, a seemingly necessary intervention capable of shaping Indigenous people into normalized ideologies of masculinity and civility. Other images featured structural improvements to bridges, walkways, and buildings; the establishment of public schools; and various other new infrastructures, such as telegraphic lines and the electrical grid. Looking again to the images of the Bontoc boy, one may also notice the differences in the environment in which the subject is photographed. Looking behind the foreground of the figure on the left, who stands barefoot on a rock next to a patch of grass, we can see a small group of out-of-focus villagers moving across the bare earth without any infrastructural improvements. Conversely, the image on the right, taken nine years later, shows a man standing in shoes in front of an ankle-height wall made of brick and mortar, which is likely a small bridge over a creek or pathway. The introduction of brick infrastructures helps subtly signify and justify the scope of US occupation in the Philippines. In establishing an archive of modernization of the Philippines through technologies of mass production and the vast distribution networks in print, the US colonial government developed a foundational visual and textual terrain that tied the Philippines to logics of the past, the uncivilized, and the savage.

Historian Aaron Abel T. Mallari writes, "The American endeavor in the Philippines was thus explicitly described as a tutelary effort seeking to prepare Filipinos for self-rule,"[16] particularly within educational and carceral spaces, but also within the political realms of the bureaucratic colonial government structures. As such, many Pilipinxs internalized US systems of power through the US-established public educational system or via the reconfigured penal system in which prisoners would try, enforce, and self-regulate through the program of a prisoner's court. As these colonial systems of constraint regulated how Pilipinx bodies could exist, especially in light of the goal for self-governance, the US colonial government established a framework that enabled the proliferation and embodiment of behaviors that would not only keep the Philippines dependent on the United States but also ensure that their bodies were oriented toward white settler colonial ideals.

Looking toward mechanisms of corporeal control via the breath, we can begin to consider how the simple components of breathing, that is, inhalation and exhalation, might be managed and constrained through a holistic and occasionally metaphoric approach to its control. Specifically, I consider four types of images of Pilipinx bodies in relation to the management and constriction of the breath, namely, the inhalation of tobacco smoke, exhalation through the wind instruments of military marching bands, the choking sensations of torture and interrogations (primarily via waterboarding and use of the garrote), and the ultimate rupture of the breath through capital punishment by hanging. As this collection of images suggests, the latter three examples highlight the conditions of the carceral system as a particularly significant apparatus through which the breath was managed and controlled. While the Bilibid prison in particular was used as a central site for US experiments of benevolent assimilation, garnering much international attention from tourists and journalists alike, the prison system across the archipelago was used as what Mallari considers an "important thread utilized by the Americans in weaving the fabric of colonial domination."[17] Within the context of an overall desire for Pilipinxs to embody white settler colonial ideals as a way to advocate for the ability to self-govern, US imperialists relied on images within the prison system to project fictions of progress onto the overall project of benevolent assimilation. Through the transnational distributive networks and circulation of these images, the US colonial government was able to cultivate a visual-textual repertoire of difference "informed by a "rhetoric of empire and colonization"[18] and where Americans could "[define] themselves through conquest,"[19] not unlike the way in which Orta's video of Garner enables the NYPD to assert its position of power.

Though not tethered to the prison system, acts of inhalation were managed in part by the overwhelming prevalence of tobacco smoke within the cultural lives of Pilipinxs. As Yoshihiro Chiba indicates, "The cigar industry employed more workers in the Philippines than any other industry" at the time and saw a significant jump in production as a result of the Payne-Aldrich Tariff Act of 1909, which effectively allowed for cigars, along with sugar, abaca, and coconuts, to be exported duty-free.[20] First set into place by Spanish colonizers in the early 1600s and later controlled by US colonial taxation and tariff laws after the monopolies were broken up, tobacco production in the Philippines was a consistently lucrative crop as an export from the archipelago. Providing a thorough look at the tobacco monopoly during Spanish rule, Edilberto C. de Jesus discusses the durability of the crop after much of the valuable land was cleared for cultivation. With the land no longer able to be used for other food-based crops, Pilipinx farmers were thus trapped into an economic corner that they could hardly escape.[21]

As tobacco was an important agricultural export during the US and Spanish colonial eras, it is understandable that images of the scale of its production became important cultural aspects to be seen by viewers across the Pacific. One such image depicts the interior of a cigar factory with dozens of workers seated in a vast room filled with long tables that seated fourteen workers each. Seen diligently working in a well-ventilated space with high ceilings not only highlighted the Spanish colonial architectural style but offered a vision of the expansive spatial arrangement needed to house the number of workers employed in the factory. As this was an established industry that permeated cultural and social life, images of the cigar's consumption among Indigenous and mestizx Pilipinx populations was another fascinating aspect of life in the Philippines to be captured. While tobacco consumption in the Philippines was a regular and banal aspect of daily life, published postcards tended to revisit gendered tropes of abjection and primitivism visualizing mostly Pilipinx women and girls smoking proportionally large cigars that sexualized their bodies as objects of desire and consumption. One example features an image of an older Indigenous woman fully clothed seen smoking a cigar roughly the length of her forearm as she grasps one end to support it at her mouth (figure 4.1). In the seemingly candid full-length portrait, we see her standing upright, facing off to the left side of the frame, barefoot and wearing a scarf around her head and a double layered, full-length patterned skirt. Positioned in front of an ambiguous background, we see two bunches of cuttings at her feet, and the shadows of two other ambiguous figures on her other side. In a second published postcard found online, the same woman is seen facing another woman similarly dressed and adorned who also

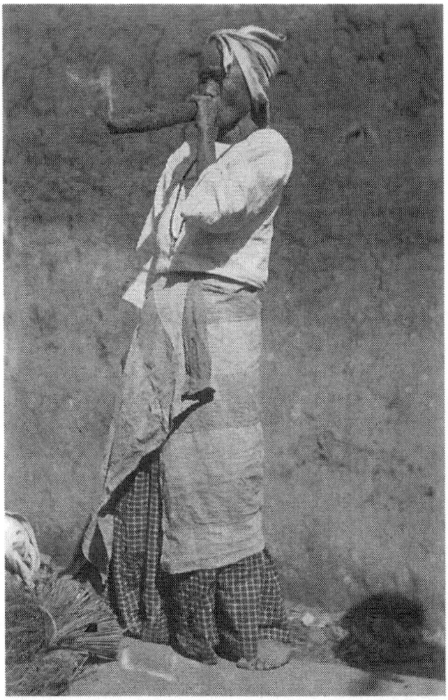

Figure 4.1. Ilocano woman smoking a cigar, date unknown. Courtesy of the author.

holds a cigar. In this image, the second woman holds the burning end of the cigar with her right hand to support its weight while also holding another cigar in her left. Within both images, the scale and size of the cigar in the hands of these women thus becomes a sexually suggestive signifier for the ways tobacco is able to take up space of the body's ability to breathe. Captured in the moments of inhalation as smoke emanates from the ends of the cigars, both images position tobacco as a tool for a kind of constraint reflecting both a physiological addiction as well as an economic one.

In turning to the act of exhalation, I consider the emergence and proliferation of military marching bands popularized after US annexation as a second technology through which the US colonial government sustained corporeal constraint. As focused exhalations turned into air streams pushed through tubes of wind instruments, the establishment of marching band culture became another aspect of civil and social life initiated by the US military as a form of social and corporeal constraint. While initially introduced by the military outside of the prison system, US officials saw an opportunity to adequately prepare Pilipinx prisoners for civilized life while they completed their sentences. Citing Pilipinx music scholar Hilarion F. Rubio, Mary Talusan notes that "to Rubio, American tutelage transformed Filipino bands into orderly disciplined entities, embracing the traits of modernity and moving toward 'progress.'"[22] Ordered by governor-general William Howard Taft to establish, train, and direct a military marching band in the Philippines, Walter Howard Loving brought his newly formed Philippine Constabulary Band to the 1904 World's Fair in St. Louis. As a projected space of the future, the World's Fair not only demonstrated the discoveries of the era but also touted the necessity for colonial contingent within the Philippines as the way to advocate for sustaining a presence and maintaining colonial control.[23] As such, the Philippine Constabulary Band continued to exist through Japanese occupation—well after formal US occupation ended—and sustained the internalized mechanisms of colonial control established during the beginning stages of its emergence. As the success of the Philippine Constabulary Band continued to flourish during the US colonial era, images and photographs of the prison became not only spaces to invite viewers into the beginning stages of military band training but also indexes for the success and necessity of the prison system as part of the larger project of benevolent assimilation, or in my view, of sustaining constraint.

One of the postcards produced and distributed at that time features a courtyard filled with prisoners wearing typically striped prison suits surrounding a building, some holding instruments and others standing at attention (figure 4.2). At the top of the postcard the caption reads "Inspection of Prisoners, Bilibid Prison, Manila, Philippines," leaving out the specificity of

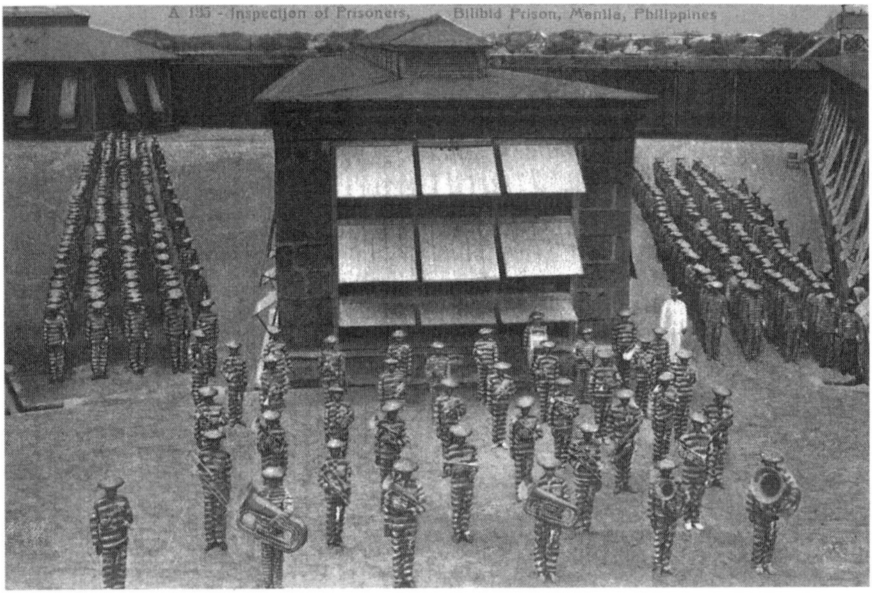

Figure 4.2. Inmates at attention, Bilibid Prison, Manila, Philippines, date unknown. Courtesy of the author.

the marching band as an inherent aspect of the roll call. As a colored photo postcard (most likely a lithograph), the image contains a parallel framing to another published black-and-white photo postcard. In the second image, fully suited cadets are seen standing in formation, half with marching band instruments, and the half standing at attention. Potentially in the midst of a color guard ceremony, indicated in part by a small group of people holding flags on the left side of the frame, both images immediately entangle the military, the prison, and the marching band as apparatuses of colonial control. As an embodied gesture of militarization, these images establish the prison not only as a site of corporeal control but also as a space for the spectacle of entertainment. Bilibid was a tourist destination in its own right. Visitors could witness the shaping of Indigenous peoples into idealized colonial subjects in real time from within the prison. As a related aside, we could also draw further parallels to the 2007 video released on YouTube colloquially known as the "Dancing Inmates," featuring hundreds of prisoners incarcerated at the Cebu Provincial Detention and Rehabilitation Center. Since the time of this writing, this viral video has amassed over fifty-nine million views and continues to be referenced in a 2019 Netflix docuseries, *Happy Jail,* directed by Michele Josue. Taken from the vantage point of a platform overlooking the prison yard that is very similar to the point of view of the camera of the postcards discussed here, this kind of carceral imagery remains consistent within the optics of constraint being discussed. Whereas the "Dancing Inmates" video presents a contemporary articulation of mediated constraint within the prison system, both the postcards and the video highlight what J. Lorenzo Perillo notes as a Foucauldian panoptic gaze. Marking the US imperial gaze, the camera's positioning "establishes a sense of objectification that reaffirms the viewer's superior position over the inmates."[24] Consistent with images of tobacco, these images also tout the colonial ability to manage and control multiple groups of people, highlighting the scale and scope of the colonial apparatus.

Aside from the two physiological aspects of breathing that could have been controlled within these logics of constraint, I am also drawn to consider the liminal and ultimate forms of constraint as part of the broader assemblage of technologies that sustained US colonial presence in the Philippines. Noting the prison system as a central institution for occurrences of constraint, I am drawn to two additional sets of images that were published as postcards during the era, ones that veer toward the macabre as they depict events of torture and execution. While these images isolate specific events framed within conditions of the prison system, they offer other glimpses into the ways control of the breath was used to project power over Pilipinx prisoners and civilians. Seen in relation to lynching postcards of African Americans produced in the continental United States, images depicting the hanging and torture of Pilipinxs carry much of the same affective weight, even apart from the conditions of the event. Though not conducted as part of a mob action that sought to circumvent the criminal justice system at large, the affective register of these postcards drew on the existence and circulation of lynching postcards that became popularized during the picture postcard era.

In a distinctly framed image of what would be an execution, a prisoner is positioned on top of a platform, seated with his arms behind him while his bare feet are being held by two officers (figure 4.3). Surrounded by half a dozen other officers, including a priest carrying a large wooden cross who looms above the scene, the prisoner is the clear subject of the photographer's gaze. Sure to capture "Bilibid Prison" stenciled on the bottom portion of the platform, the viewer is drawn to the action of the stage of execution. While it is not obvious in this postcard, a second postcard of the same event found online shows the prisoner in the midst of execution by garrote, signaling a continuation of the practice initially introduced by the Spanish. I should note here that the number "13" printed on the bottom right corner suggests that the postcard shown here is part of a series or collection of postcards, available at the time for purchase as a set. Within the economy of picture postcard images emerging from the Philippines, postcard collector Mike Price notes that there

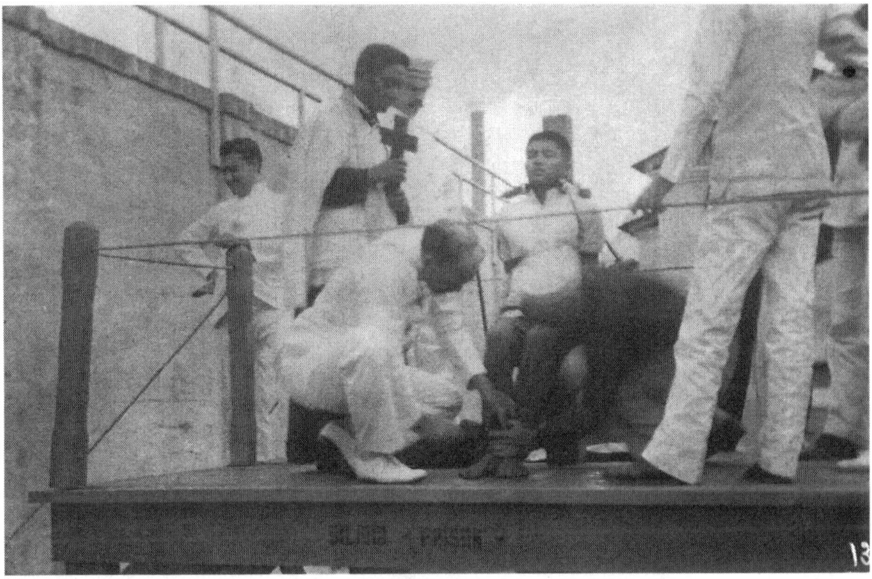

Figure 4.3. Execution by garrote, date unknown. Courtesy of the author.

could have been scores—if not hundreds—of photographers across the archipelago contracted to take photographs during US occupation.[25] As voyeurs of military operations abroad responsible for documenting daily life, tourists and service members alike could then purchase these sets to send home or assemble a scrap book–style photo album, evidenced in the various archives that contain these holdings. While the image here was purchased on eBay as an individual print, it is important to understand how these images were often consumed at the time of their initial distribution.

It is telling that images of the garrote, used as a strategic implementation of torture and execution by Spain and the United States, were often tied to a savage form of Pilipinx self-policing. While the aforementioned image of the Bilibid Prison stage falls outside of the projected state-sanctioned image archive, a popularized photograph licensed by Getty Images establishes a different narrative. At this time of racial ambiguity, especially as the United States was entangled in multiple international conflicts at the turn of the twentieth century, an image of a group of Brown men surround another criminal, who is seen looking at the camera while his neck is held inside the torture apparatus (figure 4.4). What marks this image as particularly striking, aside from the curious gaze of the subjects in the photograph, is actually the story of its circulation. In this pairing of two postcards drawn from the same image taken in the Philippines, the visual-rhetorical entanglement conflates three distinct

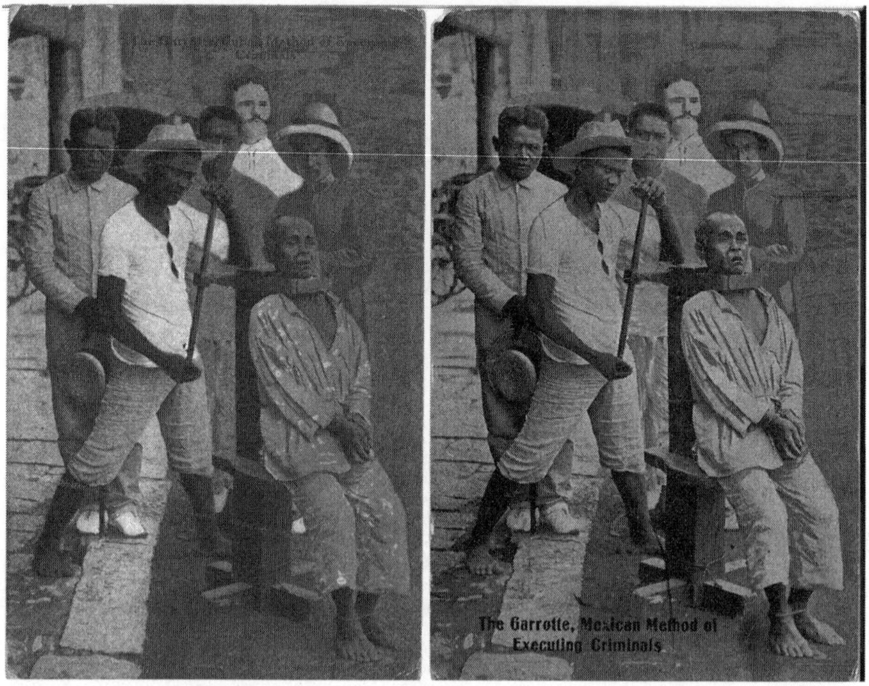

Figure 4.4. Licensed image of garrote postcard used to mark two distinct countries on separate postcards, dates of printing unknown. Courtesy of the author.

national identifiers attributed to Mexican and Cuban forms of execution. With inscriptions that read "The Garrotte, Cuban Method of Executing Criminals" on the left postcard, and "The Garrotte, Mexican Method of Executing Criminals" on the black-and-white postcard on the right, it is clear that the publishers of these postcards didn't want or need to specify the location of the photograph. While this conflation of identities inevitably constrains Pilipinxs back into the racialized matrix, disabling any foreseeable access to self-governance, it points to the broader project of white settler colonialism that cultivated an affective distance from whiteness, placing Pilipinxs further behind an ability to access civility.

In this vein, in projecting affiliations toward other racialized groups, we can then begin to understand the prevalence of hanging postcards that began to appear during the same era, particularly in their visual and affective proximity toward lynching postcards of African Americans. As seen in the group of hanging postcards, many of which depict multiple Pilipinxs being hung simultaneously from traditionally designed gallows, there are several similar aspects of spectatorship imbued within the frames of both lynching and hanging postcards of African Americans and Pilipinxs, respectively. Drawing on similar logics of the racialized spectacle, the camera positions the shot in order to capture the group of viewers, primarily US military officials, while other Pilipinx viewers watch from afar. A marked spectacle, given the architecture of the gallows and the presence of those in attendance, the recurring trope of scale is again seen in these images of constraint (figure 4.5). While the scale of constraint is seen within the literal frame, I am also drawn to a particularly fascinating set of postcards that offer a complete sequence of the hanging of a "Sulu Soltan" (figure 4.6). In a tableaux of four images captured in a series, the photographer outlines the process of a hanging, from the prisoners' approach to the gallows to their ultimate placement into a black sealed coffin. While the space of this chapter doesn't allow for a more thorough examination of this particular set of postcards, I am intrigued by the presence of other Pilipinx prisoners and constabulary officers who figure prominently in the frames, in part as a form of embodied constraint that was developed through the technologies of the prison system at large.

What emerges from these particular sets of images, due in part to the nature of the action depicted, is an immediate recognition of power and constraint. Held still between or after breaths, these images epitomize the duration of sustain. That is, to borrow from musical parlance, how long a note is

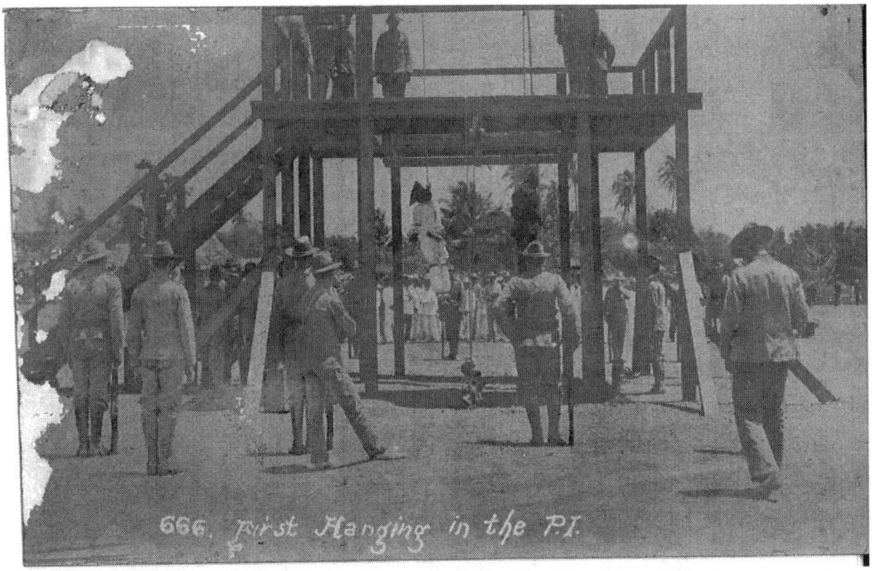

Figure 4.5. "First Hanging in the P.I.," date unknown. Courtesy of the author.

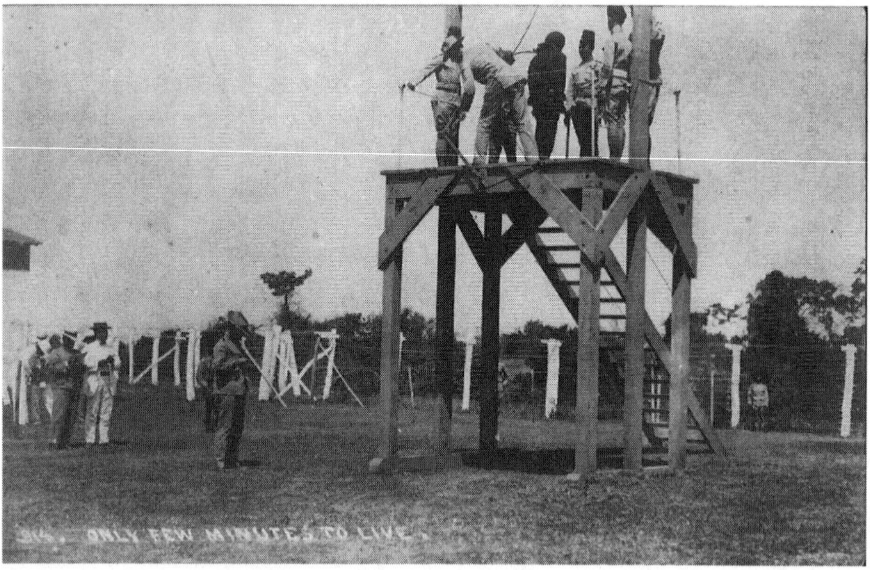

Figure 4.6. "Only a Few Minutes to Live," second in a series of four hanging postcards, date unknown. Courtesy of the author.

sustained after an instrument's key is released. As viewers and distributors of these postcards, the US consumers that carried these postcards were effectively and literally holding on to the breath of Pilipinx peoples. As images later distributed internationally through Internet auction sites such as eBay, Pilipinx breath becomes further entangled in what queer and Indigenous scholar Mark Rifkin regards as settler colonial "temporal orientations." For Rifkin, "Being temporally oriented suggests that one's experiences, sensations, and possibilities for action are shaped by the existing inclinations, itineraries, and networks in which one is immersed."[26] As constrained images that continually fix Indigenous Pilipinx peoples as criminal or savage, we can begin to understand how the transnational and transtemporal circulation of constraint is sustained under white settler colonial logics. With these postcards in hand, images of Pilipinx death can be viewed only as a recognition and elongation of their abjection, a revival of duration that pushes the temporal frame into our contemporary moment.

Noting the biopolitical entanglement between governmental powers and technologies of breath control specifically, scholar Marijn Nieuwenhuis establishes that "the iron hands of power seem to tighten themselves around the throats of fragile bodies both close and far away."[27] Those same hands of power reveal themselves through the photographs and postcards of Pilipinx bodies hanging in the gallows, just as they reappear in the viral video of Eric Garner's death in 2014. For BLM activists and other writers, "I can't breathe!" enabled a rhetoric in which Garner's last words became a signifier for sustained marginalization historically and established the metaphor that mapped the breath to the sustainability of Black, Indigenous, and nonwhite people of color. In the case of Garner, his inability to breathe spoke to the legacy of racialization that closed off the ability of nonwhite communities to exist freely. I further suggest that his words reiterated broader histories of "sustained constraint" in the formation of the United States, nationally and internationally, as seen most notably in images of the breath documented in the Philippines after the War of 1898. In both the video of Garner and the photos of Pilipinx victims of war, we see how white supremacist settler colonial power structures debilitated nonwhite communities and enabled what Lauren Berlant called a "slow death" for historically marginalized communities.[28]

The traumatic event of Garner's death thus offered a poignant instance of ongoing racialized violence, wherein the context of white supremacy is articulated through death but is not eradicated by the discourse that surrounds it. For Jasbir K. Puar, who quotes Berlant, "Slow death occurs not within the time scale of the crisis, not of the event of the suicide or the epidemic, but in 'a zone of temporality . . . of ongoingness, getting by, and living on, where the structural inequalities are dispersed, the pacing of their experience intermittent, often in phenomena not prone to capture by a consciousness organized by archives of memorable impact.'"[29] While the circulation of Garner's last moments that looped and recurred across the temporal and spatial spheres of the Internet and social media networks complicate the singularity of his death, a new kind of trigger turns Shermaine M. Jones' aforementioned affective asphyxia into an affective death. Establishing a new metaphor for ongoing racialized violence within the contemporary moment, the video of Garner's death both acts as a sped-up signifier for the slow death of Black communities at large and contributes to the vast number of archived videos that have recorded Black (and Brown) victims being killed at the hands of US military and law enforcement. Put another way, the assemblage of videos of Black death, including Orta's video, articulates an assemblage of situations that allow for the proliferation of restricting and constraining disposable communities in the eyes of the State. The photographs of the Pilipinx bodies at the turn of the century function in a similar manner. Those war-era postcards, still available for purchase on eBay today, as with the viral video of Garner and more recently George Floyd, effectively enable the slow death of Black and Brown communities to be witnessed on screen and in print. Thus, it becomes clear that slow death is reliant, in part, on the long-standing recurrence of similarly articulated events, or, in the case of this analysis, on the repetition and recirculation of specific kinds of images and footage.

Noting the ways media consumers behave with video material in the age of Web 2.0, the ability to control how and when media content is viewed obfuscates the notion of the event as being tied to a single space and time, as the moment is revisited and replayed outside of its initial broadcast and recording. Operating on a new kind of scale than previously seen, Orta's social media video, in contrast to the static postcards and photos of the Philippines, allowed for a different deployment of the nonlinearity of slow death, whereby the video that "starts and stops, redoubles and leaps ahead" shifts how an event is experienced and felt.[30] That such videos are controlled by viewers who are able to pause and replay the video instantly and wherever they may be located indicates a distinct ability to control how and when a video is seen, not to mention the multiple kinds of screens that the video can be seen on, and pushes against the temporal specificity of the broadcast.

Looking again toward Nieuwenhuis' writing, it then becomes possible for the control of the breath by the State, and its subsequent mediation and circulation, to be seen as descriptors of a larger project of ongoing settler colonial violence. While the carceral system remains a central signifier for the ultimate form of policing bodies, a focus on the breath enables an opening into other forms of corporeal control that rely on the condition of policing at large. In the instance of Garner's death, Pantaleo "cut off the supply of the medium that forms the elementary condition of life itself" and displayed how "the air is increasingly becoming the preferred technology of power to discipline, punish and kill anybody who breathes too freely."[31] The Pilipinx images of death, dying, and "sustained constraint" likewise tell us something about the temporal and historical layers of that technology and its employment not just in the United States today but also on a global scale throughout history. To constrain the body via the breath is to limit the ability and agency of how a body can behave within a broader societal framework. If breathing is the condition that signifies one's humanity, control of the breath thus becomes the "strategy for the governance of 'unwanted' bodies."[32] Within the circulation of Orta's video, Garner's death therefore became both a remnant of the conditions of anti-Black violence that predated the event and a reminder of the mechanisms utilized by settler colonial systems of the State to enact corporeal control of dispossessed and criminalized bodies. So too, the war-era images of Pilipinx bodies inhaling smoke, exhaling sound, and hung and garroted spoke to how those same systems of white supremacy were sustained through a broader history of military violence, imperialism, and respiratory constraints.

Notes

1. Wesley Lowery, "'I Can't Breathe': Five Years after Eric Garner Died in Struggle with New York Police, Resolution Still Elusive," *Washington Post,* June 13, 2019, National sec., accessed June 25, 2019, https://www.washingtonpost.com.

2. Shermaine M. Jones, "'I Can't Breathe!': Affective Asphyxia in Claudia Rankine's Citizen: An American Lyric," *South: A Scholarly Journal* 50, no. 1 (2017): 38.

3. Ibid.

4. Ibid.

5. Safiya Umoja Noble, "Teaching Trayvon: Race, Media, and the Politics of Spectacle," *Black Scholar* 44, no. 1 (2014): 21.

6. Sandra Y. Govan and Sandra G. Shannon, "From Post Racial Climate to Winter in America: Life, Literature, and the Small Screen," *CLA Journal* 58, no. 3/4 (2015): 131.

7. Ulla D. Berg and Ana Y. Ramos-Zayas, "Racializing Affect: A Theoretical Proposition," *Current Anthropology* 56, no. 5 (2015): 663.

8. Stuart Hall, "The Spectacle of the 'Other,'" in *Representation: Cultural Representations and Signifying Practices,* Culture, Media, and Identities (London: Sage, 2000), 259.

9. Jasbir K. Puar, "Introduction: The Cost of Getting Better," in *The Right to Maim: Debility, Capacity, Disability* (Durham, NC: Duke University Press, 2017), 1.

10. Aaron Abel T. Mallari, "The Bilibid Prison as an American Colonial Project in the Philippines," *Philippine Sociological Review* 60 (2012): 169.

11. Sharon Delmendo, "Marketing Colonialism: Little Brown Brothers in the Kodak Zone," in *The Star-Entangled Banner: One Hundred Years of America in the Philippines* (New Brunswick, NJ: Rutgers University Press, 2004), 47.

12. Vicente L. Rafael, *Motherless Tongues: The Insurgency of Language amid Wars of Translation* (Durham, NC: Duke University Press, 2016), 45.

13. Oscar V. Campomanes, "Images of Filipino Racialization in the Anthropological Laboratories of the American Empire: The Case of Daniel Folmar," "Comparative Racialization," special issue, *PMLA* 123, no. 5 (2008): 1694.

14. Dean Conant Worcester, "The Non-Christian Peoples of the Philippine Islands." *National Geographic Magazine* 24, no. 11 (November 1913): 1162.

15. Dean C. Worcester, *The Philippines Past and Present,* vol. 2 (New York: The Macmillan Company, 1914). See also "The Project Gutenberg EBook of The Philippines: Past and Present (Volume 2 of 2), by Dean Conant Worcester," accessed April 15, 2021, www.gutenberg.org.

16. Mallari, "Bilibid Prison," 172.

17. Ibid.

18. Nerrisa Balce, *Body Parts of Empire: Visual Abjection, Filipino Images, and the American Archive* (Ann Arbor: University of Michigan Press, 2016), 7.

19. Delmendo, "Marketing Colonialism," 48.

20. Yoshihiro Chiba, "Cigar-Makers in American Colonial Manila: Survival during Structural Depression in the 1920s," *Journal of Southeast Asian Studies* 36, no. 3 (2005): 376.

21. Edilberto C. de Jesus, *The Tobacco Monopoly in the Philippines: Bureaucratic Enterprise and Social Change, 1766–1880* (Manila, Philippines: Ateneo de Manila University Press, 1998), 85.

22. Mary Talusan, "Music, Race, and Imperialism: The Philippine Constabulary Band

at the 1904 St. Louis World's Fair," "World's Fair 1904," special issue, *Philippine Studies* 52, no. 4 (2004): 508.

23. Claiborne T. Richardson, "The Filipino-American Phenomenon: The Loving Touch," *Black Perspective in Music* 10, no. 1 (Spring 1982): 11.

24. J. Lorenzo Perillo, "'If I Was Not in Prison, I Would Not Be Famous': Discipline, Choreography, and Mimicry in the Philippines," "Rethinking Intercultural Performance," special issue, *Theater Journal* 63, no. 4, (December 2011): 610.

25. Mike Price, interview with author, January 23, 2018.

26. Mark Rifkin, "Indigenous Orientations," in *Beyond Settler Time: Temporal Sovereignty and Indigenous Self-Determination* (Durham, NC: Duke University Press, 2017), 2.

27. Marijn Nieuwenhuis, "A Right to Breathe," *Critical Legal Thinking,* January 19, 2015, accessed June 1, 2019, http://criticallegalthinking.com.

28. Lauren Berlant, "Slow Death (Sovereignty, Obesity, Lateral Agency)," *Critical Inquiry* 33, no. 4 (2007): 754.

29. Puar, "Introduction," 11.

30. Ibid.

31. Nieuwenhuis, "Right to Breathe."

32. Ibid.

Part II

Making Our Empire Beautiful

Archipelagos of Whiteness after 1898

FIVE

Architecture, Domestic Space, and the Imperial Gaze in the Puerto Rico Chapters of *Our Islands and Their People* (1899)

Paul B. Niell

A photograph from José de Olivares and William Smith Bryan's volume *Our Islands and Their People as Seen with Camera and Pencil* (1899) presents a view of the mountain town of Aibonito, Puerto Rico (figure 5.1). To shoot the scene, the photographer established a high vantage point upon the roof of "the Barracks," according to the caption, overlooking the area below. The caption describes the view as one of a "class of houses in the suburbs occupied by the peons and laboring people."[1] Human figures in the photograph return the camera's gaze, including two women on the roadway in the foreground balancing loads atop their heads and three adolescent boys in the middle on a pathway. In the background beyond, the walls and towers of the city's cathedral rise above houses of wood and a cluster of *bohíos,* or thatch-covered dwellings, framed and set on stilts. Indeed, the photograph even seems contrived in order to strike a contrast between tin-roofed houses with clean lines and the irregular appearance of the *bohíos* that meet the viewer's gaze in the picture's middle ground. These thatched buildings exhibit abundant signs of human life around them, including garments or sheets drying on clotheslines, animal pens, and footpaths. Such living spaces appear integral to the pueblo even as they are situated at the edge of urban existence in Aibonito, a town named for its pleasant mountain air. The author of the text, José Olivares, notes explicitly what he perceives as the deficiencies of these kinds of structures and their occupants: "The framework, including the bridge roof, is of poles, tied together. Then the palm leaves are laid on, and other poles, of about the thickness of a broomstick, are tied horizontally across the walls of the house, to keep the palm leaves together. The floor of the hut is of poles, so loosely put together that all the dirt drops through the cracks. The roof is so poorly made that the rain drips through, and at night the cold breezes whistle through the walls."[2]

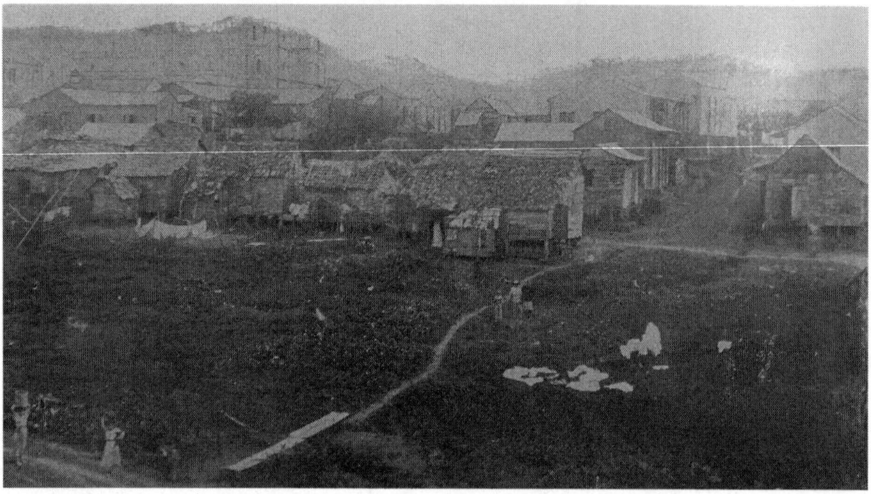

Figure 5.1. "View of the Town of Aibonito," c. 1898–1899. Photograph. Olivares and Bryan, *Our Islands and Their People,* 1:406.

Describing this "class of houses," he later writes,

> The mode of life among the lower classes is wretched in the extreme.... Their houses are made of any kind of materials they can get to piece together, principally poles and palm leaves; and it is a common sight to see six or eight persons, or even more, living in a wretched hut barely large enough for two... at night they bunch together like shivering pigs, on the dirt floors of their miserable hovels, without beds or covering, and each day and night was but a repetition of the accumulated miseries of centuries of similar days and nights that had gone before.[3]

Readers in the United States with the means available to purchase this book at fifteen dollars per volume (over $450 today) could avail themselves of over 750 pages of text interspersed with photographs and drawings. This robust volume and its literary and visual kindred at the fin de siècle purported to bring the aftermath of the Spanish-American War to a US domestic audience. Photographers presented what was explained as a panorama of the islands, place by place, featuring public buildings, agricultural landscapes, and people in their social and physical environments with occasional glimpses of gallant US troops gaining control of the situation in the aftermath of a brief conflict.[4] Olivares' dismal picture of the living conditions of the island's lower classes circa 1899 came in the wake of the US invasion and occupation of Puerto Rico. His tone of condescension pervades the volume, a view of insular impoverishment that he ties to former Spanish colonial rule. In the present chapter, I examine the ways in which the book's authors and editors used the materiality of architecture and the rhetoric of domestic space to condition the imperial gaze of a US readership, positioning its audiences in the role of a succeeding colonial master. Through an emphasis on architectural differences from the US mainland, and, by implication, the human element associated with this foreign and presumably exotic built environment, the book's images and text critique the people and places of Puerto Rico after the US acquisition of the island from Spain in 1898 with the signing of the Treaty of Paris. In situating Puerto Rico's built environment within a framework of US material and sensory expectations, the book endeavored to mobilize domestic solidarity in the valuation of the colonial differences encountered in these new territories. In this way, *Our Islands and Their People* made sense of US imperial activities in Puerto Rico and in the Tropic of Cancer by offering itself as a bridge spanning a gap of unintelligibility. That is, the book attempted to frame the material differences encountered and understood in relation to everyday living in the US metropolis, and to explain how deviations from metropolitan norms could be mobilized to validate conquest and to deepen an appreciation among readers of the usefulness of these insular residents and spaces to the expanding US empire.

Scholars of books and other publications precipitated by the Spanish-American War have noted how such materials functioned as vehicles of imperial consensus making through text and image, generating visions of new territorialities motivated by US economic interests.[5] Historian James Hevia identifies a "photography complex" in such turn-of-the-century books, referring to the expediency and synchronicity with which the medium of the photograph delivered the 1898 world to its consumer.[6] Photography not only offered an immediacy that seemed to put the reader on the scene of expanding US territorial control but also a truth value and a capacity to present foreign territories as specimens for metropolitan inspection, knowledge creation, and the negotiation of global personhood. In the introduction to *Our Islands and Their People,* major general Joseph Wheeler explicates the incredible usefulness of the book for US audiences coming to terms with these new territorial acquisitions and locates its audience at "the fireside of every American home."[7] This opening reference to domesticity in the volume is important, in fact central, to how the book was conceptualized as a guide to the things, people, and places at the edge of empire and to locating them as such. Framing the site of viewership as a domestic space on the US mainland, the book anchors imperial seeing in the nuclear family and neutralizes this activity by embedding it in everyday routine. The book's opening thereby inserts imperial seeing into processes of imperial socialization and the normalization of national looking on the home front. While focusing intently on domestic architectural settings and their human occupants in Puerto Rico through the sense of immediacy generated by the synchronizing of text and photography, the book rendered foreign environments as US territory by invoking well-worn colonial rhetorics of verbal and visual identification, of conquering and exploitation, in order to help compose the US imperial subject's privileged geopolitical position. My contention in the present chapter is that the trope of domestic space and architecture supplied an important and underinvestigated dimension of this larger process of constructing the imperial gaze.

Imperial Looking by the Fireside

Major General Wheeler's identification of an intended audience for the book, ideally at the hearth and thereby in the home, gives us insights into the volume's construction of a locus for learning how to look in imperial ways. The book's authors, image makers, and editors thereby operated with the understanding that their information was intended to inform domestic mentalities and worldviews affirmed in private as well as public space. Thus, its architects conceived the book as a vehicle of national subject formation, one that operated to make an essential unit of national belonging: the nuclear family. Imperial looking and patriotism operate inseparably in this process as viewers looked upon the war booty of "our islands." This discourse was not new, rather it informed, reshaped, and focused those hegemonic proclivities already operative in the minds of US citizens as component parts of their sense of national identity.

To broaden the horizon, we must come to see that the nationalist US rhetoric of *Our Islands and Their People* circa 1898 belonged to a much older process of empire in the West than simply those forces coalescing at this moment of history. Historian Jorge Duany has argued that *Our Islands and Their People* made Puerto Ricans into the "other" in the service of US colonial self-definitions as a rising empire on the world stage.[8] He suggests the cooptation of patterns of colonial othering from preceding empires and leaves open an opportunity to delve into the precise machinations of imagery and text as they relate to architecture and domestic spaces, given the particularities of these books and their possible sites of consumption. *Our Islands and Their People* established, after all, its categories of race, class, and gender in concert with normative and evolving US and Western conceptions of the self. At times, the text even borrows and transposes elements of North American racism toward mainland subalterns, such as African Americans, onto Puerto Ricans. Domestic equivalencies conveyed by the expediency of the photograph and within the narrative framework of the fireside book informed home audiences on how to understand and to value these new territorial acquisitions formerly colonized by Spain.

The issue of the United States as a late nineteenth-century imperial successor to Spain in the Tropic of Cancer requires a deepening of how we think of "empire" circa 1898. While the Spanish administration of Puerto Rico, along with Guam and Cuba, officially gave way to US occupation and, eventually, territorial rule, these chapters of *Our Islands and Their People,* as with the book as a whole, should be seen as part of a continuum of modern / colonial practices in the Americas, the Atlantic World, and globally. Decolonial theory's reframing of modernity, empire, and colonial power provides a means to this end. Even as colonial administrations have officially ended in many parts of the world in the last two centuries, decolonial theory looks at a deeper structure of management that continues across the colonial-national threshold, a "logic of coloniality," that operates as an inseparable component of modernity. Furthermore, modernity / coloniality arose with Occidentalism, the ideological creation of "the West" beginning in the late fifteenth century as people, political practices, and ideological constructions of western Europe violently and oppressively expanded overseas. Coloniality, according to the late Ánibal Quijano, identifies the darker and transnational side of Western modernity, that of the racism, genderism, and imperialism instrumental to capitalism's expansion worldwide.[9] The European invasion of Caribbean islands and the vast continental reaches that would be invented as "America" within an evolving order of European dominant knowledge led to a massive acquisition of land and labor through the conquest and colonization of indigenous peoples and the opening of the transatlantic African slave trade.[10] Reconsidering the publications that followed the Spanish-American War of 1898 through this idea of a continuum of modernity / coloniality across five centuries and to the present day facilitates an understanding of the discursive continuities wrought by the United States as a new world empire. The United States would not only replay the all-too-familiar "encounter with natives" narrative but would also co-opt vision and visualization of the "other" as a dominant tool of imperial thought and subjectivity. In this case, the deployment of colonial discourse operated to subalternize Puerto Ricans and to set up and validate a structure of management for their exploitation. A reformulated rhetoric of modernity, that is, the framing of the United States as a liberator from the dark empire of Spain for readers at the fireside, operated to hide or recast this brazen seizure and reconquering of islands and the subjugation of their people.

The colonialist rhetoric that drives the narrative in *Our Islands and Their People* profited from a trove of Occidentalist discursive practices and therefore illustrates specific ways in which the United States adapted and reconfigured rhetorical strategies of empire in use for centuries. First, the medium of the book, long a tool employed by Europe to identify, order, and thereby control the globe after 1492, carried the authority of the printed word and operated through presumed epistemic powers to classify and define the world.[11] The order of Western knowledge and the notion of Western-ness itself, an important legacy of printed books, reinforced the authority of such 1898 publications to describe and explain new territorial acquisitions. By invoking an established narrative of world expansion and exploration that authorized Western epistemologies, subjectivities, and identities, these narratives would thereby energize expansionist desires under the long assumption of the West as the globe's discoverer. *Our Islands and Their People* drew upon the racist inscription of the indigenous people of the Americas as "Indians," a homogenized and subalternized social category presumed to occupy a position of labor based on their perceived mental and moral frailties in comparison to the dominant Western observer. In this way, the book would cast "Puerto Ricans" as inferior and lacking modernity for a US readership, making the island's land, labor, and resources into objects for metropolitan exploitation.[12]

Of the books and their printed images deployed by the West to produce knowledge of the "other" abroad, domestic architecture and space were of keen interest from the very beginning. The Spanish historian Gonzalo Fernández de Oviedo y Valdés (1478–1557), in his writings on the "New World," included discussions and drawings of indigenous dwellings in the Caribbean. He explains the houses of the Taíno as belonging to two separate classes, *buhíos* (rectangular buildings reserved for caciques or chiefs) and *caneys* (circular or polygonal structures used by the people). His drawings depict thatched structures of wood not unlike those seen in *Our Islands and Their People* almost four hundred years later.[13] In addition to the ethnohistorical information that such accounts might offer the study of the precontact Caribbean, these early modern texts and images composed Occidentalism by developing a central and metropolitan viewpoint through which to construct oneself in relation to otherness. In other words, this constructed field of vision and its magisterial loci of observation contributed to the production of a sense of a Western self against the global others whose subjugation could be justified by virtue of their inferior standing within an evolving Occidental order of humanity.

Emergent Western image technologies, such as print even prior to 1492, allowed for the depiction of the world in association with text that offered a Eurocentric narrative of things and people "encountered," which generated a dominant locus of perception. This way of looking at the world was neither neutral nor providential, as the rhetoric of "discovery" suggests. Rather it developed quickly into an ideological project that subalternized non-European peoples, making the indigenous of the Americas into "Indians," and Africans and their descendants into "blacks" via stereotypical representations in painting, sculpture, and print. Photography carried things further, as Hevia has argued, adding new dimensions to the imperial vision, verifying homogenizing categories that aided in the control of colonial subjects. In *Our Islands and Their People,* the book's title scarcely hides its colonial intentions, beginning with a possessive pronoun in plural form, thereby affirming a collective and normative US and Western identity as the authorized locus of observation (modernity) while creating the things to be possessed and / or subordinated through bias and racism (coloniality).[14]

Descriptions and photographs of architectural materiality in *Our Islands and Their People* become an instrumental and convincing means of addressing the new lands phenomenally by emptying them of familiarity in order to make them "other" in opposition to bodily and sensory norms of the metropolis. This process was, again, far from novel. Rather, it forms in this case a continuum to the readership / viewership of sixteenth-century chronicles of the Americas by Spanish and European writers that contributed to the idea of a Western domestic space by giving account of a virgin and alien landscape for their audiences. In fact, Western domestic space was itself a construct of global imperial processes after 1492. Detailed portrayals of phenomenal spaces in Puerto Rico allowed readers / viewers to imagine those spaces with architecture serving as a key link between what was perceived as exotic, different, and strange and the comfort, familiarity, and normative sensoriality that surrounded metropolitan subjects back home. In this sense, the discussion of architecture bridged the metropolis and the would-be colony, allowing readers / viewers to think more intimately about the colonial project and to see its justification at almost every turn of the page. As clean, civilized, ordered, and capital-producing domestic spaces engulfed the reader at the fireside, the book brought forth Puerto Ricans and their architecture as a foil. The volume, in this way, functioned to construct and authorize the "American home" in the imaginary as a vital element of private social organization under capitalism and as a privileged place of viewing and making sense of a world through an Occidentalist and imperialist gaze.

In order for the colonial transformation of Puerto Rico to be successful, for capital to flow ideally through the new island(s), and for US citizens to reap the rewards of the spoils of 1898 and its potential for production, spaces needed to be sanitized and improved. US architects of empire cast Spain as a backward imperial power. As a result, subjugated people in former Spanish colonies would have to be realigned according to the grid of US capitalism, the same gridded matrix that permeated life in the United States down to the very household in which firesides could be found.[15] The focus on architecture in the book sets up a kind of equivalency of daily life so that North American readers might have a keener sense of their new colonial subjects in order, ultimately, to support policies that shaped them as subordinates. From the general, I now turn to the particular, to categories of architecture, and to photographic and textual descriptions of living spaces, that formed the argument for US imperial expansion and associated it with what are identified and framed as customary Puerto Rican people and their dwellings.

Shacks, Huts, and Hovels: The Dwellings of the *Peones*

The primary author of *Our Islands and Their People,* José de Olivares, in his analysis takes aim at poor and working-class dwellings encountered en route through Puerto Rico: "Nine-tenths of the people of Porto Rico are miserably poor. Their rude huts, scattered over the country, are meaner than the mud hovels of Egypt, and the rooms which form their tenements in the towns are more thickly crowded than the slums of the cities of China."[16] The material culture of the insular inhabitants, one gleans from Olivares' text, conveys a pervasive sense of the subcivilized. As with other islands covered in the book, the author focuses much attention on structures that he perceived as "native" in contrast to the more refined dwellings of the upper classes. Echoing the early identifications of Oviedo in the Caribbean, in the nineteenth century the Spanish government in Puerto Rico referred to such buildings as *bohíos.* In these types of dwellings, thick wooden poles set into the ground, combined with cross beams tied together with plant-derived cordage, provided a structure that was then roofed by palms leaves.[17] These buildings responded sensibly to the Caribbean climate in their strength, in their ventilation, and in how readily they could be replaced following storms if destroyed. As Europeans arrived, a colonial *bohío* emerged that incorporated European, Amerindian, and African techniques and conceptions of architecture variously through time, including the use of thatch roofing, wood siding, and rectangular volumes.[18]

While the form is the transcultural product of the colonial period, the presence of the *bohío* in the landscape over time took on a pejorative meaning. As Spain expanded urban settlement on the island in the late eighteenth and nineteenth centuries in order to move Puerto Rico toward export-oriented agriculture, a material hierarchy arose in official documentation that contrasted the *bohío* to the *casa* (house), which was increasingly a reference to domestic structures built of more substantial materials, such as wood framing or masonry. By the nineteenth century, the Spanish government kept statistics of towns' ratios of *casas* to *bohíos,* as though a fewer number of *bohíos* could speak to the prosperity and civility of the town.[19] In spite of *bohíos'* long history in the Caribbean and suitability to the climate and outdoor lifestyle, Olivares, in concert with Spanish colonial perceptions, links what he sees as the formal and material deficiencies of *bohíos* to the habits and customs of the islanders who built such dwellings. The author frames the buildings in terms of their evident lack of the necessities of civilization:

> The hut has no windows. Its door of palm leaves can be lifted away during the daytime. It has absolutely no furniture. The family sleeps on the floor. The cooking is done in a little lean-to at the back, upon a fire bed of earth, the pot being raised upon stones above the coals.
>
> In this house, which I have described from notes made in the hut itself, there were eight children, three of them stark naked, and one of the three was five years old. It was deformed, and could only crawl over the floor in its nakedness. All the children were exceedingly lean, although their heads and eyes were good.[20]

In choosing his English words for describing the dwellings of the poor and working classes in Puerto Rico circa 1898, Olivares summoned what US readers would have regarded as derogatory signifiers: "rude huts," "shacks," "miserable hovels," "homes of the peons," and "shanties." In spite of his identifying two classes of *bohío* dwellers, Olivares equates both lifeways with that of domesticated animals:

> The houses of the poor are wholly unfurnished. They sleep on mats and on the bare ground, and have neither tables nor chairs. In the huts of the middle classes, a few rude beds, and now and then a hammock, can be seen, but the dwelling places of the peons are as bare of furniture and the common conveniences and comforts of life as the stables in which an American farmer shelters his horse. They need no stoves or cooking utensils, because the mildness of the climate requires no artificial warmth, and bananas, eaten raw, constitute practically their only food.[21]

Olivares' bleak assessment of the poor and working classes is closely tied to the material conditions of their houses. The photography in the book seems likewise to promote that connection in synchrony with the author's text. In the image captioned "Coffee Picker's Hut and Family at Guanabo, Porto Rico," a woman holds her child and smiles to the camera next to the open doorway of her thatch-covered, wood-clad hut (figure 5.2). The photograph is taken or cropped so that only she and her house are visible, an effort that visually brings together the human and the habitation. The area surrounding the house is, in this way, beyond the view. The photograph thereby presents a curtailment of the fullness of Caribbean lifeways, that is, of the life lived in the spaces outside the home. The pre-Hispanic expression *batey* for a common space at

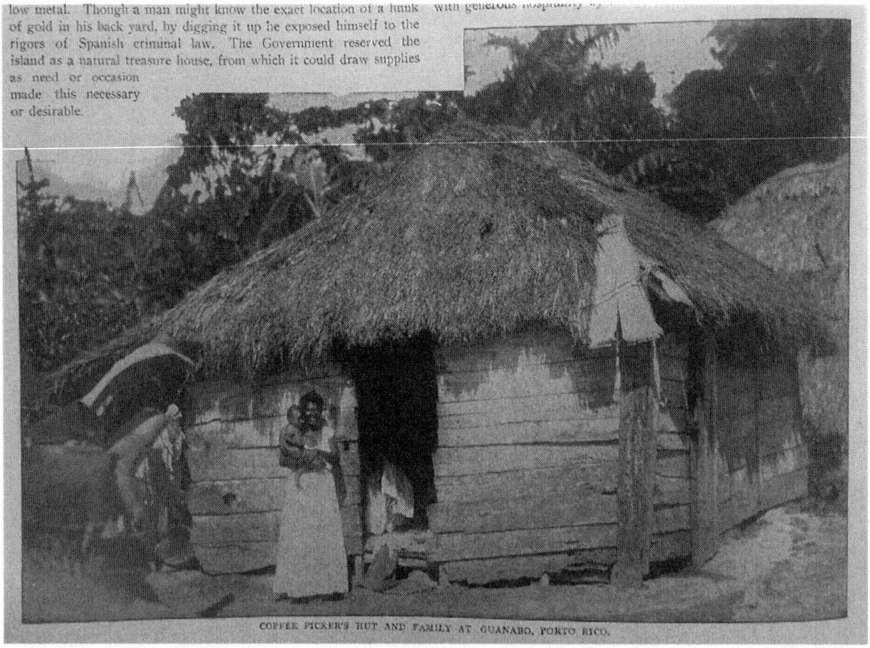

Figure 5.2. "Coffee Picker's Hut and Family at Guanabo, Porto Rico," c. 1898. Photograph. Olivares and Bryan, *Our Islands and Their People,* 1:288.

the center of an indigenous village flanked by houses survived into the colonial period as a reference, variously, to the processing areas of a sugar plantation and to the "yard" or open spaces around houses. In these areas (the kind of spaces seen in figure 5.1), people prepared food, cleaned their clothes, raised livestock, played games, and interacted socially. The author endeavors to diminish those lifeways and to reduce Caribbean people to a nonmodern stasis out of alignment with Western expectations of progress and modernity. He does so by assertively linking such people to material things that US readers would view as signs of degradation, thereby positioning the subjects in a frozen and dependent state.

We see more of a space surrounding the house in the photograph titled "Huts of Cocoanut Pickers," which includes workers from coconut plantations near Catano across the bay from San Juan (figure 5.3). A woman of African descent holds a child and turns to her right toward the photographer as various other women occupy the space between her and the "huts," which seem to consist of thatched roofs, wooden walls, doors, and contiguous units such that three open and two shuttered doorways appear along the right side of the photograph in a recessional line. A man in the group, presumably part of the

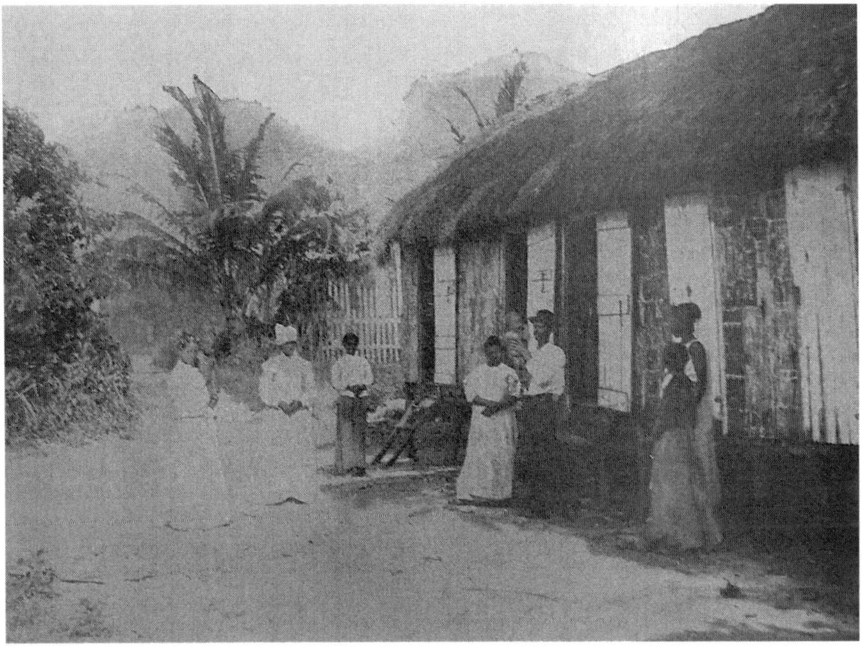

Figure 5.3. "Huts of Cocoanut Pickers," c. 1898–1899. Photograph. Olivares and Bryan, *Our Islands and Their People,* 1:268.

US surveying party, holds a baby aloft. There are two stairways into the structures providing access to rooms that likely had no interior connections. Neighbors would, therefore, exit their dwellings into a space before the structures that served as a common area between households; yet, in showing this larger space of Caribbean life, the photograph includes a mediating figure whose existence in the image provides an Anglo-Saxon person to underscore Puerto Rican difference.

The perception that these Puerto Rican laborers would need continued colonial direction from a US administration, as natives who were not entirely modern, is furthered by the author's recourse to biblical devices accumulated through centuries of European domination. "They live so close to nature that the things which would seem improper to us are with them the innocent affairs of their daily life," Olivares writes. "In many respects they are still in that Edenic state which thinks no evil and consequently knows none."[22] The author's condescending invocation of Old Testament imagery conjures sixteenth-century Spanish views of natives living innocently in a state of nature, thus valorizing Christian missionizing efforts. This rhetoric of early modern Christian salvation served to mask the darker side of labor exploitation, cultural disregard and destruction, and many other abuses. Therefore, sixteenth- and seventeenth-century discourses form a foundation for the kind of civilizing, democratizing rhetoric that we read in *Our Islands and Their People* and other evidence of late nineteenth-century US imperial activities. Framing Puerto Ricans as innocents living in an Edenic state functioned as a means of making them dependents in the declining civilization of the former empire of Spain—deficient, depraved, and thus in need of US intervention for economic, social, and material salvation. These photographs provide us with visual evidence, therefore, of a reconditioning of the Western imperial gaze in service of the promotion of US imperial interests abroad in newly conquered territories in 1898.

Our Islands and Their People utilized US material and sensory norms in order to construct a racist imaginary. Olivares uses physical and behavioral descriptions to cast "Porto Ricans" as a certain type of people, a race from which one can expect particular kinds of thought and behavior. His description of racial composition and deviance from US Anglo-Saxon Protestants allows the author to affirm the readership as the white race with a duty to govern, correct, and civilize these Caribbean subalterns. The author does so, in part, by introducing a class of "peons" on the island for which he supplies observations of their physical characteristics.

"The majority of the peons are whites, although there are many mulattos, and not a few negroes. They have good faces and are naturally intelligent. They are quiet and peaceable. They are kind to their families, and are, on the whole, good citizens. Americans who have employed them say that they are excellent workers, and that they are glad to do all they can to earn their money. They work from sunrise until sunset, and are as reliable as the average American workmen."[23]

Olivares' concern with the dwellings of the so-called peons mirrors his conception of the productive capacity of these individuals. Throughout, he maintains that the people of Puerto Rico suffer from an idleness not unlike what he sees in the subalternized working poor of the US mainland but nevertheless are enthusiastic about their new country and would make good workers: "The idle children of Porto Rico and the little negroes of the South will supply precisely the kind of labor that is needed to gather the tea leaves." He insists that correcting their material conditions and way of life would lead to productive results: "Porto Ricans are not bad people. Remove from them the terrible temptation produced by enforced hunger and nakedness; give to these people an opportunity to earn an honest living; teach them that toil is honorable; build for them factories instead of forts; teach them to handle tools instead of bayonets, and we shall produce upon them a moral effect which the Spaniards failed to produce, and make them a people whom we shall not be ashamed to recognize as fellow-citizens of our grand republic."[24]

In the towns and cities, the poor and working classes might find themselves living on the ground floor of two-story townhomes in rented spaces owned by more affluent Puerto Ricans in what amounted to a boom in real estate speculation in the nineteenth-century city of San Juan, among others. Olivares notes a similar pattern across the island: “All the houses are of two stories, the poorer inhabitants occupying the ground floors, while those who are better off live above them.”[25] Referring to such arrangements, he writes, “In such rooms families of six, ten, fifteen, and sometimes twenty, live, sleeping upon the floors, or upon cot beds, which are taken outside during the daytime.”[26] Here, he captures a sense of congestion noted by city officials and travelers in nineteenth-century Puerto Rico. As the density of urban centers increased, so did strategies of gentrification along lines of race and class.[27]

In San Juan, rising rents and property values inside the city walls pushed the lower classes into the *extramuros,* the suburbs of Puerta de Tierra and eventually Cangrejos / Santurce. In Ponce, regulations on *vagos* (the unemployed) and *amancebados* (those living together out of wedlock) allowed urban patriarchs in the nineteenth century to open up new neighborhoods on the flanks of cities in order to relocate these individuals.[28] The United States took control of an island where colonial exclusion was embedded into urban spaces and rural landscapes along lines of race, class, and gender from centuries of Spanish colonialism and nineteenth-century reforms. These social structures constituted architecture and landscape, just as the built environment, in turn, produced them. Engaging these structures in surveys, reports, and large volumes intended for the general public of the United States, such as *Our Islands and Their People,* became important means of assessing how US imperial power could plug into extant spatial divisions and practices of exclusion, and what kinds of things could be done to utilize the labor of the working poor. In the effort to assess these conditions quickly, US personnel used domestic architecture as an indication of the state of people and living conditions.

Taste and Urban Refinement: Spaces of the Upwardly Mobile

Our Islands and Their People's focus on the material conditions of the poor and working classes composed a view of fin de siècle Puerto Rico as possessing a downtrodden but adept labor force that could make the island produce for the US economy. In order to incorporate Puerto Rico's capitalists into the narrative and thereby the equation, Olivares writes about the conditions of the aristocracy and upwardly mobile classes of professionals and their material worlds of refinement. In the houses of the elite and upper middle classes, spaces such as patios, *salas* (living rooms), and the oddity of second-story living from a North American perspective populate his account. He notes also the material standards of these individuals: "The homes of the rich are usually furnished with taste and elegance, and the children of such families are reared in an atmosphere of luxury and refinement; but up to this time there has been no opportunity for them to be spoiled by an excess of riches."[29] The author appeals to an anticipated sense of North American difference in suggesting that US readers might find it odd to see second-floor parlors and receptions rooms. A photograph from the book represents a line of two- and three-story houses of the affluent along the Plaza de Colón in San Juan (figure 5.4). In these upper stories of the island's capital city in an area once enclosed by fortified walls, the refined world of the Puerto Rican social elite and upwardly mobile took shape. The elite or upper-middle-class house established important divisions between public and private as well as rented space on the ground floor. Such spaces established separation between house and street in gendered configurations. "The women of this [upper] class are rarely seen upon the streets," Olivares writes, "they do not hang out of the windows nor lean dreamily over the balconies, and only a few of them go out to walk in the plaza when the military band plays."[30] With the increase in populations of African descent, in streets of Spanish Caribbean port cities such as Havana and San Juan, especially in the nineteenth century, young women of the upper classes spent the majority of their time indoors, venturing out occasionally and usually with female chaperones and / or male attendants in order to navigate public spaces

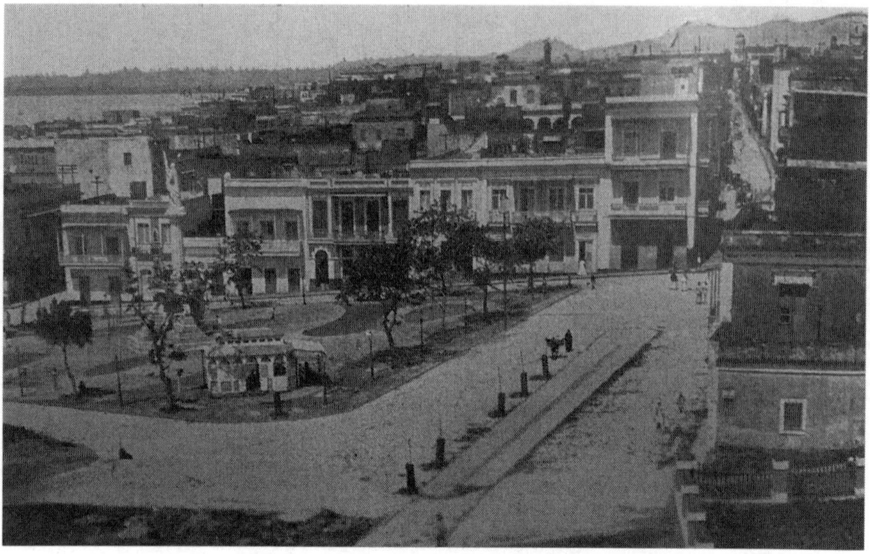

Figure 5.4. "Bird's-Eye View of San Juan, Porto Rico," c. 1898–1899. Photograph. Olivares and Bryan, *Our Islands and Their People,* 1:258.

(streets, plazas, and promenades) populated on a daily basis by racially mixed populations regarded by their families as a threat to social standing.

Traveling to the southern Puerto Rican city of Ponce, Olivares and the artists and photographers would have encountered quite different house forms than in San Juan's *intramuros* (walled cities). By the late nineteenth century, much of the human settlement outside the walls of the capital exhibited Creolized patterns of wood-framed or masonry houses with formidable balconies across the full front on the first or second story.[31] Wealthy planters kept town homes in addition to their rural *haciendas* (estates) in order to maintain an urban presence and connection to city governance. In the southwestern Puerto Rican city of Yauco in an area known for coffee production, a photograph captioned "Residence of a Wealthy Coffee Planter" displays such a house, that of Philip Pieraildis, in this case, apparently one of the wealthiest coffee planters in Puerto Rico (figure 5.5). The one-story house of brick and masonry, four bays across, is fronted by a balcony the width of the plan and supported by ironwork. Gated steps rise from the sidewalk. High-style Beaux Arts detailing (including dentils, classical door surrounds, quoining, an ornate balustrade, and rectangular paneling) set the house well apart from those of lower-class residents. Typologically, the so-called *casa criolla* (Creole house) differed fundamentally from the patio house of San Juan in which the outer wall of the building comes flush to the street with the patio as the point of connectivity

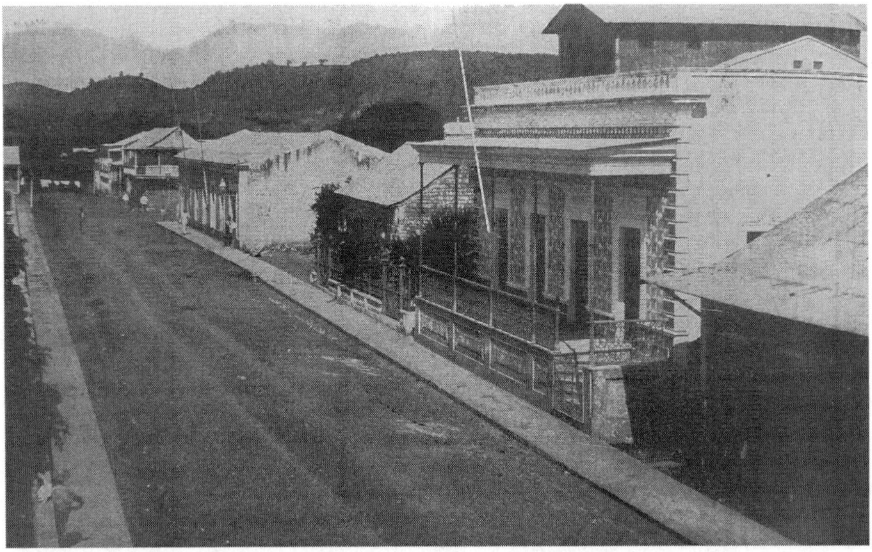

Figure 5.5. "Residence of a Wealthy Coffee Planter," c. 1898–1899. Photograph. Olivares and Bryan, *Our Islands and Their People*, 1:264.

between internal rooms. In the Creole house, by contrast, the building starts in a front porch or *balcón* that gives way to an interior *sala* and its flanking bedrooms in the grandest of houses, the number and size of such rooms depending on the means of the owner. Describing these structures, Olivares writes, "As we drive the streets we observe that the houses are nearly all built of brick, covered with stucco, and many of them have pillars in front, which lend an imposing appearance even to a common shanty. The houses are painted in all the colors of the rainbow, which in our opinion is far more attractive than the monotonous white or brown of our American towns."[32]

In spite of various architectural refinements seen in urban townhomes, Olivares seems to have come away with the perception that Puerto Rican cities and towns possessed a greater sense of congestion than their North American counterparts. The walled town of San Juan, while picturesque in its ramparts, contained a population of about twenty thousand people "densely packed in closely-built houses."[33] Olivares writes, "Porto Rican towns are more compactly built than ours; there are no distinctive suburbs, so that on leaving the outskirts of Ponce over the military road we plunge at once into the rural sections."[34] This crowding notwithstanding, daily recreation in the city could alleviate a sense of stuffiness for the more gentile and refined residents, including those of the middle classes. Here, the author exhibits the ambivalence of the imperial gaze, in which the hegemonic and profit-driven tendency to subalternize and denigrate the material life of Puerto Rico gives way to the realities of the human phenomenal encounter with the other that comprised the aftermath of 1898. In his observations, Olivares describes a stimulating and welcoming environment as a respite from the very spatial homogeneity and modest Protestant sensibilities of North America that he seems to measure Puerto Rico against in so many other passages.

In *Our Islands and Their People,* curiosity intermingles with an aggressive and brazen ethnocentrism informed by a logic of coloniality long established in the West. The book is remarkable for its absorption and reconfiguration of standard practices of colonial discourse from previous empires that the United States adopted and repurposed to conquer and colonize the Tropic of Cancer following the Spanish-American War. Spaces, at least mentally, would need to be sanitized and swept clear. People would also have to be corrected materially and in their behaviors. The book's focus on architecture and domestic spaces gave account of the roughness of the freshly acquired landscape and offered a vision of how it could be assimilated for the US consumer. The theme of domesticity served a vital role in this project, as the formidable fireside books brought the complexities of the spoils of war to the homes of North America, in which an island world that was home to a much older empire began to take a decisive turn in its history.

Notes

1. José de Olivares and William Smith Bryan, *Our Islands and Their People as Seen with Camera and Pencil,* (St. Louis, MO: N. D. Thompson, 1899), 2:406.

2. Ibid., 1:301.

3. Ibid., 1:329.

4. The book, as its title page claims, is about "embracing perfect photographic and descriptive representations of the peoples and the islands lately acquired from Spain... so complete as to practically transfer the islands and their people to the pictured page." Ibid., title page.

5. For sources that critique Western colonialism at the turn of the nineteenth century and include some discussion of *Our Islands and Their People*, see Faye C. Caronan, "Colonial Consumption and Colonial Hierarchies in Representations of Philippine and Puerto Rican Tourism," "Philippine Studies," special issue, *Representations* 53, no. 1 (2005): 32–58; Miguel A. Bretos, "Imaging Cuba under the American Flag: Charles Edward Doty in Havana, 1899–1902," Cuba-themed issue, *Journal of Decorative and Propaganda Arts* (1996): 82–103; Jorge Duany, "Portraying the Other: Puerto Rican Images in Two American Photography Collections," "Imperial Disclosures: Part II," special issue, *Discourse* 23, no. 1 (Winter 2001): 119–153; Gervasio Luis Garcia, "I Am the Other: Puerto Rico in the Eyes of North Americans, 1898," *Journal of American History* 87, no. 1 (June 2000): 39–64; Robert Martinez, "The Emergence of Imperialist Capitalism and Puerto Rican Emigration, 1879–1901," *Journal of American Ethnic History* 3, no. 2 (Spring 1984): 54–66; and Lanny Thompson, *Nuestra isla y su gente: La construcción del "otro" puertorriqueño en "Our Islands and Their People,"* 2nd ed., rev. and exp. (Río Piedras: Universidad de Puerto Rico, Centro de Investigaciones Sociales y Departamento de Historia, 2007).

6. The contribution of Hevia and those of his coauthors to the volume, in general, underscores the crucial role of visual culture—painting, prints, photography, etc.—in constituting empire in the past five centuries and vice versa. See James L. Hevia, "The Photography Complex: Exposing Boxer-Era China (1900–1901), Making Civilization," in *Empires of Vision: A Reader*, edited by Martin Jay and Sumathi Ramaswamy (Durham, NC: Duke University Press, 2014), 283–314.

7. Joseph Wheeler, "Introduction," in de Olivares, *Our Islands and Their People,* 1:5.

8. Duany, "Portraying the Other."

9. For the concept of coloniality, see Ánibal Quijano, "Coloniality and Modernity/"Rationality," *Cultural Studies* 21, no. 2 (2010): 168–178; and Walter D. Mignolo, *The Darker Side of Western Modernity: Global Futures, Decolonial Options* (Durham, NC: Duke University Press, 2011). See also Mabel Moraña, Enrique Dussel, and Carlos A. Jáuregui, eds., *Coloniality at Large: Latin America and the Postcolonial Debate* (Durham, NC: Duke University Press, 2008).

10. See José Rabasa, *Inventing America: Spanish Historiography and the Formation of Eurocentrism* (Norman: University of Oklahoma Press, 1993).

11. Michel Foucault's work on the development of Western epistemology, while highly important to our understanding of the machinations of power in the West, is blind to the colonial scene and the issue of empire. See Michel Foucault, *The Order of Things: An Archaeology of the Human Sciences* (1966; repr., London: Routledge, 1989). Decolonial theory intervenes in the Eurocentric tradition of Karl Marx, Michel Foucault, and Henri Lefebvre to begin to explain how structures of power, domination, and exploitation operate and are negotiated worldwide after 1492.

12. According to Walter D. Mignolo, this colonial way of seeing built upon centuries of Western development has always operated through a process of "fixing the center," that is, the construction of an ideological center in the territorial imagination of metropolitan audiences created and reinforced by images, texts, and performative practices. Walter D. Mignolo, *The Darker Side of the Renaissance: Literacy, Territoriality, and Colonization* (Ann Arbor: University of Michigan Press, 1995).

13. For a sixteenth-century drawing of the *bohío*, see Gonzalo Fernández de Oviedo y Valdés, *Historia general y natural de las Indias, islas, y tierra-firme del mar océano* (Madrid: Imprenta de la Real Academia de la Historia, 1852).

14. The author(s) litter the text with assertions laced with republican ideals, such as desires to make good democratic citizens of the new natives. Yet, this rhetoric of progress and modernity operates to conceal or valorize the drive to manipulate land and resources, subjugate people, and put them into unequal labor arrangements in the Western system, and to aggrandize the metropolis, the United States, in the process. This practice of imperial looking is dialectical, as decolonial theory has argued, for it constructs the margins as it simultaneously establishes the authority of the center. The book repeatedly raises the issue, speaking directly to the reader, of how people, things, and practices in Puerto Rico compare to those in the United States. In so doing, the book weaves the United States into the magisterial seat of global power, constructing a new type of imperial/colonial gaze at the dawn of the twentieth century.

15. In the context of nineteenth-century cities in the United States, architectural historian Dell Upton has identified a "republican spatial imagination" at work in the making of early US urban landscapes. See Upton's *Another City: Urban Life and Urban Spaces in the New American Republic* (New Haven, CT: Yale University Press, 2008).

16. de Olivares, *Our Islands,* 1:298–299.

17. For a scholarly treatment of the Taíno, see Irving Rouse, *The Taíno: Rise and Decline of the People Who Greeted Columbus* (New Haven, CT: Yale University Press, 1993).

18. For the African contribution to colonial *bohíos,* the work of John Michael Vlach on the shotgun house offers valuable perspectives. See his chapter "The Shotgun House: An African Architectural Legacy," in *Common Places: Readings in American Vernacular Architecture*, edited by Dell Upton and John Michael Vlach (Athens: The University of Georgia Press, 1986), 58–78.

19. Statistics that made the distinction between *bohío* and *casa* can be seen in Ánibal Sepúlveda, *Puerto Rico Urbano: Atlas histórico de la ciudad puertorriqueña* (San Juan: Carimar, 2004).

20. Olivares, *Our Islands,* 1:301.

21. Ibid., 1:302.

22. Ibid., 1:330.

23. Ibid., 1:299.

24. Ibid., 1:347.

25. Ibid., 1:329.

26. Ibid., 1:299.

27. See Edwin Quiles, *San Juan tras la fachada: Una mirada desde sus espacios ocultos (1508–1900)*, 2nd ed. (San Juan: Instituto de Cultura Puertorriqueña, 2014).

28. For practices of colonial exclusion in Ibero-American urbanism in Havana, Cuba, see Guadalupe García, *Beyond the Walled City: Colonial Exclusion in Havana* (Oakland: University of California Press, 2016).

29. Olivares, *Our Islands,* 1:336.

30. Ibid., 1:353.

31. For sources on the building typology known in Puerto Rico as *la casa criolla,* see Jorge Ortiz Colom, "The Puerto Rican Casa Criolla: Identity and Domestic Space," unpublished conference paper presented at the 2011 Vernacular Architecture Forum annual meeting in Falmouth, Jamaica, May 31–June 4, https://www.academia.edu; Edwin R. Quiles Rodríguez, *La ciudad de los balcones* (San Juan: Editorial Universidad de Puerto Rico, 2009); Jorge Rigau, *Puerto Rico 1900: Turn-of-the-Century Architecture in the Hispanic Caribbean, 1890–1930* (New York: Rizzoli, 1992); and Jay D. Edwards, "The Origins of Creole Architecture," *Winterthur Portfolio* 29, no. 2/3 (Summer / Autumn 1994): 155–189.

32. Olivares, *Our Islands,* 1:365.

33. Ibid., 1:349.

34. Ibid., 1:367.

Six

The Kilohana Art League

The Aesthetics of Annexation, 1894–1913

Stacy L. Kamehiro

In 1894, a group of European American residents of Honolulu founded an arts organization named the Kilohana Art League. Its objectives were: "First—To stimulate an interest in Art. Second—To afford opportunities for its study and advancement. Third—To upbuild as high a standard as may be here possible. Fourth—To establish a permanent Art center in Hawaii."[1] The birth of the league coincided with the dramatic and illegal transformation of the Hawaiian government from an Indigenous monarchy into a republic led by white businessmen. White settler efforts to create a new polity, culture, and national narrative that would garner positive recognition from the United States worked conjointly to further settlers' desire to become a US territory. As anthropologist Nicholas Thomas argues, colonialism is not primarily an economic or political imposition merely supported by ideologies of modernity and racial superiority but "has always, equally importantly and deeply, been a cultural process; its discoveries and trespasses are imagined and energized through signs, metaphors, and narratives; even what would seem its purest moments of profit and violence have been mediated, and enframed by structures of meaning. Colonial cultures are not simply ideologies that mask, mystify, or rationalize forms of oppression that are external to them; they are also expressive and constitutive of colonial relationships in themselves."[2]

Colonial culture in Hawai'i was integral to colonial politics. The artworks produced and exhibited by the Kilohana Art League represented its aspiration to create an American landscape, an American sense of place, and demonstrated, in a variety of ways, Anglo-Hawai'i's cultural affinities with the "mainland." The organization's paintings, photographs, and performances emphasized how white settlers had metamorphosed the archipelago into an American outpost in the Pacific, and indicated that Hawai'i was ripe for annexation and worthy of self rule as an American territory. Its work materialized and aestheticized Lorrin A. Thurston's (a descendant of American missionaries and a zealous annexationist) characterization of Hawai'i as an "American Colony" in the introduction to his *Hand-book on the Annexation of Hawaii* (1897), and his explanation of "Hawaiian Christianization, civilization, commerce, education and development [as] the direct product of American effort."[3]

The league's output was, however, also conditioned by uncertainties about the success of joining the United States and ambivalence about its members' cultural and national identities. Settler colonists in Hawai'i were well aware that many in the United States were opposed to acquiring overseas territories. They also lived with the constant reminder that Native Hawaiians and their supporters resisted and challenged their rule. They could not escape recognition of Indigenous dispossession, which troubled their linear narrative of settler achievements in Hawai'i's evolution to modernity. While historian Patrick Wolfe has famously defined settler colonialism as a "structure, not an event," cultural historian Felicity Barnes and others have argued that attention focused on its structure rather than on its complex interactions with Indigenous communities tends to diminish Indigenous resistance to, and/or accommodation of, colonial processes; overdetermines the inevitability of settler colonial projects; and masks its anxiety.[4] This chapter discusses how the history and activities of the Kilohana Art League aided in the political transformation of the Hawaiian Islands and articulated both colonial settler confidence *and* uncertainty.

On January 17, 1893, a small but powerful group of white businessmen calling itself the Committee of Safety overthrew the Native Hawaiian monarchy that had ruled the unified archipelago for over a century. Tensions between Indigenous political leaders and the white oligarchy had been building in the previous decade. On July 6, 1887, the latter, calling itself the Reform Party and led by American missionary descendant and lawyer Sanford B. Dole and Boston-born businessman Peter C. Jones, forced king David Kalākaua (reigned 1874–1891) to dismiss his cabinet and sign a revised constitution written by the committee of a secret organization called the Hawaiian League. Popularly known as the Bayonet Constitution because of the threat of violence the event entailed, the new constitution dramatically curtailed the authority of the monarchy; imposed voting restrictions based on residency, property, wealth, and literacy; extended voting privileges to all males of American or European (but not Asian) descent even if not citizens of the kingdom; and effectively delivered greater power to white businessmen.[5] During the reign of Lili'uokalani, Kalākaua's sister and successor (reigned 1891–1893), the protectionist McKinley Tariff Act of 1890 increased duties on many goods imported to the United States and, because it eliminated tariffs on all sugars, thereby removing Hawai'i's market advantage, caused several years of severe economic depression and had a devastating impact on the sugar industry. This development, combined with concerns that the queen planned to promulgate a new constitution restoring political power to the Hawaiian Crown and Native Hawaiian people, spurred the 1893 revolt against the government. The insurgents proceeded to establish a provisional government led by Americans and Hawai'i-born Americans with Sanford B. Dole as president.

The leaders of this coup d'état were members of a clandestine Annexation Club that had formed a year earlier in Honolulu. Encouraged in 1892 by the expansionist US president Benjamin Harrison, Secretary of State James Blaine, and Secretary of the Navy Benjamin Tracy, they immediately appointed a commission to travel to Washington, DC, to present a treaty of annexation to the US administration. Their plans were frustrated by the recent election of the antiexpansionist president Grover Cleveland, who, upon assuming office in March 1893, not only withdrew the treaty but also issued an investigation into the Hawaiian matter that determined the illegality of the overthrow and moved to restore the monarchy. Waiting for a friendlier administration that would recognize the mutual benefit of annexation and the creation of Hawai'i as a US territory, the provisional government called a convention to draft a constitution for a "Republic of Hawaii" in March 1894. This was adopted on the Fourth of July, with Dole appointed as president, and the newly formed American Union Party dominated the republic's first elections.[6] Between 1894 and 1898, the republic's leaders vigorously lobbied American legislators and heads of state to secure annexation.

Coinciding with this political transition was the formation of the Kilohana Art League in the spring of 1894. This was a time of both optimism and uncertainty on the part of American interests in Hawai'i, to whom annexation seemed imminent. Three of the four charter members of the league, D. Howard Hitchcock, Augusta Graham, and Annie H. Parke, were Hawai'i-born of American descent. The fourth founder, Allen Hutchinson, was a British sculptor who had been working in Honolulu since 1888. While the league was originally a visual arts organization, the executive committee eventually created subgroups focused on the fine arts, music, drama, literature, and community outdoor beautification. This chapter focuses on the "Pictorial and Plastic Circle of the Kilohana Art League." Patrons and members were very much part of the white missionary, business, and plantation social and political circles, and the majority of the initial members had, directly or indirectly, served on the Committee of Safety, promoted the proannexation cause, or participated in the creation of the republic.[7] An article describing the league in the *Hawaiian Annual and Almanac for 1896* described its membership as being "made up from the most intelligent, cultivated, and public-spirited of our citizens."[8] A cartoon accompanying an exhibition review published in the *Hawaiian Gazette* (May 21, 1901) features well-dressed white women and men viewing the paintings on display, visually confirming the intended Hawai'i American community of the league.[9] Virtually absent from the member rosters were Native Hawaiian and Asian surnames and the names of those who supported the monarchy. It is not surprising that pro-American social and political leaders eagerly supported the Kilohana Art League, whose stated goal was to "push on the good work for culture, refinement and enlightenment" and continue strides "in the right direction of a truer, higher art culture in this community."[10]

The league was fashioned as *the* national arts institution of the Republic of Hawaii. It promoted and showcased the firm establishment and progress of American social and cultural institutions in Hawai'i, and endeavored to make these visible to observers on the mainland and to themselves. In an article titled "Modern Art in Hawaii: Kilohana Art League" (1897), member Philip Henry Dodge crafted a periodized narrative of Hawaiian art history, beginning with "Past Hawaiian Art"—Indigenous visual and material forms whose "old master" makers he characterized as having passed away. Next was "Recent Modern Art," represented by European and American painters who had worked in Hawai'i during the monarchy, especially during the 1880s, such as Charles Furneaux, Jules Tavernier, Joseph Strong, and Robert Barnfield. Indigenous patronage of innovative architectural projects, public monuments, museums, and performances, contemporary with the aforementioned artists, were invisible in this art history of modern Hawai'i. "Current Art" was linked to the league (and the republic), with Mrs. Sanford B. Dole, first lady of the republic, acknowledged as its patroness. The league's cultural and artistic accomplishments supplanted those of Native Hawaiian institutions and patrons of the monarchy era. Dodge wrote that the aim of the arts organization was to cultivate a high standard of artistic quality "such that if our little gallery [was] suddenly transferred to any leading American city, comparisons need not be to the disadvantage of the works done here." Evidently, league artists sought to develop a Hawai'i American art and aesthetic.[11]

Approximately 180 European American residents of Hawai'i and visiting artists contributed oil paintings, watercolors, pastels, sculptures, architectural drawings, illustrations, woodworking, and china painting to nearly sixty biannual and special exhibitions from 1894 to 1913. Like the league's patrons, the artists represented the white social and economic elite.[12] Exhibited items reflected conservative tastes of the day—impressionist landscapes, seascapes, views of local plants and fish, portraits of leading white families members, and views of estates and plantations. As many Hawai'i Americans visited family and friends in the United States, they painted landscapes during their travels, primarily of California and the East Coast, which they brought back to Hawai'i and displayed alongside island scenes.[13] This had the effect of presenting their art as one among many American regional painting traditions. While local commentators viewed Hawai'i-born artists as equally capable of producing grand vistas and more intimate, rustic views of the American landscape, they judged the artists as better able to depict island landscapes than their peers from abroad. Exhibition reviews in Honolulu newspapers prided Hawai'i American artists for their ability to capture the intense and varied colors of the islands better than visiting artists. For instance, in February 1896, the league held an exhibition of visiting American artist William Henry Hilliard, who had traveled to the Hawaiian Islands to paint the Kīlauea volcano for the California sugar magnate Claus Spreckels. The league's historian complimented the "vigorous and bold" style, "conception of the picturesque," and "great technical dexterity" of Hilliard's paintings of the eastern United States, but with regard to his paintings of Honolulu views, the writer suggested that Hilliard failed to capture "the character of our Island landscape and his work was lacking in warmth and depth and sympathetic feeling."[14] In contrast, D. Howard Hitchcock, frequently lauded by Honolulu admirers as the foremost Hawai'i-born artist of his time, and the painter most represented in the league's exhibitions, was celebrated for producing numerous "masterpieces" of Hawaiian landscapes. In the November 1896 exhibition, his painting *Halemaumau Crater in Kilauea Caldera* (1893) was described as having "merit never reached by any previous painter of that subject in the representation of atmosphere superheated to the verge of incandescence over the fiery mound and fountains.... This is a picture whose historical worth scarcely falls below its high artistic quality."[15] While the artists claimed a space in American art, they also reserved a special attachment to and vision of Hawai'i's land.

Given that Hitchcock was by far the league's most prolific and popular artist, his oeuvre provides a good representation of the tastes and values of the organization's artists and patrons. Island landscapes painted by league artists generally depicted Hawai'i American accomplishments and hopes for continued prosperity. For instance, Hitchcock's *Haleakala: The C. R. Bishop Residence* (1899; figure 6.1), the residence of wealthy banker Charles Reed Bishop (born in Glens Falls, New York) and the high chiefess Bernice Pauahi features a large, colonnaded two-story home fronted by a wide, manicured lawn. The size and bright whiteness of the coral structure contrast with the surrounding foliage and shadows, suggesting an American civilizing presence, while the palm trees and ferns specify the island locale, as do the intense greens and blues pervading the scene. Though the structure suggests a taming of the Hawaiian wilderness, it also remains a part of it. The painting evokes the idea that Americans had adapted the landscape but also adapted to it. It is noteworthy that the title

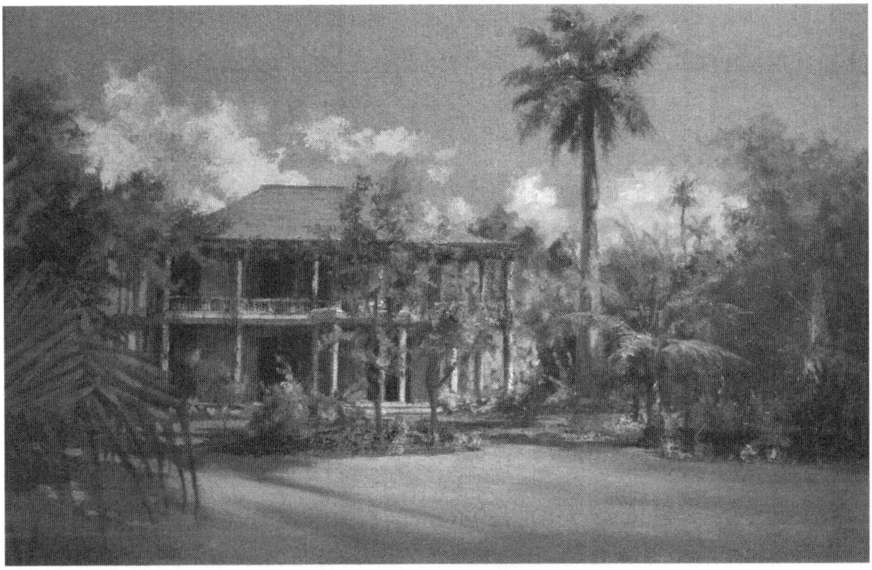

Figure 6.1. D. Howard Hitchcock, *Haleakala: The C. R. Bishop Residence,* 1899. Oil on canvas. Bernice Pauahi Bishop Museum, Honolulu. Photograph by Mark Miller, 2016. Courtesy of Wikimedia Commons.

of the picture identifies the house as Bishop's residence and does not acknowledge that the high chief Abner Kuhoʻoheiheipahu Pākī built the home and bequeathed it to his daughter, Bernice Pauahi. Upon her death in 1884, Pauahi willed the estate to Bishop to use for the duration of his life, and he quickly developed the residence as income property and added adjacent commercial buildings. From January to April 1893, during the overthrow of the monarchy, United States military personnel assisting the leaders of the coup used Haleʻākala as their headquarters, residence, hospital, and armory.[16]

Another of Hitchcock's paintings, *Coffee Plantation, Puna* (1897; figure 6.2), depicts an expansive and flourishing agricultural estate on the island of Hawaiʻi. The lush farmland occupies two-thirds of the scene, with conspicuous clusters of bright red coffee berries in the near foreground and a magnified branch emerging in the immediate foreground, from the lower left corner of the picture. A farmhouse, marking the scene as a working, cultivated landscape, is situated at the top of the sloping field, surveying the land that also dwarfs its presence. Hitchcock's paintings can be read in the spirit of W. J. T. Mitchell's observation that landscape paintings (and landscapes themselves) are closely associated with imperial expansion and articulate power relations and meanings about human-nonhuman relations. They have spatial and temporal dimensions: "Empires move outward in space as a way of moving forward

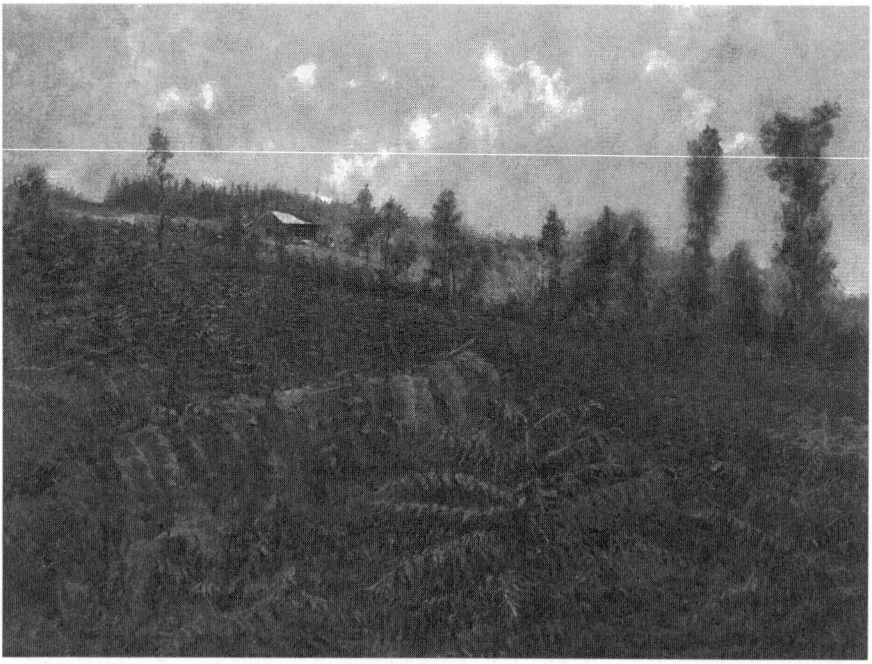

Figure 6.2. D. Howard Hitchcock, *Coffee Plantation, Puna,* 1897. Oil on canvas. Private collection. Courtesy of Bonhams, Los Angeles.

in time; the prospect that opens up is not just a spatial scene but a projected future of development and exploitation."[17] Just as Dodge's art history of Hawai'i entailed an unfolding of time to the modern present that coincided with the spatial displacement of Native Hawaiians, the paintings to which he referred materialized the myth of white progress—advances in civilization and industry—in the islands. Countering antiexpansionist arguments in the United States that whites could not flourish in hot, tropical climates and would therefore never form a self-governing majority, these images demonstrated white success and suggested opportunities for future American settlers.

A singular insistence on reading colonial landscape painting as a tool of exploitation, however, obscures the intricacy and ambiguity in colonial relationships between people and between people and place.[18] Landscapes created under the auspices of the Kilohana Art League were akin to what Miriam Aronowicz, in the context of South African colonial landscape painting, describes as "transitional objects," in which artists adapted the painting conventions they learned in the United States and Europe to local subjects, topography, light, and atmospheric conditions.[19] They also painted their dual sense of place and of belonging to a desired American landscape and a distinctly

Hawaiian one. Counter to the unequivocally pro-American rhetoric circulated by proannexationists in Hawaiʻi and US newspapers,[20] paintings of island landscapes reveal that the league and its patrons had complex national attachments. In her recent study of the bicultural identity of missionary children in Hawaiʻi, historian Joy Schulz argues that missionary descendants were raised in a Hawaiʻi that had long-standing economic and political relationships with the United States. They were reared by their parents to serve as exemplary beacons of superior American and Christian civilization for the Indigenous and migrant communities, and yet possessed a firm attachment to their Hawaiian birth land and what they considered to be their homeland. Through a study of missionary children's abundant self-documentation in letters, journals, and other writings, Schulz indicates that the children were never completely acculturated into American society, nor were they fully integrated into Native Hawaiian society. Combined with the fact that many missionary descendants were uncertain of their actual citizenship, due to interpretations of the US Naturalization Law of 1802 that excluded children born abroad to fathers born after the law went into effect, they did not feel at home in the United States, where many were sent to be educated. While abroad, they referred to themselves as "exile, stranger, expatriate, and Hawaiian," as well as "creole" and "cannibal." Almost all could speak the Hawaiian language (ʻŌlelo Hawaiʻi), and preferred gathering with other Hawaiʻi-born missionary children and conversing in Hawaiian rather than in English.[21]

Rather than mimicking New England or California landscape painting in the islands or merely documenting island views or scenes of conquest, league artists, many of whom were missionary descendants, expressed their strong, if contested and ambivalent, attachment to their Hawaiian home. Despite being based in Honolulu, urban scenes were largely absent from the league's exhibitions;[22] instead the paintings tended to depict rural, barely settled countryside and agricultural estates; Western-style homes juxtaposed with lush, tropical foliage; and brilliantly colored canyons, mountains, seascapes, and volcanoes that singularly distinguished Hawaiʻi from other American places. A watercolor by missionary granddaughter and frequent contributor to league exhibitions Helen Whitney Kelley titled *Rice Paddies* (c. 1890) shows a wide expansive terrain of rice cultivation that is emphasized by the horizontal orientation of the composition but clearly locates the scene in Hawaiʻi: four towering coconut palms extend nearly the full height of the painting in the left foreground, and a row of palms delineate the rear border of the plantation and the ocean beyond.[23] Unlike other settler colonialisms, as described by Lorenzo Veracini, which are "characterised by a persistent drive to ultimately supersede the conditions of [their] operation," ultimately driving to establish independent states and extinguish ties to metropoles,[24] annexationists in Hawaiʻi desired to strengthen political, economic, and social ties with the United States, but also wanted to maintain their cultural distinctiveness.[25]

This liminal and conflicted Hawaiʻi American identity was also evidenced in an illustrated poem titled "My Islands," produced by Hawaiʻi-born artist Annie H. Parke and missionary-granddaughter poet Mary Dillingham Frear.[26] It was created circa 1907, when Frear began her role as first lady of the Territory of Hawaiʻi (1907–1913). Framing the text of the poem are coconut palms and a seascape to identify the island setting. The text, however, adds a melancholy and nostalgic tone to the evocation "*my* islands" (emphasis added) in the words:

> On the edge of the world my Islands sleep,
> In a slumber soft and deep.
> What should they know
> Of a world of woe
> And myriad men that weep.
>
> On the edge of the world my Islands wake,
> And their languid sleep forsake.
> They long to live
> Their all to give
> And the work of the world partake.
>
> On the edge of the world dear Islands stay,
> Far from the clamorous day.
> Content with calm
> Hold peace and balm
> Be isles of the blest, for aye.

With the annexation of Hawaiʻi accomplished in 1898, the author seems to yearn for the trouble-free, "languid" pre-American / territorial past of its "blest" missionary children, prior to the clamor and disruption of having to engage in "the work of the world." Correspondingly, signs of industry and habitation are absent in the illustration, echoing concerns about changes the Americanization of the islands would bring.

Anxiety accompanied ambivalence in league art works, especially prior to 1898, when annexation was still uncertain. It seems that white artists and residents of Hawaiʻi valued images that buttressed a sense of their legitimate place and future leadership in the islands that was, in part, visualized through the absence or very limited representation of Native Hawaiians as well as the omission of Asians in the artwork promoted by the league. The Republic of

Hawaii's repeated unsuccessful bids for annexation since 1893 led to heightened efforts on the part of its leaders to convince the US Congress that annexation would be an economic and strategic boon and to dispel reservations about incorporating a territory with an "inferior" nonwhite majority. Propaganda of the day insisted the republic was no longer Native Hawaiian but American and was effectively managing the "problematic" elements of the population.[27] Although emphasis was placed on the dwindling and predicted extinction of the Indigenous population, Lorrin A. Thurston presented an additional perspective in his *Hand-Book on the Annexation of Hawaii* (1897), characterizing Native Hawaiians as peaceful, assimilable, educated in the American fashion, and supportive of annexation.[28]

Thurston said nothing of the vocal Native opposition to the provisional government and the republic.[29] The reluctance of league artists to include "inferior" nonwhite communities in their artwork was linked to their anxiety about US opposition to annexation. In June 1897, US president William McKinley submitted another Hawaiian annexation treaty to the Senate but could not immediately garner the required two-thirds majority vote to pass it. Other obstacles arose. Senator Augustus Octavius Bacon (Democrat, Georgia), concerned about the willingness of the Indigenous population to be annexed as well as the desire of Americans to acquire the archipelago, introduced an amendment that required a majority of Native Hawaiian voters to approve the treaty before the Senate would vote on it.[30] Proannexationists in Hawai'i also doubted that Native Hawaiians would acquiesce to their authority. The deposed queen Lili'uokalani had traveled to Washington in January 1897 to meet with president Grover Cleveland and other government leaders to protest annexation and was still resident there at the beginning of McKinley's administration. She conveyed her objections through interviews published in the American press and, in June 1897, submitted a written protest to the Secretary of State. In December the members of the Hawaiian Patriotic League, representing Native Hawaiian interests, met Lili'uokalani in Washington to submit to senator George Hoar and the Senate Committee on Foreign Relations a petition with over twenty-one thousand signatures in opposition to the annexation treaty, and to present to Secretary of State John Sherman another formal protest. Throughout the following month, this group continued to meet with Senate members; by the time the group departed in February 1898, barely half of the senators supported the treaty. Furthermore, anti-annexation articles continued to appear in the Hawaiian and American press, and Native Hawaiians organized anti-annexation rallies, gathered signatures for the petition, and collected donations to support the commission delivering the petition to Washington.[31]

Regarding Asian residents, Thurston was largely silent except to say the republic would restrict future immigration and that most of the laborers then residing in the country would return to their homelands upon Hawai'i's union with the United States. The "Asian problem" was a major obstacle to annexation due to anti-Chinese sentiment in the United States. As a result of a sizeable influx of Chinese workers in the 1880s, the Hawaiian government had limited their entry, even halting their immigration for a while. Simultaneously, Japanese were admitted to maintain the plantations' access to inexpensive labor, which became especially urgent when the McKinley Tariff Act was repealed in 1894 and demand for Hawaiian sugar resumed. In 1897, twenty thousand Japanese had arrived; between 1896 and 1900, the Japanese population grew to more than sixty thousand.[32] In the 1898 US congressional debates over annexation, some legislators voiced their concern about the Asian presence in Hawai'i. For instance, House representative Champ Clark stated, "How can we endure our shame when a Chinese Senator from Hawaii, with his pigtail hanging down his back, with his pagan joss in his hand, shall rise from his curule chair and in pigeon English proceed to chop logic with George Frisbie Hoar or Henry Cabot Lodge?"[33]

Kilohana Art League paintings expressed proannexation sentiments held forcefully by its artists and patrons to reassure Hawai'i Americans that they belonged in the islands and were destined to rightfully lead them. Despite constituting the large majority of the population, Native Hawaiians were not significantly depicted. Views were typically unpopulated; occasionally an Indigenous person would be pictured, but figures tended to be elderly, passive, or rendered on a small scale. Hitchcock's *Hawaiian and His Home* (c. 1895),[34] for instance, features a single male figure, whose age is signaled by his white beard and slightly hunched posture. He is seated, his pose inactive, in front of his *hale* (house), which is presented as a solitary, isolated structure. There are no other buildings represented to indicate that he is part of a larger community, nor any sign of productive activity or useful occupation of the land. Native Hawaiians are depicted as people of the past.

Other themes in the league's output related to Indigenous disappearance include the single, remote *hale* and the beached canoe. Regarding the former, pictures typically showed an Indigenous domicile with little evidence of active habitation, and omitted Native bodies.[35] Pertaining to the latter, there is an odd and disquieting surfeit of paintings of unattended Native Hawaiian outrigger canoes lodged on unpopulated shores, particularly in Hitchcock's oeuvre, but also executed by other artists, such as Hugo Anton Fisher, who was active in Hawai'i from 1894–1896. Hitchcock's *Canoe and Hala Tree* (c. 1890s; figure 6.3) is representative of this genre, depicting a lone canoe on an empty shore with no homes or activity nearby. In both genres Indigenous cultural objects are mere ornaments in the transforming landscape, lacking evi-

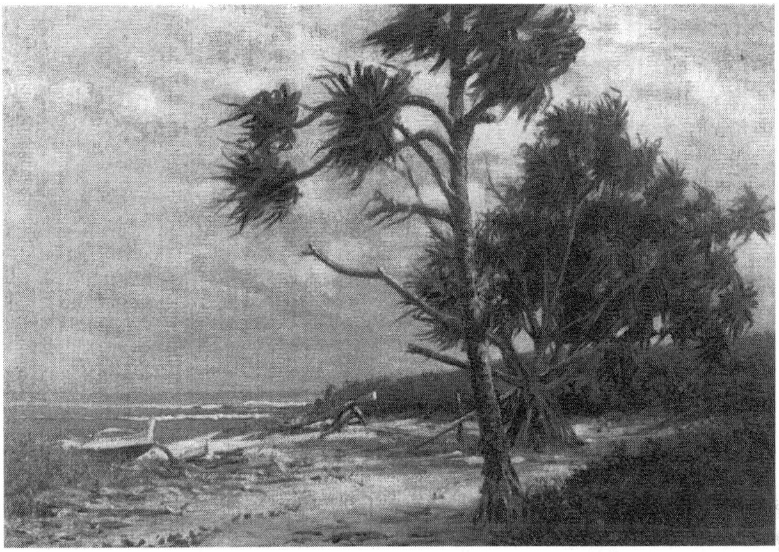

Figure 6.3. D. Howard Hitchcock, *Canoe and Hala Tree,* c. 1890s. Oil on canvas. Private collection. Courtesy of Wikimedia Commons.

dence of fruitful use or of the people who made and used them. Historian David W. Forbes notes that these pictures were very popular among Hawai'i American residents as well as visitors.[36]

It is not that Native Hawaiian and Asian figures were generally omitted in the art of Hawai'i; their near absence in the league exhibitions is in distinct contrast to pictures produced during the monarchy period (pre-1893). In mid-century, artists such as Enoch Wood Perry, Jr., freely included Indigenous subjects in their work. Perry's *Diamond Head from Waikiki* (c. 1865) shows Native Hawaiians occupied in activities such as gathering on the shore in conversation, courting, fishing, tending to a child, and guiding a canoe.[37] In *View of Hilo Bay* (1888; figure 6.4), Joseph Nāwahī, a Native Hawaiian painter, writer, and politician, depicted a lively land- and seascape populated with Indigenous people. On the near shore, young men fish, a couple converses over an outrigger canoe (not in disuse or abandoned, as in paintings produced by league artists), and another couple surveys the scene. White buildings speckle the shoreline, a variety of sea craft are present in the middle distance, and numerous people gather on Mokuola (Coconut Island) on the right side of the picture, suggesting an active and thriving community. English painter Robert C. Barnfield, who resided in Hawai'i from 1885 until his death in 1893, and who was a friend to king David Kalākaua, painted *Hawaiian Homes* (c. 1885), a watercolor showing a well-maintained and populated homestead.

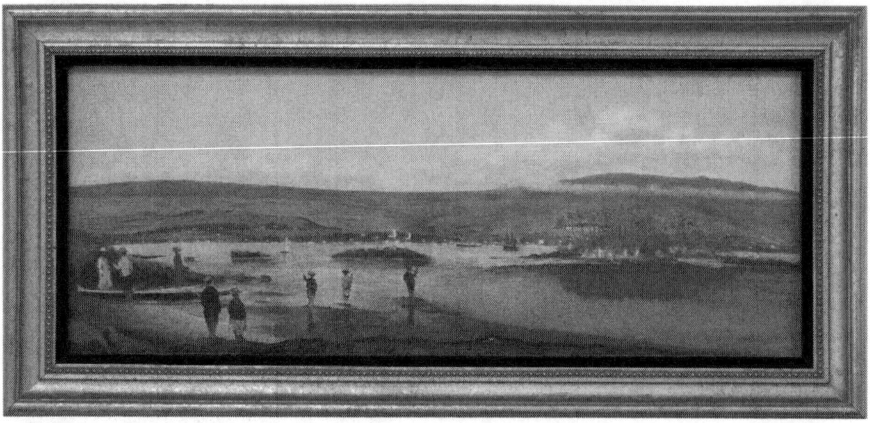

Figure 6.4. Joseph Nāwahī, *View of Hilo Bay,* 1888. Oil on canvas. Courtesy of Kamehameha Schools, Honolulu.

The title indicates a plurality of residences ("homes"), a community that is indicated by a neighboring *hale* on the opposite side of a stone wall separating the properties. Two inhabitants appear to be engaged in activities on the *lānai* (porch) of the house, and in the left foreground is a canoe, not abandoned but covered with palm leaves to protect it for future activity.[38] Kalākaua also used one of Barnfield's paintings of a Hawaiian sacred structure (*heiau*) on the cover of his book *The Legends and Myths of Hawaii* (1888). Though not populated, the illustration depicts Native Hawaiian religious structures and figures; these types of images are generally absent in league paintings, which did not depict Indigenous cultural practices. There appears to exist only one reference to an image of a *heiau* in the league's catalogues, produced by Annie H. Parke and titled *Old Heeiau* [*sic*], *Keokea* (1904). It is significant that the title, with the word "old," identifies the structure as a thing of the past.

Three years earlier, Kalākaua had commissioned Joseph Strong to paint a picture of Japanese laborers as a gift to the Japanese emperor in assurance that his subjects were thriving in Hawai'i. In the painting, titled *Japanese Laborers on Spreckelsville Plantation* (1885),[39] Strong situates a Japanese family in the near center of the canvas. A sturdy worker stands with hands on hips amid a field of cut sugar cane, perhaps inspecting the effects of his labor, and to his left, two women and a child enjoy a meal break in a moment of rest. The presence of a family unit suggests that the Japanese workers were doing well, receiving fair treatment, and enjoying health and productivity, which is pictorially emphasized by their strong, substanial bodies and the visual stability of the broad columnar male figure and the solid triangular forms of the women. In the background, industrious workers continue to harvest the field as a team of oxen haul away wagonloads of cane. Native Hawaiians are central subjects in other paintings by Strong, such as *Hawaiian Canoe, Waikiki* (1884).[40] Unlike the unattended canoes that serve as melancholy ornaments to many beachscapes, Strong's painting focuses on the vessel, which fills the frame of the picture and is echoed by a second canoe in the near distance. Perched on the sides of the canoe are two substantial figures, a young Native Hawaiian boy attired in a barkcloth *malo* (loincloth) who is partaking of a snack, perhaps something yielded from his catch, and a girl dressed in a *holokū* (missionary-inspired dress), adorned with a flower or feather head lei and resting on a finely woven mat. Their youth signals continuing generations of the Indigenous population, and their dress and active proximity to the canoes indicate Native adaptation and survival. Strong's stout and detailed nonwhite bodies contrast with those in paintings such as Kelley's *Rice Paddies* (above), which includes tiny figures dwarfed by the landscape, or hazily rendered forms characteristic of other league works.

The occasional depiction of Native Hawaiians and Asians as primary subjects by league artists tended to be confined to photography and sculpture that depicted nonwhites as racial and ethnic "types." In 1907, the sculptor J. Rosenstein exhibited *Native Girl—Bas Relief (Study from Life)* and a figure in the round of a Chinese child, *Little Ah Sid—A Study from Life*. The latter recalls phrenological casts intended to document racial difference. Earlier, in an 1894 exhibition, founding league member Allen Hutchinson had displayed six plaster casts of Hawaiian figures with titles such as *Hawaiian Type, Old Woman; Hawaiian Type, Boy;* and *Hawaiian Type, Girl*. Like Rosenstein's *Native Girl*, Hutchinson's bas-reliefs (seen in figure 6.5) feature two young Native Hawaiians in full profile reminiscent of nineteenth-century anthropometric photography.[41] While the local media praised the aesthetic qualities of portraits, views, china painting, and other works produced by league artists, images of nonwhites were complimented for their fidelity to nature and worthy contributions to scientific study. Representations of Native Hawaiians and Asians were scarce in the league exhibitions of the 1890s, and it appears that its artists became comfortable depicting nonwhite figures only after Hawaiʻi became a US territory in 1898 and some of their unease about their political future had been ameliorated.

During the postmonarchy period, it should be noted that Native Hawaiians and Asians did not completely cease to be represented; they were simply largely invisible in the art works destined for league patronage. Some artists produced pictures of Indigenous people or nonwhite residents that either were not offered for consideration for league exhibition, or evidently did not pass the jury selection process. Bessie Wheeler, for instance, who exhibited flower paintings for the Kilohana Art League, did not show paintings such as *Flower*

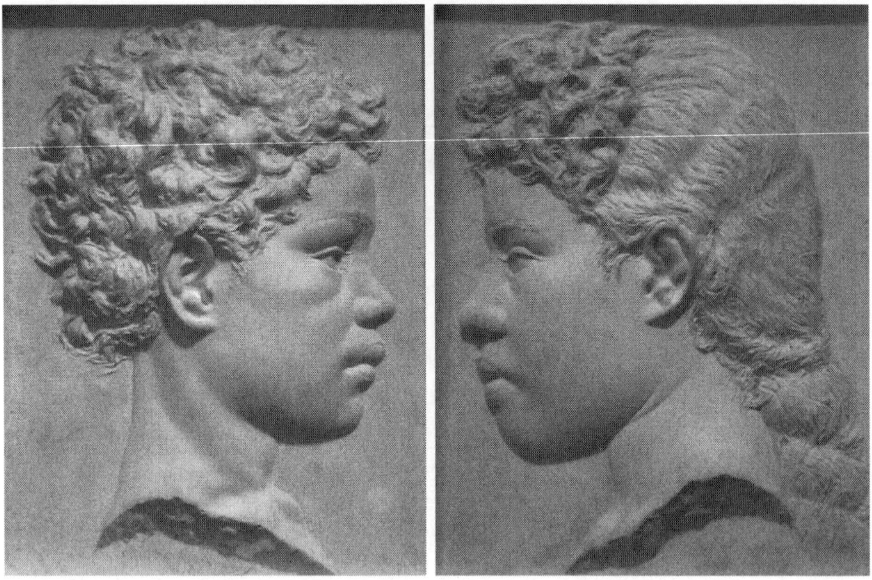

Figure 6.5. Allen Hutchinson, *Hawaiian Types,* 1891. Plaster casts. Bernice Pauahi Bishop Museum. Courtesy of Wikimedia Commons.

Lei Seller (c. 1900), a full portrait of an Indigenous vendor, or her illustrations of Honolulu street characters, which instead were featured in publications directed at tourists.[42] Matteo Sandonà, an Italian-born artist who immigrated to the United States as a child, made several trips to Hawai'i in the early 1900s.[43] Although he displayed some of his white society portraits (e.g., *Sanford Ballard Dole,* 1905) and landscapes with the league, his chalk drawings and portraits of Native Hawaiians, such as of princess Abigail Kawānanakoa (1903) and colonel Samuel Parker (1903) were not included in the league's biannual exhibitions. Similarly, California painter Theodore Wores, another league affiliate who established a studio in Honolulu for eighteen months (making trips to Sāmoa as well), displayed his portraits of the white elite in the rooms of the art league but exhibited twenty-two Hawaiian and fourteen Sāmoan pictures at the Pacific Hardware Company in Honolulu in April 1902. These included his now famous oil paintings *The Lei Maker* (1901) and *A Lagoon in Safuni, Savaii, Samoa* (1902).

Another California-based artist, Grace Carpenter Hudson (1865–1937), known for her studies of Native American children, visited Honolulu and Hilo in 1901 for eleven months and painted Native Hawaiian, Japanese, and Chinese subjects. She produced nearly thirty portraits in addition to several landscapes of the island of O'ahu. Despite the fact that Hudson received press attention for attending events related to the league's spring 1901 exhibition, she expressed irritation that Hitchcock and Wores largely monopolized the show and she was able to enter only a small landscape sketch.[44] Instead, she displayed her portraits of nonwhite subjects in the windows of the Pacific Hardware Company. Her studies, however, were appreciated in San Francisco, where they were exhibited upon her return. A reviewer for the *San Francisco Chronicle* wrote, "Grace Hudson is the first American artist of note to bring something worthwhile from the Hawaiian Islands."[45] Visiting artist Henry Nappenbach (1862–1931) produced several watercolor sketches of Chinatown during his one-month stay in Honolulu in 1898. One example, titled *Maunakea Street, Honolulu,* shows Chinese and Japanese figures moving about in a prosperous, attractive, and bustling section of Chinatown. Urban scenes, particularly of ethnic neighborhoods in Hawai'i, were rarely, if ever, hung on the league walls, especially prior to 1900, when the Hawaiian Organic Act was enacted and Hawai'i was secured as a US territory. Images like these would not become more common in the mainstream Hawaiian art scene until well after annexation.

Just as the league's preferred subjects were conditioned by the contemporary political climate, so too were the social and political attachments of its artists. As noted above, the people who participated in the league's activities, as artists and patrons, represented the white social and economic elite, with few exceptions. Several Native Hawaiian artists are conspicuously absent in the league's exhibitions. Joseph Nāwahī, an anti-annexationist activist, did not join the league. Neither did princess Victoria Ka'iulani, heir to the throne, who was studying art in England at the time of the overthrow and who later traveled to Washington to work to restore the monarchy, resuming residence in Hawai'i in 1897. Nāwahī produced volcano scenes and landscapes, while Ka'iulani painted floral subjects and landscapes. Described as "an enthusiastic flower painter," Lillie Hart Gay Torrey (1871–1956), of Native Hawaiian and British descent, produced large canvases that were popular among island residents.[46] Yet none of her works appear in the league exhibition catalogues.[47]

Non-Native artists who had connections to Hawaiian chiefs and royalty were likewise excluded, probably by choice. Hubert Vos (1855–1935), born in Holland and known for his portraits of European high society members, arrived in Hawai'i in 1897 with his wife, Eleanor (Kaikilani) Coney Graham Vos,[48] a ranking chiefess and companion to Queen Lili'uokalani. Vos painted compelling portraits of a range of Native Hawaiian society, as well as endemic plant and fish studies (e.g., *Study of Hawaiian Fish* (1898); *Ekekela: Hawaiian Flower Girl* (1899); *Kolomona: Hawaiian Troubadour* (1898); and his portraits of his wife, Kaikilani). Vos' international reputation as an artist, role as art commissioner at the Chicago World's Fair, and participation in exhibitions at San Francisco's Bohemian Club, the Union League Club in New York, the Corcoran Gallery of Art in Washington, DC, and Paris International Exposition of 1900 would certainly have been of interest to the league, which courted visiting artists and prided itself on hosting outside talent. Yet he does not appear to have been interested in associating with the league. These are a few of many others who elected to practice art outside of the league's purview.

In addition to enacting the social and political aspirations of the white oligarchy through the production and exhibition of visual art, league members and patrons involved themselves in other Americanizing cultural pursuits, especially after annexation was achieved. In 1907, the league participated in an annual Floral Parade celebrating George Washington's birthday. The float entered by the league promoted its plans to erect a larger and more permanent "temple of art" in Honolulu (figure 6.6). Described as "among the most elaborate of the wagon floats,"[49] the tableau consisted of a classical-style temple adorned with laurels and palm fronds and occupied by women of the league attired in Greek gowns and holding various symbols representing art, music, and theatre. As visualized in the float presentation, the neoclassical conception of how "Hawaiian art" was defined corresponds to the history of Hawai'i's art described in Dodge's 1897 article, which eulogized the Indigenous "art of the past" and praised truly modern art in the islands, having roots in the Western classical tradition now nurtured through the Kilohana Art League. The cultural and artistic accomplishments of the league (as well as the republic and the territory) supplanted those of Native Hawaiian institutions of the monarchy era. Indigenous patronage of innovative architectural projects, public monuments, museums, and performances were invisible in the league's art history of Hawai'i. The league also occasionally hosted Mardi Gras benefit balls and May Day celebrations in which additional transformations of national culture were enacted. At these events, a king, queen, and royal court (figure 6.7) plainly signaled the replacement of Indigenous rulers of the kingdom with the new regime.

I turn to one last example of the league's ambitions to develop an American art center in the Pacific. Late in 1907 and into 1908, league organizers vigorously rallied in the local press to obtain a large abandoned building along the Honolulu waterfront to pursue their goal of "being an effective university for the propagation of the fine arts, and the promotion of ideals of civic improvement."[50] They desired to call this the Crystal Palace and attach to it a monumental arch honoring president William McKinley, who had supported incorporating Hawai'i as an American territory and under whose

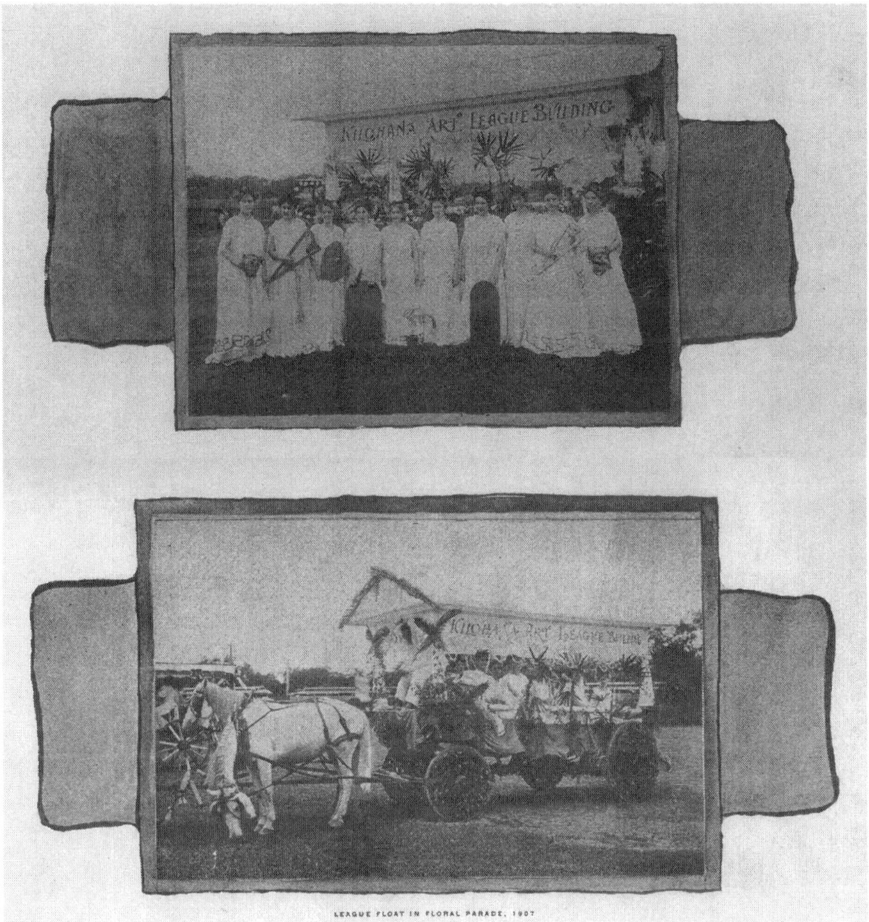

Figure 6.6. Kilohana Art League float in the Floral Parade, Honolulu, February 22, 1907. From *Mardi Tamerys Medrano Gras Grand Bal Masque Given by and for the Benefit of the Kilohana Art League,* 10–11. Courtesy of the Hawaiian Historical Society, Honolulu.

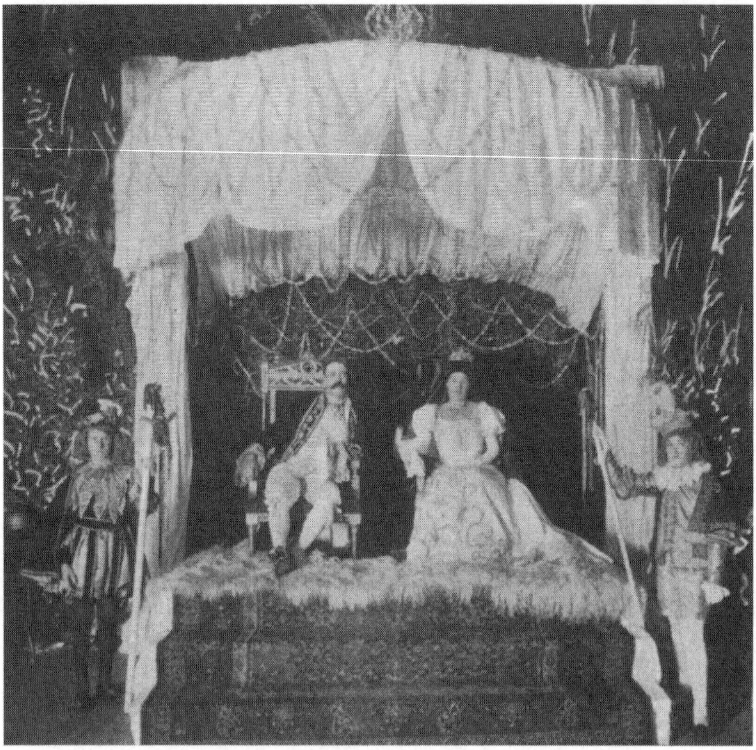

Figure 6.7. "King and Queen of Mardi Gras, 1907," Honolulu, February 12, 1907. From *Mardi Gras Grand Bal Masque,* 13. Courtesy of the Hawaiian Historical Society, Honolulu.

administration annexation was achieved. This memorial arch was to face the ocean, serving as an imposing gateway to Honolulu and marking Hawai'i as the "diamond of the Pacific."[51] In the end, members of the McKinley Memorial Committee rejected this proposal due to the high cost of the project and instead chose to erect Gordon Usborne's bronze life-size statue of the US president (figure 6.8) on the grounds of Honolulu High School, which it authorized to be renamed McKinley High School. The sculpture was elevated on a tall granite pedestal, contributing to its monumental presence. In his right hand, McKinley holds several sheets of a document, the slightly unfurled portion of which reveals the words "Treaty of Annexation." A local newspaper made special note that Usborne was a local (Honolulu) sculptor, the granite base came from Maine, and the bronze had been fabricated in New York, suggesting the successful cultural and material fusion of Hawai'i and the United States. The unveiling ceremony was held on February 23, 1911, with

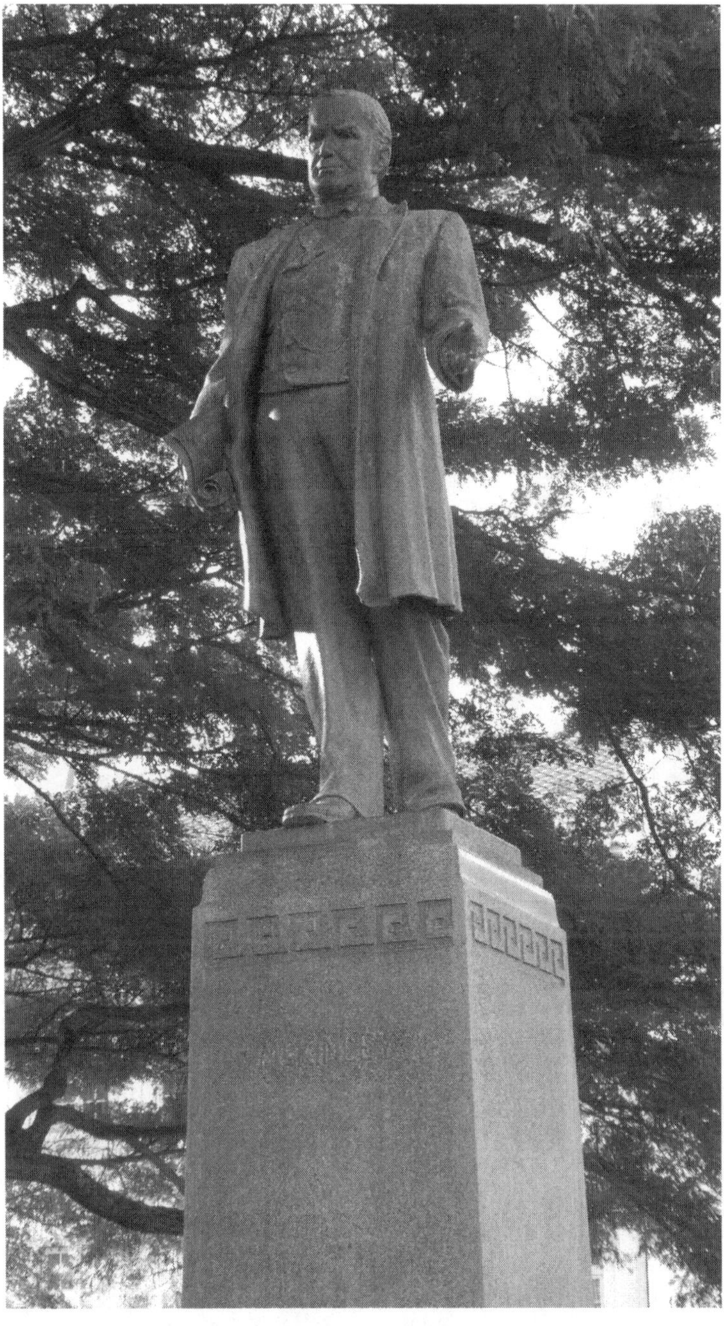

Figure 6.8. Gordon Usborne, William McKinley Memorial Monument, c. 1911. Bronze and granite. McKinley High School, Honolulu. Photograph by Maggie Wander, 2020. Courtesy of the photographer.

Sanford B. Dole delivering an address immediately prior to the revelation of the figure, which had been wrapped in US and Hawaiian flags. Perhaps to mask ongoing tensions between supporters of Hawaiian sovereignty and those celebrating the islands' territorial status, Dole's speech emphasized broad support for the monument: "There was prompt response to the suggestion that we erect a monument to McKinley's memory. Contributions came in from all parts of the Territory, from all classes, from all ages, and substantially from all races represented here. And these contributions were largely in small amounts showing how generally the heart of Hawaii was stirred."[52] Events such as Floral Parades, May Day festivals, Mardi Gras balls, and other "patriotic entertainments" (as the league called them), as well as undertakings such as the McKinley Memorial project, effectively erased and replaced the performances, processions, and monuments that, under the monarchy, publicly celebrated the births, deeds, and authority of Native Hawaiian kings and queens and their own modern aspirations.

The activities of the Kilohana Art League assisted the political transformation of the Hawaiian Islands at the turn of the century. In envisioning Hawai'i as an American community during the struggle to win annexation between 1894 and 1898, celebrating and cultivating its status as an American territory, and challenged by the ongoing protests of Native Hawaiians and the increasingly heterogeneous labor population into the early twentieth century, the white elite supported and eagerly participated in the league's exhibitions and programs. Artists and their audiences cultivated an aesthetics of annexation that manifested the ambivalence of settler colonialism in Hawai'i. Artworks expressed these desires to unite with the United States and spearhead American civilization in the Pacific as the logical outcome of American achievements in the Hawaiian Islands. At the same time, however, the league's creative output betrayed anxiety about whether Hawai'i Americans' bid to become a US territory would be successful, and if so, what changes to island life it would bring, especially as the artists and patrons embraced their difference from mainland Americans. Although the visual arts component of the league disbanded in 1913, its cultural vision, conditioned by ethnic politics and debates regarding what it meant to be "Hawaiian," continued on in new forms, such as the Cooke Art Gallery created in 1912, the Hawaiian Society of Artists founded in 1917, the Honolulu Art Society established in 1919, and the Honolulu Academy of Arts, which was inaugurated by the well-known art philanthropist and missionary descendant Anna Rice Cooke in 1922. The Kilohana Art League represents an annexation-era effort to recast Hawaiian national identity into a Hawai'i American one.

Notes

I am very grateful to the late Bob Schleck, and to Barbara Dunn, Lynne Elia, Maggie Wander, Marion Cadora, Jen Hernandez, and Viola Or for their assistance with archival and collections research. Research funding was provided by the Arts Research Institute, Clare Wedding Research Fellowship, and Committee on Research at the University of California, Santa Cruz.

1. "The Kilohana Art League, Its By-Laws and List of Its Members," Kilohana Art League Scrapbook (hereafter KAL Scrapbook), Hawaiian Historical Society.

2. Nicholas Thomas, *Colonialism's Culture: Anthropology, Travel, and Government* (Princeton, NJ: Princeton University Press, 1994), 2.

3. Lorrin A. Thurston, *Hand-Book on the Annexation of Hawaii* (St. Joseph, MI: A. B. Morse, 1897), 1.

4. Felicity Barnes, review of *Studies in Settler Colonialism,* ed. Fiona Bateman and Lionel Pilkington (Basingstoke, UK: Palgrave Macmillan, 2011), in *Settler Colonial Studies* 3, no. 1 (2013): 128, 130; cf. Aimee Carrillo Rowe and Eve Tuck, "Settler Colonialism, and Cultural Studies," *Cultural Studies* 17, no. 1 (2017): 6; and Audra Simpson, *Mohawk Interruptus: Political Life across the Borders of Settler States* (Durham, NC: Duke University Press, 2014), 19. See also Patrick Wolfe, *Settler Colonialism and the Transformation of Anthropology: The Politics and Poetics of an Ethnographic Event* (New York: Cassell, 1999), and "Settler Colonialism, and the Elimination of the Native," *Journal of Genocide Research* 8, no. 4 (2006): 387–409.

5. For a detailed description of the Committee of Safety members, see Ralph Thomas Kam and Jeffrey K. Lyons, "Remembering the Committee of Safety: Identifying the Citizenship, Descent, and Occupations of the Men Who Overthrew the Monarchy," *Hawaiian Journal of History* 55 (2019): 31–54. On the 1887 constitution, see Ralph S. Kuykendall, *The Hawaiian Kingdom,* vol. 3, *1874–1893: The Kalakaua Dynasty* (Honolulu: University of Hawai'i Press, 1967), 368–372. The main authors of this constitution were L. A. Thurston Jonathan Austin, S. B. Dole, W. A. Kinney, W. O. Smith, Cecil Brown, Rev. W. B. Oleson, N. B. Emerson, J. A. Kennedy, John A. McCandless, George N. Wilcox, A. S. Wilcox, H. Waterhouse, F. Wundenberg, E. G. Hitchcock, W. E. Rowell, Dr. S. G. Tucker, and C. W. Ashford (Kuykendall, *Hawaiian Kingdom,* 367). On the Hawaiian League, see Kuykendall, *Hawaiian Kingdom,* 347–348.

6. On the overthrow of the monarchy and the establishment of the provisional government and Republic of Hawaii, see Gavan Daws, *Shoal of Time: A History of the Hawaiian Islands* (Honolulu: University of Hawai'i Press, 1968), 265–281; and Kuykendall, *Hawaiian Kingdom,* 523–650.

7. KAL Scrapbook.

8. C. T. Rodgers, "Kilohana Art League," *Hawaiian Almanac and Annual for 1896*, ed. Thomas G. Thrum (Honolulu: T. G. Thrum, 1896), 138.

9. I use the term "Hawai'i American" to refer to people of European American descent who were born in Hawai'i or to American transplants who considered the Republic of Hawaii their home.

10. D. Howard Hitchcock, "Report of the President of the Kilohana Art League with a List of Members, November, 1897," KAL Scrapbook, 35.

11. Philip Henry Dodge, "Modern Art in Hawaii: Kilohana Art League," *Paradise of the Pacific* 10, no. 10 (1897): 149. The connection of Hawai'i's cultural modernity with white, rather than Indigenous, artistic activity is echoed in Forbes' 1992 art history of Hawai'i, par-

ticularly in his chapter titled "The Emergence of Hawaiian Modernism, 1890–1941," which, with rare exceptions, chronicles the work of white painters in the islands. His two exceptions are artists Isami Doi and Keichi Kimura, represented by works dated c. 1939. See David W. Forbes, *Encounters with Paradise: View of Hawaii and Its People, 1778-1941* (Honolulu: Honolulu Academy of Arts, 1992), 201–270.

12. In combing through Kilohana Art League exhibition catalogs, I found only three artists' surnames of non–European American derivation: Bessie Afong, Lau Sheong, and L. Teng Cheong. Afong, who briefly contributed to league exhibitions in 1896 and 1897, served as one of First Lady Dole's assistants at President Dole's reception for the first anniversary celebration of the provisional government that was set up after the overthrow of the monarchy. Because the Hawai'i press noted that supporters of the monarchy were conspicuously absent at the event, it can be assumed that Afong supported the new regime. In fact, she signed the guest registry to record her presence at the event; see United States Congress, "Executive Document No. 46," in *The Executive Documents of the Senate of the United States for the Second Session of the Fifty-Third Congress, 1893–1894* (Washington, DC: Government Printing Office, 1895), 4–5, 13. Lau Sheong and L. Teng Cheong participated in league exhibitions in 1899–1908 and 1902–1903, respectively, only after the United States annexed Hawai'i. Of course, European American surnames could be attached to Native Hawaiian or Asian people through marriage or descent, which additional research might reveal.

13. For instance, Mrs. Ogilvie, a contributor of watercolor paintings to the May 1895 exhibition, contributed primarily views of California scenery. KAL Scrapbook, 11.

14. "A History of the Kilohana Art League," manuscript, KAL Scrapbook, 20. See also "The Art Reception: Kilohana League Rooms Open to W. H. Hilliard," *Hawaiian Gazette*, February 25, 1896, 5.

15. "The Autumn Exhibition: Works on View in Various Lines of Art. Decorated China by Several Ladies—Some of Mr. Hitchcock's Paintings—New Contributors," newspaper clipping in unidentified periodical source, November 17, 1896, KAL Scrapbook, 24.

16. George He'eu Sanford Kanahele, *Pauahi: The Kamehameha Legacy* (Honolulu: Kamehameha Schools, 1986), 75–77; Harold Winfield Kent, *Charles Reed Bishop, Man of Hawaii* (Palo Alto, CA: Pacific Books, 1965), 34–35.

17. W. J. T. Mitchell, "Imperial Landscape," in *The Cultural Geography Reader*, ed. Timothy S. Oakes and Patricia L. Price (New York: Routledge, 2006), 170; see also 165–169.

18. Cf. Elizabeth Johns, "American Landscape: Manifest What?," *Journal of Interdisciplinary History* 23, no. 4 (1993): 753. See Johns' critique of Albert Boime's (1991) narrow analysis of American landscape painting produced c. 1830–1865 in terms of social historical documents of manifest destiny.

19. Miriam Aronowicz, "Terra Nulla: Contesting the South African Colonial Landscape," *University of Toronto Art Journal* 2 (2009): 5.

20. Proannexationist writers include the American missionary descendants Lorrin A. Thurston, Sereno Bishop, and William N. Armstrong.

21. Joy Schulz, *Hawaiian by Birth: Missionary Children, Bicultural Identity, and U.S. Colonialism in the Pacific* (Lincoln: University of Nebraska Press, 2017), 7–14, 125–137.

22. The current location or existence of the great majority of the paintings exhibited by the league is unknown; my observation is based on works available in collections with public access, reproductions, and lists of titles gleaned from the semiannual exhibition catalogs.

23. For a brief biography and description of Kelley's work, see Forbes, *Encounters with Paradise*, 205, 216–218. *Rice Paddies* is published in Don Severson, Michael D. Horikawa,

and Jennifer Saville, *Finding Paradise: Island Art in Private Collections* (Honolulu: Honolulu Academy of Arts, 2002), xxviii.

24. Lorenzo Veracini, "Introducing *settler colonial studies*," *settler colonial studies* 1, no. 1 (2011): 2–3.

25. Cf. Annie E. Coombes, "Memory and History in Settler Colonialism," in *Rethinking Settler Colonialism: History and Memory in Australia, Canada, Aotearoa New Zealand, and South Africa*, ed. Annie E. Coombes (New York: Manchester University Press, 2006), 3.

26. This illustrated poem was published in a souvenir booklet; Kilohana Art League, *Mardi Gras Grand Bal Masque Given by and for the Benefit of the Kilohana Art League at the Crystal Palace* (Honolulu: Hawaiian Gazette, 1908), 7.

27. Hawaiian Society of the Sons of the American Revolution et al., *An Address by the Hawaiian Branches of the Sons of the American Revolution, Sons of Veterans, and Grand Army of the Republic to Their Compatriots in Ameria Concerning the Annexaton of Hawaii* (Washington, DC: Gibson Bros., 1897), 5–6.

28. Lorrin A. Thurston cited in Eric T. Love, *Race over Empire: Racism and U.S. Imperialism, 1865–1900* (Chapel Hill: University of North Carolina Press, 2004), 138–139. See also Wolfe, "Settler Colonialism," 397ff, on assimilation as a settler colonial strategy to eliminate Indigenous peoples.

29. Love, *Race over Empire*, 138–140.

30. "The Hawaiian Resolution," *New York Times*, March 22, 1898; "The Bacon Amendment," *Los Angeles Herald*, January 22, 1898, 4; *Omaha (NE) World-Herald*, March 1, 1898, 4.

31. For example, *Aloha Aina* (Honolulu), September 18, 1897, 5; October 9, 1897, 7; December 11, 1897, 2; *Independent* (Honolulu), July 31, 1897, 2; January 6, 1898, 4; February 5, 1898, 1; February 23, 1898, 1; *Loea Kalaiaina* (Honolulu), March 14, 1898, 3; March 21, 1898, 3.

32. Daws, *Shoal of Time*, 285, 304.

33. *Congressional Record*, 55th Congress, 2nd Session, 5788–5795, in Daws, *Shoal of Time*, 290.

34. This painting is published in Severson, Horikawa, and Saville, *Finding Paradise*, 102.

35. Other examples of this genre include D. Howard Hitchcock's *Kona Coast, Hawaii* (1897) and *Ala Moana Beach, Oahu* (1899); Helen Whitney Kelley's *Beach Grass Shack* (c. 1880), *Windward Grass Shack* (c. 1880), and *Hawaiian Landscape with House* (n.d.); and Selma Kinney's *Old Post Office at Hauula, Oahu* (1904), all of which omit Native Hawaiian figures. It should be noted, however, that Kelley did produce at least one watercolor (*Hawaiian Fishing Village*, c. 1880) that includes multiple structures and an inhabitant.

36. David W. Forbes, *He Makana: The Gertrude Mary Joan Damon Haig Collection of Hawaiian Art, Paintings, and Prints* (Honolulu: State Foundation on Culture and the Arts, Hawai'i State Art Museum, 2013), 26. See, for instance, Hugo Anton Fisher's *Beach of Waikiki* (1896) in ibid., plate 17. Other examples of canoe paintings include D. Howard Hitchcock's *Mauna Kea from Hilo Bay* (1887); *The Beach at Waikiki* (1896); *Beached Canoe, Squall Beyond* (1896); *Beached Canoe* (1897); and *Diamond Head Nocturne* (n.d.).

37. This painting can be viewed in Wikimedia Commons, https://commons.wikimedia.org.

38. This painting is published in Severson, Horikawa, and Saville, *Finding Paradise*, 84. See also Robert Barnfield's *Captain Cook's Monument* (c. 1887), which shows Indigenous figures in the landscape and others conducting a canoe in the waters nearby, as well as a large village in the distance.

39. This painting is published in Forbes, *Encounters with Paradise*, plate 109. Joseph

Strong, son-in-law of Robert Louis Stevenson, arrived in Honolulu in 1882 and enjoyed considerable royal patronage. He was appointed as the official artist for Hawai'i's expedition to Sāmoa in 1887. In 1890, Strong relocated to Sāmoa with Stevenson, later returning to San Francisco in 1895 (Forbes, *Encounters with Paradise,* 188–189).

40. This painting is published in Severson, Horikawa, and Saville, *Finding Paradise,* 97. Strong's *Hawaiians at Rest, Waikiki* (c. 1884) similarly depicts three Native Hawaiians on a shore with a nondeserted outrigger canoe.

41. Photographs of Rosenstein's works are included in the KAL Scrapbook, 14, 97. On phrenological sculptures and anthropometric imaging, see Kriselle Baker and Elizabeth Rankin, *Fiona Pardington: The Pressure of Sunlight Falling* (Dunedin, New Zealand: Otago University Press, 2011); Melissa Banta and Curtis M. Hinsley, *From Site to Site: Anthropology, Photography, and the Power of Imagery* (Cambridge, MA: Peabody Museum Press, 1986); and Christopher Pinney, "The Parallel Histories of Anthropology and Photography," in *Anthropology and Photography, 1860–1920,* ed. Elizabeth Edwards, 74–95 (New Haven, CT: Yale University Press in association with The Royal Anthropological Institute, 1992).

42. Cf. Severson, Horiwaka, and Saville, *Finding Paradise,* 105.

43. Duccio Kaumualii Marignoli and Marzia Ratti, *Matteo Sandonà and Hawai'i: A Capital Ambition* (Honolulu: Honolulu Academy of Arts, 2007).

44. Karen Holmes and Sherrie Smith-Ferri, *Days of Grace: California Artist Grace Hudson in Hawaii* (Ukiah, CA: Grace Hudson Museum, 2014), 44–45. This volume contains excellent reproductions of Hudson's Hawai'i works.

45. *San Francisco Chronicle,* November 1901, in Forbes, *Encounters with Paradise,* 227.

46. Forbes, *Encounters with Paradise,* 204.

47. This, despite the fact that her husband, noted portrait painter George Burroughs Torrey (1863–1942), also known as "the painter of presidents," would likely have been courted by the league's officers.

48. See Riánna M. Williams, "Hawaiian *Ali'i* Women in New York Society: The Ena-Coney-Vos-Gould Connection," *Hawaiian Journal of History* 38 (2004): 147–164.

49. "Floral Parade a Brilliant and Successful Affair," *Hawaiian Gazette,* February 25, 1908, 3.

50. KAL Scrapbook.

51. KAL Scrapbook, 6, 11.

52. "Statue Stands as a Monument," *Evening Bulletin,* February 24, 1911, 7. See also "High School Gets the Fund: McKinley Memorial Money Will Erect Statue and Endow a Library," *Pacific Commercial Advertiser,* March 3, 1908, 1; Thos. G. Thrum, "Retrospect for 1911," in *Hawaiian Almanac and Annual for 1912,* ed. Thos. G. Thrum (Honolulu: Thos. G. Thrum), 153.

SEVEN

The 1905 *Report on Proposed Improvements at Manila* by Daniel Burnham

The American Imperium in Textual and Urban Design Form

Ian Morley

Early American colonial governance in the Philippines centered on a number of fundamentals: pacifying the local population; enlarging the national economy; developing road, rail, and bridge infrastructure; promoting public education; elevating standards of public health; and redesigning large-size cities. Critical to the process of restructuring the built fabric was Daniel Burnham, who, after visiting the Philippines from December 1904 to January 1905, imported the City Beautiful planning paradigm by composing in early 1905 grand plans for Manila and Baguio, that is, the national and summer capital cities. Helping remove the built vestiges of Spanish colonialism, the application of the City Beautiful model reshaped the form *and* meaning of Philippine urban settlements. As a result, Philippine cities, for the first time, were perceived to be "modern." However, notwithstanding the fact that Burnham and Anderson's urban planning exercises had been discussed by numerous scholars, no study of their 1905 *Report on Proposed Improvements at Manila* as an imperial city planning text exists. Consequently, this work seeks to engage with cultural theory so as to analyze the document as a proclamation of the American imperium in Southeast Asia. In so doing the study seeks not only to outline the environmental features that Burnham believed would transform Manila into a city rivaling the greatest of the Western world, but also, by taking up the ideas of intellectuals such as Theodor Adorno, to show how Burnham's report, whether purposefully or not, spoke of cultural evolution. After all, to speak of cultural change is to think of societal administration, and cultural evolution is a central element in both city planning and American imperial historiography.

Background

When examining the history of colonial urban design in the Philippines, two texts stand out. The first text, dating from 1573, was issued by King Philip II of Spain. Titled *Leyes de Indias* (Laws of the Indies), it has been described as "probably the most effective planning document in the history of mankind."[1] Comprised of 148 ordinances, the *Laws of the Indies* established uniform built environments throughout the entire geographical spread of the Spanish Empire. Central to the decree's execution was the founding of new settlements, which were organized spatially in grids. At the nucleus of these environmental configurations was an open area known as the *plaza mayor* (major plaza). This space was oriented toward the four directions marked on a compass and was lined by government offices, a church, and the homes of the colonial elites. The *Laws of the Indies* permitted colonial governmental authority, religious ideology, and Spanish culture to be expressed in chorus.[2] It fundamentally affected life in the Philippines: first, the Spaniards moved the native people (*indios*) off rural land into new settlements through the use of *reducción* (forced resettlement); second, rural land was confiscated from the *indios* and redistributed to the Spanish colonists; third, new colonial settlements were designed in accord with a *traza* (plan), and new building types constructed; and, lastly, a hierarchical social settlement system was instigated so that those of the highest social standing within colonial society had the right to reside around the centrally located *plaza mayor.*

The second text that profoundly affected the development of the Philippine built environment was *The Report on Improvement at Manila.* Published by the US Bureau of Insular Affairs in June 1905, and despite being just nine pages in length, it introduced to Philippine society notions of urban planning associated with the American City Beautiful model.[3] Composed by the United States' leading city planning practitioner at the time, Daniel Burnham (1846–1912), albeit with assistance from Peirce Anderson (1870–1924), the report helped forge a new type of urban layout in the Philippines and, in doing so, it undermined the *plaza mayor* as the physical and symbolic heart of civic society. The impact of Burnham and Anderson's report was tremendous. Among other things, it guided American and Filipino architect-planners working within the Bureau of Public Works until the 1930s.[4] With its architectural and spatial recommendations to instigate the environmental and cultural transformation of the Philippine capital city,[5] the 1905 report laid bare what Manila as a "modern planned city" should be. Yet, despite the seemingly countless descriptions of Burnham and Anderson's manuscript tendered by historians, architects, and planners alike, what did their report really say? And why did it say what it did? Notwithstanding the fact that *The Report on*

Improvement at Manila occupies a central position within the urban historiography of the Philippines, crucially, there has been no detailed textual analysis of it to date. Therefore, to comprehend the document in a new way, textual devices (such as Voyant Tools) and theoretical frameworks have been exploited within the milieu of this work. As a result, a new lens has been fashioned to read and value Burnham and Anderson's text.

Reading *The Report on Improvement at Manila*: Core Themes

The Report on Improvement at Manila, about seven thousand words in length, and comprised of seven main sections, divulges how the Philippine capital could be renewed by the application of a City Beautiful plan that is explained in 1,660 or so different word forms. The words most frequently used to describe the design, planning, and environment are, shown by figure 7.1, "city" (used fifty-two times), "Manila" (thirty-nine), "street" (twenty-five), "buildings" (twenty-three), "center" (twenty-two), "new" (twenty-one), "river" (twenty-one), "water" (twenty-one), "building" (twenty), and "parks" (nineteen). It is also notable that word trends are perceptible where particular words

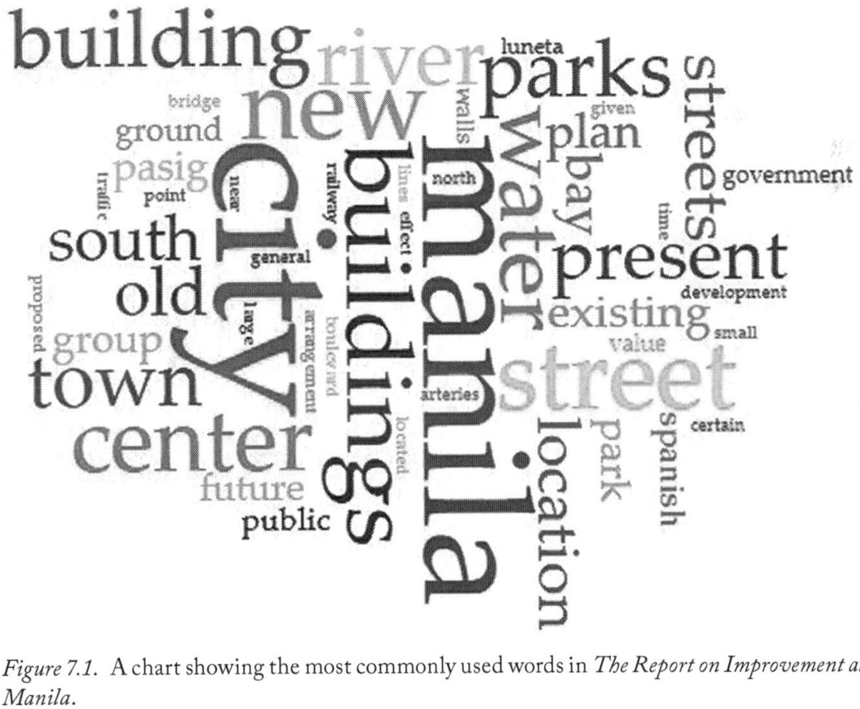

Figure 7.1. A chart showing the most commonly used words in *The Report on Improvement at Manila*.

are situated within the report: some words are used within particular sections of the document while others are consistently mentioned throughout. For example, of the five most popular word forms used, "street" features very little in the opening and closing sections, whereas, in contrast, "city" appears regularly throughout the document. Moreover, links between particular words are also recognizable.

With respect to the topic of lexical alliances within the text, when examining frequently used words such as "park," it is also possible to see the recurrent use of words such as "location," "parkways," and "boulevards." Likewise, when the word "building" was employed in the report, it was typically used in conjunction with words such as "beautiful," "sites," and "group." Hence, in order to comprehensively decipher the meaning of Burnham and Anderson's document, one must be mindful of their urban design recommendations and be aware of how vocabulary in their report was employed. Yet, before embarking on an examination of specific words and their placement, it is imperative to break down the structural form, thematic content, and historical context of *The Report on Improvement at Manila*. Without doing this, any subsequent textual analysis will simply come across as arbitrary and detached from the process of American colonization in the Philippines.

The opening section of *The Report on Improvement at Manila* clarifies the manuscript's purpose, describing in less than 550 words Manila's history since its founding as a colonial capital in 1571, the nature of the local topography, and the building methods used during the Spanish colonial era (1565–1898), as well as political conditions and the demography circa 1905. As the basic manual for the redevelopment of Manila under American colonial authority,[6] the report advocates a handful of environmental reforms (figure 7.2). These include developing the city's waterfront along Manila Bay, laying out new parks and parkways, establishing a new street system, creating suburban resorts, and using the Pasig River and *esteros* (estuarine waterways) for transportation; in addition, Burnham and Anderson proffer advice as to where new building types should be sited.[7] The bulk of their report, roughly speaking 5,500 words, discusses these environmental proposals and how they can be brought into being.

When studying Burnham and Anderson's report, it is easy to lapse into mere description of what Manila was to environmentally transform into after 1905.[8] In other words, it is possible to simply view the document as a handful of parts, each section containing key points regarding what Manila's urban design should be. For example, one could simply state that in the section titled "(2) Street Systems," Burnham and Anderson advise that the entrances through the Spanish city walls be widened, that a new road system be laid throughout Manila so as to reduce traffic congestion, and that the road layout,

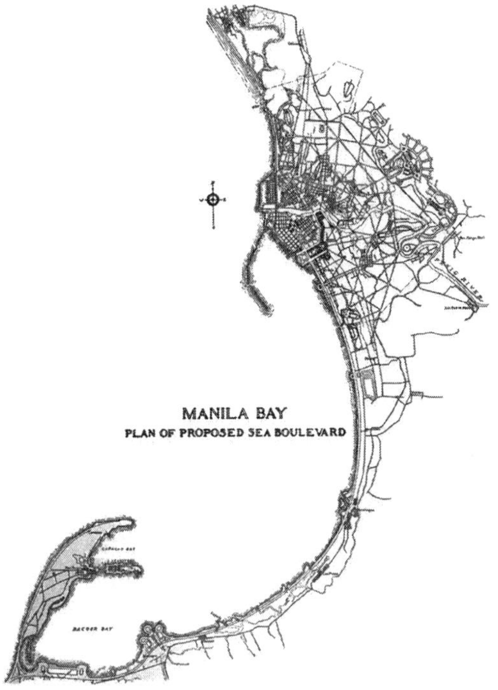

Figure 7.2. Burnham and Anderson's 1905 city plan for the renewal of Manila. Burnham and Anderson, *The Report on Improvement at Manila.*

punctuated by diagonal arteries, would help tie together previously detached inner and outer city districts. But in presenting such a description the actual meaning of the planners' recommendations are downplayed. With respect to widening the city wall entrances, while traffic flow would evidently be improved, it is also vital to note that airflow would be improved as a result. At the time when Burnham and Anderson composed their report, this was recognized as helping improve public health conditions in Manila. Furthermore, with respect to Burnham and Anderson's suggested new road configuration, one may simply read this as saying that as part of Manila's Americanization some new boulevards were to be constructed and some existing roadways (for example, the shorefront thoroughfare between Manila and the port town of Cavite) were to be revitalized. As part of such an account, basic details can clearly be put forward; for example, the aforesaid roadway between Manila and Cavite was to be widened to 250 feet and so transformed into an "Ocean Boulevard" lined with palm, bamboo, and mango trees.[9] Likewise, in the section of the report titled "(1) Development of Water Front, Parks, and Parkways," Burnham and Anderson recommend the erection of new public buildings and the laying out of green spaces throughout the built environment. It could be suggested that this was simply a ruse by the American colonial regime to visually embellish the Philippine capital. However, new open spaces such as parks and playfields were to have a number of functions. First, open space *was* to be used to "dignify important buildings,"[10] but, second, green spaces were to give the populace sites for engaging in a range of leisure activities. Third, open spaces were to provide sites for statuary and fountains. Fourth, the new fountains were to help form microclimates so that Manila's population could have new opportunities to take refuge from the tropical climate.[11] Fifth, new open space was to be created by, for instance, filling in the moat surrounding the Spanish colonial walled city (known as Intramuros). There were two reasons for doing so. First, by the early 1900s the moat had developed a reputation as a source of disease. Second, by creating a substantial lawn about the Intramuros walls, these icons of Spanish imperialism were to become devalued. No more were they to stand as grand structures of Spanish authority. Rather, now they were to be relegated to a "lounging place," that is to say a site for leisure and relaxation. And lastly, the sixth function of the open space in the frame of City Beautiful planning logic was to offer locales where different social groups could interact. This, as Burnham and Anderson clarify with reference to the example of play fields in Chicago, elevates the moral tone of urban life, because community spirit and civic pride swells, and local crime rates drop.[12]

As for infrastructure development, Burnham and Anderson indicated that there was a need not only for new roads within Manila's bounds but also for new bridges, an expanded local rail system, and an enlarged port. As to why such a major overhaul of the city's structural and transport utilities was recommended, it is vital not to overlook the political, cultural, and economic significance and standing Manila had within Philippine society at the start of the twentieth century, as well as American colonial politics' tendency to prompt societal advancement. It must not be forgotten that by the end of the Spanish colonial period, what happened politically, culturally, and economically in Manila overshadowed activities in other urban communities in the Philippines. Manila ranked first in the country in terms of size and importance.[13] Consequently, to activate reform in the capital city also activated the capacity to sway economic, political, and cultural conditions within the nation at large.[14] What is more, at the time American colonization commenced, Manila was perceived by the colonizers as "backward." Such a view was the result of numerous causes, for example, the presence of widespread poverty, Filipinos' poor diets,[15] citizens' low average life expectancy (twenty-one years at the start of the 1900s), the lack of modern-era urban infrastructure, the majority of the population's residing in nipa huts, and so on.[16] In light of president William McKinley's Benevolent Assimilation Proclamation declaring that the United States' mission in the Philippines was to "uplift" and "civilize,"

American colonizers felt that to enhance the quality of life of Filipinos they had to alter the existing cultural and economic structures and also reshape the physical environments in which people lived.[17] The new road layout in Manila would do more than enhance traffic circulation: it would also provide new sensations that articulated to Filipinos that a new colonial age, one grounded in modernity, had commenced. In this setting new roads constructed from asphalt, ones that replaced the mud-and-stone highways of the Spanish era, that is, thoroughfares that were all but impassable during the wet season, enabled people to more freely move about the city. The Americans too through using modern construction materials meant travel was to become more comfortable. This benefitted both citizens and business people alike, thereby supporting economic development. The *esteros,* which by the early 1900s comprised of a mix of stagnant, polluted mud and water, were to be dredged and widened. Their banks were also to be rebuilt. "So treated," remarked Burnham and Anderson, "they will offer an economical and unobjectionable means of freight handling that will greatly contribute to the prosperity of the city."[18] Then again, to better comprehend the American promotion of environmental change and societal betterment, a discussion of chronology is needed. It must not be overlooked that Burnham and Anderson's report was completed shortly after the American colonial government had introduced the *tranvia* (streetcar).[19] The transformation of Manila's physical appearance, alongside the introduction of an electric-powered form of transport became, according to Michael Pante, a step toward Manila showing off its modernity, namely an "achievement" that was American-inspired.[20] As a result, as Filipinos went about their daily activities, no more was life typified by horse-drawn or steam-powered carriages and bumpy thoroughfares. Instead, from the early 1900s onward, electric trams, level roadways, and, subsequently, cars were to express the progress in society born of the governmental handover between Spain and the United States in 1898.

Taking the topic of cultural change and development further, and continuing to focus on the improvement of Manila's infrastructure, a number of boulevards were to be constructed after 1905. These roadways would improve connectivity between outlying and inner-city neighborhoods, and, being lined with trees akin to parkways in American cities, were to play an important role in forging new urban vistas. New views were an important part of Manila's alteration, and Burnham and Anderson recommended building a new civic core, to be sited in the Extramuros (the area of Manila outside the Spanish walled city). The American planners proposed this because it would help to show off the improved city as a site of "advanced civilization."[21] It would also make the Intramuros politically redundant; new public institutions in the Extramuros would present the locality, not the aged walled city, "as the beating heart of a healthy democratic nation."[22] As a result, whereas before 1898 colonial rule in the Philippines had a reputation for authoritarianism, corruption, and oppression, the Americans, in contrast, aspired to present their brand of colonial governance as being in polarity. They repeatedly emphasized that they were in the Philippines not to exploit but rather to impart "development" so that, ultimately, the Filipinos would be able to successfully take on the responsibilities of self-rule.[23] From 1905 onward Manila was to have a spatial form and appearance that diverged from what it had had under Spanish colonial rule: "The creation of long, straight, and sometimes broad thoroughfares, and the integration of landscape architecture with the man-made environment, was a major component of this transition."[24] With the boulevards permitting people to see farther vistas with eye-catching new public edifices, such as the capitol with its prominent large dome, all Filipinos (irrespective of age, social standing, life experiences, etc.) were able to individually and collectively observe governmental institutions operating on their behalf as part of the alteration of local society.[25] Given this actuality, three things must now be considered: conceptually speaking, to establish views towards important architectural features permits the viewer to acquire a sense of ownership as to what they see; seeing new environmental features accentuates that what one sees is not only real but *belongs to the now;* and giving everyone the capacity to see grand architectural objects means that there is no racial discrimination as to who one is as a "Filipino." Consequently, the natives, Japanese, Chinese, and so on who under the Spanish *reducción* policy had formerly been separated into their own quarters in the Extramuros were all able to freely live and move about the reformed city, given that the American colonial regime identified them all as Manila citizens, that is, as "Filipinos." In this context Manila's new design was critical to helping the Americans showcase society's transformation and, by association, it allowed the Filipinos to acquire competence and to realize that Spanish colonial rule and all its drawbacks had been forever consigned to history.[26]

Reading *The Report on Improvement at Manila* Textually

As a text fostering social engineering, *The Report on Improvement at Manila* was to provide the means to initiate social, economic, and cultural opportunities that were unimaginable during the Spanish colonial age. The application of the City Beautiful planning paradigm in this framework illuminated how, in broad terms, American colonial governance intended to evolve society away from the allegedly "backward" state of being associated with the prior colonial era. With its symbolic and pragmatic meanings, Burnham and Anderson's planning vision for Manila sought to establish transitions that would help, for example, to embolden Filipinos to see themselves as a cohesive "us." This bonding following the implementation of the 1905 report was to be enhanced by statuary placed within newly created public spaces, for example, in the Washington, DC, style mall (today known as Rizal Park) to the west of the capitol building site. Such a deed reveals how the Americans were prepared to tie the built environment's renewal, and thus society's evolution, to notions of Filipinism. With the erection of a monument dedicated to the Filipino national hero José Rizal (1861–1896) in the aforesaid public space in 1913 (figure 7.3), the colonizers manufactured a rallying point for the local population and, in addition, founded a site to help literally and metaphorically sustain Rizal's belief that Filipinos belonged to a single political-ethnic collective.[27] Yet, to recognize why a statue of Rizal in the center of "Modern Manila" took on so much value to the Filipinos, and to the Americans as well, one must consider how people understood government after 1898. For the Americans, the purpose of democratic administration, in both North America and the Philippines, was to protect citizens, give them security, and grant social benefits. For the Filipinos, government should be formed in such a manner as to endow welfare and civil rights. In order to accomplish these ambitions, it was believed, according to George A. Malcolm, that the bureaucrats must as a rule listen to the public and follow their suggestions simply because they, the citizens, were best qualified to understand their own *and* society's wider needs.[28]

When probing the meaning of cultural change, the theory of culture can be of great worth. Examining the concepts of thinkers such as Theodor

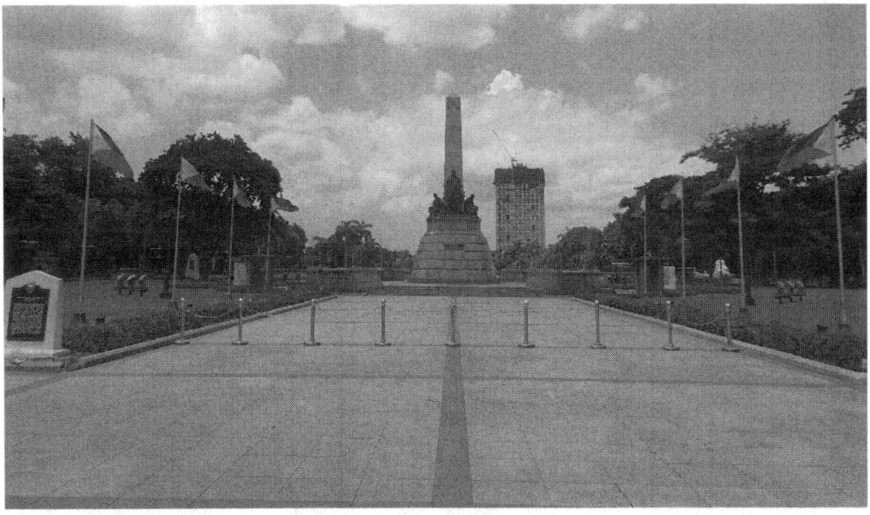

Figure 7.3. The Rizal Monument in Rizal Park, c. 2019. Courtesy of the author.

Adorno (1903–1969), can produce new insights. In Adorno's view, there is proximity between culture and administration,[29] an alliance that reveals itself within the practice of language; in consequence, by coupling governmental authority and reports on urban designing with cultural growth, a dialectic emerges that endorses the perception that social justice cannot transpire unless formerly unregulated environmental elements in society become controlled. Considering that *The Report on Improvement at Manila* summarized the existing environmental conditions in the city alongside "their most obvious possibilities,"[30] and that in the early 1900s there was "the opportunity to create a unified city equal to the greatest of the Western world, with unparalleled and priceless addition of a tropical setting,"[31] it is impossible to assess the 1905 report without referencing, if only briefly, what Manila was to become structurally, and the language that Burnham and Anderson use to express this. Interestingly, as textual analysis discloses, from the standpoint of architecture, "Modern Manila" preserved Spanish colonial design traditions. For instance tiles, mentioned six times in the 398-word section titled "Future Building Materials," were to still be used for roofing, and small window openings and overhanging second floors were to still be an elemental part of colonial housing design. In considering why Burnham and Anderson made such recommendations, it is important to consider issues of aesthetic charm, the low cost of existing building materials, their resilience against earthquakes, and the need for protection from the climate.[32] All in all, Burnham and Anderson conclude, "The Spanish traditions are deserving of acceptance."[33] Conversely, if one adheres to the opinion that as Burnham and Anderson were sanctioning modern American urban traits in Manila they were accordingly promoting the use of the construction materials used in the United States, one immediately runs into the danger of misreading what their document was actually about. For example, words such as "concrete," "iron," and "steel" are rarely employed within the report.

Proclaiming a new destiny for Filipinos, Burnham and Anderson's plan was, to interpret Hartmut Rosa, to enact "cultural acceleration."[34] But, as already indicated, even though this evolution was precious to the Americans in hegemonic terms, it was not grounded in a wholesale rejection of all things Spanish or a single-handed promotion of all things American. Hence modernization in the Philippines from 1898 onward was an amalgam of gradualistic and paradigmatic components, although there was immense propaganda value to implementing social reform for the Americans.[35] Cultural and environmental transitions helped to present the American colonizers as doers. Through the application of change as "progress," for example, in the form of a new city layout, the Americans presented themselves as "victors" in that they could introduce *and* entrench modern-era mores.[36] As noted earlier, new roads, new public spaces, and new forms of transportation articulated society's transformation in America's hands. These new urban features promised a new freedom of movement, new opportunities for leisure and improved health, and the compression of time and space in that it was now faster to travel from A to B within the Philippine capital city. As Michel de Certeau makes clear, when a new spatial system is implemented, a temporal and cultural discontinuity can be forged. With the laying down of a new spatial order, possibilities arise, which the citizen subsequently actualizes through, for instance, the use of new types of transport, seeing new buildings, and using new public spaces. This actualizing process creates a facet of culture that Ian Buchanan calls "a near and a far, a *here* and a *there*."[37]

Undoubtedly, as David Harvey has explained, it is important to realize that promotion of the modern age must be understood as a reaction to the crisis-ridden experiences of earlier years.[38] Given that when Americans arrived in Manila in 1898 they observed widespread "primitiveness," the restructuring of the colonial built fabric affected metamorphosis so that "backwardness" could be eliminated. In the view of Werner von Siemens (1816–1892), the law of cultural acceleration means that a culture's development transpires continuously, albeit at different speeds and at different times due to the varying effects of technology and organizational innovation.[39] Yet to sum up, as Fritz Reheis has observed, any cultural acceleration must always be read through two lenses (so as to come to terms with what modern society in a given place actually is): the psychological and the environmental. Altering one, Reheis argues, affects the other.[40] To simply read *The Report on Improvement at Manila* descriptively misses what it is truly saying as to what modern Filipino civilization should be from 1905 onward, from the perspective of the American colonizers.

All in all, *The Report on Improvement at Manila* was a watershed in the environmental design of Manila. As the first American document dedicated to the (re)design of a Philippine city, its implementation forged a cityscape that was no longer characterized by bell towers and church-lined plazas. In their place were to be large green open spaces, lengthy roadways, classically formed buildings, and impressive sightlines toward new public edifices. Significantly, too, even though Burnham and Anderson's plan for upgrading life in Manila has been discussed by countless scholars, and so placed at the heart of the urban historiography of the Philippines, there is still much to learn about it. As this work has revealed, by employing textual analysis tools, the document reveals itself in ways hitherto unseen. Textual tools provide a new gauge of what "Modern Manila" was to mean structurally and culturally (in the context of US colonial governance) to those who built it, and to those who would live in it. As table 7.1 presents, environmental reform along the lines recommended by Burnham and Anderson was to articulate both a spatial *and*

Table 7.1. Different urban forms and cultural meanings of Manila's built environment for American colonizers during the early 1900s.

Spanish Colonial Manila	American Colonial Manila
Environmentally modeled by the *Laws of the Indies*	Application of the City Beautiful paradigm
Intramuros (as heart of the city)	Extramuros (as the center of the "new city")
Church-lined plazas	Green spaces with statues of national heroes
Archaic cultural traditions and Catholicism	Modern, secular civic society
Politics of authoritarianism	Democratic political system
Racial separation	Filipino unity/ nationhood
Oppression	Promise of future self-rule

a cultural dichotomy, a sense of separation that held meaning for Americans and for Filipinos. As a consequence, while "Spanish Manila" was perceived by Americans as archaic and riddled with socioeconomic and environmental problems, "Modern Manila" was to be a site where development and civil liberties unattainable for Filipinos under Spanish colonial rule could readily be enjoyed.

Moreover, if to Americans the Spanish colonial era was characterized by an archaic, oppressive system of colonial governance, so, by reforming Philippine society and thereby the character of colonial built environments, civilization was to be upgraded for the Filipinos. As an upshot their day-to-day life was to be improved. Such environmental transition after 1905 transpired not only in Manila but elsewhere in the Philippines, for example, in Baguio, Cebu, Zamboanga, Lingayen, and Cabanatuan. Yet, significantly, if one wants to know what new urban form the Philippines took on, and why, one must start with *The Report on Improvement at Manila.* And one should read the language of Burnham and Anderson carefully. As cultural theorists have recurrently emphasized, to know language is to know culture, and to grasp culture is to establish a frame for coming to terms with the disposition of societal administration.

Notes

1. Axel I. Mundigo and Dora P. Crouch, "The City Planning Ordinances of the Laws of the Indies Revisited. Part 1: Their Philosophy and Implications," *Town Planning Review* 48, no. 3 (July 1977): 248.

2. Ian Morley, *Cities and Nationhood: American Imperialism and Urban Design in the Philippines, 1898–1916* (Honolulu: University of Hawai'i Press, 2018), 33.

3. Numerous texts have investigated the nature of City Beautiful urban design in the United States. These include Mel Scott, *American City Planning since 1890* (Berkeley: University of California Press, 1969), 47–109; John W. Reps, *The Making of Urban America: A History of City Planning in the United States* (Princeton, NJ: Princeton University Press, 1965), 497–525; Thomas S. Hines, *Burnham of Chicago* (Chicago, IL: Chicago University Press, 1974), 92–216; William H. Wilson, *The City Beautiful Movement* (Baltimore, MD: Johns Hopkins University Press, 1989), 75–95; and Jon A. Peterson, *The Birth of City Planning in the United States, 1840–1917* (Baltimore, MD: Johns Hopkins University Press, 2003), 55–245.

4. Ian Morley, *American Colonisation and the City Beautiful: Filipinos and Planning in the Philippines, 1916–35* (London: Routledge, 2019), 82–172.

5. Christopher Vernon, "Daniel Hudson Burnham and the American City Imperial," *Thesis Eleven* 123, no. 1 (August 2014): 88.

6. William E. Parsons, "Burnham as a Pioneer in City Planning," *Architectural Record* 38 (July–December 1915): 14.

7. Daniel Hudson Burnham and Peirce Anderson, *Report on Proposed Improvements at Manila*, in *Report of the Philippine Commission Part 1* (Washington, DC: Government Printing Office, 1906), 628.

8. The report was accompanied by just two illustrations: one image showed a map of Manila with the layout of the proposed Ocean Boulevard between the city and Cavite; the other was a plan of the city of Manila in accordance with the recommended City Beautiful inspired layout by Burnham and Anderson.

9. Burnham and Anderson, *Report*, 628.

10. Ibid.

11. Ibid., 629

12. Ibid.

13. George W. Brown, *Pearl of the Orient: The Philippine Islands* (Boston, MA: Dana Estates, 1900), 104.

14. Ian Morley, *Cities and Nationhood*, 47.

15. Daniel F. Doeppers, *Feeding Manila in Peace and War, 1850–1940* (Madison: University of Wisconsin Press, 2016), 10.

16. In 1901 almost 18,500 buildings were listed in Manila. Of this total more than 12,250 were described by the Americans as "shacks" or in "bad" condition. Ian Morley, *Cities and Nationhood*, 44.

17. The Benevolent Assimilation Proclamation was issued on December 21, 1898.

18. Burnham and Anderson, *Report*, 634.

19. The *tranvia* was introduced in April 1905.

20. Michael Pante, "Mobility and Modernity in the Urban Transport Systems of Colonial Manila and Singapore," *Journal of Social History* 47, no. 4 (June 2014): 863.

21. Ian Morley, *Cities and Nationhood*, 68–75.

22. Ibid., 69.

23. At the time their colonization began, the Americans held a fear that Filipinos were unprepared for sovereignty. With this in mind, the colonizers would offer practical lessons in democratic government, and would import American cultural mores so that Filipinos could be "our little brown brothers." William H. Taft, *Hearing before Committee on Insular Affairs, Friday, February 21, 1902* (Washington, DC: Government Printing Office, 1902), 28.

24. Ian Morley, *Cities and Nationhood*, 62–63.

25. Ibid., 78.

26. Ibid., 24.

27. Sharon Delmendo, *The Star Entangled Banner* (New Brunswick, NJ: Rutgers University Press, 2004), 22. The monument was designed by Richard Kissling, and was formally unveiled on December 30, 1913.

28. George A. Malcolm, *The Government of the Philippine Islands: Its Development and Fundamentals* (Rochester, NY: Lawyers Co-Operative, 1916), 21–22.

29. Theodor W. Adorno, *The Culture Industry: Selected Essays on Mass Culture* (New York: Routledge, 1991), 107.

30. Burnham and Anderson, *Report,* 635.

31. Ibid.

32. Ibid.

33. Ibid.

34. Hartmut Rosa, *Social Acceleration: A Theory of Modernity* (New York: Columbia University Press, 2015), 40.

35. Ian Morley, *Cities and Nationhood,* 45.

36. Ibid.

37. Ian Buchanan, "Walking in the City," in *The Certeau Reader,* ed. Graham Ward (Oxford: Blackwell, 2000), 106–107.

38. David Harvey cited in Rosa, *Social Acceleration,* 40.

39. Reference to Werner von Siemens in ibid., 42.

40. Fritz Reheis, *Die Kreativität der Langsamkeit* (Darmstadt, Germany: Primus, 1999).

EIGHT

Manufacturing American Imperial Landscapes in the Tropics
Baguio and Balboa

Christopher Vernon

Victorious in the Spanish-American-Cuban-Filipino War (1898), the United States unexpectedly entered the global imperial arena, now possessing an empire spanning from Cuba and Puerto Rico in the Caribbean to Guam and the Philippines in the Pacific. In a jubilant climate of patriotic fervor, Washington's newly minted imperial status galvanized concern for improving and reshaping the city in a fashion commensurate with its magnified role.[1] On the strength of his magisterial orchestration of the World's Columbian Exposition (1893), celebrated Chicago architect Daniel Hudson Burnham garnered the lead in Washington's metamorphosis (1901–1902). On the heels of this domestic enterprise, the nation reset its sights on its newly acquired imperial archipelago and next dispatched its "larger than life" celebrity architect to the Philippines (1904). There, along with "Americanizing" the former Spanish colonial capital at comparatively antique Manila (1571), Burnham was to configure a summer capital, Baguio, de novo. At this far-flung outpost of empire, he employed, as at Washington, urban design, or, more accurately, landscape architecture as a potent instrument of imperialist expression. Conceptualized within this heady ethos, Burnham's Philippine projects, translated across the Pacific, informed Isthmian Canal Commission architect Austin Lord's layout of a model American town, Balboa (1913), set to arise amid the jungle of its recently forged Panama Canal Zone. This chapter scrutinizes Baguio and Balboa's plans through the lens of imperialism, sifted further by an analysis of how each architect responded to the formidable challenge posed by perilous tropical environments—delirious climes then popularly held as sinister, disease-ridden, and inhabited by indolent primitives. In parallel, it also focuses on the symbolic value Burnham and Lord awarded the rugged terrain within their respective future imperial cities' layouts—arguing that architecture and urbanism are seldom, if ever, simply benign aesthetic propositions.

Burnham, L'Enfant, and Washington's Broken Terrain

With dreams of empire lingering within the popular imagination, in 1901, senator James McMillan established the Senate Park Commission (SPC) (also eponymously known as the McMillan Commission) to oversee Washington's improvement.[2] "General Burnham," as the senator later anointed him, became its de facto chairman. Landscape architect Frederick Law Olmsted, Jr. (whose widely renowned father had by then retired), architect Charles F. McKim, and sculptor Augustus Saint-Gaudens joined him. Burnham was awarded the prestigious post largely owing to his lasting World's Columbian Exposition fame. Indeed, the SPC's formation amounted to a reunion: all of its members had contributed to the Chicago Fair. Reassembled, this band of luminaries was now officially charged to restore and expand Pierre Charles L'Enfant's foundational plan for the capital (1791). In 1901, much to the SPC's consternation, Washington evinced not its original author's hand but that of his successor, pioneering, homegrown landscape architect Andrew Jackson Downing. Instead of L'Enfant's sweeping vistas, Washington's urban tapestry remained studded with the American's half-century-old sylvan mantle of picturesque groves, obliterating the original plan's spatial clarity.[3] The need for restoration being acute, the SPC's activities would entail considerable reimagining. Nonetheless, the SPC was finally poised to redress Englishman Charles Dickens' earlier mocking, if not stinging, dismissal of America's capital as but a disappointing "City of Magnificent Intentions."[4] Although Burnham did not foresee it, the SPC's analytical studies would endow him with his first object lesson of dovetailing an orthogonal grid, one meticulously interwoven with diagonals, amid undulating terrain. As he would revisit and adapt L'Enfant's topographically divined orientation technique at the Philippine summer capital, this dimension of the Frenchman's plan begs closer exploration.

Conventionally, L'Enfant's layout is matter-of-factly categorized as a Baroque plan, presumably based on André Le Nôtre's royal gardens at Versailles (1661). The SPC, for instance, straightforwardly characterized L'Enfant as "a man of position and education, and an engineer of ability" and contended that he "must have been familiar with those great works of master Le Nôtre."[5] L'Enfant's design, however, was not simply the mechanistic outcome of a derivative exercise. Alternatively, it encapsulated a finely nuanced response to the future capital's actual, not idealized, site. Although uneasily conjured today, Washington's locale was celebrated in the late eighteenth century as one of diverse picturesque beauty—an uneven mosaic of "hilly and level, wet and dry, forested and cultivated, rocky and fertile." Contemporary accounts routinely "extolled the unusual natural beauty of the area and L'Enfant was particularly sensible of its grandeur and variety." After reconnoitering the site, the architect discerned, "Nothing can be more admirably adapted for the purpose [of the federal city]; nature had done much for it, and with the aid of art it will become the wonder of the world."[6] In the Frenchman's vision, the new capital of America's "vast empire" would artfully accentuate, not subjugate, its natural setting.

When conceptualizing his plan, L'Enfant resolved to wed a geometric template with the site's undulating topography; by contrast, Le Nôtre had only to contend with comparatively level terrain at Versailles. At the outset, L'Enfant strategically located government edifices, monuments, and public squares on elevated sites, "commanding," as he put it, "the most extensive prospects." He then linked these with diagonal boulevards, establishing not only physical communication but also, again in his own words, "reciprocity of sight."[7] After demarcating these "anchors," he calculatingly overlaid them with a street grid, adjusting it so that the orthogonals and the diagonals converged upon the squares. At his plan's heart lay a bucolic parkland, its rotated "T" shape the outcome of the convergence of two interlocking axes—one north-south and the other east-west.

Vitally, L'Enfant awarded landscape foci to both of his axial armatures, fixing the composition's alignment in response to topography and view-capturing possibilities. From the commanding hilltop Congress House (now the Capitol, colloquially referred to as "Capitol Hill"), he projected an axial Grand Boulevard (today the Mall) west, directing the eye down the thoroughfare greensward, past a commemorative equestrian statue of George Washington (unlike the gargantuan obelisk memorial erected later), and then propelling it across the Potomac's middle-ground waters to finally rest upon the "wilderness" at the hazy distance.[8] Although indebted to the Anglo-French picturesque technique, L'Enfant uniquely charged his scenographic landscape appropriation with a localized symbolism. In post-Revolutionary America, the continental interior was garnering esteem as a superabundant, "limitless" frontier, one that would quickly magnetize the nascent democracy's westward spread. The nation did not blink, and seized expansion as its mission or, as it came to be known, Manifest Destiny. From the elevated President's House (White House), L'Enfant projected a second axis some seven miles (eleven kilometers) south, awarding its apogee to an aqueous prospect, the Potomac River's convergence with its eastern branch (today the Anacostia River). Above all, he "recognized that he must not sacrifice that vista to any architectural arrangement."[9] By privileging or foregrounding landscape in his cross-axial scheme, the French engineer valorized America's natural world.

In 1902, after only a year's frenetic activity, the SPC officially unveiled its revisionist capital layout (also known, after its Congressional sponsor, as "the McMillan plan"). The plan was substantially, but not entirely, informed by detailed historical analysis. At Burnham's suggestion, for instance, the SPC even made a month-long European study tour, replete with excursions to Versailles and other Le Nôtre masterworks. In the process, Burnham learned to appreciate L'Enfant's use of local topography and its underlying symbolism. As the SPC plan registered, however, the sway of neoclassical City Beautiful ideals on Burnham's design sensibilities conspired against his restoring the Frenchman's axial landscape foci. He instead replaced them with built objects, visually enclosing L'Enfant's seemingly infinite vistas. For instance, a temple memorial to Abraham Lincoln, not a "wilderness" panorama, now bookended the western end of L'Enfant's east-west axis. No less dramatic a departure, a "Pantheon" enshrining statues of "illustrious men of the nation" or "the memory of some individual" (later manifested as the Thomas Jefferson Memorial) displaced the Potomac's convergence as the north-south axis' southern terminus.[10] These substitutions underscored a crucial temporal divergence: in "L'Enfant's day, the political and architectural allusions had been to republican Rome," but now the "rhetoric and rationale were unabashedly imperial."[11] Of no less gravitas, Burnham saw through twentieth-century eyes a conceptualized landscape, not as a spatial entity in its own right as had L'Enfant but instead only as a "background setting" or architectural frame. Through time, as the SPC's plan was incrementally executed, "all sense of the surrounding countryside [was] sacrificed to Federal monumentalism."[12]

To the Philippine Colony

With the SPC's heroic vision for the imperial hearth now forged, the United States next resolved to accentuate its Manifest Destiny, newly extended even further west, in the distant Pacific. Again, it turned to Burnham. In September 1904, a newspaper in the architect's adopted Chicago heralded his post, trumpeting boastfully on its front page: "Plan Queen City for the Far East: Uncle Sam Commissions Architect Burnham of Chicago to Make Manila the Gem of the Orient: Plan a Summer Capital: Spot in Mountains to Be Made the Philippine Simla [Shimla]." Along with "Americanizing" the colony's capital, Burnham was to, no less importantly, lay out a wholly new summer capital, Baguio. Still enjoying professional prominence from his Chicago Fair success, augmented now by his Washington work, Burnham was a logical and predictable choice for the job. Indeed, the Philippine capital building enterprise had entered the government's imperial ken around 1901, when Burnham was, as this report identified, "president" of the "Washington commission of architects [SPC]."[13]

Despite his impressive qualifications, though, Burnham was not, in fact, America's first choice. Instead, seeking a *landscape* architect, not an architect, the government had initially solicited Frederick Law Olmsted, Jr., to take up the position.[14] After deliberating, Olmsted Jr. reluctantly declined the nationally prominent work, owing to his other projects' press—he later regretted his decision, reminiscing that he had "often kicked" himself for not taking the job.[15] Nonetheless, that the government first approached Olmsted reveals its vision of the Philippine project foremost as a landscape design, not an architectural proposition. Rather than just erecting an assemblage of monolithic edifices, officialdom had set out to manufacture an entire American imperial landscape.[16]

The SPC's landscape architect being unavailable, Burnham boldly resolved the government's predicament by putting none other than himself forward to direct the enterprise. Perhaps rationalizing and although he was not the Columbian Exposition's sole author (despite his popularization as such), the architect essentially considered it a work of landscape architecture. After all, it was there that the public, he was convinced, "discovered the art of Landscape Architecture and were delighted."[17] The government, equally eager to infuse its Philippine endeavor with prestige, acquiesced and awarded Burnham the job—although the thirty-four-year-old Olmsted Jr.'s star was rising, he then remained less popularly known than his father or Burnham. Expected to "afford an example to other nations" and attract associated scrutiny, the undertaking's scale and scope mandated assistance.[18] And so, Burnham conscripted his employee, École des Beaux-Arts–educated Peirce Anderson. It also dictated that the pair voyage to the Philippines to study its capitals, old and new.[19]

Tropical Nature

Arriving at Manila in December 1904 for around a month's visit, Burnham (and Anderson) was immediately overwhelmed by an exotic landscape of tropical nature, a lurid, languid "world" (actual and psychological) far removed from cacophonous, inland Chicago—seemingly permanently under construction—and its vanishing prairie hinterland. "Diving into the Orient," to use his words, must have simultaneously been an ethereal, unsettling experience.[20] The day's conventional wisdom, in America and Great Britain alike, held tropical climes to be sinister, disease ridden, and home to idle natives.[21] In short, the tropics were believed anathematic to Anglo-Celtic "civilization." Conversely, white imperialists required elevated, cool climates to ensure their mission's success. Although Burnham was certainly not unaware of this view, there is no evidence that he espoused it. The architect's outlook was likely more ambivalent. We do know that he did not simply confront the tropics as a foreboding obstacle to be strenuously overcome. A besotted Burnham, for instance, glowingly rhapsodized Manila's luxuriant "tropical setting" as "unparalleled and priceless." His esteem soon led him to envision embroidering the newly American city with an Ocean Boulevard, lushly embowered with "palms, bamboo, and mangoes," linked with a leafy parkland network riddled with "playing fountains" to "help mitigate the [admittedly] trying effects of a tropical climate."[22]

Burnham, a native New Yorker, likely first gleaned a tropical mystique while performing as the World's Columbian Exposition's director of works. His knowledge source was an authoritative one: none other than famed landscape architect Frederick Law Olmsted, by the 1890s esteemed as nothing short of a sage. Although the fair is legendarily recollected as a mirage-like, neoclassical White City, we must not forget that not all the miniature metropolis evoked the heroicized ambience of imperial antiquity. North of its celebrated Court of Honor epicenter, Olmsted, the fair's consulting landscape architect, had conjured an alternative, reclusive oasis.[23] Leaving the boisterous White City's heat and glare behind, this serene, seductively mysterious, and vividly green precinct showcased a Wooded Island and its enclosing lagoon. Foiling the stiff geometry otherwise typical of the fairgrounds, here the planting was luxuriant and composed irregularly to create visual and spatial tropical effects.[24] When laying out the island and its shimmering aqueous envelope, Olmsted instructed his superintendent of landscape "to make it appear that we found this body of water and its shores and have done nothing to them except at the landings and bridges." To achieve this, he wished the sinuous water body to be "rich, rank, luxurious, crowded with vegetation, like the banks of some tropical rivers" (figure 8.1).[25]

On the face of it, Olmsted's choice of an inspirational font for the exposition's windswept, prairie locale perplexes, if not mystifies. Given that he possessed transcendentalist esteem for tropical nature, however, makes his selection fathomable. The landscape architect's tropical preoccupation had actually begun some thirty years earlier, while traversing the Isthmus of Panama (1863). The isthmus' "scenery," he reflected, "excited a wholly different emotion from that produced by any of our temperate-zone scenery, or rather it excited an emotion of a kind which our scenery sometimes produces as a quiet suggestion to reflection, excited it instantly, instinctively and directly." "If my retrospective analysis of emotion is correct," he mused, then "it rests upon a sense of the superabundant creative power, infinite resource, and liberality of Nature—the childish playfulness and profuse careless utterance of Nature."[26] When designing the fairgrounds three decades later, Olmsted remained under a tropical spell. For him, contact with an idealized,

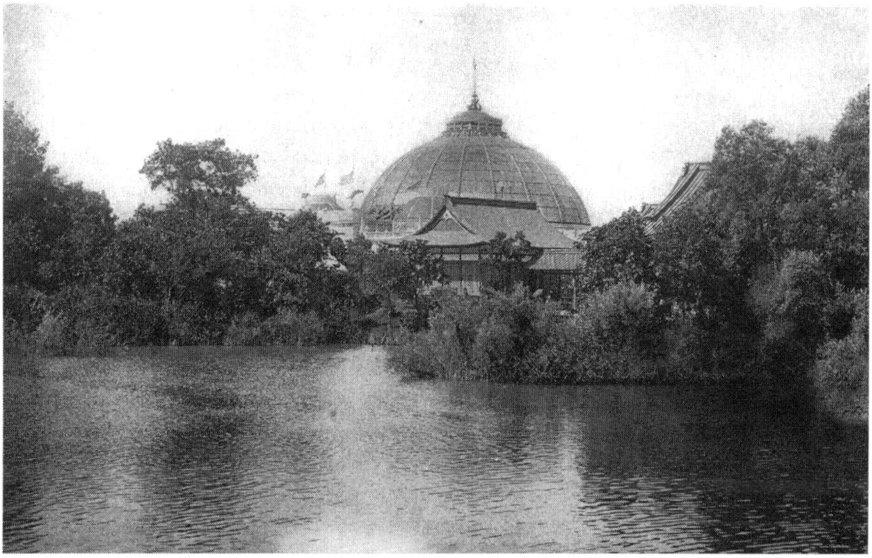

Figure 8.1. Frederick Law Olmsted's tropical planting effects at the World's Columbian Exposition as seen in this view of the "Wooded Island near Horticultural Building." Arnold and Higinbotham, *Official Views of the World's Columbian Exposition.*

superabundant natural world was still a quality of urban life requisite—no less so in the prophetic White City. Well beyond the confines of its Wooded Island precinct, Olmsted exotically punctuated even the Fair's Court of Honor heart with potted tropical palms. And it is extremely unlikely that the landscape architect did not impart his tropical enthusiasms to Burnham.

Baguio, America's Shimla

Despite Burnham's own tropical embrace, the choices of constructing a summer capital and where to locate it were not his to make. Baguio's inland, mountainous site, set amid Luzon's notoriously rugged Cordillera Central, had already been decided on and the protean city officially designated the summer capital in 1903, a year before he landed, if not quite commandeered, his official post.[27] Even earlier, the summer capital idea had, in fact, originated with the United States' Spanish foes. All too aware of this uneasy reality, Burnham marginalized Baguio's source, dismissing it with American bravado: "It was always *mañana* with the Spanish rulers, and they never got around to actual work on realizing the dream."[28] Eschewing its non-Anglo origin, the United States instead cited the British Raj's Indian summer capital as Baguio's reference, overtly likening it to a "Philippine Shimla." Unlike at Washington and Manila,

Burnham would accentuate Baguio's imperial monumentality not with grandiose architectural ensembles but through the city's configuration.

Health concerns dictated Baguio's location. With the city's new summer capital status as its catalyst, one newspaper succinctly illuminated, "Summer stations at high altitudes in tropical lands are important for the health and comfort of white immigrants from the temperate zones.... If they may have a breathing spell during the most heated period at an altitude where the air is bracing, the temperature moderate, the water pure and cold and the scenery beautiful and inspiring, they may acquire a fresh stock of health and vigor to carry them comfortably through their daily routine."[29] As Baguio's elevated locale exceeded all of these criteria, the newspaper deemed it a "Philippine paradise." America's tropical anxieties, moreover, were so great that there was even talk of making the place not just the colony's summer capital but its sole capital. Inadvertently symptomatic of this ambition, one newspaper erroneously reported that Manila had actually been "abandoned" in favor of Baguio, "the new capital of the Philippines."[30]

Along with its salubrious climate, Baguio's decidedly nontropical landscape was vital to its appeal. Period portrayals of the summer capital's environs did not fail to exalt the virtues of its variant clime. Another newspaper, for instance, discerned that Baguio's "rugged," "grass covered," and "finely [pine] forested" landscape reassuringly "resembled an American park."[31] Lacking Washington and Manila's age-old urban fabric, the summer capital's site was comparatively a tabula rasa. This allured Burnham, compelling the architect to grow "more deeply interested in the summer capital project [than in Manila]," as it would free him, or so he thought, to "formulate [his] plans untrammelled by any but natural conditions."[32] Heightening his design ambitions, Burnham learned, around the time of his appointment, that at least one government official hoped Baguio would "eventually" become the singular capital.[33]

After nine arduous days surveying the capital site's uncannily "American park-like" landscape (no easy task for the nearly sixty-year-old, portly architect), Burnham, no longer reliant on maps alone, had gained a "hands-on" site appreciation. He discovered, for instance, that the locale was not completely "untrammelled." It was already impressed with the footprints of "a few dozen structures of public and private construction," most prominently a "civil sanatorium" (1902).[34] More than anything else, however, he also now realized that Baguio's "natural conditions," aesthetically and climatically exhilarating or not, actually posed a formidable design challenge. Accustomed to working with level, more malleable canvases, Burnham was now intimidated, confronted with a dramatically broken terrain. Despite his growing repute for "thinking big," he responded—according to his plan's on-the-ground imple-

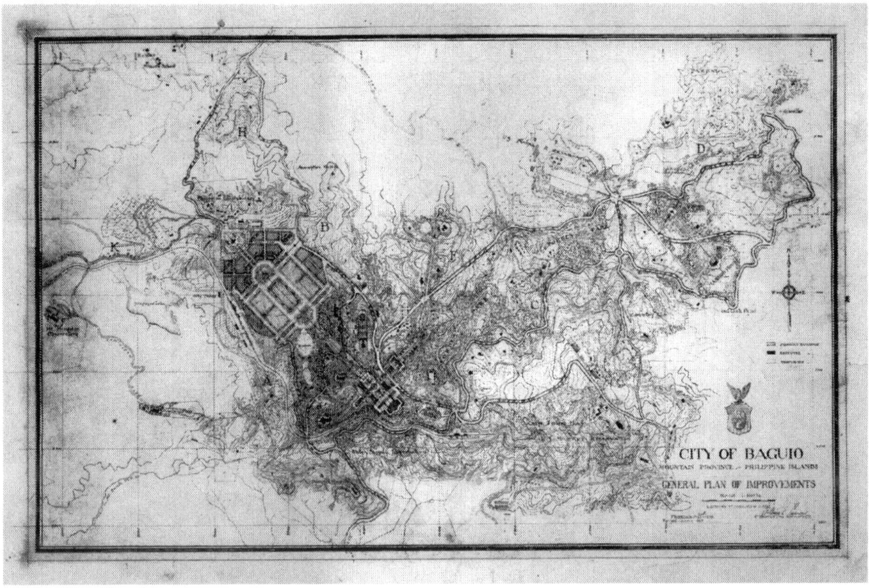

Figure 8.2. "City of Baguio: Preliminary Plan for Proposed Town Site," 1905. Avery Architectural and Fine Arts Library.

menter, William E. Parsons—by humbly adopting the "controlling principle" that his plan be "obedient to nature." Adherence to this rule, however, did not preclude a regular, geometric layout (figure 8.2).[35]

At Baguio, Burnham compliantly aligned axes "along ridges, valleys and hilltops," deferring to landforms, not an arbitrary template, to fix their alignments. This strategy reflected his decision to adopt and revivify L'Enfant's eighteenth-century topographically determined approach, one, as we now understand, he had recovered while orchestrating Washington's urban metamorphosis. Evincing the Frenchman's sensibilities, Burnham valued a pair of Baguio's higher mounts as pedestals beckoning official buildings, reserving one summit for municipal government and the second for national government. A "long main axis, expended by an open green esplanade [later known as Burnham Park]," connected the two hilltop groups.[36] "The intention is," the architect clarified, "to carry through the lines of the streets to commanding points on the hillsides and thus permit the location of monumental buildings where they command a view down neighboring streets, and count for their full value as an important element in the general effect." He awarded towering hilltops only to officialdom. Otherwise, to ubiquitously impose "formal architectural silhouettes upon the summits of the surrounding hills," Burnham cautioned, "would make a hard skyline and go far toward destroying the charm of this beautiful landscape." Alternatively, he inserted "buildings [into] the sloping hillsides," enabling them to "be seen against a solid background of green foliage" and thereby gaining the "best possible setting without mutilating their surroundings."[37] By crowning summits with monumental ensembles and subjugating all other buildings to their verdant slopes, Burnham's topographically articulated political symbolism—one indebted to L'Enfant's Washington—"Americanized" Baguio's landscape.

Unlike at Manila, the summer capital's citizenry was largely, if not exclusively, to be American civil servants. Consequently, Burnham no longer required an overtly imperial vocabulary. This liberated him to make an architecture that was monumental in scale and aspect, not in its stylistic references or materiality. That is to say, as we now appreciate, the summer capital's rugged topography, not its architecture, was his imperial medium.[38] And so, Baguio's structures were constructed of timber, not stone or concrete, in a fashion resonant with the American alpine stick style. The capital's rustic compound soon resembled an "upstate New York resort town magically transplanted to this oasis of almost familiar weather and terrain."[39] It also was evocative of Shimla itself. And by 1913, one American journalist would caution the British Raj, only half in jest, that it "had best look carefully to her laurels that Baguio may not someday not far distant outshine quaint Simla."[40]

In the end, Burnham remarkably succeeded in nestling a neoclassical City Beautiful plan within the broken terrain's warp and weft. Upon reflection, the architect hoped that his summer capital would be considered "something unusual among cities."[41] And, indeed, it was. Burnham's layout, however, was not unprecedented. Baguio's plan, as we know, was most directly informed by his adaptation of L'Enfant's topographically informed technique. This was not, however, the first time that Burnham had relied on it. Another precedent, more temporally immediate, is found within his own oeuvre. In 1903, only a year before embarking on its Philippine enterprise, the government invited Burnham (who, in turn, involved his soon-to-be partner, Edward H. Bennett) to make a competitive scheme (albeit an unsuccessful one) for the improvement and expansion of the US Military Academy at West Point, New York (figure 8.3).[42] After surveying the academy's spectacular property overlooking the Hudson River, Burnham concluded that, essentially, there was "one axis superior to all others for a monumental treatment of this post." "When one stands on the balcony of the Observatory, from which is obtained a broad view of the Government domain and the surrounding country," he explained, "this belief is confirmed, for *this axis is the natural one in the landscape.*" It would be "wrong," Burnham argued, resonant with L'Enfant's sensibilities, "to neglect the course to be pursued *when Nature herself has so plainly indicated it.*"[43] Not only were the architect's axial alignments topographically determined, his

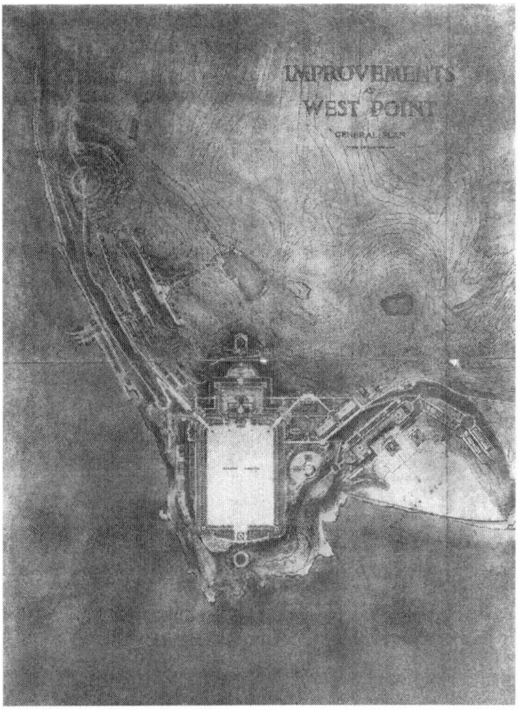

Figure 8.3. "Improvements at West Point: General Plan," 1903. *American Architect and Building News,* September 19, 1903.

axes themselves were also symbolically laden with governmental power, not only imperialistic but also overtly militaristic.

Baguio was also "unusual" in an unintended, paradoxical sense. Despite the city's imperial underpinnings, the summer capital eventually gained favor among Philippine elites—albeit actively coaxed by the Americans—as a resort destination. For instance, no less a native personage than general Emilio Aguinaldo, once the United States' Philippine-American War adversary, toured the fledging city in 1913. Thoroughly impressed, he now believed "Baguio ought to be [made] the permanent capital of the Islands."[44] And the general was apparently not the only Filipino to hold this opinion.[45] Even after independence (1946), native esteem for Burnham's achievement escalated. The Philippine government, for instance, did not erase but rather reinscribed the American appellation of Baguio's sylvan heart, Burnham Park.[46] This appreciation culminated in 1992. That year, the government erected a monolithic bust of Burnham atop an elevated platform within his namesake park.[47] With the sculpture's installation, the government palpably remembered the American "for making their city into a site of touristic pleasure." With the "stone eyes" of Burnham's "spectre" surveying the "landscape he helped to devise," the monument's position extends, if only accidentally, the "colonial gaze in[to] a postcolonial setting."[48]

From Washington to the Philippines to Panama

Back across the Pacific, the Philippines was not America's only imperial node: another new city was set to rise from within the Panamanian jungle. Soon after ascending to the office after William McKinley's assassination (1901), US president Theodore Roosevelt resolved, "No single great material work which remains to be undertaken on this continent is of such consequence to the American people as the building of a canal across the Isthmus connecting North and South America."[49] Aiming to commandingly demonstrate American might and superiority in the imperial arena, the new president grew determined to triumph in the wake of France's failure. In 1903, having "spoken softly and carried a big stick," Roosevelt controversially brokered Panama's independence from Colombia. Later that year, just months before Burnham left for the Philippines, the new republic recompensed. Panama now awarded the United States sovereignty over a strip of land across the isthmus, from then on known as the Panama Canal Zone. This area took the canal as its centerline and was approximately ten miles (sixteen kilometers) wide and fifty miles (eighty kilometers) long.[50]

In 1910, Roosevelt's successor, William Howard Taft—formerly governor-general of the Philippines (and then effectively Burnham's employer)—convened a Commission of Fine Arts (CFA).[51] Unsurprisingly, he appointed Burnham its chairman. Although the architect's health had begun to deteriorate by then, he nonetheless accepted. Other members included vice-chairman Francis Millet, a painter and sculptor who had worked with Burnham as the World's Columbian Exposition's director of decoration; fellow fair contributor and SPC veteran Frederick Law Olmsted, Jr.; sculptor Daniel Chester French; venerable neoclassicist architects Thomas Hastings and Cass Gilbert; and layman Charles Moore, earlier the SPC's secretary.

Two years later, however, the CFA withstood double blows. The first came in April. Vice-chairman Millet, en route back to the United States from Europe, tragically drowned with the sinking of the RMS *Titanic*.[52] Burnham was at sea at the same time, headed in the opposite direction. He landed at Cherbourg only days after the tragedy. In Germany that June, though, he too died, and the CFA lost its foundational chairman. "Greatly shocked," President Taft eulogized that it was he who had sent the architect to "the Philippine Islands for the beautification of Manila and for the laying out of a capitol [Baguio] in the mountains." And now, eight years later, he did not fail to recollect the capital's "fine climate" in the same breath.[53]

Despite its loss of Burnham and Millet, the CFA persevered. It filled Burnham's vacancy (albeit not in his chairman capacity) with another imperially credentialed architect, none other than Peirce Anderson.[54] Poignantly, Taft's appointment of Burnham's former Philippines assistant, otherwise professionally obscure, was the president's tribute to the late architect.[55] Although the CFA's membership (especially Olmsted) was intimately knowledgeable of Burnham's design fundamentals, Anderson's firsthand imperial city building experience now deepened the collective's wisdom.

In August 1912, only months after Burnham's death, Congress passed the Panama Canal Act. Senator Francis G. Newlands, addressing the august body that month, urged it to consider that "in finishing that great structure we should take into our councils the great men in architecture and in art who have done so much in the way of the artistic development of the country since the Chicago World's Exposition."[56] Heeding Newlands' plea, Congress amended the act, making new provision for the CFA to advise the president on the waterway's "artistic character."[57] The senator's aesthetic concerns, along with his pivotal role in securing the CFA's engagement, won accolades from Walter Burley Griffin, an architect and landscape architect hailing from Burnham's Chicago.

"Thankful" for Senator Newlands' "constructive imagination and great ideals," Griffin considered the "great national Panama undertaking" an opportunity to forge a modern architecture, one informed by "the same un-academic, untrammeled and straightforward way in which the structural advantages [of the canal itself] have been worked out." To do so, he contended, "would have a greater and more permanent value for architectural development of a new order than had the Columbian Exposition, which stimulated interest in the fruits of an old order, whose expression, magnificent as it was, represented the development of needs, materials and building facilities now both foreign and obsolete."[58] Only months before, Griffin had been declared the winner of the international competition to design Australia's national capital city, later named Canberra. The CFA, one imagines, would have welcomed the momentary celebrity's endorsement. Although his advocacy of a "new order" architecture and the Chicago Fair's obsolescence would have inevitably antagonized the CFA's neoclassical predisposition, Griffin's urban vision for the Australian capital, as we will soon understand, would nonetheless have Canal Zone import.

With the canal approaching completion, the government now indulged in contemplating the herculean engineering enterprise's aesthetic dimension. In February 1913, the CFA dispatched its new Chairman French and Vice-Chairman Olmsted to the Canal Zone. The government's "artistic" concerns, however, had actually entered the CFA's ken before Burnham's death. And the late architect would have a vicarious hand in its isthmus activities. After an intensive study tour of the Canal Zone, French and Olmsted returned home and consulted their fellow members. Afterward, the CFA determined, "The canal, like the Pyramids or some imposing object in natural scenery, is impressive from its scale and simplicity and directness.... One feels that anything done merely for the purpose of beautifying it would not only fail to accomplish that purpose, but would be an impertinence."[59] When scrutinizing the Canal Zone, however, Olmsted and French had not limited their critical gaze to the canal itself.

Balboa

The two Fine Arts commissioners did not travel to Panama alone. New York–based Isthmian Canal Commission architect Austin W. Lord accompanied them.[60] MIT-educated, Lord had effectively launched his career in 1890, taking up work in the office of McKim, Mead and White. There, the novice soon came to enjoy a special rapport with partner Charles McKim. McKim, as we know, later served with Burnham on the SPC, and the two were close friends. Lord, moreover, was in the office when his mentor designed the World's Columbian Exposition's Agriculture Building—no doubt with input from the fair's director of works. Under McKim's tutelage, inculcation with neoclassical City Beautiful ideals was inescapable. In fact, Lord's "close association" with the elder architect proved to be his career's "dominating influence." From McKim, he gained a "true understanding" of the "proper application of historic precedent to modern conditions."[61] And, by 1908, he had also already secured city planning experience, furthering it that year by coauthoring a plan for Columbus, Ohio.[62] Olmsted and French had doubtless encountered a kindred spirit.

Wasting no time, French, Olmsted, and Lord seized on their week-long Panamanian voyage as an opportunity for rigorous dialogues. When the trio convened, Lord was consumed with planning the model town of Balboa, the Panama Canal's operational headquarters. As the town's erection on a topographically broken site on the isthmus' Pacific side was to begin in only a few months, this pressing project likely monopolized their shipboard deliberations. In Lord's imperial vision up until then, a monolithic Administration Building, positioned atop Lone Tree Hill, a promontory on Ancon Hill's slope (approximately one hundred feet [thirty meters] in elevation), became, as the CFA later distinguished it, Balboa's "controlling feature."[63] From this topographically and visually commanding edifice, Lord projected, directly on axis nearly eighty feet (twenty-five meters) below, an avenue or linear parkland, christening it El Prado (the meadow) (figure 8.4).

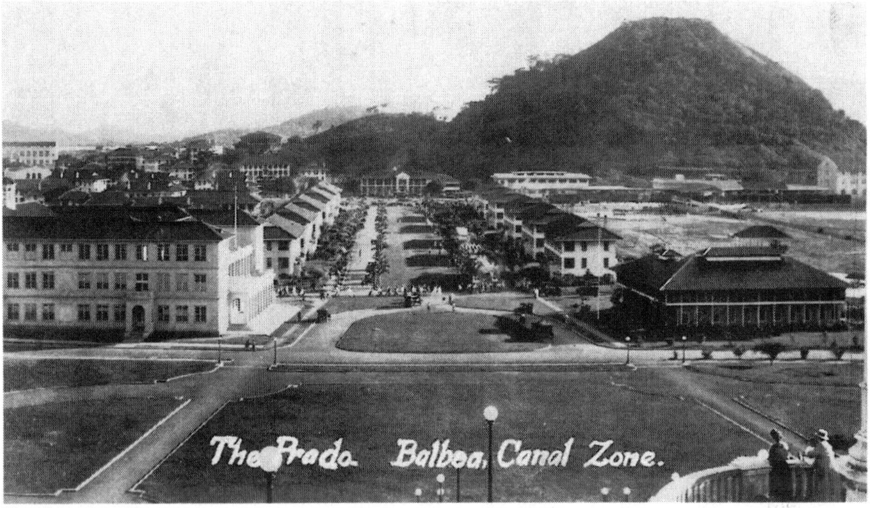

Figure 8.4. View from Balboa's Administration Building down El Prado to Sosa Hill, c. 1925. Author's collection.

Resonant with the SPC's Washington Mall plan, Balboa's Prado was to be similarly accentuated by buildings and tree plantations aligned in parallel on either side of it. Down the slope from the omnipresent Administration Building, Lord arrayed building locations hierarchically, in accordance with their civic status. He positioned the police station and post office, for instance, in closest proximity to it, distancing the lesser-important quartermaster and chief sanitary departments further down the axis. Somewhat surprisingly, Lord benignly culminated the grandiose assemblage with a diminutive bandstand.[64] Curiously, on his Canal Zone visit, Olmsted had recommended an axial focal point statue.[65] Just how a statue, however, morphed into a bandstand remains unclear.

After reviewing Lord's scheme (presumably in dialogue with fellow CFA members, including Philippines veteran Anderson), Olmsted and French were generally content with his City Beautiful plan, isolating only one appreciable deficiency. The Prado's axial alignment was "unfortunate," they assessed, as the "view of the canal when looking down the avenue would be cut off by the roofs of the navy-yard shops, and the actual terminus of the vista would be a foundry."[66] In remedy, Olmsted urged the architect to reorient his axis so that it terminated focally on a local landform, Sosa Hill. Lord did so, apparently without protest.

Olmsted's determination that Lord realign Balboa's principal axis with Sosa Hill is momentous. On the one hand, the landscape architect's decision was informed by his and Anderson's intimate knowledge of Burnham's Baguio scheme—registering the late architect's vicarious Canal Zone influence. On the other, peculiarly, it would have been more compatible with Burnham's City Beautiful tenets to next visually terminate the now topographically aligned axis with a monumental edifice—as with, for instance, the SPC's Lincoln Memorial axial focus. Olmsted's somewhat surprising advice, however, suggests another, more timely informant: Walter Burley Griffin's prize-winning Canberra design. Axial alignments that were not only topographically dictated but also—unusually, if not uniquely—focused on terminal landforms were core to the Chicagoan's layout. Equally central to his competition success, Griffin's plan was also distinguished, like Balboa's layout, by its harmonious fusion of the inner city's regular geometry with the picturesque, curvilinear plans of its contour-hugging, peripheral suburbs.[67] Griffin's victory, seen by many as an international endorsement of American city planning expertise, had already triggered media sensation. The *New York Times,* for instance, devoted an entire page to overviewing his plan (based on an interview with its unknown author) the previous year, published beneath the banner "American Designs Splendid New Capital for Australia."[68] Along with interpretative accounts such as this (ones Lord also likely did not miss), Olmsted had by now made direct contact with an indisputably authoritative knowledge source: Griffin himself.

In mid-January 1913, Olmsted attended Griffin's "Plans for a Capital City for Australia" dinner lecture at the New York annual meeting of the American Society of Landscape Architects. Some thirty leading landscape architects of the day joined the CFA's vice-chairman to listen to the Chicagoan.[69] Given the evening's social dimension, together with the audience's modest numbers, it is very likely that Olmsted and Griffin not only met personally but that the two landscape architects had also more than a passing opportunity for conversation. Complementing Griffin's firsthand analytical account, face-to-face communication would have given Olmsted far more than a superficial understanding of Canberra's layout. Conversely, it is difficult to imagine Olmsted remaining silent on his imminent Panamanian mission. Griffin was, as we have learned, already aware of and actively interested in the CFA's canal involvement. Canberra freshly ensconced in his ken, Olmsted sailed to Panama only three weeks later.

Balboa's Architecture

Akin to Baguio's demographic, Balboa was to be an American enclave, home to "white members of the [Canal's] operating force" (figure 8.5).[70] This negated, as it had for Burnham at the Philippine summer capital, Lord's need

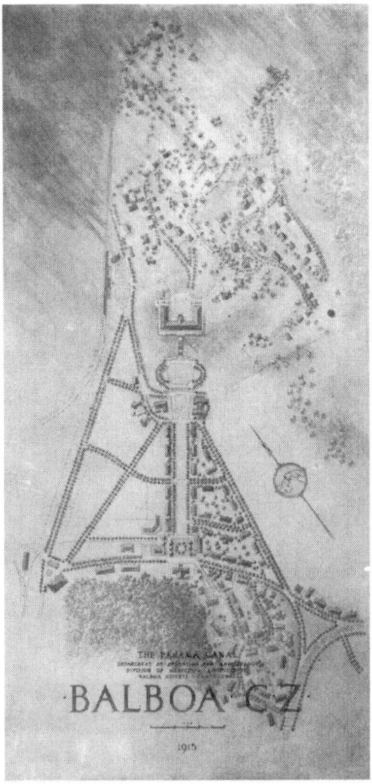

Figure 8.5. Plan rendering of "Balboa CZ," 1915. Panama Canal Authority Library, Biblioteca Roberto F. Chiari.

for a highly legible imperial idiom. Secure in his knowledge of the United States' perpetual isthmus occupation, he attempted to visually "naturalize" or "indigenize" its presence. Indeed, this rationale also likely motivated officialdom's decision to name the town after a Spanish explorer and endorse its parkland heart's Spanish appellation. Eschewing Greco-Roman antiquity, Lord now drew on Latin precedents. The outcome of his maiden Canal Zone visit a year earlier, he believed Balboa's architecture must embody a uniform "style, probably a modification of the Spanish renaissance, with appropriate adaptation of adjacent landscape."[71] The architect's new Panamanian aim to imbue the raw American presence with an enduring, timeless patina of antiquity, that is, permanence, accelerated his instinctive impulse to look backward, in excess of his core historicist sensibilities.

Nonetheless, Panama's intense, unforgiving tropical heat, torrential rains, and stifling humidity soon frustrated his efforts to concoct an architectural hybrid. This compelled him to rethink his decision. "Contrary to general opinion," Lord backpedaled; he had found it "impossible to adopt the type of architecture of southern climes—particularly of Mexico." Unlike its northern neighbor, as Olmsted had alerted him, Panama's rainfall was so great that all of Balboa's buildings would require "colonnaded fronts and connecting colonnades" so as to provide "a continuous covered way from one end of the street to the other."[72] This "confrontation with tropical weather and topography" demanded Lord identify a new reference point. Withdrawing into comfortable neoclassical territory, he opted instead to distill Balboa's architectural language from the "style" of "Italian design," later reported as an adaptation of the "Renaissance of the Fifteenth Century in Italy to modern building conditions and materials and local requirements."[73] This alternative source yielded "thick, light-colored, concrete-walled structures." And, although evocative of a "generalized classical origin," the buildings' "white stucco covering and [dark red clay] tile roofs [nonetheless] evince a Latin American influence."[74]

There was one eminent, symbolically illuminating exception to Balboa's otherwise ubiquitous Latin American idiom, albeit designed by fellow American architect Homer E. Bartlett, not Lord: Panama City's new railroad station (1912; figure 8.6). Although beyond Balboa's limits, the land upon which the building was erected was owned by the American government's Panama Railroad Company, making it part of the Canal Zone.[75] Akin to Burnham's awe-inspiring Union Station at America's capital, Bartlett likewise envisioned his monolithic edifice as the ceremonious Pacific entry portal to Balboa and the Canal Zone beyond. Constructed to "give permanency, even against the ravages of a tropical climate," the passenger terminal also accommodated the railroad's administrative offices and employee domiciles.[76] As the building's audience was by no means exclusively American, Bartlett referenced not Latin but overtly imperial Greco-Roman sources.[77] The degree to which he, MIT-educated like Lord, was aware of his colleague's Balboa enterprise is uncertain, although Bartlett could hardly have been oblivious to it.[78] Of no less symbolic gravitas, Bartlett embellished the edifice with a forecourt tropical garden, known as the Plaza Cinco de Mayo (Plaza Fifth of May)—which before the station's construction had been an undeveloped tract. Along with amplifying the terminal's civic grandiosity within its Franco-Spanish urban envelope, the

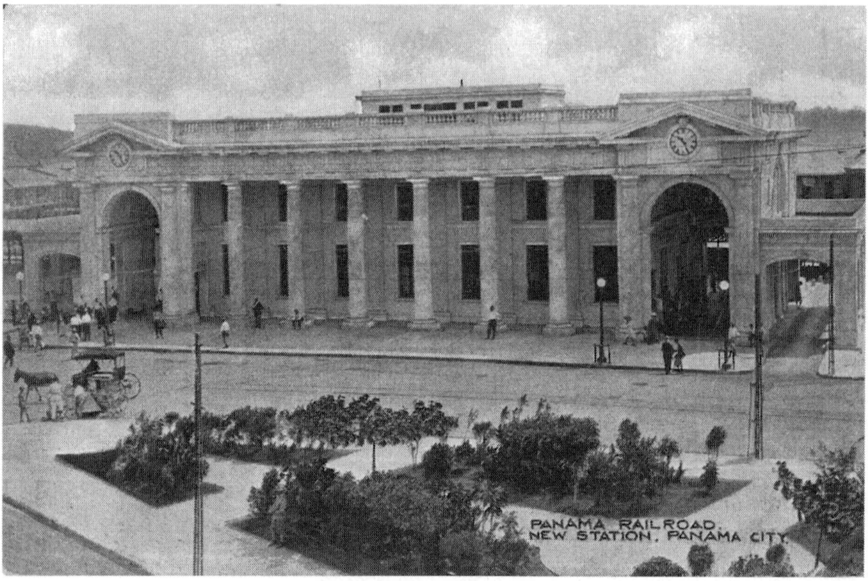

Figure 8.6. New railway station at Panama City, c. 1913. Author's collection.

garden also veiled and "indigenized" America's Panamanian presence.[79] The use of tropical vegetation to this end, as we will discover, would become commonplace throughout the Canal Zone.

The imperialistic ethos that underpinned the design of Panama City's new railroad hub did not go unrecognized by at least one popular magazine. When reviewing it, *Travel* identified that the station, curiously, featured a pair of vestibules, not just one. One vestibule, it innocuously explained, was "reserved for first class passengers [i.e., Americans]," and another for "second class.... Uncle Sam, on his one very own government railroad," the editor surmised, "does not hesitate to divide his passengers into classes.... It would be interesting to see" if Uncle Sam, the writer changed tack and speculated wryly, "would permit such a step on the part of any of the privately owned railroads within his boundaries."[80]

Balboa's Landscape Architecture

Into the Panama Canal's "making," acclaimed travel writer Paul Theroux astutely discerned, went "all the energies of America, all her genius and all her deceits."[81] One of these deceits was the calculated deployment of tropical nature. With Balboa's town plan adopted, the Isthmian Canal Commission now sought a landscape architect to orchestrate its implementation. At Olmsted's recommendation, it hired his former Harvard student and employee William Lyman Phillips.[82] Arriving at the Canal Zone in 1913, Phillips was instructed to "fine tune" Lord's layout.[83] Like the Olmsteds before him, he grew quickly enchanted with tropical vegetation and valued its use as a device, analogous to Lord's architectural strategy, to "indigenize" America's imperial presence.[84] The landscape architect, like his architect predecessor, thought Latin sources richly fertile in design potential. After scrutinizing the Canal Zone's natural and cultural landscapes, Phillips esteemed the "charming plazas, parks, and squares built by the Spanish and French" and aimed to shape Balboa in their image. "He may have been the only man on the isthmus," his biographer contended, "who understood the importance of making a visually harmonious tropical town, which would reflect the rhythm and style of life in Central America."[85] This was, however, hagiographical overstatement. Olmsted and Lord were no less aware of the value of tropical harmony, from both aesthetic and imperialistic stances. And, in the end, "Zonians," as American residents identified themselves, also grew to appreciate "their lush tropical environment" and "from hell on earth" made Panama "a paradise."[86]

Although not explicitly envisioned as such, Balboa came to function as the Canal Zone's "capital." And, through its architecture and urbanism, the town cast the zone's die as American. This default "capital," as Richard Guy

Wilson—the first scholar to consider the Canal Zone as an American imperialistic expression—diagnosed, with its "alignment of buildings, sequence of squares and tree-lined central axis with the raised focal point of the Administration Building," recalls "most especially the Mall from the McMillan [SPC] Plan for Washington, DC, and ultimately the Court of Honor at the World's Columbian Exposition of 1893." He concluded, "It personifies power."[87] Rather than existing in perpetuity, however, the United States' Canal Zone tenure proved ephemeral. In 1979, just short of seventy years after Balboa's completion, it relinquished the zone to the Republic of Panama. The handover was for some wistful, resonant of Britain's even briefer occupation of imperial Delhi. Predicated upon American permanency, the Canal Zone's former "capital" now became symbolically ambivalent, if not redundant.[88]

Notes

1. Arthur Bartlett Maurice, "The Washington of the Future," *New Country Life* 34, no. 5 (September 1918): 47; and Michael T. Klare, "The Architecture of Imperial America," *Science & Society* 33, no. 3 (Summer / Fall 1969): 278.

2. Charles Moore, ed., *The Improvement of the Park System of the District of Columbia* (United States Senate Report no. 166, 57th Congress, 1st Session) (Washington, DC: Government Printing Office, 1902), 8–9; and Jon A. Peterson, "The Senate Park Commission Plan for Washington, DC: A New Vision for the Capital and the Nation," in *Designing the Nation's Capital: The 1901 Plan for Washington, DC,* ed. Sue Koehler and Pamela Scott (Washington, DC: US Commission of Fine Arts, 2006), 1–48.

3. See Therese O'Malley, "'A Public Museum of Trees': Mid-Nineteenth Century Plans for the Mall," in *The Mall in Washington, 1791–1991,* ed. Richard Longstreth (Washington, DC: National Gallery of Art, 1991), 37–58; see also Andrew Jackson Downing's "Plan Showing Proposed Method of Laying Out the Public Grounds [the Mall] at Washington," Library of Congress, accessed January 12, 2018, http://www.loc.gov.

4. Charles Dickens, *American Notes for General Circulation* (Paris: A. and W. Galignani, 1842), 146.

5. Moore, *Improvement of the Park System,* 12.

6. Don Alexander Hawkins, "The Landscape of the Federal City: A 1792 Walking Tour," *Washington History* 3, no. 1 (Spring / Summer 1991): 11; see also Pamela Scott, "'This Vast Empire': The Iconography of the Mall, 1791–1848," in *The Mall in Washington, 1791–1991,* ed. Richard Longstreth (Washington, DC: National Gallery of Art, 1991), 37.

7. Pamela Scott, "L'Enfant's Washington Described: The City in the Public Press, 1791–1795," *Washington History* 3, no. 1 (Spring / Summer 1991): 103.

8. Thomas S. Hines, "The Imperial Mall: The City Beautiful Movement and the Washington Plan of 1901–1902," in *The Mall in Washington, 1791–1991,* ed. Richard Longstreth (Washington, DC: National Gallery of Art, 1991), 85.

9. J. P. Dougherty, "Baroque and Picturesque Motifs in L'Enfant's Design for the Federal Capital," *American Quarterly* 26, no. 1 (March 1974): 33.

10. Moore, *Improvement of the Park System,* 50.

11. Hines, "Imperial Mall," 96.

12. Dougherty, "Baroque and Picturesque Motifs," 36.

13. "Plan Queen City for the Far East: Uncle Sam Commissions Architect Burnham of Chicago to Make Manila the Gem of the Orient: Plan a Summer Capital: Spot in Mountains to Be Made the Philippine Simla," *Chicago Daily Tribune,* September 18, 1904, 1.

14. Edward Clark Whiting and William Lyman Phillips, "Frederick Law Olmsted—1870–1957: An Appreciation of the Man and His Achievements," *Landscape Architecture* 48, no. 3 (April 1958): 144–157.

15. Olmsted did not turn down the post immediately. Before doing so, he went so far as to secure "maps and surveys" of Baguio's site. Robert R. Reed, *City of Pines: The Origins of Baguio as a Colonial Hill Station and Regional Capital,* 2nd ed. (Baguio City, Philippines: A-Seven, 1999), 99. Writing to Harvard in the 1940s, Olmsted reflected, "I have often kicked myself for having been unable to accept Secretary Taft's offer to professional employment in the Philippines in the early 1900s." I am grateful to Olmsted's biographer, Elizabeth Hope Cushing, for alerting me to this reference. Elizabeth Hope Cushing, e-mail message to the author, March 27, 2013.

16. See Scott Kirsch, "Aesthetic Regime Change: The Burnham Plans and US Landscape Imperialism in the Philippines," *Philippine Studies: Historical and Ethnographic Viewpoints* 65, no. 3 (September 2017): 315–356.

17. Quoted in Charles Moore, *Daniel H. Burnham: Architect, Planner of Cities,* (Boston, MA: Houghton Mifflin, 1921), 2:169.

18. "Personal," *Construction News* 18, no. 13 (September 24, 1904): 218.

19. On Burnham's Philippine appointment, see, for instance, Thomas S. Hines, *Burnham of Chicago: Architect and Planner* (Chicago, IL: University of Chicago Press, 1979); and Moore, *Daniel H. Burnham,* 1:232–245.

20. Moore, *Daniel H. Burnham,* 1:245.

21. Nancy Leys Stepan, *Picturing Tropical Nature* (Ithaca, NY: Cornell University Press, 2001).

22. Daniel Hudson Burnham and Peirce Anderson, "Report on Proposed Improvements at Manila," in *Sixth Annual Report of the Philippine Commission 1905 (Part 1)* (Washington, DC: Government Printing Office, 1906), 635, 629.

23. Frederick Law Olmsted, "A Report upon the Landscape Architecture of the Columbian Exposition to the American Institute of Architects," *American Architect and Building News* 41, no. 924 (September 9, 1893): 151–154.

24. David Schuyler, "Frederick Law Olmsted and the World's Columbian Exposition," *Journal of Planning History* 15, no. 1 (February 2016): 3–28.

25. Charles E. Beveridge, "Frederick Law Olmsted's Theory of Landscape Design," *Nineteenth Century* 3, no. 2 (Summer 1977): 43.

26. Frederick Law Olmsted, "The Esthetic Value of Tropical Scenery," *Landscape Architecture* 5, no. 3 (April 1915): 124.

27. On June 1, 1903, the Philippine Commission resolved to make Baguio "the summer capital of the Archipelago and to construct suitable buildings, to secure suitable transportation, to secure proper water supply, and to make residence in Baguio possible for all the officers and employees of the Insular Government for four months during the year." *Second Annual Report of the Philippine Civil Service Board to the Civil Governor of the Philippine Islands* (Manila: Bureau of Public Printing, 1903), 62.

For an excellent discussion of those US infrastructural projects in Baguio, particularly the twenty-six-mile highway, first called Benguet then Kennon, that connected the lowland to the US mountain city, see Rebecca Tinio McKenna, *American Imperial Pastoral: The*

Architecture of US Colonialism in the Philippines (Chicago, IL: University of Chicago Press, 2017), 49–75.

28. "Plan Queen City," 1.

29. "A Philippine Paradise: Climate as Equable as Hawaii and as Bracing as the Adirondacks," *Evening Star* (Washington, DC), July 4, 1903, 15.

30. "To Abandon Manila as Capital of Philippine Islands," *Evening Republican* (Meadville, PA), April 11, 1904, 1.

31. "Philippine Commission Will Move the Capital," *Washington (DC) Times,* April 9, 1904, 3.

32. "Plan Queen City," 1.

33. Kirsch, "Aesthetic Regime Change," 347.

34. Reed, *City of Pines,* 97.

35. William E. Parsons, "Burnham as a Pioneer in City Planning," *Architectural Record* 38, no. 1 (July 1915): 25, 26.

36. Daniel Hudson Burnham and Peirce Anderson, "Preliminary Plan of Baguio, Province of Benguet, P.I.," in *Sixth Annual Report of the Philippine Commission (Part 3)* (Washington, DC: Government Printing Office, 1906), 405.

37. Daniel Hudson Burnham and Peirce Anderson, "Report on the Proposed Plan of the City of Baguio, Province of Benguet, P.I.," in Glenn Brown (ed.) *Proceedings of the Thirty-Eighth Annual Convention of the American Institute of Architects* (Washington, DC: Press of Gibson Brothers, 1905), 153, 155.

38. "The New Manila: What the Government Is Doing to Beautify the Capital of the Philippines," *Century Magazine* 83, no. 2 (December 1911): 248.

39. Ron Robin, *Enclaves of America: The Rhetoric of American Political Architecture Abroad, 1900–1965* (Princeton, NJ: Princeton University Press, 1992), 25.

40. Monroe Woolley, "Baguio, Simla of the Philippines," *Overland Monthly* 62, no. 3 (September 1913): 295.

41. Moore, *Daniel H. Burnham,* 1:245.

42. See "The West Point Plan" in Moore, *Daniel H. Burnham,* 1:189–196; and Mario Manieri-Elia, "Toward an 'Imperial City': Daniel H. Burnham and the City Beautiful Movement," in Giogio Ciucci, Francesco Dal Co, Mario Manieri-Elia, and Manfredo Tafuri, *The American City: From the Civil War to the New Deal* (Cambridge, MA: MIT Press, 1979), 78–80. On the competition, also see "Military Topics," *Los Angeles Times,* January 18, 1903), 36. Cram, Goodhue & Ferguson won the contest. "Boston Architects' Plans Adopted for West Point," *Boston Post,* June 1, 1903, 5.

43. Daniel H. Burnham, "A Competitive Design for the Improvements at the U. S. Military Academy, West Point, N. Y.," *American Architect and Building News* 81, no. 1447 (September 19, 1903): 95; emphasis added.

44. William Cameron Forbes, *The Philippine Islands,* vol. 1 (Boston, MA: Houghton Mifflin Company, 1928), 580.

45. "There were not lacking thoughtful Filipinos who felt, as did General Aguinaldo, that Baguio ought ultimately to be the permanent capital of the Islands." Ibid., 583.

46. It is unclear as to just when the "park around the lake" was "appropriately named for Mr. Burnham." We do know that this American commemorative gesture had taken place by 1928.

47. On Burnham Park and its bust, see David Brody, *Visualizing American Empire: Orientalism and Imperialism in the Philippines* (Chicago, IL: University of Chicago Press, 2010), 160–163.

48. Ibid., 162.

49. "Message of the President of the United States Communicated to the Two Houses of Congress, at the Beginning of the First Session of the Fifty-Seventh Congress," December 3 1901, accessed January 19, 2018, http://www.theodore-roosevelt.com.

50. See David McCullough's magisterial, classic reference *The Path between the Seas: The Creation of the Panama Canal, 1870–1914* (New York: Simon and Schuster, 1977).

51. Sue Koehler, "The Commission of Fine Arts: Implementing the Senate Park Commission's Vision," in *Designing the Nation's Capital: The 1901 Plan for Washington, DC,* ed. Sue Koehler and Pamela Scott (Washington, DC: US Commission of Fine Arts, 2006), 245–273.

52. The CFA replaced Millet with painter Edwin H. Blashfield.

53. William H. Taft, "Daniel Hudson Burnham: An Appreciation," *Architectural Record* 32, no. 2 (August 1912): 184.

54. "A Federal Appointment," *Architectural Record* 32, no. 5 (November 1912): 479.

55. No less poignantly, Anderson, when appointed, was then "on the Atlantic Ocean returning from Europe with the ashes of the body of Mr. Burnham, which was cremated at Heidelberg." "Peirce Anderson Named by Taft," *Washington Herald,* July 4, 1912, 3.

56. Francis G. Newlands, "Art Control of the Panama Canal," *Architect and Engineer of California* 30, no. 1 (August 1912): 104.

57. US Commission of Fine Arts, *Panama Canal: Message from the President of the United States transmitting a Report by the Commission of Fine Arts in Relation to the Artistic Structure of the Panama Canal,* US Senate Document no. 146, 63rd Congress, 1st Session (Washington, DC: Government Printing Office, 1913), 5.

58. Walter Burley Griffin, "Architecture at Panama," *Concrete-Cement Age* 1, no. 5 (November 1912): 64. Griffin was responding to the magazine's September 1912 editorial "Architecture at Panama."

59. French and Olmsted "sailed from New York for Colon on February 4, 1913." US Commission of Fine Arts, *Panama Canal,* 5. They were to arrive "on or about February 12." "Commission of Fine Arts," *Canal Record* 6, no. 24 (February 5, 1913): 195. Curiously, this source reported that commission members "E[dwin]. H. Blashfield," "Charles Moore," and "A[rno]. B. C. Cammerer" were also to be among the party. Whether or not these three actually made the trip is unclear.

60. Lord's assistant Mario Schiavoni also accompanied the party. On Lord, see Carol McMichael Reese and Thomas F. Reese, "The Architectural Image of Modern Industry in the Canal Zone: Architect Austin Willard Lord," in *The Panama Canal and Its Architectural Legacy, 1905–1920* (Panama City: Fundación Ciudad del Saber, Autoridad del Canal de Panamá and Fundación Arte y Cultura, 2013), 171–175, 180.

61. J. C. L., "As He Is Known, Being Brief Sketches of Contemporary Members of the Architectural Profession: Austin W. Lord," *Brickbuilder* 25, no. 1 (January 1916): 23. Also instructive is Austin W. Lord, "The Significance of Rome to the American Architectural Student," *American Architect and Building News* 82, no. 1454 (November 7, 1903): 43–45.

62. See Austin W. Lord, Albert Kelsey, Charles N. Lowrie, Charles Mulford Robinson, and H. A. McNeil, *The Plan of the City of Columbus* (Columbus, OH: Plan Commission, 1908). Earlier, Lord's submission to "The International Competition for the Phoebe Hearst Architectural Plan for the University of California" placed fifth in the contest. See, for instance, H. S. Allen, "The Phebe [*sic*] Hearst Architectural Competition for the University of California," *American Monthly Review of Reviews* 20, no. 4 (October 1899): 433–441.

63. US Commission of Fine Arts, *Panama Canal,* 12.

64. On Balboa's plan, see Lord's own account, "Architecture on the Isthmus of Panama," *Architecture: The Professional Architectural Monthly* 29, no. 5 (May 1914): 98–114. Also see US Commission of Fine Arts, *Panama Canal,* 12–14; Reese and Reese, *Panama Canal,* 186–189; and Richard Guy Wilson, "Imperial American Identity at the Panama Canal," *Modulus 1980–81: The University of Virginia School of Architecture Review* (Charlottesville: University of Virginia, 1981), 22–29.

65. "The Artistic Side of the Panama Canal," *Fort Wayne (IN) Weekly Journal-Gazette,* October 16, 1913, 10.

66. US Commission of Fine Arts, *Panama Canal,* 12.

67. With respect to Balboa's fusion of the picturesque with regular geometry, Carol McMichael Reese and Thomas F. Reese write, "In contrast to the more formal, Beaux-Arts inspired planning and design that he [Olmsted] and Lord deemed proper for the Prado, he proposed a picturesque approach to landscape planning for the residential districts"; Reese and Reese, *Panama Canal,* 188. For an overview of Griffin's design, see for instance, Christopher Vernon, "Canberra: Where Landscape Is Pre-eminent," in *Planning Twentieth Century Capital Cities,* ed. David L. A. Gordon (London: Routledge, 2006), 130–149.

68. "American Designs Splendid New Capital for Australia: City Twenty-Five Miles Square to Be Built upon What Is Now a Wilderness," *New York Times,* June 2, 1912, 39.

69. Griffin delivered the lecture on January 14, 1913; Olmsted departed for Panama on February 4. Olmsted's (and the others') attendance is recorded in Carl Rust Parker, Bremer W. Pond, and Theodora Kimball, eds., *Transactions of the American Society of Landscape Architects, 1909–1921* (Amsterdam, NY: Recorder Press, 1922), 27–28.

70. Regarding the differences between the colonial ventures of the Philippines and Panama, especially how the Panama Canal attracted far more attention from US audiences, see Alexander Missal, "Ideal Community: The Canal Zone as an American Utopia," in *Seaway to the Future: American Social Visions and the Construction of the Panama Canal* (Madison: University of Wisconsin Press, 2008), 146.

71. "Permanent Buildings for the Canal Zone," *Pan-American Magazine* 14, no. 5 (May 1912): 73.

72. Austin W. Lord, "Architecture on the Isthmus of Panama," *Architecture: The Professional Architectural Monthly* 29, no. 5 (May 1914): 101, 114.

73. "Permanent Buildings: Architects for the Commission Preparing Plans in Uniform Style," *Canal Record* 6, no. 43 (June 18, 1913): 361; and "Canal Office Building," *Canal Record* 8, no. 19 (December 30, 1914): 181.

74. R. G. Wilson, "Imperial American Identity," 26.

75. Eduardo Tejeira-Davis, *Panamá: An Architectural and Landscape Guide* (Seville, Spain: Junta de Andalucía, 2007), 249–250.

76. Edward Hungerford, "Progress in Transportation: Panama's Remarkable Terminal," *Travel* 23, no. 5 (September 1914): 37.

77. One account, probably written in consultation with Bartlett, explained that the terminal "is a free adaptation of the stucco architecture of Pilladio [*sic*] as found, for example, in Vicenza and nearby cities of north-eastern Italy"; "New Station in Panama: Modern Structure Designed in Accord with Local Operating Conditions," *Canal Record* 7, no. 36 (April 29, 1914): 340. Also see "New Station at Panama: Plans for Improvement of Railroad Terminal Have Been Approved," *Canal Record* 5, no. 41 (5 June 1912): 329–330; and "New Station in Panama," *Railway World* 58, no. 5 (May 1914): 397–399.

78. See "Alumni Notes," *Technology Architectural Record* 6, no. 2 (March 1913): 43.

79. On Panama City's Franco-Spanish architecture, see Eduardo Tejeira-Davis, "The

Architecture of the Panama Canal: Colonialism, Syncretism and Coming to Terms with the Tropics," in *Tropical Architecture: Critical Regionalism in the Age of Globalization,* ed. Alexander Tzonis, Liane Lefaivre, and Bruno Stagno (Chichester, UK: Wiley-Academy, 2001), 155–158.

80. Hungerford, "Progress in Transportation," 37.

81. Paul Theroux, *The Old Patagonian Express: By Train through the Americas* (Boston, MA: Houghton Mifflin, 1979), 219.

82. Faith Reyher Jackson, "Balboa, Canal Zone," in *Pioneer of Tropical Landscape Architecture: William Lyman Phillips in Florida* (Gainesville: University Press of Florida, 1997), 27–45; and Reese and Reese, *Panama Canal,* 191–193, 194–196, and 198–203. Also see Phillips' autobiographical account "William Lyman Phillips" in *Secretary's Second Report: Harvard College Class of 1908* (Cambridge, MA: Harvard College, 1914), 252.

83. "Personal," *Canal Record* 6, no. 40 (May 28, 1913): 335; "Official Circulars: Duties of Landscape Architect," *Canal Record* 6, no. 50 (August 6, 1913): 427; and "Balboa Town Site" in *Annual Report of the Isthmian Canal Commission and the Panama Canal for the Fiscal Year Ended June 30, 1914* (Washington, DC: Government Printing Office, 1914), 223–225.

84. W. L. Phillips, "Decorative Trees and Plants for Permanent Townsites," *Canal Record* 7, no. 21 (January 14, 1914): 200.

85. Jackson, "Balboa, Canal Zone," 35.

86. Eduardo Tejeira-Davis, "Architecture of the Panama Canal," 161.

87. R. G. Wilson, "Imperial American Identity," 26.

88. For a haunting, ethereal photographic essay on the post-American Canal Zone, see Matías Costa, *Zonians* (Madrid: La Fábrica, 2015). Within this context, also see Bjørn Berge, "The Canal Zone: A Siberia in the Caribbean," in *Nowherelands: An Atlas of Vanished Countries 1840–1975* (London: Thames & Hudson, 2017), 116–119.

Part III

Negotiating Paradise

Design, Environment, and Identity in the Modern Era

NINE

Havana's Early Modern Hotels
Accommodating Colonialism, Independence, and Imperialism

Erica Morawski

In 1941, Fox released the musical film *Weekend in Havana*. Starring Alice Faye, Carmen Miranda, John Payne, and Cesar Romero, the production offers a rather representative view of images of Cuba, Cubans, and tourism that were constructed in the US popular imagination during the first sixty years of the twentieth century.[1] Not only does the film incorporate characteristics of Cuban tourism that were common by the 1940s—such as differentiated tourism for varying socioeconomic classes, unaccompanied female travelers, and a highly developed tourist infrastructure—but it also reinforces many of the stereotypes that made Cuba popular, namely its reputation as an anything-goes destination. The plot revolves around Macy's shop girl Nan Spencer (Alice Faye), who finds herself on the finest vacation in Havana that money can buy to compensate for a grounded steamship ruining her more economical travel plans. Predictably, Nan's desire for adventure, exoticism, and romance are satiated by her vacation in Havana. But how did this plotline become so commonplace as to be represented in Hollywood film and so easily comprehended by a popular US viewing audience? The answers are complex and are partly due to shifts in the built landscape that accommodated a growing mass tourism to this Caribbean island, a tourism that was largely born of and based upon US imperialistic visions of maintaining Cuba as a subjugated nation that existed for the pleasure and profit of the United States.

While the interactions between the US and Cuban characters largely drive the plot of *Weekend in Havana,* set design and reference to location are pivotal in reinforcing US understandings of vacationing in this Caribbean locale and in justifying the characters' actions. A montage of famous locales and monuments in Havana serves as a segue between Nan's departure from the United States and her arrival at her Havana hotel room, effectively orienting the viewer to Havana's built landscape and providing a contextual "flavor" of the location to inform the viewer throughout the film. Many of these locations are never visited by characters in the film, and it is Nan's hotel that serves as one of the recurring settings. While the hotel goes unnamed, viewers are probably meant to understand that Nan stays at the Hotel Nacional de Cuba, which at the time was widely considered the finest hotel in Cuba. It presumably goes unnamed because the hotel portrayed in the movie is an amalgamation of different sets and locations. Nan's view of the Capitolio from her room is an impossible vista from the Hotel Nacional and probably realized by placing a painted screen outside of the window.[2] In addition, the lobby is in an art deco style, and is most likely a Hollywood set. Although one could easily dismiss this as an inauthentic pastiche, I would argue that it is a useful technique for succinctly conveying a certain idea of place. Nan's view from her hotel reveals a city of impressive architecture, the lobby conveys the modern nature of the city, and the sumptuous hotel rooms convey the luxurious experience possible in Havana.

Nan's experiences parallel real—and ideal—tourist experiences that had been in the making for the previous forty-plus years. The hotel, I contend, has played a significant yet understudied role in shaping these experiences. While there are many scenes of Nan taking in the sights of the city and visiting casinos, restaurants, and cafes, we often are brought back to scenes of Nan in her hotel room or in the hotel lobby. For foreign tourists, the hotel ideally needs to be inviting by speaking to the familiar and comfortable so as to serve as a home away from home. At the same time, many hotels suggested something of the local culture or society, or at least some construction of it, that owners or designers thought would appeal to the targeted clientele. Therefore, this type of hotel—the foreign tourist hotel—strives to achieve a balance between the familiar and comfortable, and the exotic and exciting.

The foreign tourist hotel developed in Havana as mass tourism and US imperial influence took hold in Cuba. This chapter considers this Cuban history, from colony through transition to a republic heavily shaped by US imperial interests and force, as it intersects with the shift in modern hotels from public civic spaces to more private spaces of consumption. The result of these overlapping historical trajectories is a movement in hotels from accessible (although by no means egalitarian) spaces for local Cubans and visitors alike to exclusive spaces restricted to paying US tourists. The shift was the result of changes to the way hotels were conceived, designed, and used, combined with changing geopolitical situations in which Cuban corruption and US interference triumphed. This chapter focuses on two hotels, the Hotel Inglaterra and the Hotel Sevilla-Biltmore, that were integral to this change because of their protracted social and design histories.

Architecture of Accommodation

Hotel design wields influence in shaping a certain experience or setting and thus plays a significant role in shaping tourists' understanding of the foreign environment. As spaces of tourism, they also inform the locals' understanding of the foreigners who visit their city and the manner in which their nation is represented to visitors. However, hotel designs do not impose a monolithic message; the many people who interact with them have the agency to interpret and negotiate them in various and sometimes quite contradictory ways. Business entities (both Cuban and US) and governments that were involved in the hotels covered in this study understood the importance of hotel design as a means to convey a certain image, the attractiveness of this image being directly related to the potential for profit.

To trace this change in hotels from public to exclusive spaces—a shift that was both shaped by outside forces and exerted influence on changes in society—I employ a framework that revolves around the concept of "accommodation." In thinking about how hotels function, we can explore the hotel as an architecture of accommodation according to the multiple definitions of the word. Most obviously, hotels adhere to the definition of "accommodation" as living spaces or lodgings for people, especially with regard to sleeping, seating, or entertainment, but we can also interrogate hotels through other definitions of the term. Hotels are an architecture of accommodation in that they can be studied in terms of the way they offer a convenient arrangement, settlement, or compromise. For example, a significant amount of hotel design in the tropical zone makes compromises in its depiction of a more accurate representation of contemporary local culture in order to present visitors with some of the stereotypes they desire. "Accommodation" also means the process of adapting or adjusting to some person or thing. In this sense of the word, for example, we can talk about tourists' accommodation of their behaviors and opinions in accordance to what the hotel design presents to them. This can take many forms, from adapting to different sleeping and living configurations to altering one's perspective of local culture based on artworks in the hotel lobby. Therefore, it is through the lens of accommodation that we can better understand how these buildings are not just receptacles for a complexity of meaning but are also dynamic spaces where new and diverse meanings can be created and changed at different moments in time, thanks to a framework that accounts for the visual, operational, and experiential. In other words, this framework supports a more cohesive consideration of such factors as hotels' negotiation as building projects, the form they take, their visual appearance, their systems and practices of operation and management, and their use by heterogenous bodies of tourists and locals.

The Modern Hotel Finds a Home in Havana

As a specific building typology, the modern hotel has its origins in the 1820s, according to scholars such as Molly W. Berger and A. K. Sandoval-Strausz.[3] It was at this time, Berger contends, that "characteristics and form emerged as the product of a deliberate design and, as a result, became radically distinct from hotels that had existed before."[4] Employing the most modern technologies as a means to ensure the satisfaction of large numbers of guests, the modern hotel was known as a machine of efficiency. The specific technologies these hotels incorporated changed over the long arc of the modern hotel's evolution from the nineteenth into the twentieth century, but hotels were consistently some of the first spaces where new technologies were integrated and employed. Some examples of these technologies included running water, bathrooms, machines to aid in laundering, equipment for cooking and cleaning on a large scale, and gas and then electric lighting systems. Also integral to the definition of the modern hotel was attention to cleanliness, privacy, and social propriety. Moreover, the development of this building typology was overwhelmingly associated with the United States, and in the twentieth century, the modern hotel was referred to as the "American hotel," nomenclature that indicated the type of hotel no matter the location.

In structure, space, and operation, modern hotels were most associated with urban areas. They first took hold in cities because they relied on water and sewage infrastructure, gas and later electricity, and other utilities, services, and systems that initially developed in urban areas. Marked by the comings and goings of large numbers of people who needed temporary lodging, cities provided modern hotels with the steady flow of guests upon which they relied. This hotel typology quickly moved outside of urban areas as destination tourism to more remote locations became increasingly accessible and popular in the nineteenth century, largely thanks to technologies of transportation, such as the railroad and steamships, and, as it relates to the United States, its imperial inclination to conquer areas that are now part of the mainland United States.[5]

Despite being credited as a US invention, modern hotels were almost simultaneously erected in other significant urban areas in the Americas. Moreover, it was not uncommon for the most modern advances in lodging to be implemented immediately in the outposts of empire—it made foreign spaces more comfortable for US visitors while also serving as a reassuring symbol of imperial dominance. The earliest modern hotels in Cuba, Havana's Hotel Pasaje and Hotel Perla de Cuba, date to the 1830s, or possibly earlier, and boast designs, amenities, and systems similar to those found in US modern hotels. The emergence of these hotels signal a moment in which Havana offered the urban infrastructure, capital, and sufficient number of travelers to support them. Many US, European, and Cuban travelers who visited Havana in the early nineteenth century and earlier lodged in *casas de huéspedes,* or guesthouses, which were residential buildings with a number of rooms available for rent.[6] While at times their name bore the word "hotel," such as Hotel West's, they were more akin to boarding houses than to modern hotels.[7]

Casas de huéspedes often had a more homelike atmosphere. Many were even in structures that were originally built as domestic spaces. Thus, it was quite easy for these to be located within the residence-rich urban zone of the walled *centro* of Havana. It was not impossible to repurpose an extant building within the walled center so that it could function as a modern hotel. However, to create a truly grand, purpose-built modern hotel, entrepreneurs looked outside of the city walls. Not only was there more space, but this area, specifically near the Monserrate Gates, was a hub for people coming and going from the Villanueva Station, a neoclassical structure built in the 1830s to support the Cuban railroad, one of the earliest instances of railroad implementation in the world. This is significant because these early modern hotels were originally utilized not by destination tourists but by foreigners and Cubans moving between the urban capital and more rural areas of the island dedicated to agricultural production and resource extraction. Locations near train stations and other transportation centers allowed hotels and guesthouses to tap into the large number of travelers who were constantly moving through these areas.[8] Thus, these early modern hotels were key nodes in a colonial project characterized by productive rural areas that served to enrich the Spanish colonial power that operated out of the urban center of Havana. In short, they were fundamental sites and structures in supporting a colonial economy. By the nineteenth-century the colonial framework was not as straightforward; private owners, both *criollos* and *peninsulares,* appear as dominant figures in the system, but various forms of taxes ensured that the Spanish Crown profited significantly off of businesses located in its colonies.[9]

Hotel Inglaterra: From Colony to Independence

While there is a debate over whether the Hotel Perla de Cuba or the Hotel Telégrafo was the oldest hotel in Havana, documentation shows that both were operating in 1835.[10] Located between these two hotels and formed by incorporating the extant Escauriza Café into the new hotel structure, the Hotel Inglaterra was built almost twenty years after the earliest modern hotels appeared in Havana (figure 9.1). Hotel names reveal the practice of the time of referring to other geographies and the associations they carry. The hotel was situated within a city block commonly known as the Acera del Louvre

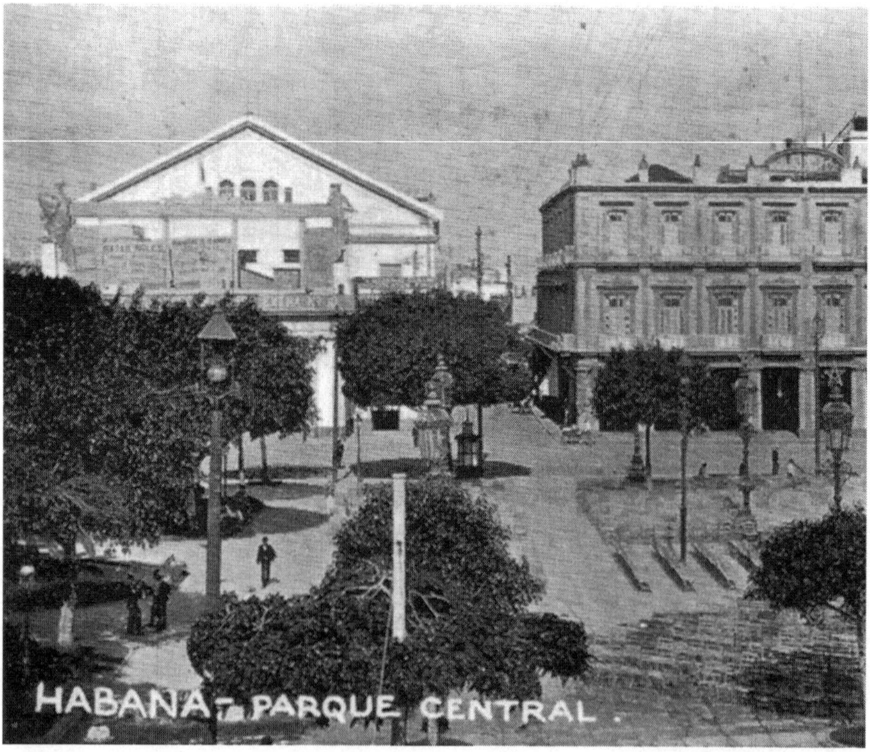

Figure 9.1. Postcard showing a view of the Parque Central with the Hotel Inglaterra on the right and the Teatro Tacón on the left, c. 1905–1930. Author's Collection.

(Sidewalk of the Louvre), which references a structure in Paris associated with the history and sophistication of royal France and the newer tradition of public museums. Likewise, the Inglaterra (England) drew upon the old-world stature of that European country, as well as its very modern condition and reputation as cradle of the Industrial Revolution at the time the hotel opened.[11] The names are important reminders of Havana's international character and cosmopolitan aspirations.

The Hotel Inglaterra was built in 1853, a moment that marked a period of rapid expansion and tumultuous transformation in the urban area in which it was located. The hotel was both a product of this change and a force in contributing to the expansion in this area. By looking beyond the moment of construction through the lens of accommodation, we can begin to unearth the complex relationships of the hotel and its visitors to the urban environment, and of the visitors to one another.

The owners of the Hotel Inglaterra recognized the importance of geographic location—in this case, this was the area known as Las Murallas (The Walls), so named for its location just outside and including the city fortifications. The walled area of the city was cramped and built up, and by the time the hotel was built, the city had long been expanding outside of the walls containing congested, narrow streets. The fashionable area of Paseo del Prado, where the social elite would promenade, was just outside of the Monserrate Gates to the north of the hotel.[12] Based on the European tradition of promenading, the Cuban practice focused especially around young unmarried females, who, according to Cuban custom, were prohibited from appearing in public except during the daily promenade. Appearing along Paseo del Prado in a two-wheeled carriage was considered a particularly stylish way to promenade. After the avenue was remodeled and expanded in 1834 under the government of Miguel Tacón, who endeavored to make Havana a symbol of urban modernity as a means to reinforce Spanish sovereignty during a period of revolution throughout Latin America, prominent buildings such as the Teatro Tacón (Tacón Theater) sprang up along this road, cementing its reputation as a place of cultural activity and entertainment.[13] The Hotel Inglaterra was located in the heart of this social and cultural activity.

On August 8, 1863, ten years after the Hotel Inglaterra opened, the demolition of the old city walls began.[14] The demolition, along with the reconfiguration of the area located in front of the hotel into the Parque Central (Central Park) in 1877, placed an emphasis on expanding city life in an orderly fashion in a way that was comparable to other modern projects carried out in such European centers as Vienna and Barcelona. Decorated with modern lighting and ornamentation from New York, the park was an impressive site to behold and became a central node in the urban landscape. One of the most desirable views of this popular new plaza was from one of the park-side rooms of the Hotel Inglaterra. The expansion of the city worked in the hotel's favor, and the hotel contributed to making this a fashionable part of the city.

Despite Tacón's attempt to solidify Cuba's standing as a Spanish colony through urban development, as well as the fact that the majority of the new urban spaces were built by men from Spain, architectural historian Jean-François Lejeune has documented how this new area of the city ultimately became associated with a proindependence spirit.[15] Many of the *criollos* were the successful businessmen and entrepreneurs responsible for the wealth and progress of Cuba. The new growth beyond the walls, such as the railroad station, factories, theaters and cafes, came to symbolize the power and accomplishments of the *criollos*. Given that the Hotel Inglaterra was in an area associated with criollo society, it is no surprise that it was a notable site in the long fight for Cuban independence.

Just as the urban area around the Hotel Inglaterra was continuously changing in form, so, too, did the hotel constantly adapt to the present moment through modifications in structure, amenities, and operations. Striving to maintain the hotel's reputation of excellence, the owners undertook continuous upgrades and renovations of the hotel, with significant expansions in 1891 and in 1915, which included the addition of a top floor. The hotel's design, both its visible design and invisible operational procedures and spaces, was of fundamental importance in providing guests with a positive experience. In terms of the unseen aspects of design, for example, the hotel had an unusual footprint on the city block that was adapted to fit into the space of surrounding buildings while still providing the service areas necessary to offer guests the amenities that garnered it a first-class ranking. The main block contained an original total of three floors, while the two secondary blocks, located to the back of the building, were of one and two stories. The secondary blocks, which were dedicated to such activities as cooking, dishwashing, laundering, and ice making, helped ensure that the restaurants, dining rooms, bars, stores, lecture halls, and lounge areas on the public first floor could operate smoothly.

The visible aspects of the hotel, in particular what might be called its decoration or ornamentation, presented a mixture of design elements that can be described as Moorish, Creole, and neoclassical. These should not be seen as a careless pastiche but rather as a strategy of accommodating many tastes and aims. For example, the 1915 remodel focused on providing the increasing number of US visitors with what they desired—comfort through modern amenities combined with an experience of the exotic. In this case, to create this interior effect, many of the materials were imported from Spain. Areas on the first floor, especially the enclosed interior courtyard, were decorated in a Sevillian style that displayed the strong Moorish influence on that part of Spain. For the US guests the Moorish interiors conjured notions of the exotic through reference to the influence of Islamic culture in Spain and the connotations of a warm climate that this type of style evoked.

Scholar Juan de las Cuevas has described the exterior of the hotel as eclectic, in which creole elements of the time are visually predominant, including cast iron balconies, *guarda vecinos* (decorated metal components located between two balconies), and *vitrales* (stained glass windows located above doors).[16] These had come to be considered signature elements of Cuban architecture and would have simultaneously accommodated a visitor's desire for the exotic and a local's desire for an expression of creole identity. Moreover, these elements addressed climatic concerns. Through its employment of colored glass, *vitrales* filtered the harsh Caribbean sunlight. Balconies and *guarda vecinos,* through their open metalwork, allow breezes to pass through, a necessity in the hot, humid tropics.

Finally, the neoclassical character of the Hotel Inglaterra's façade reveals the popularity of this style in the mid-nineteenth century.[17] Investigating the topic of neoclassicism in urban Havana, art historian Paul B. Niell has argued that this architecture played a significant role in the construction of Cuban heritage and a shared civic identity, as well as expressing the idea of *buen gusto,* or good taste.[18] This neoclassical vocabulary, which was also popular in the United States in these years, would have been familiar and inviting to US visitors as well. The original three-story construction of 1853 had more ornate pedimented windows on the second floor, and rather austere projecting pediments on the third-floor windows. With the remodel in 1915, each successive floor from the ground up was rendered more ornate than the one previous. Projecting stringcourses clearly delineated separate floors, and when considered comprehensively the floors boasted the full spectrum of neoclassical elements—pilasters, pediments, swags, and cartouches—culminating in a balustrade on the roof level that was topped with decorative urns and an arched pediment that served as the sign for the hotel.[19] Neoclassicism spoke to multiple audiences—it framed a Cuban civic and cultural identity and, at the same time, was familiar to US viewers—though resonating differently for various groups and individuals; it was a style of building that traversed cultures.

In the nineteenth century and into the twentieth century, hotels throughout the Americas, like the Hotel Inglaterra, were designed to accommodate a variety of activities and people. In the nineteenth century, lobbies, bars, and restaurants were considered part of the public domain—guests and locals were welcome to partake of what the hotel had to offer on the public floors as long as they appeared to belong to a respectable social class. The Hotel Inglaterra serves as an illuminating example of how the hotel accommodated two different groups of people—tourists and locals—who, moreover, were quite heterogenous among themselves. While visitors came from all over the globe, US travelers came to increasingly dominate the tourism industry from the late nineteenth century into the twentieth century. The hotel offered a home away from home for the US visitors who came to Cuba primarily for health, business, and/or vacation purposes. For those interested in health travel, it was not just the climate that promised a remedy to the stress of living a modern life in the United States. As historian Louis A. Pérez has chronicled, during the nineteenth century Cuba entered the US imagination as the "tropics," which conjured notions of time as much as place. Traveling to Cuba promised curative effects, partly by one's being "transported back to a simpler time, less rushed and more contemplative."[20] Despite their desire for a respite from modern life, US travelers still wanted access to the desirable features of modern life, especially when it came to their lodgings. Indeed, even if they were enchanted with the idea of "simpler times," visitors insisted on up-to-date living environments. The Hotel Inglaterra quickly developed the reputation among US visitors as the finest hotel.[21]

While a popular place for US visitors to stay, the Hotel Inglaterra was also an important site for accommodating the Cuban fight for independence. Proindependence agitators favored meeting at the Hotel Inglaterra, whose rooms provided the setting for subversive lectures that took place amid the normal hustle and bustle of the hotel.[22] The Hotel Inglaterra was also the hotel of choice for US military and political leaders who were involved in the Spanish-Cuban-American War and the site of controversial meetings of these men. It was even the site of the shooting of a Cuban by one of Theodore Roosevelt's Rough Riders.[23]

The Hotel Inglaterra became all the more important as a site of the independence movement when independence leader Antonio Maceo stayed in the hotel for five months in 1890. After establishing himself in the military during the Ten Years' War, Maceo was later involved in the other two wars for independence.[24] Maceo stationed himself in the Hotel Inglaterra for a period in 1890 as a means to further the independence cause. During his time in Havana he held interviews with journalists, connected with important men of the city, and swayed the views of labor leaders to support independence.[25] Typical of the nineteenth and early twentieth centuries, the public nature of the modern hotel made the Hotel Inglaterra's communal spaces an advantageous venue for political activity. Organizing, lobbying, and other political campaigning all took place amid the comings and goings of hotel guests, locals, and porters and bellhops. Maceo most likely stayed at the Hotel Inglaterra for a number of reasons. It was attractively located in a part of the city where proindependence activity was particularly strong. Additionally, he may have favored it because many considered it the most modern hotel in Cuba, a choice that may have been meant to express the modern nature of the Cuban independence movement. Moreover, its selection may have been due to the fact that modern hotels provided the public spaces conducive to politicking. The public qualities of hotels and the perception of them as empowering local spaces was, however, soon to shift in the twentieth century.

Sevilla-Biltmore: US Imperialism and Tourism Take Hold

Manuel López and Urbano González, proprietors of the Hotel Inglaterra and Hotel Pasaje, respectively, recognized that despite the substantial number of hotels in Havana, there remained a demand for more accommodations, so they commissioned Cuban architect José Toraya to design a hotel.[26] López and González understood that to compete in the world of hotels, one must always strive for the latest in design trends and technologies. While the example of the Hotel Inglaterra exemplifies an interest in offering spaces to accommodate both foreigners and locals, the Sevilla Hotel, later to become the Sevilla-Biltmore, illustrates a different impulse: as mass tourism took hold in Havana, hotels increasingly focused principally on the tourist's experience (figure 9.2). This was not necessarily unique to Havana; rather, it is representative of a broader trend in which hotel public spaces were refashioned for paying guests, eschewing the previously held conceptions of these zones as civic and public spaces. The Sevilla-Biltmore's history exemplifies this shift, as it does the move to a robust and predominantly US traveler–oriented tourism. Coupled together, these two changes exacerbated conflicts and tensions caused by US imperialism. The two proprietors succeeded in what was considered the ultimate in hotel design when the Sevilla Hotel opened in 1908, but the acquisition and enlargement of the hotel in 1919 by US owners signaled a significant moment in which tourism infrastructure became a popular investment, more specifically, an investment in developing tourism infrastructure that fashioned Havana as a playground for US visitors.

Publications such as *Cuba: The Loveliest Land that Human Eyes Have Ever Seen* (1925) simultaneously illustrate and work to bolster US imperialist attitudes of Cuba as a place for enjoyment by US visitors. The island is objectified as a space that exists for the pleasure of US tourists. Printed by the Cuban

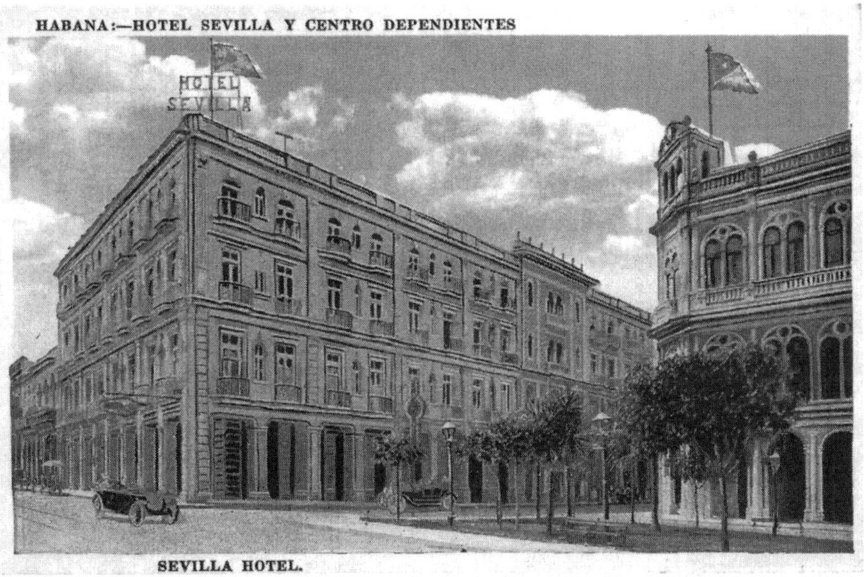

Figure 9.2. Postcard of the Hotel Sevilla with the original main façade on the right, c. 1905–1930. Author's collection.

National Tourist Commission, the brochure signals an era in which not only tourism infrastructure is organized and managed but knowledge is curated and provided to mass tourists, allowing US visitors to partake in a form of epistemic imperialism, which can be defined as the understanding that the perception of having a form of expert knowledge functions as means to establish and justify superiority, intervention, and control. Shaping an imagined understanding of what the island has to offer, promotional brochures and guidebooks offered viewers the possibility of performing a familiarity or knowledge that simulated a kind of firsthand experience. A mixture of historical and scientific "facts" and current information on travel, dining, lodging, and sightseeing, these brochures encouraged tourism to Cuba in part by making potential tourists feel it was knowable enough to visit.[27] In other words, by allowing the potential tourist to "know" Cuba through its history and facts, such as agricultural production or cultural traditions, the island became safe enough to travel to—it was no longer too foreign, its exoticness rendered understandably alluring rather than threatening. By the time this publication came out, Havana had developed into an established destination for US tourists. This increase in tourism, as well as its changed nature, can be observed across the life of the Sevilla-Biltmore and the changes in its design.

Although obscured by the later addition, the original building was markedly grand, with a prominent entrance on Calle Trocadero between Paseo del Prado and Calle Zulueta, an ideal location not far from Parque Central and its nearby attractions.[28] Composed of five floors, the hotel contained an impressive two hundred and fifty guestrooms. Private baths, quality imported furniture, the finest building materials, and modern technologies ensured efficient hotel operations and guest enjoyment. Notably, Cuba was almost a decade into official US intervention on the island when López and González undertook this business venture, positioning them in a competitive world in which US business interests and politics were a dominant force on the island.

The façade and decoration of the public spaces accommodated both US tourist desires for the exotic and Cuban aspirations to establish their relatively new nation as modern yet rich in heritage. Overflowing with decoration, the central portion of the façade was designed in a style that was clearly inspired by the Moorish architecture of Andalucía and by Spanish *modernismo*.[29] Flanking the central portion, the repetitive fenestration signals the plethora of commodious guestrooms inside the building and reveals its function as a hotel. The various elements that compose the facade reflect a typical approach of the period in which it was acceptable to combine different styles or create hybridizations in order to make new styles symbolic of the modern. The central portion of the façade was a modern interpretation clearly inspired by such iconic historic works as the Alhambra Palace in Spain. The interior design conveyed

Spanish flavor as well as Cuban traditions through such details as the interior courtyard. This recreational space was complemented by other lobby areas that relied heavily on Spanish-style tiles, arcades, and *persianas* (wooden window louvers), elements of Spanish-influenced Cuban traditions.

One day after the Volstead Act (Prohibition) became law, businessman John McEntee Bowman announced the copurchase of the Hotel Sevilla with Charles Flynn, signaling the transfer of the hotel from Cuban to US ownership.[30] Bowman already had more than five years' experience running the Biltmore chain of hotels based in the United States, was adamantly opposed to Prohibition, and saw Cuba as the next or perhaps last great hope in light of alcohol restriction in the United States. Less than four years later, Bowman publicly announced his plans to enlarge the hotel, detailing his hiring of the New York firm of Schultze & Weaver, whom he had already commissioned to design his Atlanta and Los Angeles Biltmore hotels, to add a ten-story addition to the Havana hotel.

The imposing new tower was located on the fashionable Paseo del Prado, effectively repositioning the main entrance (figure 9.3). Set perpendicular to the old building, the soaring new addition had a commanding presence on

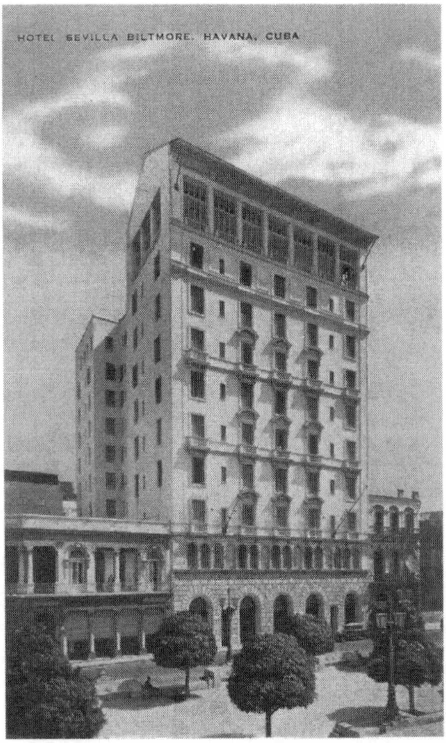

Figure 9.3. Postcard of the Sevilla-Biltmore Hotel highlights its towering presence on the Paseo del Prado, and its verso description notes its roof garden and "Spanish Patio," c. 1905–1930. Author's collection.

Paseo del Prado, and its rooftop patio offered impressive views of the city from above, allowing US tourists to visually consume the urban landscape through a position of ocular dominance. From the rooftop patio, the city spread out for guests to know and understand through vision, bringing the far-flung Morro Castle on the other side of the bay as well as great swaths of the city's coastline easily within the vista of Sevilla-Biltmore guests.

The Italianate style of Schultze & Weaver's beaux arts design did not seem to concede much to Cuban architectural heritage, and critics thought the addition clashed with the architectural character of Paseo del Prado.[31] Indeed, the most striking feature in all of the images of the remodeled hotel is the way in which the hotel dominated the urban landscape. However, the ground floor arcade along the Paseo del Prado adhered to the Cuban tradition of porticos. The visitor entered into a vaulted foyer from the new entrance on Paseo del Prado and then into an interior courtyard. Shops on the ground floor of this area provided guests and well-to-do locals with services and goods.

While many found that the exterior of the addition lacked a Cuban or Spanish tone, interior renovations accommodated guests' expectations for the foreign. Departing from the Italianate style of the addition's exterior, and more consistent with the style of the original portion of the hotel, the Palm Garden (interior patio café), the foyer of the roof garden, and other public places were decorated with Spanish tiles, *persianas,* and other details that referenced Cuba's colonial heritage. These areas were also decorated with such furnishings as wicker chairs and settees and potted palms—typical of Cuban interior decoration.[32] Such spaces became increasingly reserved for hotel guests, who were predominantly from the United States, and other US travelers. Its identity as part of a US hotel chain certainly enhanced its popularity among US tourists—Biltmore was a widely known and well-respected hotel brand—and Prohibition only encouraged more travel to Cuba, where many flocked to places that were known to be watering holes for the US visitor, including the Sevilla-Biltmore rooftop bar, Sloppy Joe's, Ballyhoo, and Dos Hermanos Bar.

Throughout the first half of the 1920s the *New York Times* ran periodic articles announcing successive record-breaking numbers of tourists to Havana. These articles always ended with a list of the social elite lodging at the Sevilla-Biltmore. Headlines in US newspapers such as "Havana's New Year's Eve Is of Pre-Volstead Style: Wine Flows Freely in Cafes and Cow Bells Aid Noisy Celebration" underscored the gaiety of a vacation in Cuba. Indeed, Prohibition helped seal Havana's fate as a destination for pleasure seekers and partiers. US citizens of all classes wanted to travel to Cuba, which resulted in a diversification of the tourism industry. Supported by a sophisticated and complex tourist infrastructure, there was an enormous increase in the number of tourists throughout the 1920s that ultimately defined the vision of Havana presented in *Weekend in Havana*.[33] The Hotel Sevilla-Biltmore helped accommodate this great influx of US tourists and contributed to the construction of Cuba as a destination of adventure, entertainment, romance, and indulgence. In 1919, the *New York Times* featured a major article that proclaimed that "the Pearl of the Antilles deems the present an auspicious occasion to establish herself as the Monaco of America—a playground at the doorstep of a puritanical nation."[34]

The romantic and wild image of a Cuban vacation helped solidify Cuba as the most popular destination in the Caribbean for US travelers. In 1928, Cuba captured about 77 percent of US travelers to the Caribbean.[35] Cuba was, by far, the most popular destination for US tourists in this decade, and, averse to missing out on potential profits, various agents ranging from US businessmen to the Cuban government sought to benefit from what was, by that point, a firmly established tourism industry. All of these visitors needed lodging, and they were accommodated by an ever-increasing number of modern hotels that spread from a core group near Parque Central to the newly developing suburban peripheries.[36]

The Legacy of Havana's Modern Hotels

Nan's visit to Cuba in *Weekend in Havana* is curious in its timing—1941 marked a slump in the tourist market brought on by the Great Depression and World War II. Perhaps it reflects a desire for fantasy in this dark moment right before the United States was officially involved in the war. It most certainly speaks to the cultural impact of US president Franklin Delano Roosevelt's Good Neighbor Policy, launched in 1933. While espousing nonintervention, the Good Neighbor Policy was a turn toward a new kind of imperialism that was driven by softer forms of coercion than military involvement. The United States now looked to its American neighbors to supply raw materials and finished goods through trade deals that were made possible by more covert efforts, such as aiding in the institution of certain political leaders in Latin American countries, and cultural initiatives packaged as promoting hemispheric unity. Therefore, while the US government nullified the onerous Platt Amendment in Cuba in 1934 and supported the overthrow of the dictatorial regime of Gerardo Machado y Morales, it was done for self-serving interests, such as a better sugar trade agreement.

As the US economy boomed in the wake of World War II, many sought to reinforce their wealth through renewed efforts to strengthen and expand the tourism industry in Cuba. Promoters effectively built off of the reputation of Cuba established during Prohibition, and 1950s Havana vacations were defined as opportunities to set aside the strictures of everyday life in the United

States in favor of all types of transgressions and indulgences. Gambling, partying, and entertainment took center stage in the spectacle of Cuban tourism, and a new spate of modern hotels was built in the 1950s to house this activity. This was the notorious era of the US mafia in Cuba tolerated by the corrupt regime of Fulgencio Batista, and many Cubans, including Fidel Castro, saw this as an insidious form of imperialism that was damaging to the cultural, social, and economic welfare of Cuba.

The "frozen in time" image of Cuba that still haunts the popular imagination of US mainlanders is that of Nan's vision of Havana in the 1940s and the decade that followed. By this post–World War II period, the official age of US imperialism had ended, and the United States was at that point looking to a new form of imperialism disguised as Pan-American unity amid the growing threats of the Cold War. Nan's version of Havana became fixed in the US popular imagination because the United States could no longer control Cuba in the way it wanted after the Revolution in 1959. Instead, the US government has sought to manipulate and influence Cuba through embargoes and other means that have left the island nation only more mysterious and alluring to many US mainlanders. This is worth mentioning because hotels continue to be a significant and highly contested space in contemporary US-Cuban relations. With president Barack Obama's opening overtures in 2014, more US travelers were able to go to Cuba and stay in hotels, and US hotel operators had renewed opportunities to do business on the island, albeit within the framework mandated by the Cuban government. The Trump administration's changes to Cuban policy also targeted hotels and tourism, severely restricting which US citizens can travel to Cuba and what shape their travels take, including prohibiting lodging at a long list of hotels that are partially or fully run by the Cuban state. In short, US-Cuban relations of today are the result and continuation of a long history of US imperialism, one in which tourism played no small part. The modern hotel shaped this history as it transitioned from a more civic and public space to a more exclusive space for US tourists at the same time that Cuba ceased being a Spanish colony and slipped into the grip of US imperialism.

Tourism is the secondlargest industry in the world, after oil, and the Cuban government is very much thinking about that today. New hotel projects, which are often the result of mixed businesses (part Cuban state and part foreign company) reflect how accommodation is still a major concern in hotels. The government and private businesses each make accommodations in order to do business, and both take into account adaptations necessary to address tourist desires. In this sense, what continues today is similar to practices that have been going on for much more than a century. If we view modern hotels through the lens of accommodation, we can come to a better understanding of the power of these hotels in projecting identity, shaping cross-cultural encounters and opinions, and addressing a complex diversity of desires.

Notes

1. A note on language: Determining appropriate and fair nomenclature for these different groups and nations is not easy, and there is no perfect solution. I use "United States" and "US" to refer to the mainland United States of America as a means of purposefully avoiding the problematic terms "America" and "Americans"; however, this is an imperfect practice that privileges the notion of white mainland United States over a more racially and culturally diverse US empire, or greater United States. For a brief discussion of the historic shift in use from the term "United States" to "America," see Daniel Immerwahr, *How to Hide an Empire: A History of the Greater United States* (New York: Farrar, Straus and Giroux, 2019), 75–76.

2. I have yet to uncover documentation that proves that scenes were shot in the Hotel Nacional, but based on the interior views of Nan's room, it appears that they did use the hotel as a set location for her room, in particular, the interiors of the Suite of the Republic, which were reserved for high-ranking politicians, influential businessman, and other VIP guests.

3. Molly W. Berger, *Hotel Dreams: Luxury, Technology, and Urban Ambition in America, 1829–1929* (Baltimore, MD: Johns Hopkins University Press, 2011); and A. K. Sandoval-Strausz, *Hotel: An American History* (New Haven, CT: Yale University Press, 2007).

4. Berger, *Hotel Dreams,* 12.

5. More specifically, I am referring to the western areas and territories of the United States that in the nineteenth century were not yet incorporated into the United States as states.

6. The manager of operations was usually the owner of the building and ran relatively small-scale hospitality operations.

7. Hotel West's was the operation of a Mistress West from North America, and scholarship has documented that *casas de huéspedes* with North American proprietors had the reputation of being the best operated. Arturo A. Pedroso Alés, "Las hospederías habaneras en el siglo XIX," *Palabra Nueva* no. 210 (September 2011), accessed August 19, 2013, http://www.palabranueva.net.

8. The introduction of the railroad in Cuba in 1836 was vital in supporting the growth of the sugar industry in the country by providing a means for products to come from rural areas to the port city in order to be shipped out to the rest of the world. Effective and efficient transportation was essential to Cuba's economy.

9. *Criollos,* or Creoles, were those born in Cuba. They considered themselves distinctly different from *peninsulares,* who were born in Spain.

10. For example, see Juan de las Cuevas, *500 Años de construcciones en Cuba* (Madrid: D. V. Chavín, 2001), 90. Some historians contest the Perla de Cuba's claim as the oldest hotel because some cite that it was originally designated as military lodging. The nearby Campo de Marte, now Parque de la Fraternidad (Fraternity Park), was where military exercises and parades took place. See Evaristo Villalba Garrido, *Cuba y el turismo* (Havana: Editorial de Ciencias Sociales, 1993), 11.

11. When the Hotel Inglaterra opened, England was considered one of the centers of the modern world. New understandings of the modern world and modernity were defined in terms related to England's Industrial Revolution. Transportation technologies such as the railroad first took hold in England; and new social and cultural events, such as the first World's Fair in 1851, were held in London.

12. The Paseo del Prado is now officially the Paseo de Martí but is still commonly referred to as the Paseo del Prado.

13. For a brief discussion of the impact of the Tacón government on the built environment of Havana, see Jospeh L. Scarpaci, Roberto Segre, and Mario Coyula, *Havana: Two Faces of the Antillean Metropolis* (Chapel Hill: University of North Carolina Press, 2002), 32–37; and Roberto Segre, "Havana, from Tacón to Forestier," in *Planning Latin America's Capital Cities, 1850–1950,* ed. Arturo Almandoz (New York: Routledge, 2002): 193–213.

14. Engineer Mariano Carillo de Albornoz proposed the Plano de Ensanche (Expansion Plan, 1849–1850) shortly after Tacón's reform program for this area of Havana, but its call for the demolition of the walls was not realized until thirteen years later. Influenced by the tearing down of the old walls in Vienna (1858) and Barcelona (1859–1860) and the modern urban planning that ensued, the Spanish Crown ordered the development of two parallel streets, Monserrate and Zulueta, each fifteen meters wide, running alongside the walls' former location. Currently, the buildings along the east side of the Paseo del Prado are where the former walls once stood.

15. Jean-François Lejeune, "The City as Landscape: Jean Claude Nicolas Forestier and the Great Urban Works of Havana, 1925–1930," *Journal of Decorative and Propaganda Arts* 22 (1996), 157. According to Lejeune, apparently many erroneously believed that the buildings constructed by Spaniards were built by Creoles.

16. De las Cuevas, *500 Años,* 91. The balconies and *vitrales* were part of the original construction and the *guarda vecinos* were added during the 1915 expansion. The purpose of *guarda vecinos* is to prevent movement from one balcony to another.

17. An interest in neoclassical architecture started to grow in 1828, when a small Greco-Roman inspired temple was built in Plaza de Armas. Known as El Templete (the Temple), this structure was, according to popular belief, built on the site where the city was founded and the first mass was held.

18. See Paul B. Niell, "El Templete: Classicism and the Dialectics of Colonial Urban Space in Early-Nineteenth Century Havana, Cuba," in *Buen Gusto and Classicism in the Visual Cultures of Latin America, 1780–1910,* ed. Paul B. Niell and Stacie G. Widdifield (Albuquerque: University of New Mexico Press, 2013), 49–71; and Paul B. Niell, *Urban Space as Heritage in Late Colonial Cuba: Classicism and Dissonance on the Plaza de Armas of Havana, 1754–1828* (Austin: University of Texas Press, 2015).

19. The balustrade and pediment decoration at the roof level were the same in the 1915 construction as in the original 1853 design.

20. Louis A. Pérez, *On Becoming Cuban: Identity, Nationality, and Culture* (Chapel Hill: University of North Carolina Press, 2008), 22.

21. US news articles from the nineteenth century always mentioned when a member of the elite was lodging at the Hotel Inglaterra.

22. Villalba Garrido, *Cuba y el turismo,* 11–12.

23. For example, see "Lee Is on His Mettle," *Chicago Daily Tribune,* May 27, 1897, 3; and "Rough Rider Shoots a Cuban," *Chicago Daily Tribune,* March 21, 1899, 1.

24. The Ten Years' War (1868–1878) ended with the Pact of Zanjón, which did not provide independence from Spain nor universal emancipation, the two major concerns of the independence movement. The Cuban quest for independence spans a period of decades in which, after the Little War (1879–1880), independence from Spain was only finally achieved with the US-named Spanish-American War of 1898, which Cubans often refer to as the Necessary War that was fought from 1895 to 1898.

25. Villalba Garrido, *Cuba y el turismo,* 12.

26. Rosalie Schwartz, *Pleasure Island: Tourism and Temptation in Cuba* (Lincoln: University of Nebraska Press, 1997), 22. Compañía Cubana "El Guardián" constructed it.

27. The facts and information presented in these types of publications were certainly questionable at times. Most notably, in an effort to attract visitors, certain aspects or characteristics of the island were misrepresented, most likely in order to seem appealing. For example, in *Cuba: The Loveliest Land,* the weather in Havana is described as "always pleasant" and it is said that "no one has ever had sunstroke"; *Cuba: The Loveliest Land That Human Eyes Have Ever Seen* (Havana: Cuban National Tourist Commission, ca. 1925), 2. If it were true that no one ever suffered sunstroke, it would have only been because it was too hot and humid in the summers to stand outside in the sun. Downplaying the severity of the summer weather in Cuba is consistent across all of the publications of this type.

28. Calle Zulueta is now called Calle Agramonte.

29. An artistic movement in Spain during the late nineteenth and early twentieth centuries, *modernismo* had its counterparts in the Art Nouveau of Belgium and France, Jugendstil in Germany, and Stile Libertá in Italy. Lluís Domènech i Montaner, Josep Puig i Cadalfach, and Antoni Gaudí were prominent architects of *modernismo* who were concerned with expressing a particular Catalonian spirit through this new style of architecture. Indeed, *modernismo* was particularly tied to the region of Catalonia, and based on the large number of Catalonians who immigrated to Cuba in this period, it is no surprise that this style entered into the built landscape of Havana.

30. Bowman made the announcement on October 29, 1919.

31. De las Cuevas, *500 Años,* 218.

32. Since the nineteenth century, wicker and rattan furniture had come to be accepted as appropriate furniture for tropical climates and had a long tradition in Cuban interior decorating.

33. For example, fifty thousand US travelers went to Cuba in 1920, and by 1928 the number of US tourists topped ninety thousand. Dennis Merrill, *Negotiating Paradise: U.S. Tourism and Empire in Twentieth-Century Latin America* (Chapel Hill: University of North Carolina Press, 2009), 107.

34. Brown and Dawson, "Cuba, Refuge of the Frivolous and Thirsty," *New York Times,* August 31, 1919, 69. Shortly after Prohibition started in the United States, bars and drinking establishments became greater in number and focus in Cuba. Many US bar owners packed up and moved down to Cuba, where they reopened their business and catered to US tourists. Pérez, *On Becoming Cuban,* 168.

35. This amounted to approximately 90,000 of 116,500 travelers.

36. The spread of hotels outside of the urban core also coincided with an attention to urban planning outside of the historic center, in particular under president Gerardo Machado y Morales. On hotels, see Erica N. Morawski, "Negotiating the Hotel Nacional de Cuba: Politics, Profits, and Protest," *Journal of the Society of Architectural Historians* 78, no. 1 (March 2019): 90–108. On urban planning, the most recent scholarship is Joseph R. Hartman, "Silent Witnesses: Modernity, Colonialism and Jean-Claude Nicolas Forestier's Unfinished Plans for Havana," *Journal of the Society of Architectural Historians* 78, no. 3 (September 2019): 292–311.

Ten

Forest Formats

Photography, Puerto Rico, and the *Caribbean Forester*

Chris Balaschak

> Human societies are, indeed, the culminating forms of the evolution of life rising out of the warm sea-margins on a primitive planet. And the subtle and complex form of human association already attained forecast even more highly organized patterns for the future.
> —Rexford Tugwell, *The Place of Planning in Society*

The opening scenes of the film *Doña Julia* (1952), directed by Skip Faust for the Division of Community Education in Puerto Rico, situate the viewer in a rural, mountainous landscape. Panning across the horizon, the film cuts, and the camera comes to rest on a dirt road on which we find Julia, played by Lucy Boscana. The plot sees Julia on her way to visit her daughter, who has become ill and is staying at the local rural hospital. Suspicious of modern medicine, Julia steals away her child, throwing out the doctor's orders, only to purchase a questionable homemade remedy that is fated to be ineffective. Wrapped within this plot is a doctor from said hospital, whom we find traveling through rural communities, discussing the advantages of vaccination and modern medicine. *Doña Julia* runs around forty-five minutes and is typical of films produced by the Division of Community Education (DIVEDCO) that aimed to positively represent the Puerto Rico Reconstruction Administration's (PRRA) efforts to modernize Puerto Rico. Established by president Franklin D. Roosevelt's executive order on May 28, 1935, the Puerto Rico Reconstruction Administration was "the New Deal in Puerto Rico," and held the goal of "constructing a new public health and public works infrastructure on the island."[1] *Doña Julia* indicates one aspect of the PRRA's "bio-colonialism," that is, the ways in which its social programming and modernization project were ecologically invasive. While vaccination was one aspect of the United States government's application of science in its management of Puerto Rico, the PRRA also advocated and supported the use of pesticides and fertilizers, and the distribution and apportionment of land in rural areas.

In order to make visible the PRRA's social and ecological program, we must look outside DIVEDCO's dramatic films. In particular, we can consider photographs made by Frank Wadsworth, a forester and one-time director of the Tropical Forest Experiment Station at the El Yunque National Forest. Throughout the PRRA, Wadsworth produced numerous photographs within the national forest, and oversaw the production of the *Caribbean Forester*, a bilingual publication covering issues in tropical forestry throughout the region. Wadsworth's photography primarily served to document his study of sustainable forest practices. However, when viewing photographs from his archive, it is clear that his research was inclusive not only of the forest, but also of the social conditions resulting from the PRRA's management of the island's formerly landless rural population.

El Yunque National Forest is the only tropical rainforest in the US National Forest System. The area was first declared public land in 1903 by president Theodore Roosevelt, who transformed all formerly Spanish Crown lands into the Luquillo Forest Reserve.[2] The reserve became part of the National Forest System in 1935, when the Caribbean National Forest and the Tropical Forest Experiment Station, established in 1939, began publishing the *Caribbean Forester*, which continued until 1964.[3] The concurrent establishment of the PRRA directly affected the forestry studies conducted at the national forest, especially with regard to agricultural diversification, soil conservation, and reforestation.[4] In particular, the PRRA's "Land Law" of 1941, which sought to distribute land to landless families, establishing *parcelas* (agricultural land distributed to landless families for subsistence farming), became an enduring subject of Wadsworth's studies.[5] Wadsworth's history roughly parallels the development of the national forest; he accepted a position at the Tropical Forest Experiment Station in 1942, became director in 1956, and retired in 1979. Unlike his predecessors, though, Wadsworth was thoroughly invested in photography as a research tool, and was the primary photo contributor to the *Caribbean Forester*, which rarely reproduced photographs until 1950.

Of particular interest to Wadsworth, and as discussed at length in his photographically illustrated research, was the concept of natural systems as climax communities. "Climax community" was an idea first developed by Frederic Clements in his *Plant Succession: An Analysis of the Development of Vegetation* (1916).[6] As quoted by Donald Worster, Clements described climax communities as follows: "The unit of vegetation, the climax formation, is an organic entity. As an organism, the formation arises, grows, matures, and dies. . . . The climax formation is the adult organism, the fully developed community." As such, Clements continued, "the climax community marches toward an automatic, predetermined fate."[7] As Worster makes clear, Clements developed the concept by studying the work of Herbert Spencer, particularly his *Principles of Biology* (1864), a title that would also become foundational in the field of "social Darwinism."[8] During the 1930s, as ecologists studied the Dust Bowl, "climax ecology" reached its height of influence, and contributed to a broad discussion about the impact of human civilization on natural climax communities.[9] From the Dust Bowl until Wadsworth's day, however, "climax ecology" inherited aspects of social Darwinism; for instance, in Clements' understanding of the Dust Bowl, the "Plains Indians" were part of the natural "biome," whereas "the white man" had "overturned and disobeyed natural laws."[10]

Climax communities were central to Wadsworth's research in Puerto Rico. As he wrote in his research, his work focused on "four forest sites" in the Luquillo Mountains wherein "the climax vegetation expresses the more important and stable soil and climatic conditions."[11] What becomes increasingly clear when reading Wadsworth's articles for the *Caribbean Forester* is that the climax communities of the Luquillo Mountains contained social as well as natural systems. Consider Wadsworth's text in the *Caribbean Forester* in 1944 titled "The First Year in the Cambalache Experimental Forest." The research was published roughly a year following the signing of a "memorandum of understanding" between the Forest Service and the Land Authority of Puerto Rico, which would put "on record the desire of these two agencies to cooperate in the development of the best silvicultural policies and techniques to be used in the management of the forest of the dry limestone region along the north coast." The area in question was "a tract of non-agricultural land for research on forest problems common to thousands of acres of other lands owned or soon to be bought by the authority."[12] Wadsworth's year-long study of the forest, which was photographically documented (though not reproduced in the *Caribbean Forester*), intended to lead toward "improved forest management practices on Authority forest lands."[13] As such, Wadsworth's study focused on the potential utilization and regeneration of the forest, but also on the value the forest would have as a source of timber, fuel, and labor for the resettlement communities within the forest. Wadsworth writes, "The presence of small tracts of agricultural land between the hills provides an excellent opportunity for class study of a combination of woodlot forestry and agriculture. Four sites have been chosen for homesteads and permission has been received from the [Land] Authority to rent to four families 5 acres for agriculture and pasture. Houses will be constructed of forest materials and rental will be paid in the form of forest work. In addition to the income from crops these families will have an opportunity to cut and prepare forest products as a profit to themselves."[14] In quoting Wadsworth's summary statement on the experimental forest at length, it is perhaps necessary to emphasize two things: on the one hand, the experiment sought to disclose a sustainable forest practice that balanced native vegetation and its regeneration with the agricultural needs of the local community; on the other, the experiment's subjects were equally the native vegetation and the local community.

The "Land Authority" Wadsworth referred to was established under the Land Law of 1941, authored by Luis Muñoz Marín. As described by anthropologist Ismael García-Cólon, under the Land Law "the government of Puerto Rico established communities, popularly known as *parcelas,* with the intention of distributing small plots to landless families."[15] García-Cólon continues, "The Land Authority had the powers to acquire land, implement the 500-acre limitation law, promote agriculture among small landowners, and resettle landless families."[16] As García-Cólon argues, the Land Authority made "an attempt at reforming land tenure, [and] was part of an effort to 'modernize' the country."[17] Much of the visual culture produced by the PRRA, notably through the Division of Community Education, propagated this ideology of modernization by resettlement. While aspects of DIVEDCO will be addressed further on, it is important to note that Wadsworth's photographic output not only precedes DIVEDCO's visual material by several years but was also already attempting a visual representation of *agregadas/os,* the landless workers the Land Authority targeted for reformation. Furthermore, one cannot understand the Land Authority's efforts without also seeing its relation to Rexford Tugwell's broader efforts at social planning during the New Deal, such as part of the Resettlement Administration's "Greenbelt Towns" program, which could then be mapped onto Puerto Rico.[18]

Although Wadsworth's work in the Cambalache Experimental Forest mentioned the families of *parceleros* who were an increasingly visible part of the forest landscape, these families are not explicitly depicted in the *Caribbean Forester.* Despite their absence, we can ascertain that Wadsworth was interested in documenting not only the families who had been resettled in Cambalache but also several other similar experimental forests on the island. Consider the following three photographs, dated 1945, and taken on the site of the Toro Negro division of the Caribbean National Forest in Villalba, Puerto Rico. The three photographs are common in subject, each depicting a different *parcelero* family (figures 10.1, 10.2, and 10.3). The first is noted as a family and their "government constructed house"; the second as a "parcelero house"; and the third as a "newly rented parcel showing government constructed house." There is also a fourth photograph that is noted as showing "typical native rural construction," thus illustrating a contrast between "government" and "native" housing (figure 10.4). Each of the photographs captures the house in full, such that we can see its situation within the forest and topography, as well as at least some members of the family that inhabit the home. Though two of the photographs produce a strong sense of contrast that might speak to the needs for the modern "hurricane-proof housing program" and "rural

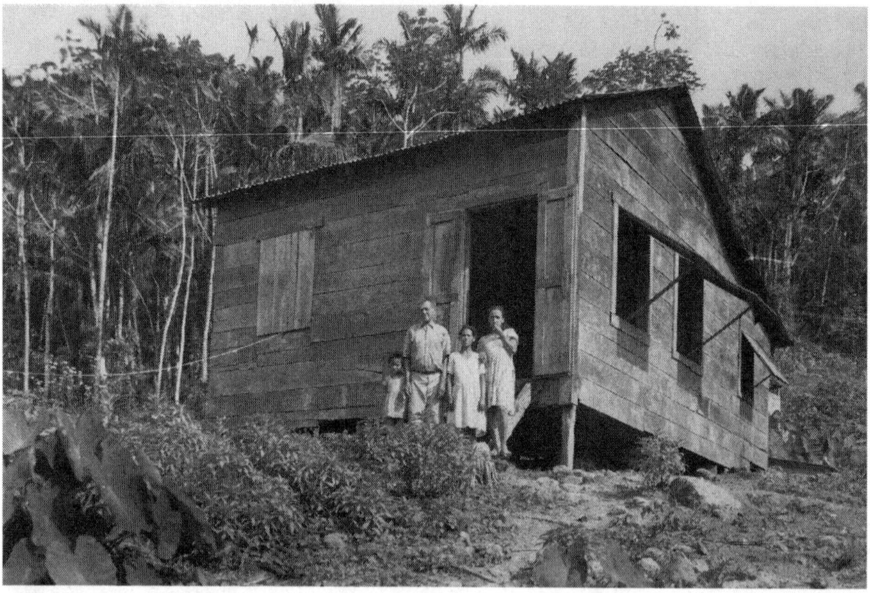

Figure 10.1. Frank Wadsworth, "Parcelero family and government constructed house, Toro Negro Div.," 1945. Records of the Forest Service, National Archives, College Park, MD.

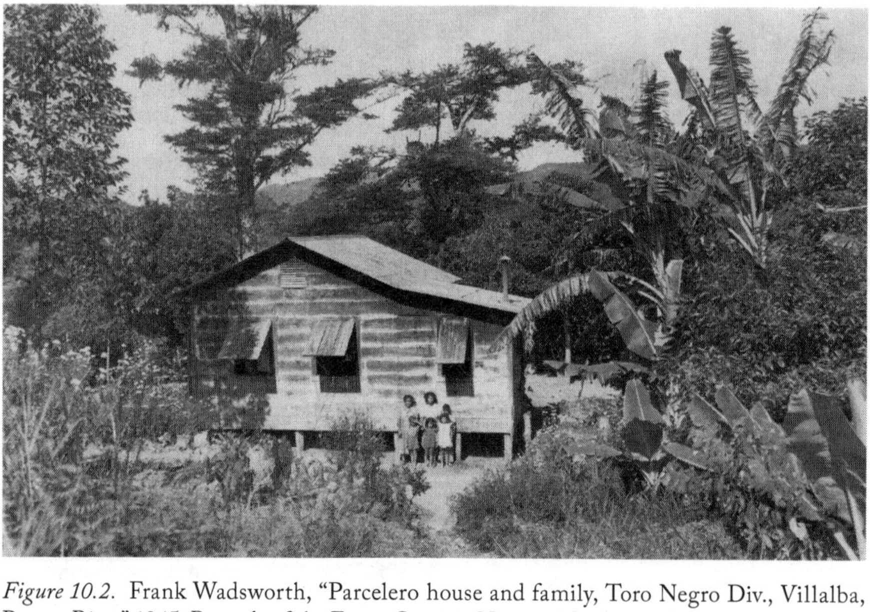

Figure 10.2. Frank Wadsworth, "Parcelero house and family, Toro Negro Div., Villalba, Puerto Rico," 1945. Records of the Forest Service, National Archives, College Park, MD.

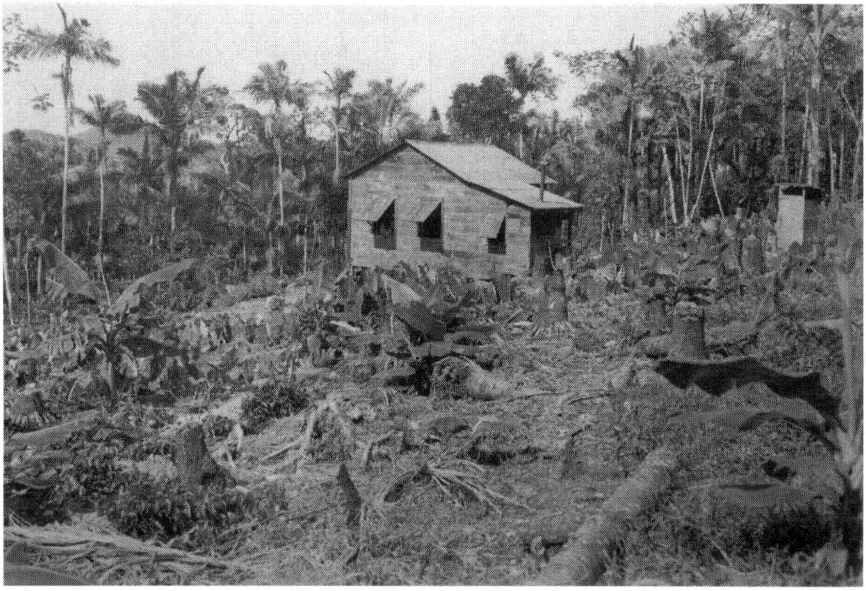

Figure 10.3. Frank Wadsworth, "Newly rented parcel showing government constructed house, land clearing, and young plantation of bananas, Toro Negro Div. Villalba, Puerto Rico," 1945. Records of the Forest Service, National Archives, College Park, MD.

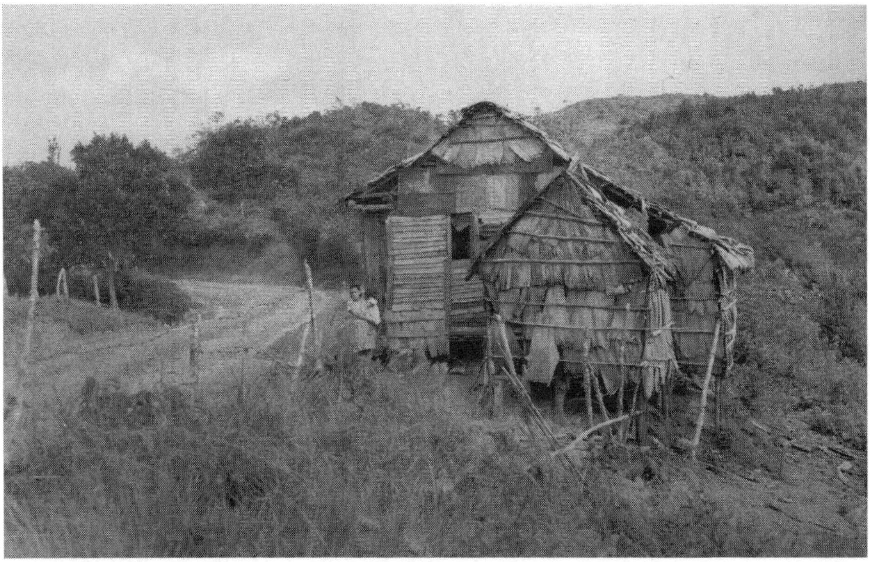

Figure 10.4. Frank Wadsworth, "Typical native rural construction, using palm sheaths, poles, and vines, near Toro Negro Div., Villalba, Puerto Rico," 1945. Records of the Forest Service, National Archives, College Park, MD.

electrification" that were part and parcel of the PRRA,[19] it would not be under Wadsworth's purview to document such conditions. As forester Peter Weaver writes, "Parceleros had a house, cistern, and access to land for a period of time. They occupied tracts where they were allowed to intercrop foodstuffs with trees (i.e., a system called taungya or agroforestry), gradually reforesting Federal land."[20] It appears this latter concern—agroforestry—was a primary motivation for Wadsworth's photographs.

Though the above photographs were not reproduced in the *Caribbean Forester*, Wadsworth reported on his Toro Negro research in an essay titled "Population and Employment Problems in the Toro Negro Forest" (1949). Wadsworth's work at Toro Negro built upon his work in the Cambalache Experimental Forest, as it "exemplifies inter-relationships between public forestry, employment, and the rural community of Puerto Rico."[21] Yet the tone is one of progress rather than hypothesis. Wadsworth writes, "The plight of parceleros in 1943 made immediate action urgent," implying that those without modern housing required such.[22] Wadsworth then lays claim to a more sustainable use of forest space, and proposes the creation of an agroforestry system whereby arable land would be situated within a climax forest. In Wadsworth's view, if families were to be settled in the forest, cultivation practices would need to be such as to regenerate the forest. Further expanding a communion between the forest, agriculture, and residency, members of the local community could also be employed by the Forest Service. But this was not simply a suggestion on Wadsworth's part, as he saw agroforestry as necessary in order to sustain the Land Authority's *parcelas* project. As Wadsworth states, in order to have a basic "standard of living," "a certain amount of timber harvesting work" would always need to be available.[23] He concludes the passage by stating, "There still remains some question, however, concerning the actual 'permanence' of this use.... With no erosion control or soil amendments, cultivation will reduce soil productivity. The inevitable result will be further reduction of farm acreage, and additional emigration, unless compensatory employment is found."[24] In short, Wadsworth was attempting to reconcile the PRRA's social program and modernization efforts with the forest ecology in order to render a stable climax community. When James C. Scott writes, in *Seeing Like a State,* that one element in "state-initiated social engineering" is "the administrative ordering of nature and society,"[25] Wadsworth is not only directly witnessing and photographing such administration but also seeing it as socially and ecologically unsustainable.

Wadsworth is nowhere on record about his photographic choices, nor is it clear where he learned to make photographs, whether he had any direct knowledge of photographic practices occurring simultaneously on Puerto Rico, or if he knew the work of his predecessors in the Farm Security Administration or Resettlement Administration. However, Wadsworth's proclivity for a front-porch realism is reminiscent of Walker Evans' work published in *Let Us Now Praise Famous Men* (1941). Evans' evocative photographs of tenant farmworkers, their bodies and faces often framed by the textures of wood-sided houses, if not the posts and beams of porches and interiors, resonate with Wadsworth's aesthetic decisions. The families in Wadsworth's photographs often occupy a space in front of the house but never beside it. They are both framed and defined by the structures they occupy, and Wadsworth appears to recognize their social conditions in a manner often occluded in the pages of the *Caribbean Forester.*

While the discourse within the *Caribbean Forester* may have acknowledged the Land Authority's placement of the landless into communities in and around the Caribbean National Forest, Wadsworth's acceptance of the *parceleros* as part of climate community ecology was indicative of the PRRA's ideology. At the helm of the PRRA, as previously noted, was Rexford Tugwell. Tugwell approached the PRRA in a manner that equated social planning with, in his words, "biological evolution."[26] Arising out of the Land Authority would be social planning by means of "orderly growth."[27] The biological metaphors were intentional. As Tugwell wrote in his essay *The Place of Planning in Society* (1958), "Human societies are, indeed, the culminating forms of the evolution of life rising out of the warm sea-margins on a primitive planet."[28] For Tugwell, society has "the nature of biological structures," and it is not natural but social evolution that leads toward a climax community.[29] He continues, "The generalization the ecologists use to describe the forces in motion among plants by any environmental disturbance... is class succession; and the end of the process is called the climax."[30] It is perhaps no surprise to understand that Tugwell sees the place of his planning, and the role of Washington in particular, as managing "organisms" toward such a climax.[31] Yet the process is one of subjugation. According to Tugwell, "There are men who come very close to the level of their animal relatives in forethought and the management of their lives; there are others who seem to us to have, almost, the characteristics of reasoning perfection."[32]

Coached as it is in the rhetoric of climax community ecology, we might understand Tugwell's planning as an ideology of biocolonialism. Biocolonialism is an extension of Michel Foucault's biopolitics, a "technology of power" that he defines as "control over relations between the human race, or human beings insofar as they are a species, insofar as they are a species, insofar as they are living beings, and their environment."[33] Foucault continues on to state that biopolitics deals "with the population as a political problem" and introduces certain mechanisms such as "forecasts, statistical estimates, and overall measures" to implement controls between a population and its environment.[34] The biopolitics of Tugwell's PRRA is apparent in the implementation of a resettlement program in which "thousands of formerly landless families redefined their lives and their means of livelihood under the new social and economic conditions as *parcela* residents."[35] However, the tactics of redefining the lives of the landless are likewise premised on understanding the island as an ecological biome, a climax community inclusive of natural and social forces. As such, Wadsworth's experimental forests might be understood as a "colonial conservation" that sought to not only preserve the generative natural forests of the island but also see the *parceleros* as part of the climax community being maintained.[36]

Although the biocolonialism apparent in Wadsworth's photographs from the 1940s is indicative of Tugwell's understanding of social planning and his subjugation of the *agregados,* Wadsworth's work is exceptional relative to that made by his predecessors in the Resettlement Administration and the Farm Security Administration, as well as his peers in the PRRA. Consider the work of filmmaker Pare Lorentz, and his film *The Plow that Broke the Plains* (1936). Produced by the Resettlement Administration, *The Plow* depicts the fate of the Great Plains during the Dust Bowl, and offers social planning as a solution. As historian Finis Dunaway wrote of the film, "Lorentz viewed the grasslands as an example of what New Deal conservationists and ecologists called a 'climax community,' a pristine, timeless realm where 'Nature' is 'minding its own knitting.'"[37] Lorentz's ecological vision was indicative of the understanding that agriculture was unsustainable. As Dunaway writes, "Lorentz focused on the interaction between humans and the natural world, tracing the fall from grace initiated by the pioneers."[38] Unlike Wadsworth, Lorentz, and indeed the Resettlement Administration more broadly, did not seek a course of sustainable and symbiotic relations in which social plans were integrated within natural systems. Instead, *The Plow,* much like Lorentz's subsequent film, *The River* (1937), celebrated "rational planning," what Dunaway describes as "the sublime power of the New Deal to use technology to control the natural world."[39] Dunaway continues, "Lorentz encouraged audiences to see government planning as a sublime spectacle of power and control leading to the landscape's orderly perfection."[40]

In the twilight of the Farm Security Administration (FSA), and following establishment of the PRRA, a number of photographers were reassigned from the FSA to the governor's office in San Juan. Edwin and Louise Rosskam were charged with, in Edwin's words, "setting up a file very much like Roy's file."[41] Edwin was likewise responsible for having Jack Delano, another photographer who had worked for the FSA's Roy Stryker, and his wife Irene "sent to Puerto Rico."[42] As with their work for the FSA, the Rosskams and the Delanos were, at least initially, making photographs "to inform the people of Puerto Rico about their government and their problems."[43] When considering Delano's photographs, for instance, the archive creates a clear division between images of what Tugwell had seen as the island's "wretched, unsanitary and overcrowded" aspects and the ways and means of "land distribution, urban planning, and expanding civil society."[44]

Yet photography was far from the primary material produced by the PRRA, and but one part of the agency's broader visual agenda. Rosskam founded the Division of Community Education, or DIVEDCO, in 1949. The division grew out of the Film and Graphic Arts Program of the Public Parks and Recreation Commission, run by Irene and Jack Delano between 1946 and 1949.[45] DIVEDCO would be directed by Rosskam, with Jack running the "film section," and Irene "in charge of the Printmaking Workshop."[46] As is clear from the organizational structure, DIVEDCO produced myriad visual materials, from film to pamphlets to posters, all of which were part of a single image ecology. Like the PRRA more broadly, DIVEDCO was based upon standards already practiced in the United States. As García-Cólon writes, "DIVEDCO was inspired by North American ideas of using community clubs to 'democratize' society. In the United States, settlement programs and the U.S. Housing Authority presented movies, lectures, music, and other entertainment with the purpose of assimilating immigrants into mainstream society and forming exemplary citizens."[47] Delano's film section was at the top of the chain, producing education films that would be promoted by way of posters produced in Irene Delano's workshop, and further accompanied by pamphlets that would allow for the discussion and dissemination of ideas promoted by the films. As García-Cólon writes of the program, "Every movie was accompanied by a book that [the] community educator distributed to the neighbors. Topics in the books and films sought to transmit 'democratic' values such as community involvement, social justice, and women's rights. The government wanted Puerto Ricans to understand the concept of liberal democracy and participation in the electoral process. The purpose was to introduce new forms of behavior and facilitate the transition from a rural order to an urban one."[48] DIVEDCO's visual campaign might thus be understood as its own climax community, a mature ecology of visual media intended to sustain the PRRA's broader modernizing ideology.

Typical of the DIVEDCO program, *Doña Julia* was promoted with a poster, which would have been printed within the workshop run by Irene Delano. As historian Marimar Benítez has stated, "Irene Delano trained the artists of the Generation of the Fifties that turned silk-screen into one of the most popular graphic mediums in Puerto Rico."[49] The workshop produced not only this poster but also the accompanying booklet, one of a series of *Libros para el pueblo,* that was intended to be distributed alongside the film's screening to prompt further discussion among the community. The booklet in question here, *La Ciencia contra la superstición* (dated 1951), is not only illustrated with linocut prints but also contains a number of articles detailing the benefits of vaccination as well as an explanation on how science discovers "truth." The booklet's opening article ("La historia de Juanita") reiterates *Doña Julia*'s narrative, one in which modern science invalidates the use of a homemade remedy.

DIVEDCO's educational booklets were a means to spread modernization efforts while also offering instructions for establishing community centers. In 1952, DIVEDCO produced a booklet that included a story titled "El Amigo desconocido." "The unknown friend" in this case is a representative of DIVEDCO sent to a rural community to educate that community as to the creation and mission of the division. The story, which is largely a dialogue, features illustrations alongside an explanation of the division's production of movies, booklets, and posters. "The unknown friend" elaborates the need for DIVEDCO's very existence, stating that the division desires to "learn as much as possible about the problems of the whole island, and about the government's efforts to solve them for the good of the people."[50] Further along in the booklet, the reader is given elaborate instructions on how to construct a community center, along with a list of the necessary supplies. The community center building is both economical and adaptable, and uses wood "from our native trees."[51] One might thus imagine such a community center as the ideal site to display the division's posters, to screen its films, and to discuss its booklets (perhaps even to take the multiple-choice test included at the back of the 1951 booklet previously discussed). It is unclear in my research how many, if any, such community centers were shown, nor where, how, or how often DIVEDCO's films were screened. However, it is clear in the context of this chapter that the audience was quite distinct from those we have discussed within the pages of the *Caribbean Forester.* DIVEDCO intended its work to be seen by the community it depicted, while Wadsworth's publication was aimed at a broader discourse and a community of foresters within the greater Caribbean.

Despite differences in their received audiences, Wadsworth's work in the *Caribbean Forester,* and DIVEDCO's campaign played equal roles in a broader biocolonialism that was not only invested in shifting understandings of land use but also in other scientific campaigns, such as vaccinations and the use of pesticides and fertilizers. What they likewise hold in common is a failure to represent what writer Rob Nixon has called the "unimagined communities." As Nixon elaborates, these are "those unimagined communities internal to the space of the nation-state, communities whose vigorously unimagined condition becomes indispensable to maintaining a highly selective discourse of national development."[52] We must recognize, for instance, that although DIVEDCO focused their efforts on the rural poor, they were represented as fictive characters within the division's own campaign. Similarly, though Wadsworth actively photographed the *parcelera* families who were inhabiting government parcel plots with the island's public forests, they were subjugated, "recast as 'surplus'" to borrow from Nixon, in Wadsworth's experimental forestry. Finally, of course, we must recognize that Tugwell's discussion of Puerto Rico and its inhabitants, posits the island as an unevolved biological entity. One cannot also help but see this view of Puerto Rico—one of a landscape to be modernized—as indicative of the neo-environmentalist aspects of New Deal ecology, in which industrial technology and capital investment are the signs of progress toward a "climax community."

Though Wadsworth's photographs presage the visual culture of the PRRA in the 1950s, by 1953 an alternate view of the PRRA's role on the island was becoming visible. While Irene Delano had "trained the artists of the Generation of the Fifties,"[53] including her successors Lorenzo Homar and Rafael Tufiño, it was also this generation of artists who "were tuned to the Nationalist ideals and identified social inequality with the United States colonial regime in Puerto Rico."[54] Many of these artists formed a collective, the Center for Puerto Rican Art, which, beginning in 1951, produced portfolios of prints that

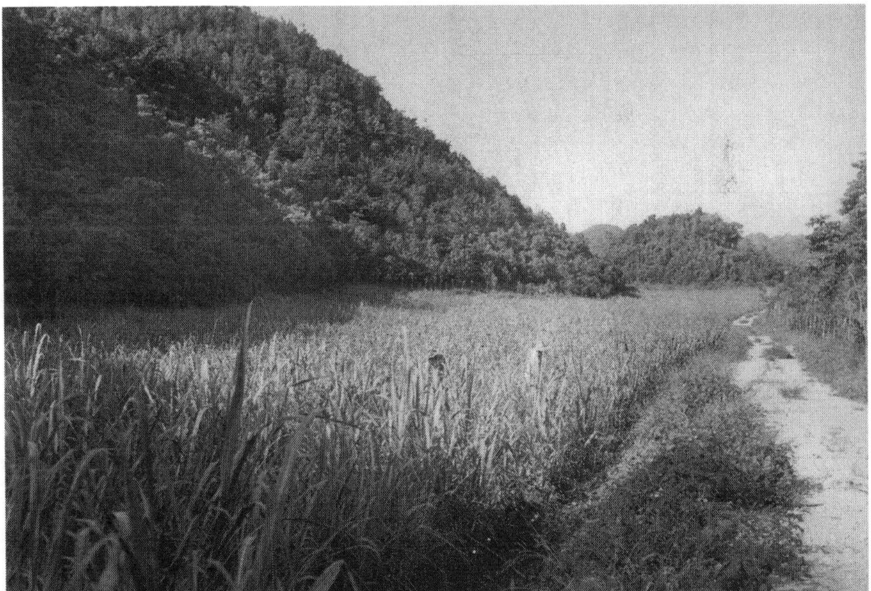

Figure 10.5. Frank Wadsworth, "Entrance to Cambalache Experimental Forest from south showing sharp line between forest and sugar cane agriculture. Garrochales, Puerto Rico," 1945. Records of the Forest Service, National Archives, College Park, MD.

recognized the subjugated, and in particular the rural poor. This included, for instance, Juan Diaz, who had worked on the *Doña Julia* poster for DIVEDCO, and many others.

When viewing Wadsworth's archive, what goes unseen is the force of American capital at play; there is scarcely a trace of the coffee, tobacco, or sugar industry that in fact spawned Puerto Rico's New Deal. As we know, economic reform of the island predated the PRRA by several years, dating to the Sugar Act of 1934 that sought "the rationalizing of the sugar industry."[55] Tugwell had visited the island as early as 1934, and "land redistribution" was an outcome of the Sugar Act's implementation.[56] Consider, finally, a telling Wadsworth photograph, made in the Cambalache Experimental Forest, and showing a "sharp line" between agriculture (a field of sugar cane) and the forest beyond (figure 10.5). Two laboring figures are hidden from view, their attire (so much as we can see) an uncanny resemblance to the two figures in Tufiño's print. While we must recognize that Wadsworth's photograph is a product of the forceful biocolonialism that the PRRA represented, we might also recognize his efforts at imaging a sustainable community between the natural and the social as ecologically progressive. The question, however, becomes, who benefits from the sustenance of such a community?

Notes

Epigraph: Tugwell's text equates social planning with "biological evolution," noting that "organized communities . . . are organisms." Rexford Tugwell, *The Place of Planning in Society* (San Juan: Puerto Rico Planning Board, 1958), 17, 21.

1. Geoff Burrows, "The New Deal in Puerto Rico: Public Works, Public Health, and the Puerto Rico Reconstruction Administration, 1935–1955" (PhD diss., City University of New York, 2014), 89.

2. Peter L. Weaver, *The Luquillo Mountains: Forest Resources and Their History* (San Juan: International Institute of Tropical Forestry, 2012), 9.

3. Ibid., 2, 18.

4. As noted by Burrows, "New Deal in Puerto Rico," 133, 150.

5. *Parcelas* are discussed at length in Ismael García-Cólon, *Land Reform in Puerto Rico: Modernizing the Colonial State, 1941–1969* (Gainesville: University Press of Florida, 2009), 3.

6. Frederic Clements quoted in Donald Worster, *Nature's Economy: A History of Ecological Ideas* (London: Cambridge University Press, 1994), 211.

7. Ibid.

8. Ibid., 212.

9. Ibid., 218.

10. Ibid.

11. Frank Wadsworth, "The Development of the Forest Land Resources of the Luquillo Mountains, Puerto Rico" (PhD diss., University of Michigan, 1949), 82.

12. Frank Wadsworth, "The First Year in the Cambalache Experimental Forest," *Caribbean Forester* 6, no. 1 (October 1944): 34.

13. Ibid.

14. Ibid., 38.

15. García-Cólon, *Land Reform in Puerto Rico,* 3.

16. Ibid., 48.

17. Ibid., 63.

18. For further connections between Tugwell's social planning in the continental United States and Puerto Rico, see Linda Levin Moreen, "Midcentury Planning in San Juan, Puerto Rico: Rexford Guy Tugwell, Henry Klumb, and Design for 'Modernization,'" master's thesis, Washington University in St. Louis, 2013).

19. Burrows, "New Deal in Puerto Rico," 90.

20. Weaver, *Luquillo Mountains,* 14.

21. Frank Wadsworth and Emilio Solis, "Population and Employment Problems in the Toro Negro Forest," *Caribbean Forester* 10, no. 1 (January 1949): 59.

22. Wadsworth, "Development of Forest Land Resources," 63.

23. Wadsworth and Solis, "Population and Employment Problems," 67.

24. Ibid.

25. James C. Scott, *Seeing Like a State: How Certain Schemes to Improve the Human Condition Have Failed* (New Haven, CT: Yale University Press, 1999), 4.

26. Tugwell, *Place of Planning in Society,* 17.

27. Ibid., 7.

28. Ibid., 17.

29. Ibid.

30. Ibid., 18–19.

31. Ibid., 53, 22.

32. Ibid., 20.

33. Michel Foucault, *"Society Must Be Defended": Lectures at the Collége de France, 1975–1976* (London: Picador, 2003), 245.

34. Ibid., 245, 246.

35. García-Cólon, *Land Reform in Puerto Rico,* 96.

36. Rob Nixon, *Slow Violence and the Environmentalism of the Poor* (Cambridge, MA: Harvard University Press, 2013), 138.

37. Finis Dunaway, *Natural Visions: The Power of Images in American Environmental Reform* (Chicago, IL: University of Chicago Press, 2005), 47.

38. Ibid., 54.

39. Ibid., 44, 78.

40. Ibid., 79.

41. Edwin Rosskam and Louise Rosskam, transcript of an oral history interview conducted August 3, 1965, Smithsonian Archives of American Art, Washington, DC, 2002.

42. Ibid.

43. Ibid.

44. As quoted in García-Cólon, *Land Reform in Puerto Rico,* 31, 3.

45. Ibid., 86.

46. Teresa Tió, "The Graphic Arts of Puerto Rico," *Puerto Rico: Art and Identity* (San Juan: Universidad de Puerto Rico, 1998), 254.

47. García-Cólon, *Land Reform in Puerto Rico,* 87.

48. Ibid., 88.

49. Marimar Benítez, "The Fifties: Affirmation and Reaction," in *Puerto Rico: Art and Identity* (San Juan: Universidad de Puerto Rico, 1998), 142.

50. *Almanaque del pueblo* (Puerto Rico: Departmento de Instruccion, Division de Educacion de la Comunidad, 1952), 26; author's translation.

51. Ibid., 40–41; author's translation.

52. Nixon, *Slow Violence,* 150.

53. Benítez, "Fifties," 142.

54. Ibid.

55. César J. Ayala and Rafael Bernabe, *Puerto Rico in the American Century: A History since 1898* (Chapel Hill: University of North Carolina Press, 2007), 101.

56. Ibid., 102.

Eleven

Making Islands Beautiful (Again?)

Rhetorics of Neoclassicism in the US Insular Empire

Joseph R. Hartman

On February 4, 2020, US media outlets leaked a draft of an executive order titled "Making Federal Buildings Beautiful Again." According to the policy section of the controversial document, any new structure built with federal funds for government purposes had to be "beautiful," with "special regard for classical architecture." The classical canon, the order stated, was best suited to express the nation's democratic ideals. History told us so. President George Washington and Secretary of State Thomas Jefferson first employed the forms of "democratic Athens" and "republican Rome" to "physically symbolize our then-new nation's self-governing ideals." Washington and Jefferson were not just revolutionary leaders and politicians. They were amateur architects. They personally oversaw the competitions to design both the neoclassical Capitol Building and the White House. Washington and Jefferson saw in the structures of Greece and Rome an imagined heritage for their Enlightenment-era vision of an American democracy.[1]

The architectural community's reaction to the Trumpian decretal was swift and largely critical. The American Institute of Architects responded within the day with a two-part tweet: "The AIA strongly opposes uniform style mandates for federal #architecture. Architecture should be designed for the specific communities that it serves, reflecting our rich nation's diverse places, thought, culture and climates. Architects are committed to honoring our past as well as reflecting our future progress, protecting the freedom of thought and expression that are essential to democracy." The National Civic Arts Society, by contrast, lobbied for the executive order. It argued that, after World War II, the US government had blindly embraced modernist styles such as brutalism and deconstructivism, as evidenced in the imposing concrete face of the FBI headquarters in Washington, DC. The result, they said, was a rash of "ugly, inexpensive, and inefficient" buildings that marred the national landscape and offended the general populous. "This executive order," argued Marian Smith, NCAS chairwoman, "gives voice to the 99 percent—the ordinary American people who do not like what our government has been building."[2]

Today's Twitter battle between classicists and modernists, government officials and architectural professionals, reveals something about the historic stakes of neoclassic architecture, both in the United States and globally. The document makes clear the real and perceived relationship between neoclassicism and nationalism. In the broader context of the Americas, since at least the sixteenth century, architects and intellectuals have made similar appeals to Greco-Roman culture as evidence of "good taste" (*buen gusto*) in local civic societies.[3] So, too, for emergent democracies in the ex-colonies of Spain during the nineteenth and twentieth centuries, neoclassic administration buildings gave the illusion of a long majestic national past, seemingly distinct from older Spanish colonial models. In the context of the United States, and in other former Spanish territories such as Argentina, Cuba, and the Philippines, neoclassic architecture aimed to legitimize a young nation, now unencumbered by the yoke of monarchical rule.

By extension, many architects and politicians believed that classical traditions reflected the spirit of a "new" society after European colonialism. Classical architecture embodied the paradoxical ideals of democracy alongside emergent capitalist ambitions, historically based on the economic model of the plantation and chattel slavery.[4] It is no coincidence that enslaved Black bodies laid the very foundations of the White House and US Capitol Building on land originally inhabited by displaced Indigenous, specifically Nacotchtank, peoples. A brutal and often unacknowledged history of human exploitation haunted those "beautiful" neoclassical façades, once prized by Washington and Jefferson, and still admired by many citizens and tourists today.

The history of neoclassicism in the context of US nationalism intersects with histories of slavery, colonialism, and imperialism. The following chapter builds on that fact to reconsider the use of neoclassicism in the US imperial context, especially as it affected the emergence of a national consciousness in the former Spanish territories after 1898. Neoclassical works produced in that context, I argue, can be read both as examples of the double consciousness of coloniality within modernity as well as spaces of fantasy and emerging national identities. My discussion begins, as did the US insular empire, in Cuba, just after the War of 1898. The first section examines how political elites used neoclassicism in public monuments in Havana. Whether representing Cuban revolutionary José Martí or New York's Statue of Liberty, Cuban officials employed neoclassicism to reify dreams of national sovereignty around legacies of Spanish colonialism and US imperialism. The following section expands on that dialogue between neoclassicism, nationalism, and imperialism through a comparative set of case studies in Cuba, Puerto Rico, and the Philippines. Employing the philosophic concept of the simulacrum, in particular, I reassess symbolic reproductions and visual correspondences between the US Capitol in Washington, DC, and the capitol buildings of San Juan, Havana, and Manila built in the late 1920s. My chapter concludes that these neoclassical monuments do not represent mere mimicry but are rather "dreams of dreams," as artists and architects simultaneously identified their works with universal symbols of democracy and with specific local heritage.

Once called the "federal style" of the United States, neoclassical formalism represented an organized discourse of persuasion in the US-controlled islands of the Caribbean and Pacific, particularly after the War of 1898. Similar to, but not quite the same as, their "original" models from Europe and the United States, neoclassic works in the colonies and new island territories of the United States operated on various levels of mimicry, simulacra, and ambivalence. Neoclassic works in the insular context offered a discourse unto themselves, transcending while also colliding with colonialist paradigms of representation and power. Neoclassic monuments in the islands affected by the US empire expose the rhetoric of modernity as fiction, which ultimately hides the logic of colonialism underneath it. The persistence of US imperial patterns in the insular context may even reveal why US citizens don't seem to take note, to care, or to advocate for these regions still today. In these histories of art, architecture, and visual culture, we find an equally layered history of concealment, ultimately based on the colonial powers of rhetoric and representation.

The complex history of neoclassical formalism, moreover, tells us something about its power today, in the United States and in the nations, colonies, commonwealths, and territories of the Caribbean and Pacific. To understand how appeals to classicism might operate in our current political age calls for a diachronic understanding of the history of art and architecture as well as a synchronic consideration of the context in which that art and architecture emerges. That is, neoclassical forms carry historic baggage with them, which affect their meaning. As does any style. The coda of this chapter thus aims to expose the fundamental impossibility of "making federal buildings beautiful again." For the aesthetic value of such civic monuments are best determined and redetermined according to specific times and places, whether Manila in 1926, Havana and San Juan in 1929, Hagåtña in 1949, Honolulu in 1965, or Washington, DC, in 1793 and today.

Give Me Liberty or Give Me Martí: Neoclassism, Nationalism, and Colonialism

Neoclassical works engaged a nuanced rhetoric of power in the ex-colonies of Spain after 1898. Neoclassical art and architecture embodied a new US dominion in places such as Cuba, Puerto Rico, and the Philippines. Yet, those seemingly US-style monuments also acted as vehicles for asserting emergent national identities, distinct from a shared Spanish colonial past. To see how this dynamic between US imperialism and nationalism has operated historically in the Caribbean and Pacific context, we begin our discussion where the US insular empire arguably began: in Cuba just after the War of 1898.

It was following Spanish rule, but before Cuba gained its full sovereignty from the United States, that a neoclassic, Italian Carrara marble statue of poet and revolutionary José Martí first appeared in the streets of Havana on February 24, 1905. Mixed-race Cuban artist José Vilalta Saavedra, then working from his studio in Florence, Italy, took credit for the statue's facture (figure 11.1).[5] The statue represented Martí in a heroic pose with arm outstretched. The famous and handsomely mustachioed face of the revolutionary stares determinately ahead. His right arm reaches forward, index finger extended,

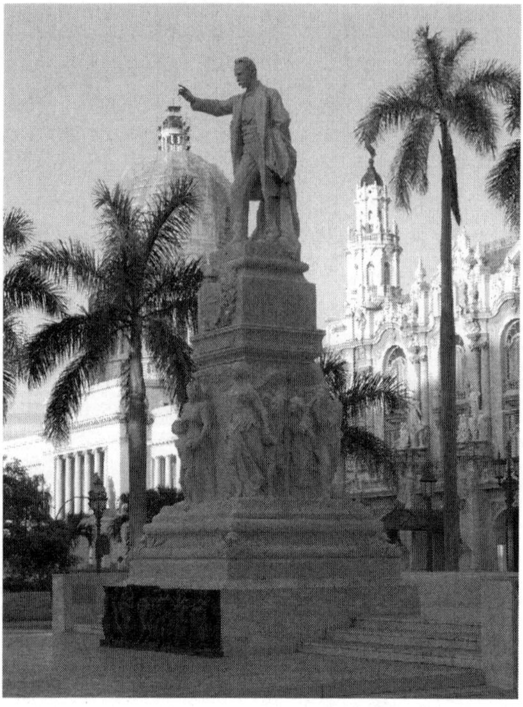

Figure 11.1. Statue of José Martí in Parque Central of Havana pictured next to El Capitolio and the Gran Teatro Nacional, 2018. Photograph by the author.

as though leading the charge—perhaps pointing Cuba's citizenry toward the very foundations of the Cuban republic. In relationship to the city, Martí appears to be pointing, either accusatively or indicatively, at the old Spanish colonial district (La Habana Vieja). On the pedestal at the base of Martí's feet are finely crafted allegorical representations, drawn from the classical canon. Two robed and winged women lead a huddled group of individuals, representing both the spirit of Victory and the populous of the new Cuban nation. Above these figures rests the Cuban crest—a triangular shield adorned in universal symbols of democracy, a fasces and a Phrygian cap, as well as signs of local cultural geography, the rising sun and the national palm tree.[6]

Cuba's government had the patriotic icon of Martí barged across the Atlantic in large wooden crates from Florence to Havana. It came to stand, as it does today, on a prominent pedestal in Havana's Parque Central, located just across from iconic architectural monuments such as Cuba's neoclassic Capitolio and the eclectic Gran Teatro Nacional. The statue remains a popular spot for selfie-snapping tourists and for locals who meet daily in the "hot corner" of the park to debate politics and baseball. Few, however, stop to ponder the convoluted history of the neoclassical work or its relationship to US imperial presence in Cuba at the turn of the twentieth century.

Fewer still may know that a miniature Statue of Liberty actually once stood on that same prominent pedestal, now occupied by Martí, the "apostle" of the Cuban Revolution.[7] Havana's own Lady Liberty was a near-replica of the US icon. Perhaps better stated, she embodied a simulacrum of US imagery, a concept to which we shall return later. Havana's Liberty presided in the city's park during the formal declaration of Cuba's Independence on May 20, 1902. She was there that same day when the nation's first constitution took effect. The United States used that national document to legalize its colonial relationship with Cuba. The nation's 1901 Constitution included a dubious appendix called the Platt Amendment. The amendment leased Guantanamo Bay to the United States indefinitely, allowed for unbridled military intervention, and left Cuba as a vassal state of its northern neighbor until the document's official abrogation in 1934.

The pedestal upon which Lady Liberty stood was, fittingly enough, a colonial-era placeholder for power in Cuba. Many had stood there before her throughout the nineteenth century.[8] A childlike bronze representation of the Spanish Queen Isabel II first stood there in 1850, lending the park its original title of La Plaza de Isabel. Then a marble figure of Christopher Columbus took her place. After him came Noble Habana, a neoclassic representation of a mythic Taína princess in the 1860s. In 1875, a marble statue of Isabel II, now depicted as a grown woman, returned to her childhood place in the park's center. Following the third Cuban War of Independence (1895–1898), the

Cuban government had the Spanish queen permanently removed by crane. This happened on March 12, 1899, a scant three months after the US flag came to rise over the iconic Spanish fort known as the Morro on Havana Bay.

The pedestal stood empty for years. Yet the symbolic center of the park was never truly vacant. The space was always already filled with an obsession to fill it.[9] The question was . . . with whom or what? The Cuban journal *El Fígaro* placed a giant question mark over a photograph of the empty pedestal on one of their covers that year (figure 11.2). The provocative image monumentalized Cuba's uncertain future.

The vacancy of the pedestal after the removal of Isabel II was a larger metaphor for the power vacuum left by the Spanish colonial government. US imperial interests soon filled it. Cuba's first president, Tomás Estrada Palma, allegedly subscribed to a form of "pro-Imperialist nationalism." His contemporaries called him an "undercover annexationist."[10] Feeding his opponents suspicions, Estrada Palma's government spent two thousand dollars to place a miniature Statue of Liberty on the park's iconic pedestal, just in time to celebrate Cuba's formal Declaration of Independence. With the United States' crest in one hand and light-bearing torch in the other, the neoclassic statue embodied a complicated sign of Cuban nationalism, to say the least.

Cuba's citizens had little time to contemplate her troubling semiotics, however. A well-timed tropical storm on October 10, 1903 (the anniversary of Cuba's first War of Independence in 1868) rendered the pedestal bare once more. Two years later, poet and revolutionary José Martí would come to take her spot. Placing Martí, a Cuban martyr killed fighting for the island's freedom only years before, in Havana's civic center seemed a clear rejoinder to the nation's history of Spanish colonialism as well as its ongoing struggle with US imperialism. With Martí, a new network of nationalist signs came to topple old visual regimes.

True enough, but the story of the statue's commission had more dimensions, too, relevant to our discussion. It was not long after the original statue of Queen Isabel II left her post in 1899 that *El Fígaro* Magazine organized a straw poll over which statue should occupy her vacant pedestal. Somewhat surprisingly, the marble likeness of Martí won by only a razor-thin margin of four votes. The next closest contender? Cuba's own Statue of Liberty! Whether Havana's Lady Liberty would have been an exact replica of New York's colossus remains unclear. But the symbolic weight of that iconic neoclassical monument, originally designed by French sculptor Frédéric Auguste Bartholdi, was certainly not lost on a young Cuban nation in transition. The Cuban people looked to US symbolism as inspiration for their own modern republic, now freed from Spanish colonial rule.

The Cuban magazine's poll included ten different statues in all. Among

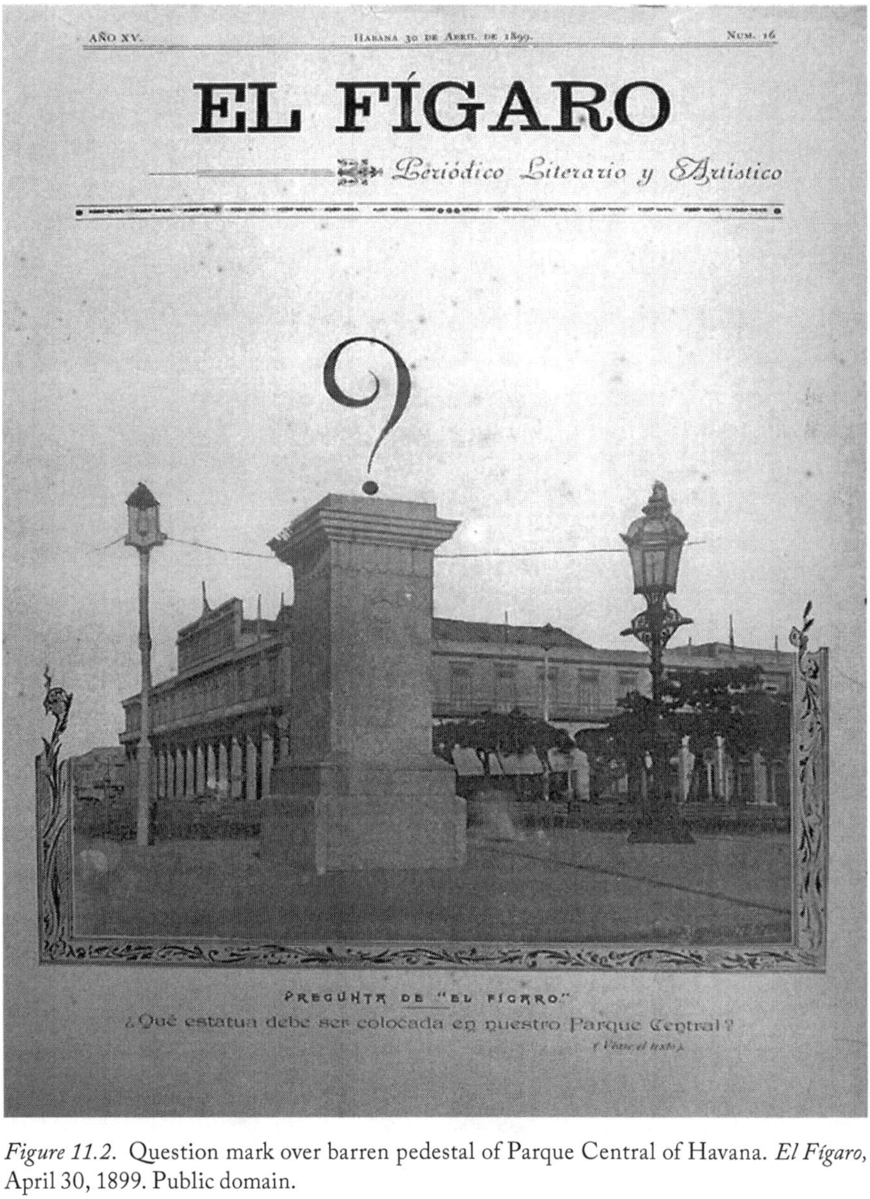

AÑO XV. HABANA 30 DE ABRIL DE 1899. NUM. 16

EL FÍGARO

Periódico Literario y Artístico

PREGUNTA DE "EL FÍGARO."

¿Qué estatua debe ser colocada en nuestro Parque Central?

(Véase el texto.)

Figure 11.2. Question mark over barren pedestal of Parque Central of Havana. *El Fígaro*, April 30, 1899. Public domain.

the more shocking results, a triumphant design dedicated to Christopher Columbus—Spanish colonial icon par excellence—won a significant share of the votes just behind Martí and Lady Liberty. Other compositions included Cuban leaders and war heroes (Máximo Gómez, Antonio Maceo, José de la Luz y Caballero, and Carlos Manuel de Céspedes). Stranger still, some votes were cast for multifigural works, including one image of the US president signing Cuba's Declaration of Independence, and another allegorical group representing Cuba, the United States, and Spain.[11] The inclusion of Cuban revolutionaries alongside US symbols and Spanish colonial icons tells us something about the conflicting visions of national identity in Cuba's nascent republic.

Though the subjects of the proposed monument varied, the use of neoclassical styles and Italianate materials was never presumably in question. Neoclassicism, it seemed, was best suited to navigate the split consciousness born of Cuba's recent colonial past, its US imperial present, and the nation's vision of a sovereign future. The use of neoclassicism helped Cuban political elites construct an image of the nation as both "white" and "civilized," a pattern dating back to the colonial period. The style of the new monument would combat and intermingle with racist views of the island, then espoused by the US press (and related to older colonial paradigms of race and power). US satirical cartoons at the turn of the century were rife with racist and sexist images of Cuba, Puerto Rico, the Philippines, and Guam. Some cartoons anthropomorphized the islands, caricaturing them as damsels in distress or helpless infants with stereotypical African, Asian, and Indigenous facial features. They were gendered and racialized babies crying out to Uncle Sam for support. Perhaps that is why, in the same poll, Cubans snubbed the suggestion of making a monument for Antonio Maceo—the famed mixed-race general of Cuba's War of Independence.[12] Maceo received the least votes. Such an appeal to whiteness, embodied in the neoclassical forms of both Martí and Liberty (not to mention Columbus!), was part of a larger social program to sanitize Cuba's history of blackness. Put otherwise, Havana's statuary engaged both historical and contemporary issues of race and racism on the island and on the US mainland. The neoclassic statue expressed white bourgeois anxieties profoundly tied to prejudiced views of African heritage in both Cuban and American cultures.

The Martí statue shows us how constructs of Cuban national identity revolved around Spanish colonialism and US imperialism, particularly in terms of race, gender, and identitarian politics after 1898. The statue also unveils the role of neoclassical art and architecture in that conversation. Neoclassicism engaged multiple layers of replication, simulacrum, and self-making. The unresolved meanings of the Martí statue, as a sign of colonial resonance *and* emergent nationalism, remained in tension for decades to come, even while the urban core around the sculpture transformed. On May 20, 1929, precisely twenty-seven years after Lady Liberty presided over the formal declaration of Cuba's Independence in Havana's Parque Central, Cuba would unveil its own domed and column-rimmed neoclassical capitol building. It was deceptively similar in appearance to the Capitol of Washington, DC. Martí's finger still pointed ambiguously toward the Spanish colonial city, but it could now, from a certain angle, also be seen to bless the dome of a new US-style capitol building, built by a Cuban dictator and funded by US banks (see figure 11.1).

The neoclassic Capitolio of Havana confronted the statue of Martí, as it took part in an ongoing dialogue regarding Cuban identity vis-à-vis US commercial and political influence. The classical-style statue of Martí and Havana's Capitolio addressed historical and political realities unique to Cuba. The political expediency of neoclassicism as a tool to navigate national identity in the ex-colonies of Spain, however, was a much wider-ranging phenomenon. Political actors, artists, and architects throughout the United States' insular empire employed neoclassical art and architecture to traverse similar terrains of nationhood and colonial identity during the early twentieth century. This is most evident in the forms of those neoclassic legislative buildings that emerged not just in Havana but also in San Juan and Manila at nearly the same time. A comparative study between Havana's legislative palace and those of San Juan and Manila helps us to feel out those reverberations of colonialism within the modern nation-state that echoed alongside local dreams of sovereignty and resistance.

Oh Capitol, My Capitol! Neoclassicism, Simulacra, and the Limits of Empire

Three civic buildings constructed in Havana, San Juan, and Manila share an interwoven history. They are the Capitolios of Cuba and Puerto Rico, and the Legislative Building of the Philippines (figures 11.3, 11.4, and 11.5).[13] Each building originally served as the legislature seats for the islands' local governments. Local civic leaders patronized the foundation of each building, too, under the auspices of the United States during the late 1920s.

The federal style of neoclassicism exhibited in those exemplars of Caribbean and Pacific civic architecture activated a complicated network of reproduction and simulacrum. They operated within the urbanization efforts of the American imperium. At the same time, they expressed local assertions of nationalism and self-governance. The buildings were inaugurated within three years of one another under the administration of US president Calvin Coolidge. Each served, variously, as sites for political ceremony and law. Cuba's

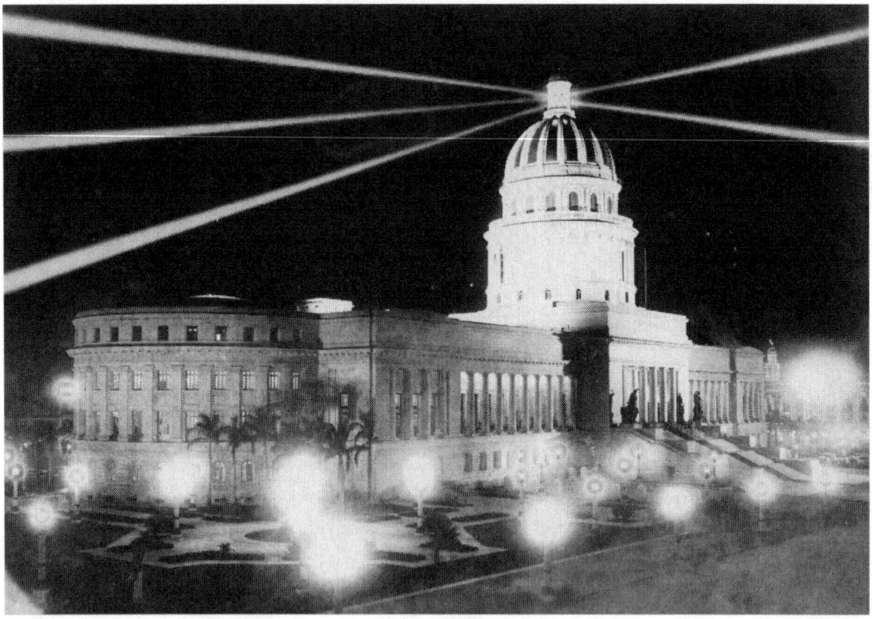

Figure 11.3. El Capitolio de la Habana at night, 1929. Photograph. Courtesy of the Wolfsonian–Florida International University, Miami Beach, Florida, the Mitchell Wolfson, Jr., Collection.

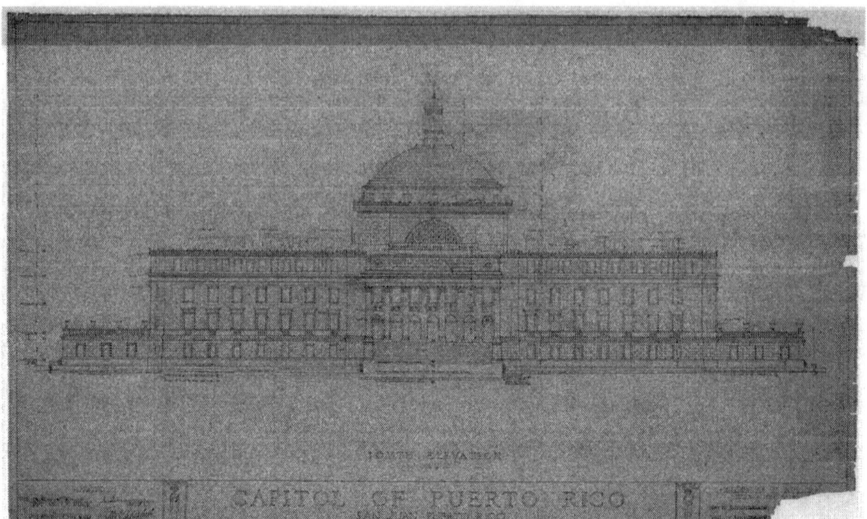

Figure 11.4. Plans for El Capitolio de Puerto Rico, 1925. Courtesy of Archivo de Arquitectura y Construcción de la Universidad de Puerto Rico.

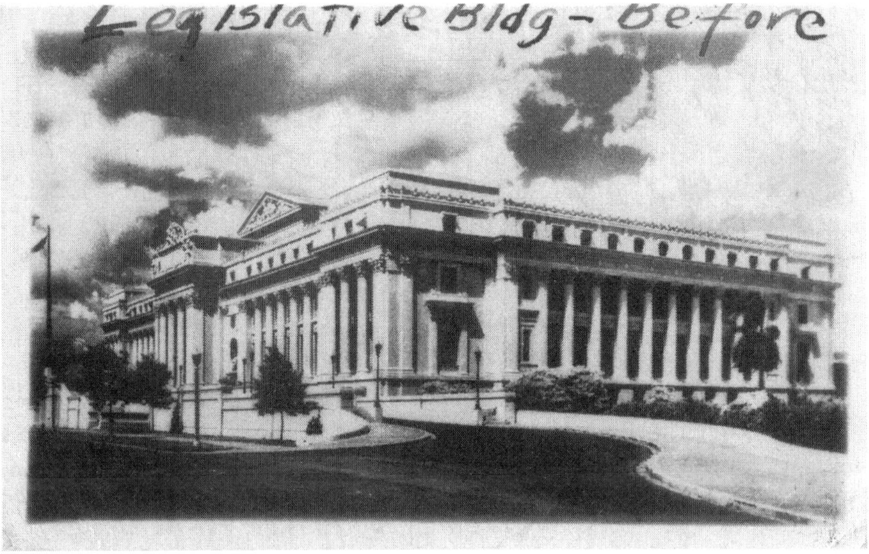

Figure 11.5. Manila Legislative Building before World War II. Personal caption on photo front: "Legislative bldg—before"; on reverse: "Pre-war legislative bldg. W. R. Brown," c. 1930. Photograph. Courtesy of the National World War II Museum, New Orleans, Louisiana.

Capitolio, unveiled in 1929, was an amalgam of the Capitol in Washington, DC, the Pantheon of Paris, and St. Peter's Basilica in Rome, among others. Puerto Rico's Capitolio, opening the same year, employed designs similar to that of Cuba's, combined with the locally imported Spanish revival styles then popular on the US mainland. The Philippines' Legislative Building, completed in 1926, featured a more distinguished beaux-arts temple façade. Famed US architect Daniel Burnham originally envisioned the building as a Carnegie-style library next to a grand-domed Kapitolyo in his unfinished 1905 plans for Manila.

Drawn from shared geographies and cultures, the Spanish Caribbean examples were necessarily distinct from the Legislative Building of Manila. Nevertheless, the three buildings displayed remarkable parallels in their respective histories and formal traits. With the support of US financial and political interests, local architects trained in the United States and Europe created the design for each building in collaboration with both national and foreign professionals. Principal architects included Raúl Otero in Cuba, Rafael Carmoega in Puerto Rico, and Juan M. Arellano in the Philippines. Those same designers employed a mixture of Indigenous symbolism with signifiers of Western democracy, from marble palms and pineapples to the Phrygian caps of the French Revolution. Likewise, each building exemplified, to varying degrees, typologies of quintessential North American capitols, statehouses, and legislative buildings, as seen in the neoclassical porticos, copulas, rotundas, and symmetrical wings of legislative houses in Minnesota, Texas, and many other states.

The similarities of the three buildings go beyond the visible surface, however. Together these architectural works reveal an untold history that transgresses the limits of geography and common narratives of monument cataloguing and Western appropriations. While operating within the cultural and political contexts of Cuba, Puerto Rico, and the Philippines in the late 1920s, the buildings speak to a broader theoretical discourse related to the replication and repurposing of imperial signs and representative modes. Local designers recrafted native and homegrown icons in the neoclassical style (such as Martí in Cuba or the humanoid island of Luzon in the Philippines). In so doing, those works also symbolized an interrogation of nationalist narratives and shared histories of US imperial hegemony and Spanish colonialism. Yes, it is true that the three neoclassic buildings each registered the political and economic ambitions of the United States. But they also effectively communicated Cuban, Puerto Rican, and Philippine assertions of identity and autonomy in the period context of the early twentieth century.

Those almost-but-not-quite identical works in Cuba, Puerto Rico, and the Philippines recall the conceptual framework of postmodern Cuban theorist and writer Antonio Benítez-Rojo in his novel *La Isla que se repite* (The Repeating Island).[14] Benítez-Rojo used the concept of the machine to describe the Caribbean as a metamachine, emerging first in the colonial plantation system. The plantation flows through the history of those islands, and, at the same time, it interrupts their past, present, and future. Benítez-Rojo's analysis was focused on the Greater Caribbean, encompassing the Antilles, the Gulf Coast, and the West Atlantic. But in light of their shared history of forced Indigenous labor (*encomiendas*), the enslavement of African peoples, the Manila Galleons and Silver Fleet, Spanish colonialism, and US imperialism, we might also include the archipelago of the Philippines as the furthest extent of those islands that repeat themselves. In many ways, the historic discourse on nationalism in the ex-Spanish colonies of the Pacific and Southeast Asia paralleled that of the Caribbean and the Americas. In their designs and urban integrations, the neoclassic civic buildings of Havana, Manila, and San Juan each evoked a similar repeating vision, born from the hauntings of coloniality within modernity—that is to say, the stubborn persistence of colonial social structures (racism, sexism, and classism) in the modern present.[15] The buildings, in that sense, offered interpretations of both imperial and republican spaces. They were simulacra, both phantasmal and concrete, of cultural and political identities negotiated through the aegis of the US empire.[16]

Hoping to employ the concept of the simulacrum even further in these distinct cultural contexts, the history of that philosophic term in Western discourse merits discussion. In 360 BCE, Plato employed the roots of the term as a derogatory label for the "phantastic" verbal distortions of his rivals. Far more recently, and famously, contemporary philosopher Jean Baudrillard argued that simulacra were not copies of the real but instead constituted a "realm of truth" in their own right. He called it the hyperreal. It was a negative reality parabolized in the Hollywood film *The Matrix,* and best represented by the vapid dreamscapes of Florida's Disney World. Philosopher Gilles Deleuze, on the other hand, argued for a more nuanced, and perhaps even positive, view of the phenomenon. He posited that simulacra were more than copies or negative realities. Instead, they were radical agents of change, with the power to overturn an original "model or privileged position."[17]

When "copies," inspired by older "models," proliferate, an occurrence ubiquitously evident in the case of neoclassic works, the distinction between an "original" and its "reproduction" becomes harder to discern. That indiscernibility presents a threat to the status quo. In this case, neoclassical simulacra threatened as much as they reinforced the colonial order of the US empire, established after 1898. Scholar Homi K. Bhabha describes the discourse of mimicry in a similar vein: "[It] is constructed around an *ambivalence;* in order to be effective, mimicry must continually produce its slippage, its excess, its difference."[18] The slippage between resemblance and excess produces a rupture, a double vision. The mimicking qualities of simulacra likewise suggest a camouflaged menace, which threatens, even as it underpins, the divide between colonized and colonizer. Architectural objects, such as those of Havana, Manila, and San Juan, so visibly plucked from the classical canon, thus become symbolically powerful in the local realm of cultural politics, precisely because they deceptively simulate, more than exactly reproduce, their so-called models.

To acknowledge the evident ambiguity between a "model" and its many copies offers us new ways of looking at ideologically charged buildings such as those of Cuba, Puerto Rico, and the Philippines. To call those legislative monuments simulacra is not to question their value. Nor is it to place the United States and Europe at the center of some imagined Leviathan that branches out to ex-colonial sites. Rather, I hope to use the concept to challenge the "privileged position" of such traditional and Eurocentric discourses that would claim to define originality and beauty. Viewing the neoclassic architecture of Havana, San Juan, and Manila in a broader history of simulacra calls into question stale paradigms such as "model" and "copy," thereby allowing us to confront the stagnation of popular center-periphery models that have attempted to explain colonial and national artifacts outside Europe and North America. Styles, designs, and technologies appropriated from those of the United States and Europe take on markedly different valences in the specific context of ex-colonial states such as Cuba, Puerto Rico, and the Philippines. Rapidly reproduced classical monuments, financed by US banks, show us the double-consciousness of coloniality within modernity. These insular works allow us to question Western myths of origin associated with Greco-Roman forms. The cultural politics of those three legislative buildings emerge from unresolved crossroads, wherein the distinction between model and copy, real and imagined, empire and nation, is less important than their intermingling.

With our theoretical stakes established, let us now turn to look, albeit briefly, at each building and its cultural context. A book could be, and in the Cuban and Puerto Rican cases has been, dedicated to each monument. For our purposes, it is instructive to focus on the receptions and resonances of those monuments. Havana's Capitolio, for instance, offers a rich history of artistic mimicry and unknowable models. The form of El Capitolio has invariably elicited the authority of other objects, from the Capitol in Washington, DC, to the Pantheon of Paris to St. Peter's Basilica in Rome. Already in 1927, during the building's construction along Havana's Prado Boulevard, Spanish polemicist Luis Araquistáin noted that El Capitolio would surely rival the US version in its splendor. He then cynically quipped, "I only hope that its inner greatness matches its material."[19]

Cuba's minister of works, Carlos Miguel de Céspedes, located El Capitolio's heritage more in the European tradition. Cuban architect Raúl Otero and technical director Eugenio Rayneri y Piedra based their design on the eighteenth-century French architect Jacques-Germain Soufflot's vision for the Pantheon of Paris. Michelangelo's famed designs for St. Peter's in Rome offered the model for the building's dome. The very name of the building recalled the legendary Temple of Jupiter that topped the Capitoline Hill during the Roman Republic.[20] In all those circumstances, whether evoking an architectural symbol of US governance, authoritarian France, the Italian Renaissance, or the glories of ancient Rome, El Capitolio repeatedly emerged as a symbolic reproduction of something else, removed in time and space. This is despite the fact that many of its architectural and decorative components reflected local traditions, including the colored glass windows (*mediopuntos*) of the building's patio as well as the historic themes of Indigenous labor and sugar cane harvest on the building's exterior metopes. According to critics, though, El Capitolio had an inescapable look of elsewhere about it. Built under the administration of Gerardo Machado, one of the nation's most notorious dictators, El Capitolio rose both menacingly and inspiringly over its citizenry. It was a nationalist mirage in stone and steel of distant uncertain origins.

A similar architecture of fata morgana nationhood and empire emerged in the Capitolio of San Juan. Frank Perkins, the New York–based architect of the original (and never finished) 1908 designs for El Capitolio of Puerto Rico asserted the emblematic power of Greco-Roman replications in the Caribbean context. In Perkins' assessment, those almost-but-not-quite forms met practical as well as symbolic ends. For an island like Puerto Rico, afflicted by tropical hurricanes and earthquakes, adapting the architecture of the Greeks was highly sensible. The buildings of that ancient culture, after all, had resisted similar threats for thousands of years. The same architect, though, used an equally ancient history of imperialism to justify El Capitolio, "that edifice from which wise legislation will emanate for the benefit of the people of a new colony."[21] That is, the building's architecture reenacted the social hierarchies and histories of empire in the ancient tradition, with the United States taking the place of Rome.

Controversy over costs, style (there was a more popular Renaissance design by Carlos del Valle Zeno), and the intervention of World War I led Perkins' project to be abandoned for over a decade.[22] After the passage of the Jones Act in 1917, however, Puerto Ricans officially became US citizens, and the construction of El Capitolio took on renewed symbolic importance. Architect Adrian Finlayson drafted a new plan in the vein of the Spanish Renaissance, but he had to abandon it after becoming ill. Rafael Carmoega, one of the most renowned Puerto Rican architects of the twentieth century, replaced Finlayson on the project. Carmoega, along with a team of architects, drafted a new plan that combined the California Mission style with Frank Perkins' original neoclassic designs.

The new building was a heavily marble-laden government center, the luxuriousness of which San Juan (and few US states) had ever seen. The new design also changed the orientation of the Capitolio from the city to the sea. The building would now look northward across Puerto Rico's Central Highway to the Atlantic Ocean (and presumably the United States beyond). Adorned with a quote by Abraham Lincoln, the building's northern entrance now had its gaze fixed on the island's imperial possessor. While Puerto Rican officials advocated for the building as a symbol of local sovereignty, critics were quick to point out the Capitolio's fraught politics. Puerto Rican–based Czech architect Antonin Nechodoma called it "simply a forest of Corinthian pillars, a mile or so of railings and cornices, about sixteen or so of vases and endless platitudes in its design and interminable clichés in ornament."[23] Like Havana's domed building, Puerto Rico's Capitolio used simulacra to negotiate identity, challenging while also appropriating the projections of US imperial power.

The Legislative Building of Manila spoke to those same projections, as well as their limitations. The building was first conceived under the aegis of the US government after the Philippine-American War (1898–1902). Plans for the building began even as US forces continued to struggle against resistance fighters in the Philippines up until 1913. Daniel Burnham's 1905 City Beautiful plan envisioned the building as a library, situated just south of a massive, and never completed, capitol building—a domed edifice not unlike Havana's and San Juan's and much in the same spirit as Burnham's Chicago plan and the 1901 McMillian plan for Washington, DC. US architect Ralph H. Doane, working for the Bureau of Public Works with Pilipino architect Antonio Toledo, first designed Manila's Legislative Building as a national library. In the Battle of Manila of 1945, the deadliest urban conflict in the Pacific theatre, the building suffered irreparable shelling and bombing damage, as US forces fought to gain back the Philippine capital from Japanese troops. Painstakingly reconstructed after World War II, the building serves today as the National Museum of Fine Arts.

Similar to Havana's and San Juan's Capitolios, located just outside the old colonial city, Doane's design situated Manila's imposing edifice along Burgos Drive, across from the old walled city of Manila (Intramuros). The Philippine legislature, established just two years earlier, decided to make use of Doane and Toledo's library in lieu of Burnham's costly and unfinished Kapitolyo. They hired renowned Pilipino architect Juan M. Arellano to redesign the space. Arellano decorated the neoclassic edifice with locally and universally symbolic signs: the humanoid forms of the principle islands of Luzon, Visayas, and Mindanao, alongside representations of Commerce, Agriculture, Law, and Learning. The second regular session of the 7th Philippine Senate occurred there in 1926 during the building's formal inauguration. US dignitaries, including general Leonard Wood, attended the event, as well as the nation's first and future president, Manuel Quezon, who also used the building for his oath of office in 1935.

Writing of Manila's Legislative Building in 1926, A. V. H. Hartendorp, editor of the journal *Philippine Education*, praised its replications but also its originality: "Dominantly Roman in architecture, but Greek in grace, Renaissance in its wealth of ornament, modern in its freedom from academic restraint, and Oriental in its richness in color. The whole may be said to typify Philippine culture at its best—not a mixture, but a merging of native and foreign, of East and West, the two combining to make a new and richer harmony."[24] The editor noted, in other words, how those seemingly foreign neoclassic designs communicated multiple messages in the cultural context of Manila. Like the architectural discourse emerging in Havana and San Juan, neoclassical formalism embodied the specter of US imperialism. Yet local architects also saw in those traditionalist designs a means to test that authority, asserting and legitimizing new expressions of nationalist and protonationalist identity in the Caribbean and Pacific.

Coda: Dreams, Nightmares, and Impossibilities

The short story "The Circular Ruins" by Argentine fabulist Jorge Luis Borges presents a fitting metaphor for the lessons to be learned from those almost-but-not quite works of neoclassic art and architecture in Cuba, Puerto Rico, and the Philippines. In the story, a mage dreams another man to life only to discover that he himself is the dream of another.[25] Like the repeating wizards of Borges' tale, the repeating Liberties and Martís of Havana and their architectural counterparts, the legislative buildings of Cuba, Puerto Rico, and the Philippines, oscillated in a circle of simulacra, found in their form and history. In a formal sense, the neoclassic works of Havana, Manila, and San Juan recalled the spirit of other classical statuary, monuments, and architecture, which in turn found their own shadows in earlier works. Truly, the Greco-Roman Statue of Liberty, the US Capitol building, the Pantheon of Paris, St. Peter's Basilica, or any neoclassical statehouse for that matter could be called simulacra. They all replicated the fantasies of the Roman Republic and Empire. The Romans, meanwhile, reproduced the grandeur of both the Etruscans and the Greeks. Ancient Greece, in turn, aimed to revive the spirit of Mycenae and Egypt. In that space of rupture between imitation and adaption, one begins to understand what worried Plato and what yet captivates historians of visual and material culture like myself. The Liberties, Martís, Capitolios, and Legislative Buildings of the Caribbean and Pacific may well have been (and still are) dreams of dreams, copies of copies. But they are ultimately Cuban dreams. Philippine dreams. Puerto Rican dreams. Dreams in which context quells any aesthetic debates that might surround the ambivalence of model and copy, real and imagined, nation and empire.

Our story of art, architecture, empire, and nationalism does not end there, however. We may conclude that neoclassical works were emblematic of nationalist dreams in the US insular context. Neoclassicism represented an ideal of US-style democracy, but also the darker side of US imperialism, from the 1790s until the end of World War II. At that point, federal modernism, associated with the likes of Ludwig Mies van der Rohe and Walter Gropius, replaced neoclassicism as the preferred style for US civic monuments at home and abroad. The change in style, however, did not result in a resolution between local sovereignty and imperialism in the US insular empire; the capitols of Hawai'i and Guam are prime examples.

The US Navy constructed the Legislative Building of Guam in Hagåtña in 1949. It was a concrete, rectangular building, typical of the modern movement style. The massive steel-and-concrete structure was hardly reflective of native architecture, more often constructed from bug-resistant Ifit trees and later Philippine hardwoods. But it would soon come to symbolize hard-won autonomy for native Chamorro peoples. Just a year after the building's inauguration, local civic leaders, including Leon Guerrero and Antonio C. Cruz, used the building as a site for staging public protests. Their walkout campaign succeeded in changing Guam's civil status, eliminating navy military rule in 1950. In so doing, they also effectively reinscribed the US-style Congress Building as an icon of Indigenous resistance efforts.[26]

Years later, in 1965, the Hawaiian firm Belt, Lemon, and Lo, working with John Carl Warnecke and Associates, conceived their plans for the State Capitol in Honolulu using Bauhaus architecture, known locally as Hawaiian international architecture. The open-air design of the entire building gave a vision of Indigenous geographies, as much is it represented Hawai'i as a relatively new state in the American Union. A pool around the building symbolized the Pacific Ocean. Volcano-shaped legislative chambers connoted geologic origins. Palm-like columns emblemized the eight principal islands of the state. Native trees (*kukuis*) in the building's courtyard evoked major gods: Kāne, Kanaloa, Kūka'ilimoku, and Lono. Rainbows that formed in the same courtyard manifested the celestial path of the gods. The design program carried multiple valences. As an icon of federal modernism, Hawai'i's capitol symbolized US federal control. Yet the iconography of the building's architectural features also conveyed cultural belief systems associated with Hawaiian sovereignty, spirituality, and history.[27]

These latter-day examples of federal architecture in the US insular context offer nuance to ongoing debates about what makes a federal monument attractive in the United States today. According to the document noted at the beginning of this chapter, there are some who believe we ought to turn back to Greece and Rome, as Washington and Jefferson once did. What that viewpoint fails to acknowledge is the impossibility of such a return. Architectural styles are contradictory at best. They are at once meaningless in themselves and yet freighted by complex histories. Neither modernism nor neoclassicism is an inherently democratic art form. Both may just as easily serve imperial interests as autocratic ones.

After World War II, modernist styles such as brutalism became emblematic of both Joseph Stalin's repressive Communist regime in the Union of Soviet Socialist Republics and the conspiracy-driven deep state of the United States. Before that, modernist styles such as art deco dominated US commercial architecture, from the Rockefeller Center of New York to the Bacardi Building of Havana. Neoclassicism, at the same time, reigned supreme as the federal style of the United States, as emblemized in the Lincoln Memorial of 1922. Yet neoclassicism also acted as the primary inspiration for fascist architecture in the 1930s and 1940s. Albert Speer's unrealized 1938 plans for the massive Volkshalle of Berlin, with its domed façade flanked by seminude colossal sculptures, was highly reminiscent of the capitol buildings of the United States and those later built under US imperial influence in the Caribbean and Pacific in the 1920s. Adolf Hitler created a sketch of the Volkshalle using neoclassical designs in 1925, just years before Cuba, Puerto Rico, and the Philippines erected their own legislative buildings.[28] The obvious links forged between neoclassicism and fascism would perhaps even explain why modernism gained such favor as the new face of the US government after the fall of Nazi Germany.

Placed in the broader field of history, the classical canon did, and still does, possess a certain power for the United States and the islands affected by its empire after 1898. Prior to World War II, neoclassical art and architecture was especially effective at representing an emergent sense of national identity, recognizable to both local and foreign audiences. What the particular case studies in this chapter show, however, is that neoclassicism is not sufficient in itself. Nor is modernism. No style possesses the ideological claims to make nationalism, imperialism, or local island cultures "beautiful again." Rather, the meanings of civic art and architecture continually oscillate around multiple stakes and stakeholders, dreams and dreamers: from autocrats and empires to artists and architects to the multitude of dispossessed Indigenous, Black, and Brown voices left out of official narratives. Both neoclassicism and modernism will no doubt play a role in those nationalist dreams to come. We should always beware, however, of the political and historical context in which such styles emerge. Disguised in marble, stone, and steel, history tells us, democratic dreams can also resemble despotic nightmares.

Notes

1. "Deliberative / Predecisional / Privileged Executive Order: Making Federal Buildings Beautiful Again," February 4, 2020, accessed April 17, 2021, https://architexturez.net/system/files/Draft_of_Trump_White_House_Executive_Order_on_Federal_Buildings.pdf, 1–7. Retitled "Promoting Beautiful Federal Civic Architecture," the executive order became a short-lived law on December 18, 2020. The following administration rescinded the order, February 24, 2021.

2. For analysis, see Katie Rogers and Robin Pogrebin, "Draft Executive Order Would Give Trump a New Target: Modern Design," *New York Times,* February 5, 2020.

3. Paul B. Niell and Stacie G. Widdifield, eds., *Buen Gusto and Classicism in the Visual Cultures of Latin America, 1780–1910* (Albuquerque: University of New Mexico Press, 2013).

4. Vivien Green Fryd, *Art and Empire: The Politics of Ethnicity in the United States Capitol, 1815–1860* (New Haven, CT: Yale University Press, 1992).

5. Saavedra regularly contracted out his work to the lesser-known Italian artist Giuseppe Neri. It is possible that the statue may have been the work of Neri, a viewpoint reinforced by

the inaccuracies in the crest held by Martí, which features seven blue stripes rather than five. Florencia Peñate, "Apuntes sobre la escultura en Centro Habana y su entorno," *Arquitectura y Urbanismo* 31, no. 3 (2010): 91, accessed January 5, 2015, http://rau.cujae.edu.cu.

6. A Caribbean sunrise over an icon of a key also adorns the top of the crest—connoting Cuba's location between Yucatan, Europe, and the United States, known in the colonial period as "The Key to the Indies." See Rolando Pujols and Teresa García Ortiz, *Guía de El Capitolio* ([Spain]: Com-Relieve, 1998), 24. On the inconsistencies of the crest on the Martí statue, see footnote 5.

7. See Marial Iglesias Utset, *Las metáforas del cambio en la vida cotidiana: Cuba, 1898–1902* (Havana: Ediciones Unión, 2010), 46–50; translated in English as Marial Iglesias Utset, *A Cultural History of Cuba during the US Occupation, 1898–1902* (Chapel Hill: University of North Carolina Press, 2011), 25–28; Jorge Oller Oller, "Primera estatua en homenaje a José Martí," *Grandes momentos del fotorreportaje cubano,* Cuba Periodistas, January 19, 2012, accessed 5 Jan. 2015, http://www.cubaperiodistas.cu.

8. Emilio Roig de Leuchsenring, *La Habana: Apuntes históricos* (Havana: Municipio de la Habana, 1939), 18–21; Abel Fernández y Simón, "Las fuentes de las plazas, parques y paseos públicos de la Habana colonial," in *Cuba: Arquitectura y urbanismo,* ed. Felipe J. Préstamo y Hernández (Miami, FL: Ediciones Universal, 1995), 337–351; Joaquín E. Weiss, *La arquitectura colonial cubana: Siglos XVI al XIX* (Havana: Instituto Cubano del Libro, Agencia Española de Cooperación International, and Consejería de Obras Públicas y Transportes Junta de Andalucia, 1996), 361–366; and Eduardo Sánchez de Fuentes and Rafael Montoro, *Cuba monumental, estatuaria y epigráfica: Comprende la historia verídica y completa, por orden cronológico, de los monumentos, esculturas, y lápidas, que existieron y existen en todo el territorio nacional, dividida en las épocas: Precolombina, colonial, interventoras y republicanas* (Havana: Impr. Solana, 1916), 139–153.

9. Francisco Morán, "José Martí o el convidado de piedra: desenfoques de la identidad nacional," *Arr—idéhistorisk tidsskrift* 1–2 (2013): 1–30.

10. Carlos Ripoll, *José Martí, the United States, and the Marxist Interpretation of Cuban History* (New Brunswick, NJ: Transaction Books, 1984), 53. See also Enrique Collazo, *Los americanos en Cuba* (Havana: Editorial de Ciencias Sociales, Instituto Cubano del Libro, 1972).

11. "¿Qué estatua debe ser colocada en el Parque Central?," *El Fígaro,* no. 16 (April 30, 1899): 18.

12. Utset, *Cultural History,* 26; see also discussion of cartoons in Louis A. Pérez, Jr., *Cuba in the American Imagination: Metaphor and the Imperial Ethos* (Chapel Hill: University of North Carolina Press, 2008). The cover image of this volume, "Well, I hardly know which to take first!" printed in the *Boston Globe,* May 28, 1898, comes from that same milieu. In this case, the cartoon depicts the ex-island colonies of Spain as consumable goods, ready to be served to a beard-stroking Uncle Sam by President McKinley.

13. On Havana's Capitolio, see Rolando Ancieto Ramos, *El capitolio de La Habana* (Havana: Centro Capitolio de La Habana, 1998); for a primary source on the same neoclassical edifice, see Carlos Miguel de Céspedes, *Libro del Capitolio* (Havana: Talleres tip. de P. Fernández y compañía, 1933).

For the Puerto Rican Capitolio, see the Archivo General de Puerto Rico, Fondo Obras Públicas, Serie Edificios Públicos, files 116–118, boxes 689–690; and the "Capitolio Collection" of the Archivo de Arquitectura y Construcción de la Universidad de Puerto Rico (AACUPR). See also Enrique Vivoni Farage, *El Capitolio de Puerto Rico, 1907–1929: Origen y transformación de un ideal puertorriqueño* (San Juan, Puerto Rico: [n.p.], 1991).

For US colonial architecture in Manila and the Legislative Building, destroyed in 1945 during World War II and reconstructed in 1949, see A. V. H. Hartendorp, "The Legislative Building," *Philippine Education* 22–23 (1926): 264–267; Gerardo Lico, *Arkitekturang Filipino: A History of Architecture and Urbanism in the Philippines* (Quezon City: University of the Philippines Press, 2008), 308-311; Norma Alarcón, *The Imperial Tapestry: American Colonial Architecture in the Philippines* (Manila: University of Santo Tomas Publishing House, 2008); and Ian Morley, *Cities and Nationhood: American Imperialism and Urban Design in the Philippines, 1898–1916* (Honolulu: University of Hawai'i Press, 2018).

14. Antonio Benítez-Rojo, *The Repeating Island: The Caribbean and the Postmodern Perspective* (Durham, NC: Duke University Press, 1992).

15. See Anibal Quijano, "Coloniality of Power, Eurocentrism, and Latin America," *Nepantla: Views from the South* 1, no. 3 (2000): 533–580; and Walter Mignolo, "Delinking: The Rhetoric of Modernity, the Logic of Coloniality, and the Grammar of De-coloniality," *Cultural Studies* 21, no. 2 (2007): 449–514.

16. The following discussion of simulacra expands on earlier arguments made by the author. See Joseph R. Hartman, *Dictator's Dreamscape: How Architecture and Vision Built Machado's Cuba and Invented Modern Havana* (Pittsburgh: University of Pittsburgh Press, 2019), 22–58.

17. See Jean Baudrillard, *Simulacra and Simulation* (Ann Arbor: University of Michigan Press, 1994), 4; and Jean Baudrillard and Francesco Proto, *Mass, Identity, Architecture: Architectural Writings of Jean Baudrillard* (Chichester, UK: Wiley Academy, 2003); and Gilles Deleuze, *Difference and Repetition*. Translated by Paul Patton (New York: Columbia University Press, 1968), 69. See also Michael Camille, "Simulacrum," in *Critical Terms for Art History*, ed. Robert S. Nelson and Richard Shiff (Chicago, IL: University of Chicago Press, 1996), 31–44.

18. Homi K. Bhabha, *The Location of Culture* (New York: Routledge, 1994), 122.

19. Luis Araquistáin, *La Agonia antillana: El Imperialismo yanqui en el mar Caribe (Impresiones de un viaje a Puerto Rico, Santo Domingo, Haiti y Cuba)* (Madrid: Espasa-Calpe, s.a., 1928), 180.

20. Céspedes, *Libro del Capitolio*, 284. On the capitol building's inauguration on May 20, 1929, see Secretaría de la Presidencia, Fondo 87, no. 36, Archivo Nacional de la República de Cuba. On technical director Eugenio Rayneri y Piedra, the first graduate of Notre Dame's School of Architecture (an institution founded by his father, Eugenio Rayneri y Sorrentino), see Notre Dame Scrapbook B, box 1, no. 2; Notre Dame Presidents' Letters, 1856-1906 (hereafter cited as UPEL), box 89, nos. 1 and 3; UPEL, box 105, nos. 5 and 7; and UPEL, box 100, nos. 15 and 16, all in the Notre Dame Archives. Many thanks to Havana's late city historian, Dr. Eusebio Leal Spengler, for providing me with access to the building during its restoration.

21. Frank F. Perkins, "The New Capitol of Puerto Rico," *Architectural Record* 25 (1909): 273.

22. Vivoni Farage, *El Capitolio de Puerto Rico;* and Archivo General de Puerto Rico, Fondo Obras Públicas, Serie Edificios Públicos, files 116–118, boxes 689–690.

23. Antonin Nechodama, "Concerning Architecture in Porto Rico," unfinished manuscript in "Antonin Nechodama Collection" of the AACUPR; and Antonín Nechodama, "Concerning Architecture in Porto Rico," *Western Architect: A National Journal of Architecture and Allied Arts* 36, no. 12 (December 1927): 193.

24. Hartendorp, "Legislative Building," 264.

25. Jorge Luis Borges, "The Circular Ruins," in *Labyrinths: Selected Stories and Other Writings* (New York: New Directions, 1964), 45–50.

26. Anne Perez Hattori, "Righting Civil Wrongs: The Guam Congress Walkout," *Isla: A Journal of Micronesian Studies,* no. 3 (1995): 1–27; For more on architecture in Guam, generally, see also H. Mark Ruth, J. B. Jones, and Morris M. Grobins, *Guidebook to the Architecture of Guam* (Taipei, Taiwan: The Institute, 1977).

27. Kelema Moses, "Almost, but Not Quite: Architecture and the Reconstruction of Space in the Territory of Hawaii," *Colonial Frames, Nationalist Histories: Imperial Legacies, Architecture, and Modernity,* ed. Madhuri Desai and Mrinalini Rajagopalan (Burlington, VT: Ashgate, July 2012), 161–184.

28. For classical styles in Nazi Germany, see Alexander Scobie, *Hitler's State Architecture: The Impact of Classical Antiquity* (University Park: Published for College Art Association by the Pennsylvania State University Press, 1990); and Lutz P. Koepnick, "Fascist Aesthetics Revisited," *Modernism/modernity* 6, no. 1 (January 1999): 51–73. For the use of modernist architecture alongside appropriations of the classical past in Fascist Italy, see Simonetta Falasca-Zamponi, *Fascist Spectacle: The Aesthetics of Power in Mussolini's Italy* (Berkeley: University of California Press, 1997); and D. Medina Lasansky, *The Renaissance Perfected: Architecture, Spectacle, and Tourism in Fascist Italy* (University Park: Pennsylvania State University Press, 2004).

Part IV

War, Resistance, and Spatial Experience in the Pacific

TWELVE

Colonial Concrete

American Architectures of Containment and Marshallese Reinscription of Space as Resistance

Brenda S. Gardenour Walter

During the arms race that escalated through the mid-twentieth century, Western powers sought out spaces that were "empty," and therefore "safe," to serve as nuclear test sites.[1] The United States, for example, began atomic testing in the deserts within its own boundaries, including Socorro, New Mexico, the site of Trinity (1945), and the Nevada Test Site outside of Las Vegas. Beyond its borders, the United States looked to other "empty spaces" such as the Marshall Islands in the Pacific Ocean. In 1946, the US military conducted the Able and Baker tests, both of which were centered on the Marshallese atoll of Bikini. The Castle Bravo test in 1954 released fifteen megatons of TNT on Bikini and produced atomic fallout for seven thousand square miles.[2] The political decision to conduct atomic testing in the desert Southwest and the Pacific Ocean was shaped by American cultural constructions of civilization, the hallmarks of which included population density, permanent infrastructures, and technological advancement. Areas that did not possess these characteristics were seen as uncivilized and primitive wildernesses devoid of life—empty spaces.[3] Of course, neither the desert nor the islands of the Pacific were empty; both were full of life and had long histories of human habitation. American authorities knew that the Pacific atolls were populated, but saw the Indigenous Marshallese as nomadic, impermanent, and therefore fungible within an expendable natural world. From an American military perspective shaped by cultural politics, this rendered the Marshallese as viable test subjects for experimentation, and their islands open to occupation.[4]

After World War II, the American military and their civilian contractors occupied Kwajalein Atoll, the main island of which served as headquarters for anti-ballistic missile research, development, and testing. The American occupation of Kwajalein was marked by an aggressive building program, grounded in spatial politics. From airstrips, missile silos, and radomes to the self-contained housing units installed for the families of military contractors, the extensive use of reinforced concrete on Kwajalein and its surrounding islands reflected American Cold War fears and the cultural politics of containment. Back on the midcentury mainland, affluent whites abandoned urban areas imagined to be "polluted" by poverty, crime, and racial strife, and retreated to gated suburban communities that functioned as white bubbles in a troubled world. There, they lived in middle-class fortresses that reflected Western constructions of the human body as mechanical and impenetrable, both building and body serving as strong outer shells to preserve patriarchal order and protect vulnerable interiors from infection and corruption.[5] These obsessive patterns of segregation and containment pertained to the American-occupied Pacific. The first phase of building on Kwajalein entailed the forcible removal of the Marshallese people who lived there. Relocated to the adjacent island of Ebeye, they joined other Indigenous persons from the Mid-Atoll Corridor who had been displaced by missile testing. By the 1970s, Kwajalein was a privileged white bubble, a strangely dislocated but familiar American suburb, featuring a country club, restaurants, and a movie theater, as well as a high school, hospital, and firehouse—all built from concrete and founded on Western architectural principles. Beyond the concrete cultural bubble, on the overcrowded island of Ebeye, the Marshallese were left to rebuild their communities from waves of rubble left by American colonizers.

The Marshallese construction of space, including its visible architectures and the invisible cultural networks flowing through them, was (and is) antithetical to the American imperial architecture that disrupted it. Where American architecture was built from tons of immovable concrete that smothered delicate island ecosystems, traditional Marshallese architecture was constructed from loosely woven pandanus fronds that often floated away on the trade winds. Like the Marshallese construction of the body, pandanus structures were open to the environment and fully integrated into the natural world. The architecture of American-occupied Kwajalein was highly specialized, restricted movement, and focused on the nuclear family; traditional Marshallese architecture, however, consisted of a single multipurpose space that facilitated continual contact between extended family members, the larger community, and nonhuman island life. This traditional architecture and the cultural patterns that it embodied were disrupted by the dislocation of the Marshallese to Ebeye, where they lived in increasingly cramped and squalid conditions, with little land for growing taro and few pandanus trees for building homes. Hemmed in by the debris of two world wars, toxic waste from nuclear testing, and endless heaps of American garbage and concrete, the

Marshallese were confronted with a new architectural environment, born of Western detritus, designed to contain them. In response, the Marshallese have continued to resist concrete colonialism and maintain the fluidity of body and community so central to their culture by inscribing these values within and upon their architectural environment—both at home in the Marshall Islands and in diasporic communities on the American mainland. Through the lens of architectural theory, the persistent openness of Marshallese construction of space becomes a powerful locus of Indigenous resistance and an agent for social change.

Permeable Pandanus

Creation accounts from traditional Marshallese cosmology exist in various permutations, but each of them situates the first act of creation in the ocean. All beings were born of Lowa, an ocean god, who "spoke to the sea," calling forth the reefs, plants, and birds.[6] From a boil on Lowa's leg were born Wulleb and Lejman; their blood generated still more creatures, until the islands were populated.[7] Lowa likewise created the deities of the four cardinal directions—Irojrilik, Lakameran, Rerek, Lalikian—the giants of Kili Island, and the *anjinmar* (nature spirits) who dwell on each atoll.[8] All of these acts of creation bound living creatures and their natural environments to a common ancestor in the spiritual world. For the Marshallese, gods and spirits continue to inhabit earth and human body alike, flowing through land and flesh, binding them forever through a fluid network of connections. Much like the coral that serves as a skeletal system for the atolls themselves, the Marshallese body is permeable, leaving it vulnerable to *anjilik,* or evil spirits, that can "bring illness to people and even abduct the soul from the body."[9] Such illnesses were traditionally treated by local healers who specialized in spiritual and physical care. If the cause of the affliction was divined to be spiritual, a priest (*drikanan*) would construct a small canoe of pandanus leaves and send the *anjilik* back out to sea.[10] Physical conditions, however, were treated by compounding medicines, altering diets, and massage. Just as the body was healed with natural substances during life, so too did it return to the natural world after death. While the fleshy husk remained on its home island, the soul departed in a canoe, first to the outermost atoll, Nadikdik, and then on to Eoerök, "the islands of the dead."[11] There, some souls persisted in spirit form while others became animals, plants, or rocks—a return that took them back to their cosmological origins, at one with sacred earth and sea.

The permeability of the Marshallese body and its connectedness to the natural environment is reflected in traditional Marshallese architecture. Family homes were constructed from wooden poles wrapped with loosely woven pandanus leaves or coconut fronds. Floors consisted of pounded earth covered with pandanus mats for comfort.[12] Rarely larger than twelve by fifteen feet, homes centered on a central, open, multipurpose space shared by extended family, with activities often spilling out into the surrounding yard, and community members flowing inward. Partial walls left these structures open not only to human activity but also to trade winds, rain, and the rare typhoon that might sweep them off into the Pacific. This architecture was likewise used in the construction of the royal compounds that housed members of the *iroij* (traditional male leaders) and the meetinghouses for men. Despite being a matriarchal society in terms of lineage and inheritance, the cultural politics of the Marshallese was patriarchal, from local decision making to royal leadership, from the crafting of political alliances to the conduct of war.[13] Like their bodies and buildings, their social structure was permeable and interconnected, with clans vying for power on and between atolls, traders traveling from island to island exchanging goods and cowrie shells, and families relocating through marriage or in search of resources. Very few material artifacts and even fewer architectural structures have survived to bear witness to Marshallese history. Pandanus buildings were never intended to be permanent but were rather quickly constructed and reconstructed as needed. Permeable and temporary, Marshallese architecture acknowledged human impermanence while affirming human connections to the natural world. Through war, weather, and decay, most of them have disappeared.[14] What remains as a testament to the past are the living Marshallese people, their culture, their stories, and their atolls—their truest home, an extension of their embodiment in life and death.

Unbounded, the Marshall Islands and its people have been repeatedly penetrated by imperial "others," first the Germans and then the Japanese, each group bringing with them diseases and invasive nonindigenous plants and animals who disrupted atoll ecosystems.[15] World War II introduced Western soldiers, bombs, and warships, the wreckage of which still lies at the bottom of lagoons and reefs from Kwajalein to Truk.[16] The damage done by all of these forces, however, cannot compare to the long-lasting physical and cultural destruction resulting from nuclear testing. In 1946, the United States commenced Operation Crossroads—two atomic detonations near Bikini meant to test the effects of nuclear weapons on ships at sea. This was only the beginning of a twelve-year nuclear program involving sixty-seven tests, the radiation and infection of multiple island bodies, and the subsequent relocation of populations to other atolls, including Kwajalein, which served as headquarters for the American nuclear project. One of the "leading environmental crimes of all times," nuclear testing in the Pacific disrupted the complex and interconnected environmental and bodily worlds of the Marshallese.[17] Bombing not only killed flora and fauna and crushed coral, the very bones of the atoll, but also irradiated the earth itself.[18] The 1954 Bravo test, a ground detonation on Bikini, was so powerful that it resulted in the fusion of soil, sand, water, and radioactive particles, and this toxic dust rose up and fell on the neighboring atolls of Rongelap and Utrik.[19] Inhabitants breathed in the fallout, consumed it in food and water, and quickly developed radiation sickness. According to one survivor who later testified at citizens' hearings, "our people began to be very sick, they vomited, burns showed on their skin, and people's hair began to fall out."[20] The US government secretly enrolled survivors in Project 4.1, an unethical medical experimentation program designed to study the longitudinal effects of radiation on the human body, all for the benefit of weapons designers.[21] American authorities eventually evacuated the people of Rongelap to Kwajalein and Majuro, but they were returned to their irradiated home island within three years of the initial blast. For almost thirty years they remained on Rongelap, where they suffered the long-term effects of atomic testing, including increased cases of thyroid disease and leukemia, miscarriages, "jelly-fish babies" born with translucent skin that survived for only hours, and other genetic birth defects.[22] Marshallese healers prepared traditional compounds to ease this suffering, but the plants and the soil from which they grew were similarly contaminated. In 1985, with the help of Greenpeace, the people of Rongelap finally left the island of their ancestors and were relocated to Majuro and Mejatto near Kwajalein. For the people of Rongelap, nuclear testing altered the very architecture of their bodies, breaking and rearranging strands of DNA, "a nuclear history threaded into their bloodlines."[23] It likewise severed them from the island, now irradiated, that embodied their historical and cultural identity. In the words of one Rongelap survivor, "You cannot put enough value on land.... How do you put a value on something that people consider as a living thing that is part of your soul?"[24]

Concrete Containment

American destruction in the North Pacific and the displacement of the Marshallese did not end with the Nuclear Test Ban Treaty of 1963. While atomic testing was no longer permitted, the Marshall Islands remained a strategic proving ground for the US military. In 1964, the US Department of Defense negotiated a ninety-nine-year lease on Kwajalein. Like fallout from an atomic bomb, Americans settled across Kwajalein Atoll, further disrupting an already destabilized environment. Under American occupation, the Marshallese who once called Kwajalein home were removed to the adjacent island of Ebeye. This new era of American imperialism was marked not only by the displacement of Indigenous populations and their relocation to local islands for later use as disposable resources but also by the claiming and control of appropriated space through aggressive building programs. Having taken possession of the atoll, Americans built modern airstrips, docks for naval vessels, research buildings, missile launch towers, and multiple radar facilities with globular radomes on several of the islands. On Kwajalein, housing and other suburban amenities were added for personnel and their families. Almost all of these structures were built of reinforced concrete, a building material chosen less for utility than for reasons related to cultural politics.

In *Building Change: Architecture, Politics, and Cultural Agency,* Lisa Findley argues that "from the scale of the buildings and cities to the scale of the landscape," architecture embodies "cultural practices and ideologies" bound to power.[25] On Kwajalein, the American imperial building program is a permanent expression of containment, an ideology deeply rooted in Western constructions of the body. Unlike the Marshallese, who see their bodies as interconnected with the environment and temporary in form, the American construction of the body is mechanical, durable, and clearly bounded. The healthy body is a well-ordered machine, reparable through biomedical intervention. The internal organs function like tubes and pipes, the muscles and heart like mechanical pumps, all regulated by electrical impulses from nerves wired to a computer brain.[26] Externally, the skin serves as a form of containment, preventing the invasion of disease and potential defeat. It likewise functions as a biological perimeter cordoning off the human body from nature, which is seen as both a terrifying wilderness and a resource to be exploited—an "empty space" full of potential. In twentieth-century America, the Cold War exacerbated long-standing cultural obsessions with bodily containment and environmental control. Fear of subtle infiltration by communist spies and devastating penetration by foreign bombs led to the construction of fallout shelters and subterranean chambers. Racist fears of nonwhite urban populations served as a catalyst for the growth of the white suburbs, gated communities that protected inhabitants from contact with potentially infectious "danger."[27] Within these insulated microcosms, the middle-class home became a refuge from atomic age fears, a patriarchal fortress with shuttered windows, locked doors, and self-contained heating, cooling, and filtration systems—a building constructed to function much like American bodies. An isolated bunker among bunkers, suburban house-bodies were arranged like a barracks, their foundations forged from impenetrable and immovable concrete.

The cultural politics of concrete containment that shaped architecture on the American mainland were exported to Kwajalein throughout the second half of the twentieth century. The three refurbished airstrips on Kwajalein no longer delivered military personnel alone but also the employees of defense contractors such as Raytheon and their families. To entice researchers to Kwajalein, which was imagined by Americans to be in the "middle of nowhere" or "at the ends of the earth," military-style housing was replaced by a replica of an American suburb familiar from the mainland (figure 12.1).[28] Because of the space required, a decision was made to extend the northern end of the island by pouring a substrate of concrete as a footing. This act not only drowned aquatic life in cement but also restrained the island's edges, which naturally shifted with changing currents and fluctuations in sea level. Upon this now-permanent foundation, engineers designed the first American family neighborhood on Kwajalein, known as Silver City, which featured paved roads laid out in a grid pattern and small plots of land.[29] At the center of each plot was a new trailer home featuring all of the modern conveniences, such as top-of-the-line kitchen appliances—including a dishwasher, which was seen as a luxury back in the states—a washer and dryer, an AT&T telephone, and, of course, air conditioning (figure 12.2). Replicating the middle-class homes on the mainland, the trailers of Silver City were self-contained body units that breathed filtered air, consumed purified water, and discretely excreted waste through hidden pipes.[30] Each of these structures was kept alive with a steady stream of electricity powered by fuel delivered across thousands of miles of ocean by tanker and plane.

American-occupied Kwajalein featured other structures familiar to suburban life on the mainland, including a school, a hospital, a firehouse, a

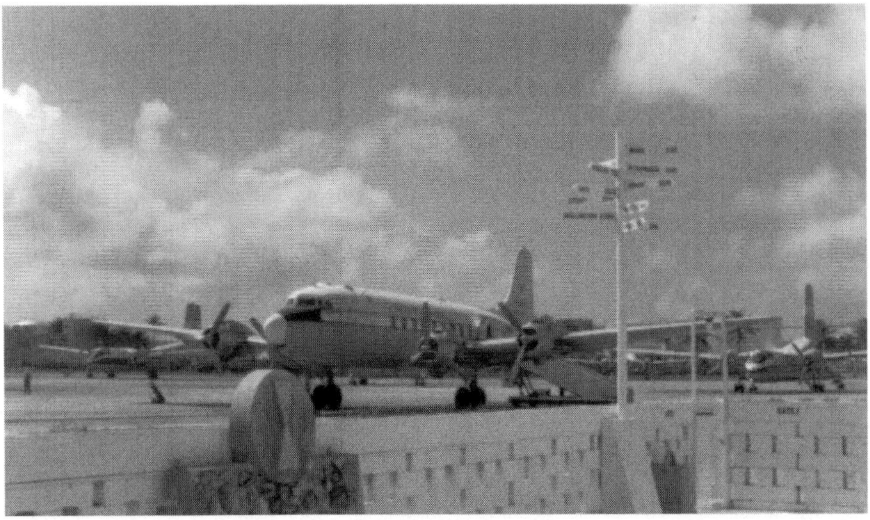

Figure 12.1. Kwajalein test site airport, 1975. The sign at the edge of the runway indicates the distance between Kwajalein—"the middle of nowhere"—and more familiar places on land. Photograph by James Kaiser, the author's father.

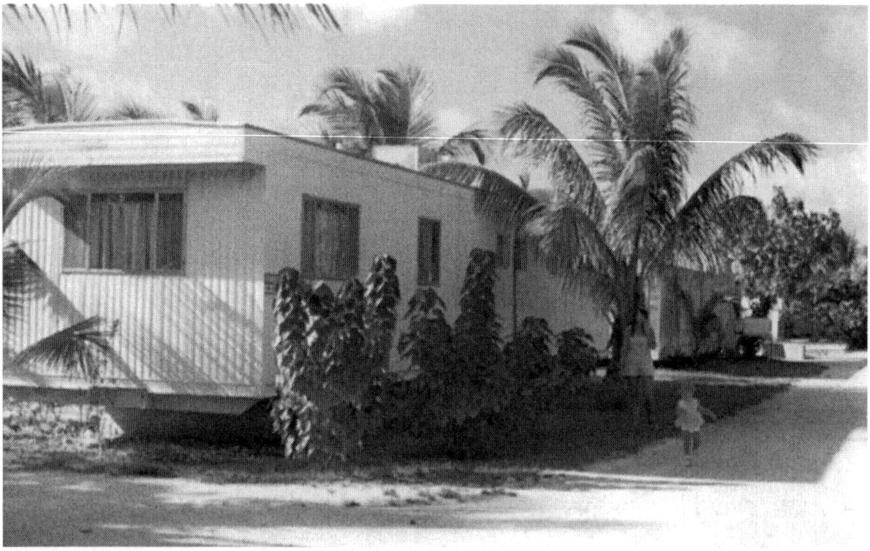

Figure 12.2. Trailer homes for Raytheon employees and their families, c. 1973. The trailers were arranged in a gridded neighborhood called Silver City because of their reflection when seen from the air. Single employees lived in an apartment complex called "The Bachelor's Quarters." Photograph by James Kaiser, the author's father.

hotel called the Kwaj Lodge, and a small department store (actually a commissary) lovingly nicknamed "Macy's." With little else to worry about, much of life on Kwajalein was dedicated to recreation. A "Guide to Recreation" published by Special Services in 1972 advertised baseball, tennis, bowling, ham radio, a hobby shop, and deep sea fishing. Families enjoyed bicycling, picnicking on Emon Beach, swimming in the lagoon, and watching movies at the outdoor Richardson Theater; they were likewise treated to a yearly carnival and Fourth of July fireworks. Further adding to the privileged ethos of the island, there was an upscale bar called the Yokwe Yuk Club, which hosted an annual military ball, and the Kwajalein Country Club—a refurbished army bunker—that featured a meticulously maintained golf course. Almost all of the community structures associated with bourgeois life on Kwaj were built from reinforced concrete—safe, contained, and purportedly permanent. One exception was the Yokwe Yuk Indoor Theater, designed to look like a traditional Marshallese meetinghouse with a steep-pitched roof and open sides but constructed from wood shakes over a steel skeleton rooted in concrete. Heavy and permanent, it is a Marshallese structure appropriated and reconstructed in Western form, a body building rendered "safe" for American occupancy (figure 12.3). Another exception is the Marshallese Cultural Center, funded

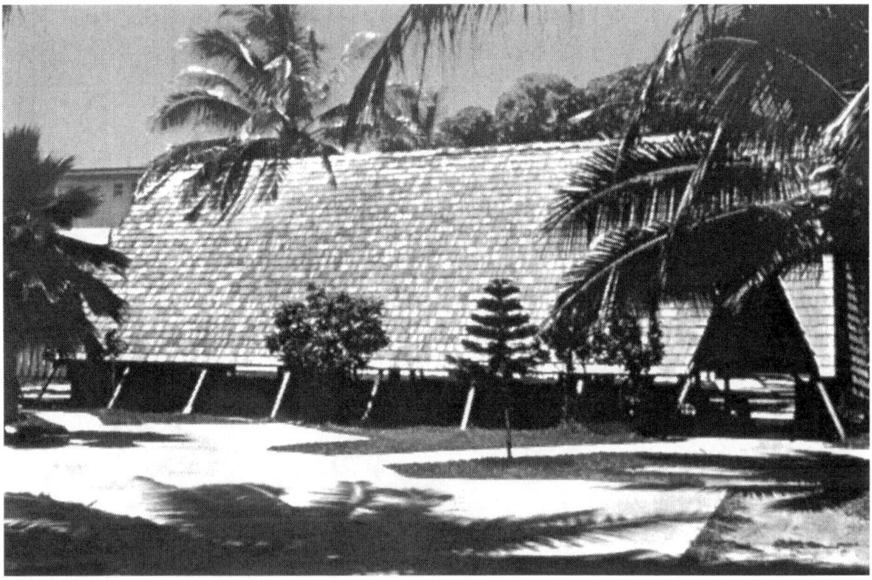

Figure 12.3. Yokwe Yuk Theater, 1973. Written on the back: "This is one of our fine movie theaters. It looks enclosed, but if you look closer you will see the sides are open!" Barbara Kaiser to her mother back in New Hampshire. Postcard by Dexter Color California.

by the US Army in 1998, which features traditional Indigenous architecture, a canoe, and an exhibit area featuring artifacts from "early European contact in the Marshalls and Japanese reign to WW2 Operation Flintlock and Bikini nuclear testing."[31] Since it is on American occupied land, Marshallese have limited access to their own traditional village. With sanitized structures somehow trapped in time, it is meant to commemorate a culture seen by colonizers as having already passed despite its continued existence, its history forever linked with the American agenda in the Pacific.[32]

The American use of colonial concrete to permanently claim space metastasized to other islands in the atoll. The conjoined islets of Roi-Namur, now famous for the size of its rats, house cement research buildings and an enormous ALTAIR radar, an all-seeing mechanical eye that tracks the flight of missiles across the atoll's lagoons. Most of those who work on Roi-Namur fly in by airplane or helicopter from Kwajalein Airport, but the island still has amenities, including a saltwater swimming pool and the "back nine" of the golf course on Kwajalein. Meck Island, an antiballistic missile test launch site, is composed almost entirely from concrete, from its extensive runway and helipad to its missile silos and windowless monitoring bunkers (figure 12.4). Like the island itself, once open to the free passage of Marshallese in their

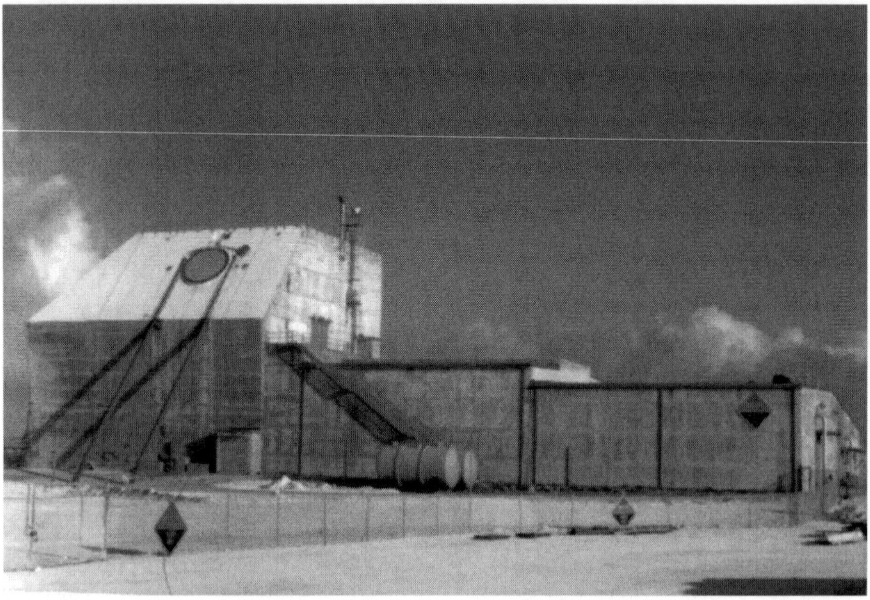

Figure 12.4. Meck Island observation and radar station, 1974. This concrete structure is an expression of colonial containment—outsiders cannot penetrate its shell, but those inside can reach out via radar and missile to control others. Photograph by James Kaiser, the author's father.

canoes, the concrete buildings on Meck are impenetrable and tightly controlled. Containment is likewise evidenced in the most ubiquitous structure on the atoll—the radome. Rising up from large concrete footings, radomes are spherical structures that encase sensitive radar equipment, thereby protecting it from weather and contaminants. Like a strange form of technological skin, radomes contain radar systems while allowing them to reach out into the world from a position of safety. The ultimate goal of all of these concrete structures is not merely to claim Kwajalein Atoll as a permanent space for American occupation in the Pacific but also to test missile systems to be used in defense of the American mainland. Like the concentric perimeters surrounding the Nike Zeus radomes on Kwajalein, concrete containment in the Pacific is an outer defensive wall behind which lay multitudes (figure 12.5).

The continued use of concrete architecture on Kwajalein is a manifestation of American imperialism, a form of occupation that exerts "explicit and implicit control over the shaping and occupation of space," separating body from environment, self from "other."[33] Concrete structures not only contain Americans within an impenetrable and inorganic safe space of their own but also exclude the organic Marshallese, who are seen as dangerous outsiders,

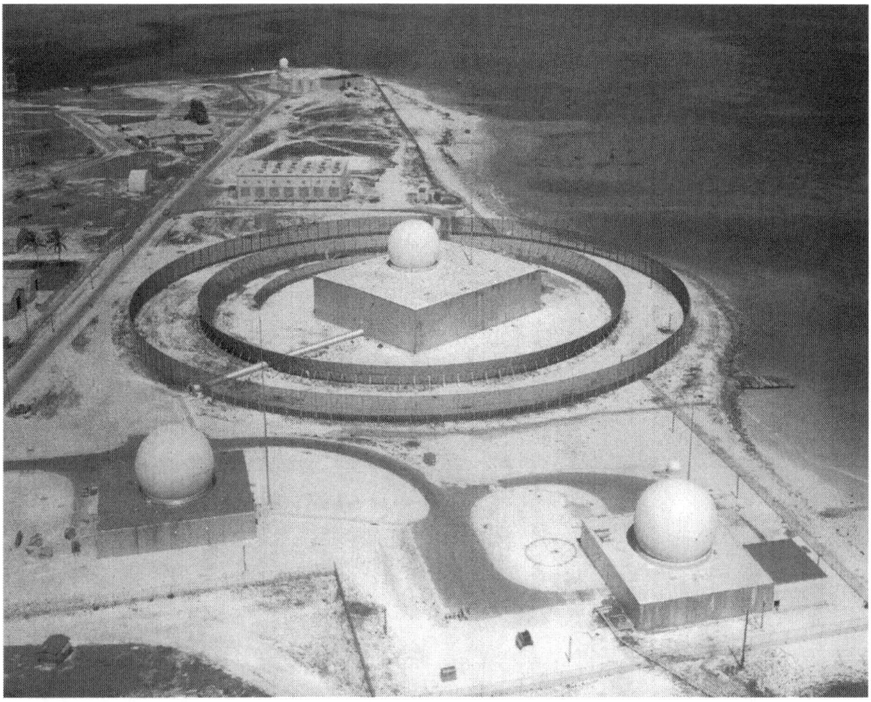

Figure 12.5. Radome complex associated with the Nike Zeus program in the 1960s and 1970s. No date given. Concentric barriers surround a radome that in turn surrounds a mechanical radar eye—a reflection not only of an American construction of the body but also an architectural expression of containment and the cultural politics that it inspired both on the American mainland and in its colonies. Public domain.

porous and unpredictable, and as belonging to the natural world and not the orderly civilization of now-American Kwajalein. In 1951, the Marshallese who once sailed the lagoons in leaky canoes rather than in self-contained steel ships were first exiled to Ebeye, a small island adjacent to Kwajalein.[34] During the day, they were permitted to work on the Big Island, first as laborers to help pour concrete, and then later as maintenance men, groundskeepers, and maids.[35] To allay American fears of bodily and domestic contamination, Marshallese women hired as servants were "given physical examinations at the hospital before being employed."[36] Marshallese workers were transported to Kwajalein on an army ferry known as "The Tarlang," which docked in the morning at 7:00 a.m. and departed each evening by 6:00 p.m. (figure 12.6). No Marshallese were permitted to remain on Kwajalein after the curfew. The same holds true today, although the curfew has shifted to 7:00 p.m. Marshallese caught on the island after curfew are charged with trespassing and sent

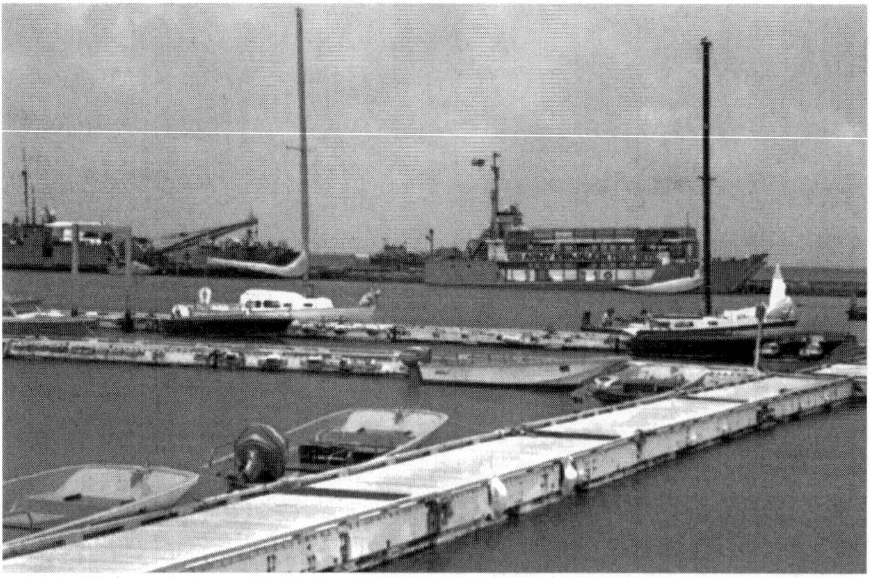

Figure 12.6. US Army Kwajalein test site ferry, nicknamed "The Tarlang," 1974. Written on the back: "The Tarlang is used to transport the Marshallese every day to the island they live on called Ebeye. They come to Kwaj every day about 7:00 AM and leave by 6:00 PM. The small boats are provided for the people on Kwaj by whichever company they work for. As usual, it's free!" Barbara Kaiser to her mother back in New Hampshire. Postcard by Dexter Color California.

back to Ebeye. This applies even to Marshallese married to Americans, as well as to their children; this means that Americans must either live separately from their spouses or move to Ebeye. The choice is not a simple one. On Kwajalein, evenings are given to barbeques and parties backlit by stunning sunsets, all on a meticulously ordered island, sealed and safe from contamination. On Ebeye, conditions are very different.

Lauren Hirschberg has drawn correlations between the white suburbs and redlined inner cities on the mainland to the privileged community on Kwajalein and the disenfranchised Marshallese on Ebeye.[37] Just as people of many colors were left behind in American cities stripped of resources, so too were the Marshallese exploited for their labor and contained in increasingly desperate living conditions. Ebeye is known as the "Slum of the Pacific," with over fifteen thousand people living on an island of less than eighty acres, creating chaos. Shoddily constructed shanties house extended families of forty or more. Several homes have now been constructed on one of the island's garbage dumps, where piles of debris tumble into the sacred sea. In response to the housing crisis on Ebeye, the American-led Kwajalein Atoll Development

Authority proposed a sort of "urban renewal" entailing the construction of three-story apartment blocks made entirely of cement. As of 2018, the twenty-seven-million-dollar project has not yet begun.[38] There are few utilities on Ebeye; waste water treatment is limited, and clean water must be brought back in five-gallon buckets or twenty-four-gallon "water hippos" from other islands, including Kwajalein. Plans have been introduced for a desalination plant, but how to fund it—and where to put it—remain unresolved. Overcrowding and pollution have trapped the Marshallese in a foreign world of concrete and metal debris, the detritus of American imperialism. Traditional Marshallese culture was predicated on fluidity, freedom of movement, the construction of permeable impermanent housing, and daily food production from land and sea. On Ebeye, there is no clean soil to farm; the reefs are strewn with garbage, and the fish are contaminated with toxic chemicals.[39] For sustenance, the people depend on prepackaged processed foods such as ramen and tinned meat, including tuna and Spam—foodways that cause high rates of obesity and diabetes and exacerbate pollution problems.[40] Disconnected from their islands, and restricted in their movement, the Marshallese have been cast into new architectures, bodies, and buildings not of their design, through the slow violence of American occupation.[41] Yet even concrete can crack, and Western structures be inscribed with new meaning, through the resilience of Indigenous culture.

Marshallese Resistance: Cracking Concrete

Despite American imperial attempts to marginalize and constrain Indigenous voices, Pacific islanders have never been silent. Since 1946, Pacific peoples have actively protested nuclear testing, resisted colonization, and advocated for their human rights to health and freedom from oppression. Despite this, Indigenous sociopolitical resistance has been routinely ignored in Western scholarship and politics.[42] In 1985, a multitude of Pacific Island nations came together to declare and ratify the Treaty of Rarotonga, which established a nuclear-free zone in the Pacific. While the Marshall Islands were exempt because of their occupation by the US military, they found other ways to protest nuclear colonialism.[43] In 1979 and again in 1982, the Marshallese staged *jodiks,* peaceful invasions of Kwajalein by boat. The 1982 *jodik,* Operation Homecoming, protested the American occupation of Kwajalein and the continued abuse of the Marshallese people under the pending Compact of Free Association, which would extend US control over the Kwajalein for another fifty years. Marshallese sailed into Kwajalein Lagoon and came to occupy Emon Beach, the shores of their ancestors. As they arrived in ever-greater numbers, military police on Kwajalein cordoned off the area and sent the island into lockdown. The Marshallese occupation of *their own land* persisted until they received concessions, including control over several small islands. Kwajalein, however, would not be returned. It probably never will be. In 2014, Lockheed Martin won a $1.6 billion contract to construct Space Fence, a defensive tracking system to be headquartered on Kwajalein. As of 2018, the concrete has been poured and systems were set to go online by 2019.[44] In the twenty-first century, American obsessions with containment and control persist, and powerfully.

On Ebeye, the Marshallese continue to resist the slow violence of American occupation and environmental degradation, countering it not only through political activism but also through the reinscription of space as a form of cultural resilience. For decades, American imperialists have used Ebeye as a dumping ground for all that did not belong within their culturally constructed concrete bubbles on Kwajalein and surrounding islands.[45] Today, the displaced Marshallese on Ebeye are hemmed in by garbage, not only their own, which has no place to go, but also that produced by American colonies and the defense industry. From the beginning of the occupation, Ebeye received leftover building supplies and scraps from American projects. From this refuse, the people of Ebeye have built their homes on increasingly scarce land. While traditional pandanus architecture cannot be built on this densely populated island stripped of natural resources, the invisible cultural architectures that once served as the foundation for pandanus housing persists.[46] For those whose clans hold *weto,* or land rights, homes are built from a bricolage of corrugated tin, plywood boards, linoleum tiles, and cement bricks, all woven together like pandanus fronds. Despite these modern materials, the cultural structuring of homes remains in keeping with Marshallese tradition. Homes typically feature a single multipurpose room where extended family engage in a wide range of activities. Large openings allow family gatherings to spill into courtyards and facilitate free communication with the larger community.[47] While traditional relationships between body, building, and culture remain fluid and alive, many family compounds are surrounded by scrap-built walls—attempts to delineate clan space in an impossibly overcrowded environment so foreign to a traditional Marshallese culture predicated on "the freedom to move around, fish, plant, and build living structures from the surrounding elements."[48] Those whose families do not have land rights cannot build their own homes, and so must occupy decaying abandoned structures open to wind, weather, and a rapidly encroaching ocean—a watery world upon which children surf and ride canoes made of old refrigerators, Styrofoam rafts, and other flotsam. As global warming causes sea levels to rise, Ebeye is disappearing, inch by inch. Homes are routinely flooded, and some are swallowed by the ocean entirely, exacerbating the housing crisis.[49] One colonial proposal to protect Ebeye from inundation includes building a six-foot-high concrete wall around the island. This wall—a prototypical American response to external threat—would sever the people of Ebeye from the fluid ocean world that is the foundation of their cultural embodiment.

Despite these layers of slow violence, Marshallese culture, with its fluid network of poetry, songs, rituals, and history, is very much alive on Ebeye, written onto postcolonial space designed to dislocate, contain, and silence it. Similar patterns remain among the communities of the Marshallese diaspora.[50] Facing inundation and in search of a more sustainable life, over 70 percent of all Marshallese now live in Hawai'i and on the American mainland, in suburban areas such as Spokane, Washington, and Springdale, Arkansas. For those relocating to mainland suburbs, the environmental shifts are seismic. Beyond adaptation to radically different climates requiring layers of clothing and restrictive footwear, Marshallese are faced with industrial and domestic architectures that are grounded in Western cultural values. In Spokane, many Marshallese men work in construction, several of them for CXT Concrete, building self-contained and immovable structures like those found on Kwajalein.[51] In Springdale, a large number of Marshallese work at the Tyson Chicken processing plant, a mechanized factory constructed from concrete that is cold, damp, and hermetically sealed. Like the buildings that contain them, the work lives of laborers are highly regulated, dominated by schedules and production goals. Models of containment and regulation are likewise embodied in Western domestic architecture, with its insulated walls, locked windows, and internal division of space into areas designated for specialized purposes. Designed as self-contained nuclear family units, mainland suburban housing (such as that found on Kwajalein) privileges Western values such as individualism and privacy, and does not coalesce with Marshallese values of fluidity and connectivity within and beyond the home. As on Ebeye, the Marshallese occupying these Western structures reinscribe them with Indigenous meanings, and repurpose them to suit their own values. In larger homes, living rooms serve as gathering spaces much like those of traditional pandanus architecture and open to the extended family. Garages can likewise serve a similar function, with wide-open doors connecting family to the greater community and the natural world. In warmer seasons, local parks become communal areas for cooking, eating, celebrating, and commemorating Marshallese survival, resilience, and resistance. In mainland diasporic communities, Marshallese culture has spilled out of contained spaces to form networks of exchange and care, places where Marshallese is spoken, where a shared history exists beyond words. Separated from their atolls and the sacred waters from which they were born, the Marshallese and their culture live on amid the concrete of American towns and cities—resisting dissolution, bending like pandanus fronds beneath the winds of change.

Notes

1. Nic Maclellan, "The Nuclear Age in the Pacific Islands," *Contemporary Pacific* 17, no. 2 (2005): 362.

2. "Castle Bravo," Atomic Heritage Foundation, Wednesday, March 1, 2017, https://www.atomicheritage.org.

3. Maclellan, "Nuclear Age," 363. Uma Kothari and Rorden Wilkinson, "Colonial Imaginaries and Postcolonial Transformations: Exiles, Bases, Beaches," *Third World Quarterly* 31, no. 8 (2010): 1395–1412. On the imaginary of emptiness, see Courtney J. Campbell, Allegra Giovine, and Jennifer Keating, *Empty Spaces: Perspectives on Emptiness in Modern History* (London: University of London Press, 2019), 1–13.

4. Kathy Jetñil-Kijiner, Marshallese activist, says, "These are situations where the Marshallese people are almost Guinea pigs, or they are just seen as disposable. We're seen as disposable in both of these situations [nuclear testing and global warming]. Our lives don't matter, the war matters, nuclear bombs matter. Our lives don't matter, oil matters, money matters, gas matters, profits matter." Kathy Jetñil-Kijiner, interview in "This Concrete Dome Holds a Leaking Toxic Timebomb," ABC News Australia, November 27, 2017, www.youtube.com.

5. On the architectural correlations between Western architecture and the body, see Kent Bloomer and Charles Moore, *Body, Memory, and Architecture* (New Haven, CT: Yale University Press, 1977); and Juhani Pallasmaa, *The Eyes of the Skin: Architecture and the Senses* (New York: Wiley and Sons, 1995).

6. Carmen Petrosia-Husa, "Traditional Medicine in the Marshall Islands," in *Republic of the Marshall Islands Ministry of Internal Affairs Historic Preservation Office, Alele Museum* (Majuro Atoll: Republic of the Marshall Islands Alele Museum, 2004), 26.

7. Ibid., 27–28.

8. Ibid., 34.

9. Ibid., 32.

10. Ibid., 35.

11. Ibid., 37.

12. E. H. Bryan, Jr., *Life in the Marshall Islands* (Honolulu, HI: Pacific Scientific Information Center, 1972), 157.

13. Petrosia-Husa, "Traditional Medicine," 24.

14. Stephen A. Royle, "Conservation and Heritage in the Face of Insular Urbanization: The Marshall Islands and Kiribati," *Built Environment* 25, no. 3 (1999): 212–213.

15. Walden Bello, *People and Power in the Pacific* (London: Pluto Press, 1992), 61.

16. Some of these wrecks were sunk in battle, while others, such as the airplanes in Kwajalein Lagoon, were simply dumped there as military refuse.

17. Bello, *People and Power,* 63.

18. Scars to the living coral reefs can be seen even today. For example, consider the Lacrosse Crater at Runik.

19. Jodi Stevens Releford and Will C. McClatchey, "Survivor Rongelap: Health Issues and Use of Traditional Medicine among the Women of Rongelap Atoll," *Ethnobotany Journal* 9 (2011): 289.

20. Harvey Wasserman, *Killing Our Own: The Disaster of America's Experience with Atomic Radiation* (New York: Random House, 1982).

21. The Marshall Islands Nuclear Commission, *Nuclear Justice for the Marshall Islands: A Strategy for Coordinated Action FY 2020–2023,* accessed April 17, 2021, https://rmi-data.sprep

.org/dataset/national-nuclear-commission-strategy-justice/resource/16ab6a56-3409-4a82-b44b-531d17bccd1d.

22. Bello, *People and Power,* 64.

23. Kathy Jetñil-Kijiner "Two Degrees," quoted in Michelle Keown, "Waves of Destruction: Nuclear Imperialism and Anti-Nuclear Protest in the Indigenous Literatures of the Pacific," *Journal of Postcolonial Writing* 54, no. 5 (2018): n.p.

24. Stuart Kirsch, "The Double Exposure of the Marshall Islands," *Architectural Review* (March 23, 2018), accessed April 17, 2021, https://www.architectural-review.com.

25. Lisa Findley, *Building Change: Architecture, Politics, and Cultural Agency* (New York: Routledge, 2005), 5, 9.

26. Cecil Helman, *Culture, Health, and Illness* (London: Hodder Arnold, 2007), 14–16.

27. Elaine Tyler, *Homeward Bound: American Families in the Cold War* (New York: Basic Books, 2008).

28. Greg Dvorak, "Detouring Kwajalein: At Home between Coral and Concrete," *Touring Pacific Cultures,* ed. Kalissa Alexeyeff and John Taylor (Acton: Australian National University Press, 2016), 98.

29. Bachelors' quarters were maintained separately from family housing on Kwajalein; bachelors even had their own segregated beach, so obsessive was the American desire to compartmentalize, control, and contain.

30. Fresh water systems delivered drinking water, but waste water systems used ocean water. "This is our swimming pool. It's great, except it's salt water! Come to think of it, so is our toilet! So we have two different plumbing systems." Postcard from Barbara Kaiser to her parents, December, 1973, in the author's collection. Today, the trailers of Silver City have been replaced by modern townhomes.

31. Marshallese Cultural Center, Facebook, accessed April 17, 2021, https://www.facebook.com.

32. The problem of treating Indigenous cultures as "lost worlds" rather than living cultures is not an issue limited to the Marshall Islands but one faced in many museums around the world. On the commemoration of nuclear testing at the expense of Marshallese history in the Pacific, see Steve Brown, "Poetics and Politics: Bikini Atoll and World Heritage Listing," *Transcending the Culture-Nature Divide in Cultural Heritage: Views from the Asia-Pacific Region,* ed. Sally Brockwell, Sue O'Connor, Denis Byrne (Acton: Australian National University Press, 2013), 35–52.

33. Findley, *Building Change,* 9.

34. Bryan, "Life in the Marshall Islands," 149.

35. Dvorak, "Detouring Kwajalein," 107–108.

36. Lauren Hirshberg, "Nuclear Families: (Re)producing 1950s Suburban America in the Marshall Islands," *OAH Magazine of History* 26, no. 4 (2012): 36–43. See also Leon Fink, Julie Greene, and Lauren Hirshberg, "Domestic Containment in the Marshall Islands: Making a Home for Cold War Workers in the US Imperial Pacific," *Labor* 13 (2016): 177–196.

37. Hirshberg, "Nuclear Families," 40.

38. "Ebeye Developments Move Forward," *Marshall Islands Journal,* April 13, 2018, http://marshallislandsjournal.com.

39. Ron S. Nolan, Ron R. McConnaughey, and Charles R. Stearns, "Fishes Inhabiting Two Small Nuclear Test Craters at Enewetak Atoll, Marshall Islands," *Micronesia* 11, no. 2 (1975): 205–217.

40. Ingrid Ahlgren, Seiji Yamada, and Allen Wong, "Rising Oceans, Climate Change,

Food Aid, and Human Rights in the Marshall Islands," *Health and Human Rights* 16, no. 1 (2014): 73; Bryan, "Life in the Marshall Islands," 134.

41. On slow violence in this context, see Kirsch, "Double Exposure."

42. Maclellan, "Nuclear Age in the Pacific Islands," 364–365. This is in spite of very strong Indigenous voices, such as Kathy Jetñil-Kijiner and Darlene Keju. See Giff Johnson, *Don't Ever Whisper: Darlene Keju, Pacific Health Pioneer, Champion for Nuclear Survivors* (Charleston, SC: Creative Space, 2013).

43. Martha Smith-Norris, *Domination and Resistance: The United States and the Marshall Islands during the Cold War* (Honolulu: University of Hawai'i Press, 2016).

44. "Space Fence," Lockheed Martin, accessed March 14, 2021, https://www.lockheedmartin.com.

45. "Since the early 1960s," Ebeye became "a convenient site for the placement of all of the unexpected, barely imaginable, and little-cared-about problems that testing in Kwajalein caused, all of the problems that America's military and later civilian administrations had not time to confront or resolve." David L. Hanlon, *Remaking Micronesia: Discourses over Development in a Pacific Territory* (Honolulu: University of Hawai'i Press, 1998), 187.

46. On cultural considerations on the definitions, meanings, and extension of space beyond Western definitions, see Paul Memmott and James Davidson, "Exploring a Cross-Cultural Theory of Architecture," *Traditional Dwellings and Settlements Review* 19, no. 2 (2008): 51–68.

47. Overpopulation has exacerbated the spread of infectious diseases such as tuberculosis.

48. Kotak Loeak, quoted in Hanlon, *Remaking Micronesia,* 211.

49. Coral Davenport, "Rising Seas Are Claiming a Vulnerable Nation," *New York Times,* December 12, 2015.

50. Craig Santos Perez, "New Pacific Islander Poetry," *Poetry* 208, no. 4 (2016): 373–377.

51. Tom Sowa, "Marshallese Making a New Life in Spokane," *Spokesman-Review,* March 4, 2012, https://www.spokesman.com.

THIRTEEN

Images of Empire and Visualizing Resistance in Guam (Guåhan)

Sylvia C. Frain

The United States' contemporary Pacific empire is maintained through colonial political arrangements and enforced through expansive military bases. In historical literature discussing World War II, particularly within American academies, Pacific militarization is portrayed as something of the past. If the Indigenous experience is even mentioned, it is a superficial narrative that presents the Indigenous residents as "patriotic" and "loyal" to the United States.[1]

In Guam (Guåhan), an unincorporated territory belonging to the United States, images of the continuous empire are framed and promoted as militaristic patriotism.[2] This chapter examines the visual production of imperial control as it manifests during the "Liberation Day" parade in Guam. The annual event commemorates the "liberation" of the island by the US Marines from the Imperial Japanese Army on July 21, 1944, during the last days of World War II.[3] This celebration is devoted to the US-imposed narrative of Indigenous Chamorro gratitude and American loyalty. It is visualized through American flags and weaponry, formations of marching young Indigenous troops, and the honoring of World War II survivors.

However, the post-WWII narrative of Americans as "saviors" and "liberators" is continuously challenged by the current realities of subpar medical services for the high number of returning veterans, the ongoing denial of financial compensation for World War II survivors (and their families), and the refusal of the United States to return ancestral Chamorro land (*tåno'*). Instead, the storylines of loyalty and gratitude have been appropriated by the US military and federal government to ensure continuing and expanding militarization in Guam.

Simultaneously, the Chamorros continue to resist the US-militarized empire through their cultural frameworks and principles, captured with new media technologies and visualized across digital platforms. The images of resistance feature *latte* stones (pronounced "laddy"), limestone pillars that served as foundations for ancient houses. Today, the sacred formations serve as the visible foundation of resistance to continued political colonization and expanding militarization by the United States.[4]

Imperial Control

Guam remains as a non-self-governing island and is "hegemonically constrained by dominant American ideologies."[5] Due to the "remote location" of the islands in the Western Pacific, colonizers and war planners have been able to carry out their objectives in the region without visibility and with little outside questioning.[6]

The United States' imperial project in the Pacific began in 1893 with the overthrow of the Hawaiian Kingdom, followed by the Spanish-American War of 1898.[7] The United States strategically acquired the islands of Guam and the Philippines, Cuba and Puerto Rico, and US sovereignty was established over Eastern Sāmoa (today American Sāmoa).[8] The new island territories were exploited for US military and commercial purposes, and the United States did not consider extending the American ideals of "freedom," "democracy," or "US citizenship" to the local residents.[9]

In 1898, with the first arrival of the Americans, the Chamorro people were forced under US naval command, which controlled the island as "USS Guam," similar to "USS" naval battleships.[10] While the naval command claimed its mission during the US naval era (1898–1941) was "benevolent assimilation," a paradoxical policy of simultaneously denying Chamorro civil rights and making a determined effort to bring Chamorros more in line with American cultural sensibilities" was implemented.[11] Chamorros were introduced to American ideals and were encouraged to be "good Americans" by speaking English. However, they were not legal citizens; instead, the US federal government ignored and dismissed numerous petitions created by Chamorros calling for a civil government.[12] The naval command claimed that exercising self-determination to create a civilian government would render the island vulnerable, and they would not be able to "protect" the island from foreign powers.[13]

The US naval command's imperial ideology expanded from denying civil rights to abandoning the Indigenous population. Guam had been a communications outpost up though 1941, when the US military "deserted the island and its people."[14] While white US dependents and families were evacuated, Chamorro wives and children of US servicemen were left behind.[15] This history is left out of the dominant narrative promoted by the US military, and instead the "return" of the US troops in July of 1944 is deemed heroic.

The Imperial Japanese Army attacked Pearl Harbor, O'ahu (locally known as Wai Momi ["Pearl Waters"] or Pu'uloa ["Long Hill"]), Hawai'i, on December 8, 1941, while also simultaneously bombing the Philippines, Hong Kong, Singapore, the Dutch East Indies, and Guam.[16] On December 10, 1941, Guam was invaded by the Imperial Japanese Army and remained under brutal occupation until July 21, 1944. The Chamorros were the only civilian population held by "the enemy" during World War II, and they state that "the atrocities and daily humiliations of that time are burned forever into our psyches."[17] Today's discourse of militaristic patriotism, Chamorro gratitude, and American loyalty is founded on these experiences and on transgenerational trauma.

Liberation Day

Liberation Day is a legal holiday in commemoration of the anniversary of the liberation of Guam from Japanese occupation on July 21, 1944. The "liberation" of Guam began with the US Marine 3rd Expeditionary Force dropping hundreds of pounds of bombs on the island for thirteen days. The US military did not consider the Chamorro population in the (re)occupation. Today, there is "overwhelming evidence that America's return had more to do with military strategy then some altruistic desire to free the Chamorros from enemy occupation."[18]

When the US military forces returned to the island, the Chamorros felt an immense sense of appreciation.[19] Chamorro scholars have explained how Chamorro gratitude for "survival became synonymous with American Military Forces" and the United States (mis)understood their appreciation and ongoing thankfulness as "hyperloyalty."[20] They have suggested that it was "the only political language available to the Chamorros that could be heard and understood by the Americans."[21]

Chamorro scholar Laura Torres Souder-Jaffery further explains how the return of the US military fostered gratitude and promoted militaristic patriotism. She states, "It was the sheer largesse of their material possessions and supplies—the cases of Spam, surplus Jeeps, tents, boots, clothes, and more—[that] activated an Indigenous code of indebtedness, obligation, and reciprocity."[22] This "code of obligation" evolved into young Chamorro men enlisting in the US Armed Forces and young Chamorro women marrying servicemen. The post-World War II narrative surrounding Liberation Day is still used to support the empire through militaristic patriotism and enduring American loyalty.

Micronesian scholar and filmmaker Vince M. Diaz recapitulates, "Liberation Day has been certified as the official celebration of war... this official discourse combines the memories of Chamorro survivors and American soldiers and the political imperative of a postwar American colonial history and historiography to canonize America's return as one of liberation and to fashion a story of intense Chamorro patriotism and loyalty to the United States."[23]

This narrative continues to be visually and publicly demonstrated through American flags, the display of US military weapons, honoring World War II survivors, and encouraging young Chamorro troops. The discourse that the US military "rescued" and "freed" the Chamorro people is reenacted through the parade demonstration.

Parade

The annual "Liberation Day" parade, held every year on July 21, serves as a crucial enactment to honor the United States' empire. The procession moves along a one-mile stretch of Marine Corps Drive, the main road on Guam, named after the "Liberators." Built from coral after World War II, the road runs from the US Naval Station in the south, locally referred to as "Big Navy," north to Andersen Air Force Base, which encompasses the majority of the northern part of the island.[24]

The parade, accompanied by weeks of ongoing memorials across the island, serves as a public display of the imperial "official narrative... and [US] dominant paradigm."[25] US flags, military weaponry, and marching troops are paired with BBQ and red rice, Budweiser and plastic plates. Families camp out the night before to ensure their prime viewing spot, and the floats line up very early in the morning. Late summer in Guam is extremely hot, and Marine Corps Drive is a portion of the island that consists mainly of buildings and concrete.[26]

The annual celebration is a visual salute to the US empire, consisting of images that visually support imperial ideologies. An examination of the semiotics of this form of militarization reveals a "paradox of invisibility and visibility."[27] While many elements of militarism are seen out in the open, there are additional and less obvious influences that remain hidden under the surface.

Parade floats are constructed by each village on the back of semitrucks. The World War II–era US military jeep sitting atop an American flag the length of a semitrailer shown in figure 13.1 speaks to the promotion of US military might and militaristic patriotism. It is a combination of American hardware, the iconic jeep, surrounded by the symbolic *latte* stone, an ancient Chamorro technology.

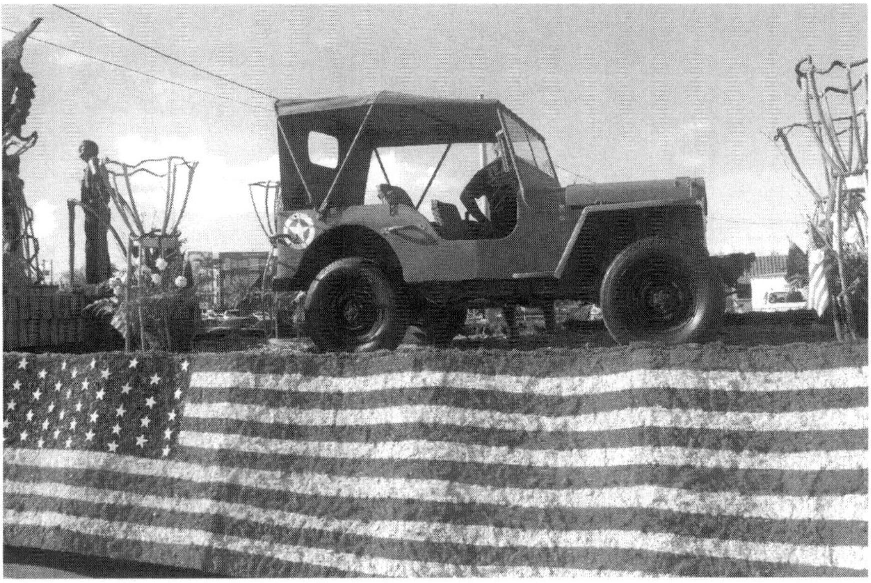

Figure 13.1. A restored World War II–era US Army jeep is placed on the back of a semitruck flatbed decorated as an American flag in hopes of earning the "best float" award during the 71st Liberation Day Parade in Guam, 2015. Photograph by the author.

"Honoring" the Survivors and War Repatriations

The parade begins midmorning by honoring the World War II survivors, many of whom are in their late eighties, and each year the community loses more. The survivors have a special seating area from which to watch the parade. One float presented the phrase "We honor them," professional-style portraits of World War II survivors, and a star cutout with the markings of the US flag commemorate the themes of militaristic patriotism, survivors' gratitude, and loyalty to the United States (figure 13.2). The visible young children in the seating area are the descendants of war survivors and some have learned of wartime survival and the postwar experience through traumatic oral stories passed from generation to generation. The current generation of young Chamorros is continuing the work of their elders in the quest for compensation from the US government.

Each Liberation Day has a theme. For the 71st anniversary in 2015, the theme was "The Spirit of Hope, the Colors of Freedom—Espiriton Diniseha, meskla na kulot Libettat." The theme centers around American ideologies, and while it may not speak to actual tangible things, the "colors of freedom," or colors that *brought* freedom, visibly confirm the heroic efforts of

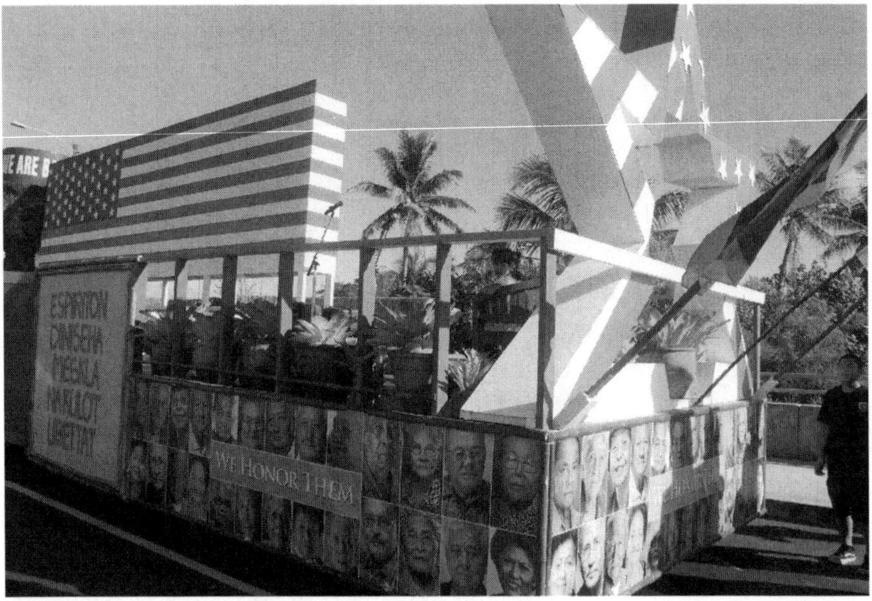

Figure 13.2. "Espirion, Dinsena, Meskla, Nakulot, Libetiat" means "The Spirit of Hope, the Colors of Freedom," and was the 71st Liberation Day's theme in 2015. Photographic portraits of World War II survivors are accompanied by the words "We Honor Them" and appear on numerous floats in the parade, as well as throughout the months of June and July in the local newspapers commemorating them. Photograph by the author.

red, white, and blue. The recognition of the "spirit of hope" references Chamorro survivors who never lost hope during the occupation, and is also written in Chamorro for the survivors. The image in figure 13.2 both captures the past (with the portraits of the survivors and the theme given in Chamorro) and supports future patriotism (through the dominating American flag and the participation of younger generations).

This visual remembrance does not translate into the material or financial realm. While World War II survivors are symbolically and publicly honored, true compensation continues to be delayed. The dominant narrative produced by the US military and federal government seizes upon the traumas of Chamorro World War II survivors' suffering and appropriates their gratitude. The empire's "honoring" is limited to public symbolism, as the survivors continue to wait for legally mandated financial compensation.

The US federal government has failed to release compensation for Chamorros who survived the Japanese occupation during World War II.[28] The group Guam World War II Reparations Advocates, formed in March 2016, filed a lawsuit on behalf of the survivors. Guam's nonvoting congresswoman, Madeleine Bordallo, proposed the Guam World War II Loyalty Recognition Act bill in the House five times. On December 8, 2016 (a symbolic seventy-five years after the US naval command abandoned and Japanese imperial forces occupied Guam), the US Senate passed the 2017 National Defense Authorization Act, which included World War II repatriations.[29] On December 23, 2016, president Barack Obama signed into law the Guam World War II Loyalty Recognition Act, Title XVII, Public Law 114–328. While Congresswoman Bordallo's office frames this as "a historic day for our island," Michael Lujan Bevacqua, assistant professor of Chamorro studies at the University of Guam, points out that the war reparation funds will be "distributed from taxation paid by employees of the US federal government stationed on Guam," and thus the United States will "compensate people with the money they would have gotten back anyways."[30]

Compensation was based on what survivors "endured," and claimants had one year to file for compensation if they had "suffered rape, injury, forced labor, internment or flight to evade imprisonment during that period."[31] The amounts of financial compensation are unexceptional. Victims of rape or severe injury, such as loss of limb or paralysis, may receive fifteen thousand dollars. Forced labor or injury, such as scarring or burning, may merit twelve thousand. Those who endured forced marches, internment, or hiding could potentially receive ten thousand.[32]

The shallowness and limitations of the empire's narrative of militaristic patriotism has been exposed. Chamorros have been fighting for compensation, which they are legally entitled to, for over seventy years. As the survivor population passes on, their grown children continue to (re)tell their parents' and grandparents' memories of massacres. In addition, accounts of gratitude and loyalty are tested when there is a lack of veteran services for those returning from war, and when the US military continually expands its footprint in the region. Within this imperial and militarized space, the lines between military and civilian populations are blurred.

Indigenous Reciprocity through US Military Service

After World War II, Chamorros "temporarily" sacrificed their land to the military to rebuild Guam. The United States constructed military bases—which remain today. Further, Chamorros enlisted in the US military in extremely high numbers, with nearly an entire generation of young people heading overseas. "Reciprocity meant that Chamorros became duty-bound to 'give the best they had'. And so, our people gave precious land and continue to offer our sons and daughters to show their appreciation to Uncle Sam [United States]. Obligation being a sacred duty, Chamorros have since been caught in a never-ending cycle of 'paying back.'"[33] After July 21, 1944, the Chamorros who survived the wartime massacres, rape, and starvation under the Imperial Japanese Army occupation had their houses bulldozed by the US military. Land was obtained through eminent domain even though the Chamorros were not yet US citizens.[34] Families were removed to construct military installations and allow access for recreational sites for US servicemen.[35] Almost three-fourths of the island came under military control after World War II.[36]

The determination to have Chamorro ancestral land returned and families compensated after "liberation" now spans several generations. Much of the land remains restricted or has been approved for private commercial use, including a McDonald's restaurant. Jose Garrido, a Chamorro who continues to work to have his family's land returned, states in the documentary film *War for Guam,* "For many of us, the war is not over."

In addition to land, the enlistment rates of Indigenous peoples from Guam serving in the US Armed Forces are the highest, second only to American Sāmoa, with the Micronesian region serving as a "recruiter's paradise."[37] People of the Mariana Islands serve in every branch of the US Armed Forces, particularly the US National Guard, which is continuously deployed and redeployed to ongoing operations in the Middle East and North Africa.[38] Chamorros have defended US democracy in foreign wars at rates three times higher than those of any other state or territory, with one in eight inhabitants currently serving or having served in the US Armed Forces.[39]

While Chamorros serve in overseas US conflicts and have done so "in every war the US has fought since World War II; Vietnam, the Gulf War and the current War on Terror," the truth is that "more Chamorros have died per capita than any other soldiers."[40] As a result, the Mariana Islands communities have high "loss of life" ratios and suffer "killed-in-action" rates up to five times the national average.[41] Nearly every family in the islands has at least one family member who is either on active duty, a veteran, or has died in combat or by suicide.

The "support our troops" call is a fallacy, as veterans on Guam are without adequate medical care or mental health services. This is possible through imperial logic that uses the islands and its people to maintain the US empire overseas, but when those people return, a substandard system with underfunded resources fails veterans and is inappropriate for Indigenous and women veterans.[42] The closest full Veterans Association hospital facility is on O'ahu, Hawai'i, nearly four thousand miles away.[43] Many returning soldiers who have been away from their families for months or longer do not want to leave again for treatment. The lack of funds available for Chamorro veterans directly confronts the narrative of "loyalty" and "patriotism" to an empire that does not give a person "freedom," "democracy," or support upon returning from the frontlines.[44] The monetary wealth of the US military is evident "inside of the fence" and demonstrates how "communities adjacent to military bases generally obtain the least investment of any community under the US flag."[45]

While on Liberation Day there is visible "support" and the empire salutes the marching troops during the parade, this becomes meaningless in view of the lack of care for the veteran population. Health statistics reveal a much darker situation beneath the positive and proud themes of militarization displayed in the Liberation Day parade. The onerous sacrifices of military personnel affects entire families and communities.[46] The image of young Chamorro soldiers marching, the young girl potentially recording the parade and the onlooker kids sitting across the street, signify the next generation of loyal Indigenous soldiers, serving the United States flag (figure 13.3). The cycle of serving in the US forces is for many a family tradition and an expectation.

The imperial ideology of "patriotic" and "loyal" soldiers defending the

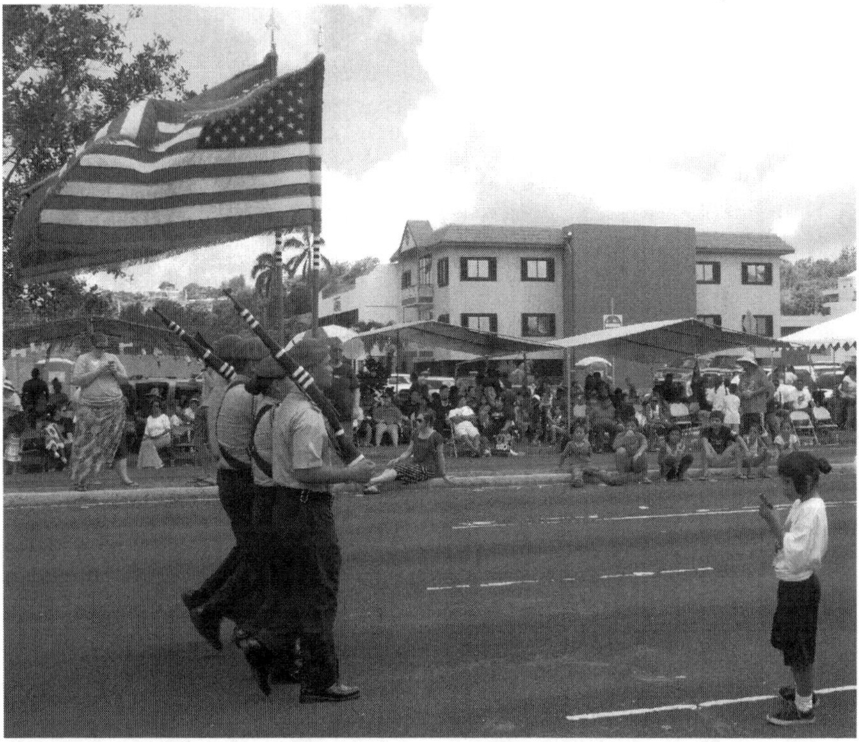

Figure 13.3. Indigenous youth serve in the US Army Reserve Officers' Training Corps program at very high rates, creating multigenerational military families of survivors, veterans, those on active duty, and those intending to enlist. Here, they march with American flags as younger generations look on, 2015. Photograph by the author.

US overseas has proven contradictory. The soldiers return home to the (militarized) Mariana Islands, where they are without a vote for commander in chief and where they receive the lowest financial and mental support for service war veterans in the United States.[47] As their contemporary war experiences follow Chamorro service members home, the resulting trauma and post traumatic stress disorder (PTSD) creates a high number of medical and mental health issues. The Chamorros absorb the impact of the invisible trauma of returning from war while the highly visible training for preparation for war continues to militarize the islands. World War II trauma persists today and is compounded by the high rate of Chamorro service people returning from defending the United States in foreign wars. The current generation of Chamorro scholars frame it as the "ambivalent nature of Chamorro 'loyalty'" that informs "the false rhetoric of 'liberation.'"[48]

Other images from Liberation Day capture expressions that validate the narrative of Chamorros displaying gratitude and demonstrating loyalty. These include the large US flag towering over young people smiling and waving, dressed in general "Pacific attire." That is, clothing specific not to the Marianas but instead to the American concept of "the Pacific."[49]

"Reoccupation Day" and the "Invasion of Guam"

Liberation Day and its accompanying imperial discourses have been and are "contested even as [they are] commemorated."[50] While the annual event is designed to promote loyalty and patriotism to the United States—it has also been used to support narratives of demilitarization and decolonization.[51]

Chamorro political activist groups galvanized in the 1990s and publicly challenged Liberation Day's "narratives of triumph and loyalty, suggesting that the name 'Reoccupation Day' would better reflect the colonial reality of Guam."[52] In 1991, Angel Santos, founder and spokesperson of Nasion Chamoru, or Chamorro Nation, an Indigenous rights organization, wrote, "True freedom for the Chamorro people does not exist on Guam."[53] The Chamorro rights activists pushed for the removal of the US military from Guåhan and the return of ancestral land to the locals.[54]

Today's generation remains critical of the "liberator" and "savior" narrative. They question the concept of US "liberation" and refer to July 21 as the "invasion of Guam." They ask, "How can it be Liberation Day if the liberators never left, and instead, took our *tåno'* and still continue to militarize the island(s)?"[55] Nearly one-third of the island remains restricted for the use of the federal government and of all branches of the US Armed Forces. Guåhan has the "highest ratio of US military spending and military hardware and land takings from Indigenous populations of any place on earth."[56]

Contemporary Resistance

The US military and US-owned media outlets frame public forms of resistance to colonization and militarization as "unpatriotic." The longest-running newspaper on the island, the *Pacific Daily News* (*PDN*), began in 1947 as the *Navy News*. It was purchased in 1971 by the Gannett Corporation, an America-based company that publishes, among others, *USA Today*. Under this colonial control, the *PDN* consistently uses "discursive strategies to rally support for pro-American ideologies."[57]

News items surrounding Liberation Day in particular "favor[ed] continued American control of Guam and marginaliz[ed] prolocal demands for self-determination."[58] The *PDN* assists in maintaining the island as unincorporated American territory while reinforcing dominant American ideologies, including expressions of gratitude and praise to the American Marine liberators and the reaffirmation of Guam residents' loyalty to the United States.[59] The understanding of gratitude to the US military and loyalty to the United States is complicated by Chamorro activists today. Today's generation continues to support the subaltern perspective of Santos' editorial through new media platforms, a contemporary form of "guerrilla-like tactics."[60]

This generation understands that (self-)representation and the "political and cultural economy of images and modes of production that determine how Indigenous people represent themselves (aesthetic production) and are represented (who speaks for Indigenous peoples in the political arena)" are interrelated.[61] People from the Mariana Islands use "this [Western] tool to leverage and to support" their own culture, as they visualize their resistance in an effort to recover ancestral land and exercise self-determination.[62] Indigenous peoples of Guåhan who resist the US militarized empire likewise promote ancient cultural practices through photography and new media technologies.[63]

Ancient Technologies Visualized across New Technologies

The majority of visual resistance on Guåhan occurs in digital form, online, and is circulated across new media platforms.[64] "Community building occurs through a web-based arena, where blogs, websites and alternative media publications address issues of self-determination . . . blogs connect to alternative new coverage of military planning, interviews with activists."[65] Within the last five years, political groups in the Mariana Islands archipelago have been "pioneering a new format of Chamorro activism" by using online social media platforms for public advocacy and information dissemination.[66] Chamorro grassroots organizations are able to reach audiences beyond traditional mainstream media outlets, enabling alternative perspectives and providing space for "those who would otherwise not have a voice against oppression."[67]

The symbol of that resistance is the *acha latte* stone, ancient limestone pillars that served as the foundation of homes and indicate ancient gravesites of the ancestors. These precontact carvings consist of two pieces (figure 13.4). The top, or *tåsa,* is a capstone with its curved side down, and the *haligi* is an upright slab from three to twenty feet high.[68] These *acha latte* stones are "recognized as sacred and have been adopted as icons of Chamorro culture and heritage."[69]

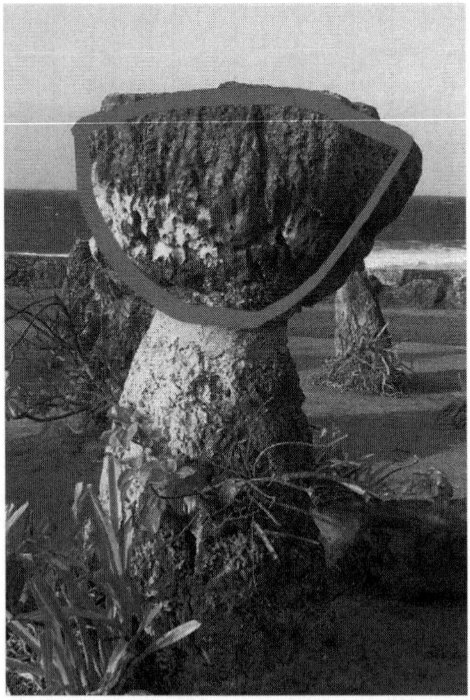

Figure 13.4. Latte stones are found only in the Marianas Archipelago and consist of two separate rock formations, 2015. The outline indicates the *tåsa* cap, or top portion, supported by the *haligi* base, or bottom portion. Photograph by Zea Nauta.

Inafa'maolek (To Make Good and Restore the Balance)

The Chamorro struggle against the US federal government and military is grounded in the Indigenous concept of *inafa'maolek,* roughly translated as to "make good for each other" by treating people well and to "restore the balance" with nature and the community.[70] This reciprocal principle is based on a commitment to family and the environment. Respect (*respetu*) must be applied to social relationships as well as the land, sea, and air so all can benefit from the gifts of the land and the sea (*i guinahan I tåno' ya tåsi*).[71] The importance of respect for the environment in Chamorro culture is further demonstrated through Indigenous protective frameworks formulated in response to the loss of land, language, and cultural practices to the United States.

Inifresi: *Prutehi yan Difendi* (The Chamorro Pledge: Protect and Defend)

Chamorros are "committed to protecting and defending the beliefs, the culture, the language, the air and the water of our cherished land."[72] The late Saena Bernadita Camacho-Dungca developed the Chamorro pledge in 1991 as an alternative to the Pledge of Allegiance to the flag of the United States, which is seen by some as imperialistic propaganda imposed on the people of the Mariana Islands.[73] Camacho-Dungca is remembered for her dedication "to the preservation of the Chamoru culture and language . . . [she] worked timelessly to pass down her knowledge to future generations."[74] Chamorros continue to recognize their role as protectors and defenders of their environment and culture for future generations. With the Inifresi as a guiding pledge, resistance is driven by the deep connection to the environment and culture. The Inifresi verbalizes the responsibility to safeguard what is Chamorro:

> The Chamorro Pledge
>
> From the highest of my thoughts, from the deepest of my heart, and with the utmost of my strength, I offer myself to protect and to defend the beliefs, the culture, the language, the air, the water, and the land of the Chamorro, which are our inherent God-given rights. This I will affirm by the holy words and our banner, the flag of Guåhan!
>
> The Inifresi
>
> Ginen i mas takhelo' gi Hinasso—ku, i mas takhalom gi Kurason—hu, yan i mas figo' na Nina'siñå—hu, Hu ufresen maisa yu' para bai hu Prutehi yan hu Difende i Hinengge, i Kottura, i Lengguahi, i Aire, i Hanom yan i tano' Chamoru, ni' Irensiå—ku Direchu ginen as Yu'os Tåta. Este hu Afitma gi hilo' i bipblia yan i banderå—hu, i banderan Guåhan![75]

The Inifresi uses the robust language of sacrifice, such as "with all my might," similar to US military slogans. However, it paradoxically calls for protection and defense *against* US political colonization, militarization, and destruction. It directly confronts how the "US" residents of the islands are denied Indigenous political rights of self-determination as US citizens without a vote for the US president.

The Inifresi is an Indigenous framework, separate from the imposed US political structure. In both written and oral form, it is recited, shared, debated, and honored at community gatherings. It appears in YouTube videos and in artwork, and is referred to in letters to the editor of the local newspapers. The Inifresi serves as a symbolic and cultural form of resistance, and provides this generation with dignity and a way to remember and tie into struggles of the past and support resistance for the future. The resistance to protect and defend (*prutehi yan difendi*) is visualized through the slogan written across the *latte* stone (figure 13.5).

While the US military claims to be protecting and defending the Mariana Islands archipelago and its people, many residents know that neither the

Chamorros peoples nor their rights to their lands are a priority. The images of imperial control are promoted as Indigenous gratitude, US loyalty, and militaristic patriotism. Yet these are ideologies that render Guåhan as not completely part of the United States, due to its nonvoting status, and enable further US militarization.

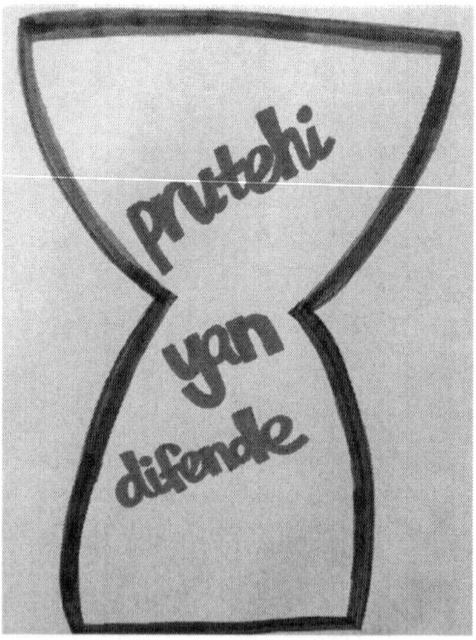

Figure 13.5. The phrase *prutehi yan difende* is from the Inifresi and means to "protect and defend" Chamorro culture, lands, and seas. This image demonstrates the connection between this framework and the *latte* stone as a form of Chamorro identity. Photograph by the author.

America's Continuing and Expanding Empire

As the US empire project in the Western Pacific continues, the Mariana Islands archipelago remains politically divided as two "insular areas" of the United States. Guåhan (imperially referred to as "Guam") is the most southern and populated island, and is an "organized, unincorporated territory" of the United States under the federal jurisdiction of the Office of Insular Affairs at the Department of the Interior. Guåhan continues to be the "longest colonized possession in the world."[76] The fourteen islands north of Guåhan are politically constructed as the Commonwealth of the Northern Mariana Islands. These political arrangements consider the islands as *belonging* to the United States rather than as a *part* of it.[77] Continuing imperial control of the archipelago renders the islands (and people) politically and legally "dependent" due to the insular area and its non-self-governing status. This grants the US military unchecked power over the land, sea, skies, and even the people.

Although the archipelago is divided politically, US Department of Defense (DOD) planners make no distinction between political entities. The DOD conceptualizes every island in the Mariana Islands archipelago as a potential live-fire training range complex, as well as the current one-million-square-mile training area that surrounds the archipelago.[78] The DOD is "refocusing" on the Pacific region to meet the "challenges of America's Pacific Century" and further militarize Guåhan.[79] This invisible and visible expanding militarization is justified in the name of US "national security."

Increased militarization signifies how the empire's perspective of "peace" is possible only through militaristic means. The Liberation Day parade floats demonstrate the appropriation of Chamorro cultural representations of local

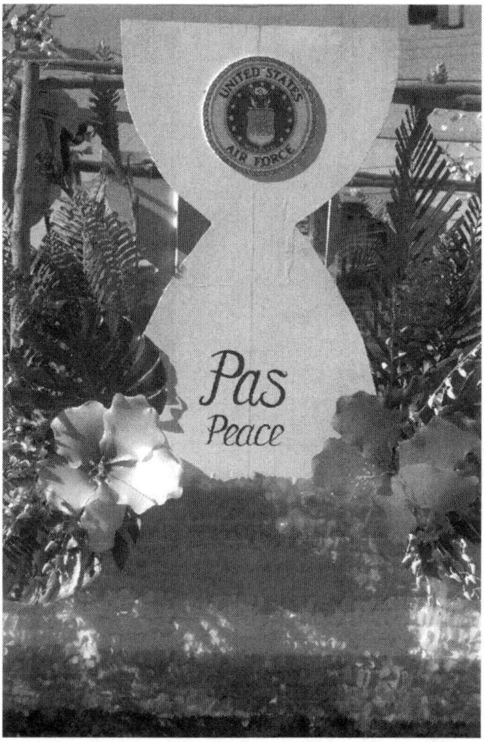

Figure 13.6. The US Air Force inserted their logo on top of a *latte* stone cutout and painted the words *pas,* Spanish for "peace," with the English "peace" on the bottom, 2015. The base is surrounded by flowers and rainbow decorations, which visually softens the theme. Photograph by the author

flowers and *latte* stones, with their theme of "hope" (*diniseha*) and "freedom" (*libettat*). The floats are supposed to signify peace, which the empire enforces through a "continuous bomber presence," including the B-1 Lancer bombers deployed to Andersen Air Force Base.[80] In addition to the appropriation of peace, the US Air Force has also taken the *latte* stone to clarify that "peace" accompanies the military presence. The US Air Force has placed their seal on top of a *latte* stone, visually imposing US militarism on Chamorro culture. This further instills the narrative that the US military symbolizes "peace" by attempting to reach out to the Chamorro community by spelling peace in Chamorro as "*pas* or *pås* (figure 13.6).

While on Liberation Day the US Air Force appropriates and militarizes the Chamorro symbol of resistance, the *latte* stone, in the name of "peace," the reality is that Guåhan has been selected as the "preferred destination" for the relocation of five thousand marines from the American Expeditionary Force (the same division that "liberated" the island) and their families from Okinawa, Japan.[81] This relocation is considered the largest and most expensive and expansive militarization plan of our time. As a result, the current generation of activists is combining cultural symbols of ancient technologies of the *latte* stone with new media technologies to visualize their resistance efforts.

Conclusion

This chapter discussed how the United States constructs the narrative of American loyalty, Indigenous gratitude, and militaristic patriotism to empire in the unincorporated territory of Guåhan. Images captured during the annual Liberation Day parade expose a visual production of imperial discourse through the demonstration of flags, weapons, and marching Indigenous troops, as well as the remembrance of civilian prisoners of war. The US military promotes itself as a provider of peace for the region. Yet, peace is ultimately conceptualized through US militaristic means. Guåhan's non-self-governing political status accommodates further militarization. Narratives of loyalty and gratitude have thus been appropriated by the US military and federal government, including the US appropriation of Indigenous culture.

Activists today remind the community that when the Liberation Day celebrations are over, the World War II survivors are still fighting for financial compensation and their ancestral land. Veterans returning from the empire's wars are still without access to complete medical and mental health services. The foundations of resistance must remain as strong as the *latte* stone.

Notes

I express my gratitude to those working for decolonization and demilitarization across the Mariana Islands archipelago and Oceania. I hope my scholarly solidarity and academic activism contributes to the quest for Chamoru self-determination and upholds *tino rangatiratanga o te iwi Māori* (Māori self-determination). I completed the final revisions of this work on Waiheke Island in Aotearoa (New Zealand). I recognize the *tangata whenua* (people of the land) as Paoa Pukunui, descendants of Ngāti Paoa Mana Whenua ki Waiheke who continue to uphold the *rangatiratanga* (autonomy) of Tāmaki Makaurau (Auckland), Tīkapa Moana (Hauraki Gulf), and Te Waitematā (Bay).

1. Vicente M. Diaz, "Deliberating 'Liberation Day'": Identity, History, Memory, and War in Guam," in *Perilous Memories: The Asia-Pacific War(s),* ed. Geoffrey M. White, L. Yoneyama, and T. Fujitani (Durham, NC: Duke University Press, 2001); Timothy P. Maga, "Democracy and Defense: The Case of Guam (1918–1941)," *Journal of Pacific History* 20, no. 3 (1985): 156–172; Laurel Anne Monnig, "'Proving Chamorro': Indigenous Narratives of Race, Identity, and Decolonization on Guam," PhD diss., University of Illinois, 2007; Amy Owen, "Guam Culture, Immigration and the US Military Build-Up," *Asia Pacific Viewpoint* 51, no. 3 (2010): 304–318; John Ries and Mark Weber, "The Fateful Year 1898: The United States Becomes an Imperial Power: The Great Debate over American Overseas Expansion," *Institute for Historical Review* 13, no. 4 (1993): 4–13; Miyume Tanji, "Chamorro Warriors and Godmothers Meet Uncle Sam," in *Gender, Power, and Military Occupations: Asia Pacific and the Middle East since 1945,* ed. Christine De Matos and Rowena Ward (Hoboken, NJ: Taylor and Francis, 2012); Teresia K. Teaiwa, "Militarism, Tourism and the Native: Articulations in Oceania," PhD diss., University of California, 2001; and Valerie Woodward, "'I Guess They Didn't Want Us Asking Too Many Questions': Reading American Empire in Guam," *Contemporary Pacific* 25, no. 1 (2013): 67–91, 218.

2. For a continental US-centric project, see documentary photographer Nina Berman's collection *Homeland* (Great Britain: Trolley, 2008), which visually examines the militarization of American life post-9/11, in particular the "burgeoning homeland security state."

3. Stripes Guam, "72nd Guam Liberation Queens Results," *Stripes Guam,* June 16, 2016, ://guam.stripes.com.

4. Sylvia C. Frain, "Resisting Political Colonization and American Militarization in the Marianas Archipelago," *AlterNative: An International Journal of Indigenous Peoples* 12, no. 3 (2016): 298–315.

5. Francis Dalisay, "Social Control in an American Pacific Island: Guam's Local Newspaper Reports on Liberation," *Journal of Communication Inquiry* 33, no. 3 (2009): 242.

6. Simon Winchester, *Pacific: Silicon Chips and Surfboards, Coral Reefs and Atom Bombs, Brutal Dictators, Fading Empires, and the Coming Collision of the World's Superpowers* (New York City: HarperCollins, 2015).

7. Francis Hezel, "From Conversion to Conquest: The Early Spanish Mission in the Marianas," *Journal of Pacific History* 17, no. 3 (1982): 115–137.

8. Noenoe K. Silva, *Aloha Betrayed: Native Hawaiian Resistance to American Colonialism* (Durham, NC: Duke University Press, 2004); Judith Selk Flores, *Estorian Inalahan: History of a Spanish-Era Village in Guam* (Hagåtna, Guam: Irensia, 2011).

9. Ross Dardani, "Weaponized Citizenship: A Critical Race Theory Analysis of U.S. Citizenship Legislation in the Pacific Unincorporated Territories" (PhD diss., University of Connecticut, 2017), 95.

10. Michael Lujan Bevacqua, "America-Style Colonialism," web log post, Guampedia, November 11, 2014, http://www.guampedia.com.

11. Michael R. Clement, Jr. "*Kustembre,* Modernity and Resistance: The Subaltern Narrative in Chamorro Language Music" (PhD diss., University of Hawai'i at Mānoa, 2011), 67.

12. Anne Perez Hattori, "Righting Civil Wrongs: The Guam Congress Walkout of 1949," *Isla: A Journal of Micronesian Studies* 3 (1995): 1–27.

13. Christine Taitano DeLisle, "Navy Wives / Native Lives: The Cultural and Historical Relations between American Naval Wives and Chamorro Women in Guam, 1898–1945" (PhD diss., University of Michigan, 2008), 41.

14. Ralph Stoney Bates, Sr. *An American Shame: The Abandonment of an Entire American Population* (CreateSpace, 2016).

15. Sahuma, "10 Things to Think about Each July," web log post, *Mumun Linahyan,* October 21, 2015, https://mumunlinahyan.com.

16. Don A. Farrell, *History of the Northern Mariana Islands* (Saipan: Commonwealth of Northern Mariana Islands Public School System, 1991), 343.

17. Joseph F. Ada, "Guam: Equal in War, but Not in Peace; Elusive Emancipation," *New York Times,* October 19, 1991, http://www.nytimes.com.

18. Diaz, "Deliberating 'Liberation Day,'" 157.

19. Cecelia Perez, "A Chamorro Retelling of Liberation," in *Kinalamten Pulitikat-Sinehten I Chamorro/Issues in Guam's Political Development: The Chamorro Perspective,* 70–77 (Mangilao, Guam: Guam Political Status Education Coordination Commission, 1996).

20. Diaz, "Deliberating 'Liberation Day,'" 161.

21. Ibid., 165.

22. Laura Marie Torres Souder-Jaffery, "Psyche under Siege: Uncle Sam, Look What You've Done to Us," in *Uncle Sam in Micronesia: Social Benefits, Social Costs,* ed. Donald H. Rubinstein and Vivian Dames (Guam: Micronesian Area Research Centre, University of Guam Press, 1991).

23. Diaz, "Deliberating 'Liberation Day,'" 156.

24. There are five additional naval sites on Guam, including Ordnance Annex, or "Naval Magazine," which contains the only freshwater reservoir and stores nuclear materials.

"Big Navy" is built on the ancient Chamorro village of Sumay, which was bombed, the survivors relocated, and the land confiscated. The Santa Rita-Sumay Peace Memorial, located at the original Santa Rita Village entrance, is dedicated to the "Chamorros of Sumay Village and all those who died during World War II." Santa Rita was established in April 1945 by the US Naval Government as a World War II temporary refugee camp for the displaced Chamorros of Sumay Village. See James Perez Viernes, "Fanhasso i Taotao Sumay: Displacement, Dispossession, and Survival in Guam" (master's thesis, University of Hawai'i at Mānoa, 2008), 103. Once a year in early April, Naval Base Guam allows families and the descendants of those lost and buried at Sumay to visit their land (*tåno'*) and ancestors for one day during the "Back to Sumay" event. Kevin Tano, "Revisiting History: Going Back to Sumay," *Pacific Daily News*, April 7, 2018, https://www.guampdn.com.

25. Diaz, "Deliberating 'Liberation Day,'" 159.

26. On a personal note, I attended the seventy-first Liberation 2015 parade on Marine Corps Drive. I, along with Chamorro women scholars Dr. Tiara Na'puti and Dr. Lisalinda Natividad, handed out decolonization information with several female social work students from the University of Guam. To my surprise, many people attending the parade understood and spoke about the hypocrisy of US "liberation" and land takings and further militarization, but they said they were at the parade to see family, friends, enjoy the barbecue, and celebrate summer. See Lisalinda Natividad and Gwyn Kirk, "Fortress Guam: Resistance to US Military Mega-Buildup," *Asia-Pacific Journal: Japan Focus* 19, no. 1 (2010): 1–17.

27. Kathy E. Ferguson and Phyllis Turnbull. *Oh, Say, Can You See? The Semiotics of the Military in Hawai'i*, (Minneapolis: University of Minnesota Press, 1999).

28. In January 2020, the first 205 World War II claims were processed by the administration of the current governor of Guam, Lou Leon Guerrero. See Haidee Eugenio Gilbert, "'They Took Everything from Us': Survivors Say War Pay Not Worth the Torture, Suffering," *Pacific Daily News*, February 7, 2020, https://www.guampdn.com. Sabrina Salas Matanane, "WWII Reparations Group Plans to Take Uncle Sam to Court," *Kuam News*, March 28, 2016, http://www.kuam.com.

29. Madeleine Z. Bordallo, "War Claims Passes," December 8, 2016, https://bordallo.house.gov.

30. Radio New Zealand, "Guam War Reparations Questioned," December12, 2016, http://www.radionz.co.nz.

31. US Department of Justice. "Guam Claims Program," last modified June 12, 2018, https://www.justice.gov.

32. Wyatt Olson, "Compensation Claim Period Opens for Guam Victims of WWII Japanese Occupation," *Stars and Stripes*, June 21, 2017, https://www.stripes.com.

33. Souder-Jaffery, "Psyche under Siege."

34. Laura Thompson, "Guam's Bombed-Out Capital," *Institute of Pacific Relations* 16, no. 6 (1947): 66–69.

35. Anne Perez Hattori, *Colonial Dis-Ease: US Navy and Health Policies and the Chamorros of Guam, 1898–1941, Pacific Islands Monograph Services* (Honolulu, Hawai'i: University of Hawai'i at Mānoa, Center for Pacific Islands Studies, 2004).

36. The 2015 documentary film *War for Guam*, directed by Frances Negrón-Muntaner, provides a Chamorro perspective of the World War II experience and lingering US military legacy. The lack of compensation for World War II survivors as well as land taken by the United States, is highlighted. The film's website is www.warforguam.com. See also Frances Negrón-Muntaner, "End the War in Guam," web log post, June 5, 2016, http://www

.huffingtonpost.com; and Sylvia Frain, "War for Guam (Film Review)," *Asia Pacific Inquiry* 7, no. 1 (2016): 126–129, https://www.uog.edu.

37. Justin Nobel, "A Micronesian Paradise—for U.S. Military Recruiters," *Time*, December 31, 2009.

38. Rick Cruz, "National Guard Airmen Prepare to Deploy," *Pacific Daily News*, January 4, 2016, http://www.guampdn.com; Neil Pang, "23 Guam Army Reservists Deploy to Afghanistan," *Guam Daily Post*, October 3, 2016, http://www.postguam.com; Jerick Sablan, "Guam Air Guard Headed to Afghanistan," *Pacific Daily News*, September 25, 2015, http://www.guampdn.com.

39. Ross Tuttle, "Island of Warriors," video file, *America by the Numbers*, PBS, October 11, 2014, http://www.pbs.org.

40. Leon Guerrero, Victoria-Lola, Kerri Ann Naputi Borja, Sabina Flores Perez, and Fanai Cruz Castro, "Hita Guåhan," in *Chamoru Testimonies Presented to the United Nations Special Political and Decolonization Committee, New York, NY* (2006), 11. https://issuu.com/guampedia/docs/hita_2006.

41. Tiara R. Na'puti and Michael Lujan Bevacqua, "Militarization and Resistance from Guåhan: Protecting and Defending Pågat," *American Quarterly* 67, no. 3 (2015): 857.

42. Women are the fastest-growing population of US veterans and homeless citizens, with a suicide rate two and a half times higher among veterans than among civilian women, and over 70 percent of them are single mothers. See Samatha Kubek, "The Invisible Veterans," web log post, *Huffingtonpost*, December 20, 2016, http://www.huffingtonpost.com; and Lily Casura, "There's a New Face for Veteran Homelessness, and It's Female: Over Seventy Percent Are Single Mothers," *Garnet News*, February 1, 2017, http://garnetnews.com. Mary F. Calvert, a US-based documentary photographer, has worked to publicize and humanize the hidden statistics through a series of photography projects. Access the photographs from "Missing in Action: Homeless Female Veterans" is available at http://maryfcalvert.com. Calvert also produced "The Battle Within: Sexual Violence in America's Military," available at http://maryfcalvert.com/the-battle-within-examining-rape-in-america's-military. She wrote, "Women who join the US Armed Forces are being raped and sexually assaulted by their colleagues in record numbers. An estimated 26,000 rapes and sexual assaults took place in the armed forces last year; only one in seven victims reported their attacks, and just one in ten of those cases went to trial." See the two-part series online at https://www.maryfcalvert.com/usa-military-sexual-assault-the-women.

43. Tuttle, "Island of Warriors."

44. Sylvia C. Frain, "Women's Resistance in the Marianas Archipelago: A US Colonial Homefront & Militarized Frontline," *Feminist Formations* 29, no. 1 (2017): 97–135.

45. Negrón-Muntaner, "End the War in Guam," 5.

46. Sylvia C. Frain and Betty Frain, "'We Serve Too!' Everyday Militarism of Children of US Service Members," *Childhood* 27, no. 3 (August 2020): 1–15.

47. For short digital films' perspective on the lack of veterans' services in the Mariana Islands, see the PBS special by Tuttle, "Island of Warriors" and the 2018 documentary *Island Soldier* (http://www.islandsoldiermovie.com) about the role Micronesian soldiers play in the US Armed Forces.

Two visual exhibitions were held on Guåhan in 2014 to honor Micronesians and Chamorros who both served and are currently serving. The first photo exhibition to "highlight the largely unrecognized role played by Pacific Island soldiers and contractors in the recent wars in Iraq and Afghanistan" was Ben Bohane's war photography exhibition *Desert Islanders*. See

"Exhibition Highlights Pacific Soldiers in Afghanistan," Waka Photos, accessed March 15, 2021, http://www.wakaphotos.com.

The second was *Sindålu: Chamorro Journeys in the U.S. Military*, a local exhibition curated by Humanities Guåhan in partnership with the Smithsonian that explored "the many significant and oftentimes unrecognized journeys of Chamorro men and women who currently serve or have served in the U.S. Military." See Sahuma, "Sindalu: Chamorro Journey Stories in the US Military," web log post, January 22, 2015, https://mumunlinahyan.com.

Note: Due to the lack of women's voices within the exhibit, Humanities Guåhan then launched the Guam Women Warriors project; an oral history and digital exhibition dedicated to active duty service and women veterans. Lacee Martinez, "Humanities Council Helps Female Veterans Share Their Stories," *Pacific Daily News*, January 31, 2015, http://www.guampdn.com. Also see the Guåhan Humanities Council Facebook page, https://www.facebook.com/guam.council.

48. Craig Santos Perez, "Cultures of Commemoration: The Politics of War, Memory, and History in the Mariana Islands by Keith L Camacho," review, *Contemporary Pacific* 25 (2013): 191.

49. To view ancient Chamorro style recreated as contemporary fashion, see the photo gallery at Lacee A. C. Martinez, "FestPac Fashion Eyes Three Eras of Style," February 18, 2016, *Pacific Daily News*, https://www.guampdn.com.

50. Diaz, "Deliberating 'Liberation Day,'" 156.

51. Keith L. Camacho, *Cultures of Commemoration: The Politics of War, Memory, and History in the Mariana Islands*, Pacific Islands Monograph Series 25 (Honolulu: Center for Pacific Islands Studies and University of Hawai'i Press, 2011).

52. C. S. Perez, "Cultures of Commemoration," 191.

53. Angel Santos, "United States Return Was Re-occupation, Not Liberation," *Pacific Daily News*, July 21, 1991, 21–22. The *PDN* may "sympathize with the resistance of prolocal actors but may only do so after first reaffirming the actors' loyalty to the United States." See Dalisay, "Social Control," 245.

54. Robert F. Rogers, *Destiny's Landfall: A History of Guam* (Honolulu: University of Hawai'i Press, 1995).

55. Sahuma, "Rethinking July 21st," web log post, July 21, 2016, https://mumunlinahyan.com.

56. Catherine Lutz, "US Military Bases on Guam in Global Perspective," *Asia-Pacific Journal: Japan Focus* 30, no. 3 (2010): 8.

57. Dalisay, "Social Control," 240.

58. Ibid., 254.

59. Ibid., 247–249. Dalisay's analysis of items published in the *Pacific Daily News* between the fiftieth and sixtieth anniversaries (1994–2004) of Liberation Day "reveals how a local, mainstream newspaper in a US colonial context could serve to influence colonized actors into consenting with their subordinate positions . . . and the PDN may legitimize the importance of adhering to the norm of American loyalty by framing this norm under the guise of colonial reciprocity." Ibid., 253. "Guamanian" is a term created in the 1950s to recognize everyone living on Guåhan at that time—including the settler and military populations.

60. Diaz, "Deliberating 'Liberation Day,'" 157).

61. Hokulani K. Aikau, "Indigenous Theory," Department of Political Science, University of Hawai'i, 5 May, 2015, http://www.politicalscience.hawaii.edu.

62. "Mary T.," personal communication with the author, October 5, 2015. I presented *Hashtag Guam/#Guam #Guahan: How Digital Photography and Social Media on Guam Is Redefining Who Photographs the Pacific* at the twenty-second Pacific History Association in 2016.

The "Photographing the Pacific" panel, chaired by Max Quanchi, a leader in Pacific Islands photographic research, traces the history of photography in the region directly to colonialism. I discussed how young people on Guåhan use the new media platform Instagram for cultural, political, and spiritual purposes. Chamorro historian and scholar Dr. Anne Hattori has also written about the role of photography as a form of remembering; see Anne Perez Hattori, "Re-membering the Past," *Journal of Pacific History* 46, no. 3 (2011): 293–318.

63. Tonia San Nicolas-Rocca and James Parrish, "Capturing and Conveying Cultural Knowledge Using Social Media," *International Journal of Knowledge Management* 9, no. 3 (2013): 1–18.

64. Sylvia C. Frain, "Fanohge Famalåo'an & Fan'tachu Fama'lauan: Women Rising: Indigenous Resistance to Militarization in the Marianas Archipelago," ebook, Guampedia, 2018, https://www.guampedia.com.

65. Tiara R. Na'puti, "Speaking the Language of Peace: Chamoru Resistance and Rhetoric in Guahan's Self-Determination Movements," *Anthropologica* 56, no. 2 (2014): 311n9.

66. Manuel L. Cruz III and Lilnabeth P. Somera, "I A'adahi: An Analysis of Chamorro Cyberactivism," unpublished paper discussed on "Public Radio Guam," February 3, 2016, https://www.podbean.com/site/EpisodeDownload/PB5C56ACSYHU5, 6, 22.

67. Ibid., 21.

68. Zea Nauta, "Hami i Tåsa," web log post, July 17, 2015, Hagan Guåhan, https://haganguahan.com.

69. Viernes, "Fanhasso i Taotao Sumay," 103n149.

70. Christine Taitano DeLisle, "Destination Chamorro Culture: Notes on Realignment, Rebranding, and Post-9/11 Militourism in Guam," *American Quarterly* 68, no. 3 (2016): 565; Dipåttamenton I Kaohao Guianhan Chamorro, *Chamorro Heritage: A Sense of Place*, ed. Research Department of Chamorro Affairs, Publication and Training Division, The Hale'-ta Series (Hagåtña, Guåhan: Political Statues Education Coordinating Commission, 2003), 23.

71. Na'puti and Bevacqua, "Militarization and Resistance," 848.

72. Leevin T. Camacho, "Resisting the Proposed Military Buildup on Guam," in *Under Occupation: Resistance and Struggle in a Militarised Asia-Pacific*, ed. Daniel Broudy, Peter Simpson, and Makoto Arakaki (Newcastle upon Tyne, UK: Cambridge Scholars, 2013), 189.

73. Bevacqua, "America-Style Colonialism," web log post, Guampedia," 2014, last updated March 21, 2021, http://www.guampedia.com.

74. Roselle Romanes, "Author of Inifresi Dr. Bernadita Camacho Dungca Passes Away at Age 75," *Pacific News Center*, February16, 2016, accessed March 3, 2016, http://www.pacificnewscenter.com.

75. L. T. Camacho, "Resisting the Proposed Military Buildup," 183.

76. Kisha Borja-Kicho'cho and A. Ricardo Aguon Hernandez, "Guam (Guåhan)," in *The Indigenous World 2012*, ed. Cæcilie Mikkelsen (Copenhagen: International Working Group for Indigenous Affairs/IWGIA, 2012), 232.

77. Julian Aguon, "On Loving the Maps Our Hands Cannot Hold: Self-Determination of Colonized and Indigenous Peoples in International Law," *UCLA Asian Pacific American Law Journal* 16, no. 1 (2011): 67.

78. US Marine Corps Forces Pacific, "Draft Environmental Impact Statement/Overseas Environmental Impact Statement for Commonwealth of the Northern Marianas Islands Joint Military Training," ed. United States Department of the Navy (Honolulu, HI: Naval Facilities Engineering Command, Pacific, 2015).

79. Hillary Rodham Clinton, *America's Pacific Century*, ed. US Department of State (Honolulu, HI: East-West Center, 2011); and Michael Green, Kathleen Hicks, and Mark

Cancian, "Asia-Pacific Rebalance 2025: Capabilities, Presence, and Partnerships: An Independent Review of U.S. Defense Strategy in the Asia-Pacific" (Washington, DC, Center for Strategic and International Studies, 2015).

80. John M. Smith, "Continuous Bomber Presence in Guam," Military.com, February 10, 2017, http://www.military.com.

81. James Perez Viernes, "Won't You Please Come Back to Guam? Media Discourse, Military Buildup, and Chamorros in the Space Between," *Contemporary Pacific* CPIS (Negotiating Culture, Place, and Identity in the Pacific) occasional paper 44 (2007): 103–118.

Selected Bibliography

Acosta Cruz, Maria. *Dream Nation: Puerto Rican Culture and the Fiction of Independence*. New Brunswick, NJ: Rutgers University Press, 2014.

Adorno, Theodor W. *The Culture Industry: Selected Essays on Mass Culture*. New York: Routledge, 1991.

Agamben, Giorgio. *Homo Sacer*. Stanford, CA: Stanford University Press, 1998.

Aguon, Julian. "On Loving the Maps Our Hands Cannot Hold: Self-Determination of Colonized and Indigenous Peoples in International Law." *UCLA Asian Pacific American Law Journal* 16, no. 1 (2011): 46–72.

Ahlgren, Ingrid, Seiji Yamada, and Allen Wong. "Rising Oceans, Climate Change, Food Aid, and Human Rights in the Marshall Islands." *Health and Human Rights* 16, no. 1 (2014): 69–80.

Aikau, Hokulani K. "Indigenous Theory." Department of Political Science, University of Hawai'i. Accessed May 5, 2015. http://www.politicalscience.hawaii.edu.

Almanaque del Pueblo. Puerto Rico: Departmento de Instruccion, Division de Educacion de la Comunidad, 1952.

Amador, José. *Medicine and Nation Building in the Americas, 1890–1940*. Nashville, TN: Vanderbilt University Press, 2015.

———. "The Pursuit of Health: Colonialism and Hookworm Eradication in Puerto Rico." *Southern Spaces*, March 30, 2017. https://southernspaces.org.

Ancieto Ramos, Rolando. *El capitolio de La Habana*. Havana: Centro Capitolio de La Habana, 1998.

Arnold, C. D., and H. D. Higinbotham. *Official Views of the World's Columbian Exposition*. Chicago, IL: Press Chicago Photo-Gravure Company, 1893.

Aronowicz, Miriam. "Terra Nulla: Contesting the South African Colonial Landscape." *University of Toronto Art Journal* 2 (2009): 1–25.

Aruca, Lohania, Narciso G. Menocal, and Edward Shaw. "The Cristóbal Colón Cemetery in Havana." Cuba-themed issue, *Journal of Decorative and Propaganda Arts* 22, 1996: 36–55.

Ayala, César J., and Rafael Bernabe. *Puerto Rico in the American Century: A History since 1898*. Chapel Hill: University of North Carolina Press, 2007.

Baker, Kriselle, and Elizabeth Rankin. *Fiona Pardington: The Pressure of Sunlight Falling*. Dunedin, New Zealand: Otago University Press, 2011.

Balce, Nerrisa. *Body Parts of Empire: Visual Abjection, Filipino Images, and the American Archive*. Ann Arbor: University of Michigan Press, 2016.

Ballard, Barbara J. "African-American Protest and the Role of the Haitian Pavilion at the 1893 Chicago World's Fair." *Multiculturalism: Roots and Realities* (2002): 108–124.

Banta, Melissa, and Curtis M. Hinsley. *From Site to Site: Anthropology, Photography, and the Power of Imagery*. Cambridge, MA: Peabody Museum Press, 1986.

Bates, Ralph Stoney, Sr. *An American Shame: The Abandonment of an Entire American Population*. CreateSpace, 2016.
Baudrillard, Jean. *Simulacra and Simulation*. Ann Arbor: University of Michigan Press, 1994.
Baudrillard, Jean, and Francesco Proto. *Mass, Identity, Architecture: Architectural Writings of Jean Baudrillard*. Chichester, UK: Wiley Academy, 2003.
Baum, L. Frank. *The Wonderful Wizard of Oz*. London: Harper Press, 2010.
Bello, Walden. *People and Power in the Pacific*. London: Pluto Press, 1992.
Benítez, Marimar. "The Fifties: Affirmation and Reaction." In *Puerto Rico: Art and Identity*. San Juan: Universidad de Puerto Rico, 1998.
Benitez-Rojo, Antonio. *The Repeating Island: The Caribbean and the Postmodern Perspective* Durham, NC: Duke University Press, 1992.
Berg, Ulla D., and Ana Y. Ramos-Zayas. "Racializing Affect: A Theoretical Proposition." *Current Anthropology* 56, no. 5 (2015): 654–677.
Berge, Bjørn. "The Canal Zone: A Siberia in the Caribbean." In *Nowherelands: An Atlas of Vanished Countries 1840–1975*, 116–119. London: Thames & Hudson, 2017.
Berger, Molly W. *Hotel Dreams: Luxury, Technology, and Urban Ambition in America, 1829–1929*. Baltimore, MD: Johns Hopkins University Press, 2011.
Berlant, Lauren. "Slow Death (Sovereignty, Obesity, Lateral Agency)." *Critical Inquiry* 33, no. 4 (2007): 754–780.
Berman, Nina. *Homeland*. Great Britain: Trolley, 2008.
Beveridge, Charles E. "Frederick Law Olmsted's Theory of Landscape Design." *Nineteenth Century* 3, no. 2 (Summer 1977): 38–43.
Bhabha, Homi K. *The Location of Culture*. New York: Routledge, 1994.
Bloomer, Kent, and Charles Moore. *Body, Memory, and Architecture*. New Haven, CT: Yale University Press, 1977.
Bolton, Richard, ed. *The Contest of Meaning: Critical Histories of Photography*. Cambridge, MA: MIT Press, 1989.
Borges, Jorge Luis. "The Circular Ruins." In *Labyrinths: Selected Stories and Other Writings*. New York: New Directions, 1964.
Bosse, David. *A Historical Atlas: Civil War Newspaper Maps*. Baltimore, MD: Johns Hopkins University Press, 1993.
Braddock, Alan C., and Dr. Christoph Irmscher, eds. *A Keener Perception: Ecocritical Studies in American Art History*. Tuscaloosa: University of Alabama Press, 2009.
Braddock, Alan C., and Karl Kusserow, eds. *Nature's Nation: American Art and Environment*. Princeton, NJ: Princeton University Art Museum, 2018.
Bretos, Miguel A. "Imaging Cuba under the American Flag: Charles Edward Doty in Havana, 1899–1902." Cuba-themed issue, *Journal of Decorative and Propaganda Arts* 22, (1996): 82–103.
Briggs, Laura. *Reproducing Empire: Race, Sex, Science, and US Imperialism in Puerto Rico*. Berkeley: University of California Press, 2003.
Brody, David. *Visualizing American Empire: Orientalism and Imperialism in the Philippines*. Chicago, IL: University of Chicago Press, 2010.
Brown, George W. *Pearl of the Orient: The Philippine Islands*. Boston, MA: Dana Estates, 1900.
Brown, Steve. "Poetics and Politics: Bikini Atoll and World Heritage Listing." In *Transcending the Culture-Nature Divide in Cultural Heritage: Views from the Asia-Pacific Region*, edited by Sally Brockwell, Sue O'Connor, and Denis Byrne, 35–52. Acton: Australian National University Press, 2013.

Brückner, Martin. *The Social Life of Maps in America, 1750–1860.* Chapel Hill: University of North Carolina Press / Omohundro Institute of Early American History and Culture, 2017.

Bryan, E. H. Jr. *Life in the Marshall Islands.* Honolulu, HI: Pacific Scientific Information Center, 1972.

Buchanan, Ian. "Walking in the City." In *The Certeau Reader,* edited by Graham Ward, 101–118. Oxford: Blackwell, 2000.

Burnham, Daniel Hudson, and Peirce Anderson. "Preliminary Plan of Baguio, Province of Benguet, P.I." In *Sixth Annual Report of the Philippine Commission (Part 3).* Washington, DC: Government Printing Office, 1906.

———. *Report on Proposed Improvements at Manila.* In *Report of the Philippine Commission Part 1,* 627–635. Washington, DC: Government Printing Office, 1906.

Burrows, Geoff. "The New Deal in Puerto Rico: Public Works, Public Health, and the Puerto Rico Reconstruction Administration, 1935–1955." PhD diss., City University of New York, 2014.

Camacho, Keith L. *Cultures of Commemoration: The Politics of War, Memory, and History in the Mariana Islands.* Pacific Islands Monograph Series 25. Honolulu: Center for Pacific Islands Studies / University of Hawai'i Press, 2011.

Camacho, Leevin T. "Resisting the Proposed Military Buildup on Guam." In *Under Occupation: Resistance and Struggle in a Militarised Asia-Pacific,* edited by Daniel Broudy, Peter Simpson, and Makoto Arakaki, 183–190. Newcastle upon Tyne, UK: Cambridge Scholars, 2013.

Camille, Michael. "Simulacrum." In *Critical Terms for Art History,* edited by Robert S. Nelson and Richard Shiff, 31–44. Chicago, IL: University of Chicago Press, 1996.

Campomanes, Oscar V. "Images of Filipino Racialization in the Anthropological Laboratories of the American Empire: The Case of Daniel Folmar." "Comparative Racialization," special issue, *PMLA* 123, no. 5. (2008): 1692–1699.

Cao, Maggie M. "What Is the Place of Empire in the History of American Art?" Bully Pulpit, *Panorama: Journal of the Association of Historians of American Art* 6, no. 1 (Spring 2020), doi.org/10.24926/24716839.9804.

Caragol, Taína and Kate Clarke Lemay. "Imperial Visions and Revisions." Bully Pulpit, *Panorama: Journal of the Association of Historians of American Art* 6, no. 1 (Spring 2020), doi .org/10.24926/24716839.10096.

Carmack, Edward W. "Civil Government for the Philippine Islands." *Congressional Record Permanent Digital Collection.* Last modified May 8, 1902. Accessed June 2, 2019. https:// congressional.proquest.com.

Caronan, Faye C. "Colonial Consumption and Colonial Hierarchies in Representations of Philippine and Puerto Rican Tourism." "Philippine Studies," special issue, *Representations* 53, no. 1 (2005): 32–58.

Céspedes, Carlos Miguel de. *Libro del Capitolio.* Havana: Talleres tip. de P. Fernández y compañía, 1933.

Chambers, John W. *The Eagle and the Dove: The American Peace Movement and United States Foreign Policy, 1900–1922.* 2nd ed. Syracuse, NY: Syracuse University Press, 1991.

Chiba, Yoshihiro. "Cigar-Makers in American Colonial Manila: Survival during Structural Depression in the 1920s." *Journal of Southeast Asian Studies* 36, no. 3 (2005): 373–397.

Clement, Michael R. Jr. "*Kustembre,* Modernity and Resistance: The Subaltern Narrative in Chamorro Language Music." PhD diss., University of Hawai'i at Mānoa, 2011.

Coates, Ta-Nehisi. "Letter to My Son." *Atlantic,* July 4, 2015.

Collazo, Enrique. *Los americanos en Cuba*. Havana: Editorial de Ciencias Sociales, Instituto Cubano del Libro, 1972.

Coombes, Annie E., ed. "Memory and History in Settler Colonialism." In *Rethinking Settler Colonialism: History and Memory in Australia, Canada, Aotearoa New Zealand, and South Africa*. New York: Manchester University Press, 2006.

Costa, Matías. *Zonians*. Madrid: La Fábrica, 2015.

Coursey, Oscar William. *History and Geography of the Philippine Islands: For General Reading and Use in Our Public Schools*. Mitchell, SD: Educator School Supply, 1903.

Dalisay, Francis. "Social Control in an American Pacific Island: Guam's Local Newspaper Reports on Liberation." *Journal of Communication Inquiry* 33, no. 3 (2009): 239–257.

Dardani, Ross. "Weaponized Citizenship: A Critical Race Theory Analysis of U.S. Citizenship Legislation in the Pacific Unincorporated Territories." PhD diss., University of Connecticut, 2017.

Davenport, Coral. "Rising Seas Are Claiming a Vulnerable Nation." *New York Times*, December 12, 2015.

Davis, Richard Harding. *The Cuban and Porto Rican Campaigns*. New York: Charles Scribner's Sons, 1898.

Daws, Gavan. *Shoal of Time: A History of the Hawaiian Islands*. Honolulu: University of Hawai'i Press, 1968.

Dedek, Peter B. *The Cemeteries of New Orleans: A Cultural History*. Baton Rouge: Louisiana State University, 2017.

de Jesus, Edilberto C. *The Tobacco Monopoly in the Philippines: Bureaucratic Enterprise and Social Change, 1766–1880*. Manila, Philippines: Ateneo de Manila University Press, 1998.

de la Cruz, Enrique B., and Pearlie Rose Baluyut. *Confrontations, Crossings, and Convergence: Photographs of the Philippines and the United States, 1898–1998*. Los Angeles: UCLA Asian American Studies Center, 1998.

de las Cuevas, Juan. *500 Años de construcciones en Cuba*. Madrid: D. V. Chavín, 2001.

Deleuze, Gilles. *Difference and Repetition*. Translated by Paul Patton. New York: Columbia University Press, 1969.

DeLisle, Christine Taitano. "Destination Chamorro Culture: Notes on Realignment, Rebranding, and Post-9/11 Militourism in Guam." *American Quarterly* 68, no. 3 (2016): 563–572.

———. "Navy Wives / Native Lives: The Cultural and Historical Relations between American Naval Wives and Chamorro Women in Guam, 1898–1945." PhD diss., University of Michigan, 2008.

Delmendo, Sharon. "Marketing Colonialism: Little Brown Brothers in the Kodak Zone." In *The Star-Entangled Banner: One Hundred Years of America in the Philippines*, 47–85. New Brunswick, NJ: Rutgers University Press, 2004.

———. *The Star Entangled Banner*. New Brunswick, NJ: Rutgers University Press, 2004.

Diaz, Vicente M. "Deliberating 'Liberation Day': Indentity, History, Memory, and War in Guam." In *Perilous Memories: The Asia-Pacific War(s)*, edited by Geoffrey M. White, L. Yoneyama, and T. Fujitani, 155–180. Durham, NC: Duke University Press, 2001.

Dillon, Diane. "Consuming Maps." In *Maps: Finding Our Place in the World*, edited by James Akerman and Robert Karrow, Jr., 289–343. Chicago, IL: University of Chicago Press / Field Museum of National History and Newberry Library, 2007.

Dodge, Philip Henry. "Modern Art in Hawaii: Kilohana Art League." *Paradise of the Pacific* 10, no. 10 (1897): 149.

Doeppers, Daniel F. *Feeding Manila in Peace and War, 1850–1940.* Madison: University of Wisconsin Press, 2016.

Dougherty, J. P. "Baroque and Picturesque Motifs in L'Enfant's Design for the Federal Capital." *American Quarterly* 26, no. 1 (March 1974): 23–36.

Drinnon, Richard. *Facing West: The Metaphysics of Indian-Hating and Empire-Building.* Norman: University of Oklahoma Press, 1997. First published in 1990 by Schocken Books.

Duany, Jorge. "Portraying the Other: Puerto Rican Images in Two American Photography Collections." "Imperial Disclosures: Part II," special issue, *Discourse* 23, no. 1, (Winter 2001): 119–153.

———. *The Puerto Rican Nation on the Move: Identities on the Island and in the United States.* Chapel Hill: University of North Carolina Press, 2002.

Dudoit, D. Māhealani. "Against Extinction: A Legacy of Native Hawaiian Resistance Literature." In *Voices of Social Justice and Diversity in a Hawai'i Context,* 45–62. Leiden: Brill, 2019.

Dunaway, Finis. *Natural Visions: The Power of Images in American Environmental Reform.* Chicago, IL: University of Chicago Press, 2005.

Dvorak, Greg. "Detouring Kwajalein: At Home between Coral and Concrete." In *Touring Pacific Cultures,* edited by Kalissa Alexeyeff and John Taylor, 97–140. Acton: Australian National University Press, 2016.

Edney, Matthew H. "The Irony of Imperial Mapping." In *The Imperial Map: Cartography and the Mastery of Empire,* edited by James R. Akerman, 11–45. Chicago, IL: University of Chicago Press, 2009.

Edwards, Jay D. "The Origins of Creole Architecture." *Winterthur Portfolio* 29, no. 2/3 (Summer / Autumn 1994): 155–189.

Edy, Carolyn M. *The Woman War Correspondent, the U.S. Military, and the Press, 1846–1947.* Lanham, MD: Lexington Books, 2017.

Falasca-Zamponi, Simonetta. *Fascist Spectacle: The Aesthetics of Power in Mussolini's Italy.* Berkeley: University of California Press, 1997.

Farrell, Don A. *History of the Northern Mariana Islands.* Saipan: Commonwealth of Northern Mariana Islands Public School System, 1991.

Ferguson, Kathy E., and Phyllis Turnbull. *Oh, Say, Can You See? The Semiotics of the Military in Hawai'i.* Minneapolis: University of Minnesota Press, 1999.

Fernández de Oviedo y Valdés, Gonzalo. *Historia general y natural de las Indias, islas, y tierra-firme del mar océano.* Madrid: Imprenta de la Real Academia de la Historia, 1852.

Fernández y Simón, Abel. "Las fuentes de las plazas, parques y paseos públicos de la Habana colonial." In *Cuba: Arquitectura y urbanismo,* edited by Felipe J. Préstamo y Hernández, 337–351. Miami, FL: Ediciones Universal, 1995.

Findley, Lisa. *Building Change: Architecture, Politics, and Cultural Agency.* New York: Routledge, 2005.

Fink, Leon, Julie Greene, and Lauren Hirshberg. "Domestic Containment in the Marshall Islands: Making a Home for Cold War Workers in the US Imperial Pacific." *Labor* 13 (2016): 177–196.

Fletcher, Lisa. "'Some Distance to Go': A Critical Survey of Island Studies." *New Literatures Review* 47 (2011): 17–34.

Flores, Judith Selk. *Estorian Inalahan: History of a Spanish-Era Village in Guam.* Hagåtna, Guam: Irensia, 2011.

Folkmar, Daniel. *Album of Philippine Types: Found in Bilibid Prison in 1903.* Manila, Philippines: Bureau of Public Printing under the Auspices of the Philippine Exposition Board, 1904.

Foos, Paul. *A Short, Offhand, Killing Affair: Soldiers and Social Conflict during the Mexican-American War.* Chapel Hill: University of North Carolina Press, 2002.

Forbes, David W., ed. *The Diary of Queen Liliuokalani of Hawaii, 1885–1900.* Honolulu, HI: Hui Hanai, 2020.

———. *Encounters with Paradise: View of Hawaii and Its People, 1778–1941* Honolulu: Honolulu Academy of Arts, 1992.

———. *He Makana: The Gertrude Mary Joan Damon Haig Collection of Hawaiian Art, Paintings, and Prints.* Honolulu: State Foundation on Culture and the Arts, Hawai'i State Art Museum, 2013.

Foucault, Michel. *The Order of Things: An Archaeology of the Human Sciences.* 1966; repr., London: Routledge, 1989.

———. *"Society Must Be Defended": Lectures at the Collége de France, 1975–1976.* London: Picador, 2003.

Frain, Sylvia C. "Fanohge Famalåo'an & Fan'tachu Fama'lauan: Women Rising: Indigenous Resistance to Militarization in the Marianas Archipelago." PhD diss., University of Otago, 2017.

———. "Resisting Political Colonization and American Militarization in the Marianas Archipelago." *AlterNative: An International Journal of Indigenous Peoples* 12, no. 3 (2016): 298–315.

———. "War for Guam (Film Review)." *Asia Pacific Inquiry* 7, no. 1 (2016): 126–129. https://www.uog.edu.

———. "Women's Resistance in the Marianas Archipelago: A US Colonial Homefront & Militarized Frontline." *Feminist Formations* 29, no. 1 (2017): 97–135.

Fryd, Vivien Green. *Art and Empire: The Politics of Ethnicity in the United States Capitol, 1815–1860.* New Haven, CT: Yale University Press, 1992.

García, Gervasio Luis. "I Am the Other: Puerto Rico in the Eyes of North Americans, 1898." *Journal of American History* 87, no. 1 (June 2000): 39–64.

García, Gervasio, and A. G. Quintero Rivera. *Desafío y solidaridad: Breve historia del movimiento obrero puertorriqueño.* Río Piedras, Puerto Rico: Ediciones Huracán, 1982.

García, Guadalupe. *Beyond the Walled City: Colonial Exclusion in Havana.* Oakland: University of California Press, 2016.

García-Cólon, Ismael. *Land Reform in Puerto Rico: Modernizing the Colonial State, 1941–1969.* Gainesville: University Press of Florida, 2009.

García Muñiz, Humberto. *Sugar and Power in the Caribbean.* San Juan: Editorial de la Universidad de Puerto Rico and Ian Randle, 2010.

González, Robert Alexander. *Designing Pan-America: U.S. Architectural Visions for the Western Hemisphere.* Austin: University of Texas Press, 2011.

Govan, Sandra Y., and Sandra G. Shannon. "From Post Racial Climate to Winter in America: Life, Literature, and the Small Screen." *CLA Journal* 58, no. 3/4 (2015): 127–138.

Guha, Ramachandra. "Radical American Environmentalism and Wilderness Preservation: A Third World Critique." *Environmental Ethics* 11, no. 1 (Spring 1989): 71–83.

Hall, Stuart. "The Spectacle of the 'Other.'" In *Representation: Cultural Representations, and Signifying Practices,* 225–279. Culture, Media, and Identities. London: Sage, 2000.

Hanlon, David L. *Remaking Micronesia: Discourses over Development in a Pacific Territory.* Honolulu: University of Hawai'i Press, 1998.

Helman, Cecil. *Culture, Health, and Illness.* London: Hodder Arnold, 2007.

Harley, John B. "Deconstructing the Map." *Cartographica* 26, no. 2 (Summer 1989): 1–20.

———. "Maps, Knowledge and Power." In *The Iconography of Landscape: Essays on the Symbolic Representation, Design, and Use of Past Environments,* edited by Denis Cosgrove and Stephen Daniels, 277–312. Cambridge: Cambridge University Press, 1989.

Hartman, Joseph R. *Dictator's Dreamscape: How Architecture and Vision Built Machado's Cuba and Invented Modern Havana.* Pittsburgh: University of Pittsburgh Press, 2019.

———. "Silent Witnesses: Modernity, Colonialism and Jean-Claude Nicolas Forestier's Unfinished Plans for Havana." *Journal of the Society of Architectural Historians* 78, no. 3 (September 2019): 292–311.

Hattori, Anne Perez. *Colonial Dis-Ease: US Navy and Health Policies and the Chamorros of Guam, 1898–1941.* Pacific Islands Monograph Serices. Honolulu: University of Hawai'i at Mānoa, Center for Pacific Islands Studies, 2004.

———. "Re-membering the Past." *Journal of Pacific History* 46, no. 3 (2011): 293–318.

———. "Righting Civil Wrongs: The Guam Congress Walkout of 1949." *Isla: A Journal of Micronesian Studies,* no. 3 (1995): 1–27.

Hawaiian Society of the Sons of the American Revolution et al. *An Address by the Hawaiian Branches of the Sons of the American Revolution, Sons of Veterans, and Grand Army of the Republic to Their Compatriots in Ameria Concerning the Annexaton of Hawaii.* Washington, DC: Gibson Bros., 1897.

Hawkins, Don Alexander. "The Landscape of the Federal City: A 1792 Walking Tour." *Washington History* 3, no. 1 (Spring / Summer 1991): 10–33.

Hermandad de Artistas Gráficos de Puerto Rico. *Puerto Rico—Arte e identidad / Puerto Rico: Art and Identity.* San Juan: Editorial de la Universidad de Puerto Rico, 1998.

Herscher, Andrew, and Ana María León. "At the Border of Decolonization." *E-Flux,* May 6, 2020. Accessed May 21, 2020. https://www.e-flux.com.

Hevia, James L. "The Photography Complex: Exposing Boxer-Era China (1900–1901), Making Civilization." In *Empires of Vision: A Reader,* edited by Martin Jay and Sumathi Ramaswamy, 283–314. Durham, NC: Duke University Press, 2014.

Hezel, Francis. "From Conversion to Conquest: The Early Spanish Mission in the Marianas." *Journal of Pacific History* 17, no. 3 (1982): 115–137.

Hines, Thomas S. *Burnham of Chicago: Architect and Planner.* Chicago, IL: Chicago University Press, 1979.

———. "The Imperial Mall: The City Beautiful Movement and the Washington Plan of 1901–1902." In *The Mall in Washington, 1791–1991,* edited by Richard Longstreth, 78–99. Washington, DC: National Gallery of Art, 1991.

Hirshberg, Lauren. "Nuclear Families: (Re)producing 1950s Suburban America in the Marshall Islands." *OAH Magazine of History* 26, no. 4 (2012): 36–43.

Hoganson, Kristin L. "Cosmopolitan Domesticity: Importing the American Dream, 1865–1920." *American Historical Review* 107, no. 1 (February 2002): 55–83.

———. *Fighting for American Manhood: How Gender Politics Provoked the Spanish-American and Philippine-American Wars.* New Haven, CT: Yale University Press, 1998.

Holmes, Karen, and Sherrie Smith-Ferri. *Days of Grace: California Artist Grace Hudson in Hawaii.* Ukiah, CA: Grace Hudson Museum, 2014.

Horsman, Reginald. *Race and Manifest Destiny.* Cambridge, MA: Harvard University Press, 1981.

Iglesias Utset, Marial. *A Cultural History of Cuba during the US Occupation, 1898–1902.* Chapel Hill: University of North Carolina Press, 2011.

———. *Las metáforas del cambio en la vida cotidiana: Cuba, 1898–1902.* Havana: Ediciones Unión, 2010.

Immerwahr, Daniel. *How to Hide an Empire: A History of the Greater United States*. New York: Farrar, Straus and Giroux, 2019.

Jackson, Faith Reyher. "Balboa, Canal Zone." In *Pioneer of Tropical Landscape Architecture: William Lyman Phillips in Florida*. Gainesville: University Press of Florida, 1997.

Jacob, Christian. *The Sovereign Map: Theoretical Approaches in Cartography throughout History*. Chicago, IL: University of Chicago Press, 2006.

Jay, Martin, and Sumathi Ramaswamy, eds. *Empires of Vision: A Reader*. Durham, NC: Duke University Press, 2014.

Jenks, Albert Ernest. *The Bontoc Igorot*. Manila, Philippines: Bureau of Public Printing, Department of the Interior, 1905.

Johns, Elizabeth. "American Landscape: Manifest What?" *Journal of Interdisciplinary History* 12, no. 4 (1993): 751–754.

Johnson, Giff. *Don't Ever Whisper: Darlene Keju, Pacific Health Pioneer, Champion for Nuclear Survivors*. Charleston, SC: Creative Space, 2013.

Johnson, Willis Fletcher. *America's Foreign Relations*. New York: Century, 1921.

Jones, Shermaine M. "'I Can't Breathe!' Affective Asphyxia in Claudia Rankine's Citizen: An American Lyric." *South: A Scholarly Journal* 50, no. 1 (2017): 37–45.

Kam, Ralph Thomas, and Jeffrey K. Lyons. "Remembering the Committee of Safety: Identifying the Citizenship, Descent, and Occupations of the Men Who Overthrew the Monarchy." *Hawaiian Journal of History* 55 (2019): 31–54.

Kanahele, George He'eu Sanford. *Pauahi: The Kamehameha Legacy*. Honolulu: Kamehameha Schools, 1986.

Kaplan, Amy, and Donald E. Pease, *Cultures of United States Imperialism*. Durham, NC: Duke University Press, 1999.

Kent, Harold Winfield. *Charles Reed Bishop, Man of Hawaii*. Palo Alto, CA: Pacific Books, 1965.

Keown, Michelle. "Waves of Destruction: Nuclear Imperialism and Anti-Nuclear Protest in the Indigenous Literatures of the Pacific." *Journal of Postcolonial Writing* 54, no. 5 (2018): 585–600.

Kilohana Art League, *Mardi Gras Grand Bal Masque Given by and for the Benefit of the Kilohana Art League at the Crystal Palace*. Honolulu: Hawaiian Gazette, 1908.

Kirsch, Scott. "Aesthetic Regime Change: The Burnham Plans and US Landscape Imperialism in the Philippines." *Philippine Studies: Historical and Ethnographic Viewpoints* 65, no. 3 (September 2017): 315–356.

———. "Insular Territories: US Colonial Science, Geopolitics, and the (Re)Mapping of the Philippines." *Geographical Journal* 182, no. 1 (March 2016): 2–14.

Kirsch, Stuart. "The Double Exposure of the Marshall Islands." *Architectural Review* (March 23, 2018). Accessed April 17, 2021. https://www.architectural-review.com.

Klare, Michael T. "The Architecture of Imperial America." *Science & Society* 33, no. 3 (Summer/Fall 1969): 257–284.

Klein, Naomi. *The Battle for Paradise: Puerto Rico Takes on the Disaster Capitalists*. Chicago, IL: Haymarket Books, 2018.

Koepnick, Lutz P. "Fascist Aesthetics Revisited." *Modernism/modernity* 6, no. 1 (January 1999): 51–73.

Kothari, Uma, and Rorden Wilkinson. "Colonial Imaginaries and Postcolonial Transformations: Exiles, Bases, Beaches." *Third World Quarterly* 31, no. 8 (2010): 1395–1412.

Kramer, Paul A. "Race-Making and Colonial Violence in the US Empire: The Philippine-American War as Race War." *Diplomatic History* 30, no. 2 (2006): 169–210.

Kuykendall, Ralph S. *The Hawaiian Kingdom*. Vol. 3, *1874–1893: The Kalakaua Dynasty*. Honolulu: University of Hawai'i Press, 1967.
Lasansky, D. Medina. *The Renaissance Perfected: Architecture, Spectacle, and Tourism in Fascist Italy*. University Park: Pennsylvania State University Press, 2004.
Lejeune, Jean-François. "The City as Landscape: Jean Claude Nicolas Forestier and the Great Urban Works of Havana, 1925–1930." *Journal of Decorative and Propaganda Arts* 22 (1996): 150–185.
Leslie, Camilo Arturo. "Territoriality, Map-Mindedness, and the Politics of Place." *Theory and Society: Renewal and Critique in Social Theory* 45, no. 2 (April 2016): 169–201.
Leuenberger, Christine, and Izhak Schnell. "The Politics of Maps: Constructing National Territories in Israel." *Social Studies of Science* 40, no. 6 (2010): 803–842.
Levy, Josh. *Micronesian Government: Yesterday, Today, and Tomorrow*. Edited by SJ Francis X. Hezel, *A Micronesian Civics Textbook*. Palikir, Pohnpei, Federated States of Micronesia: National Department of Education, 2008.
Lico, Gerard. *Arkitekturang Filipino: A History of Architecture and Urbanism in the Philippines*. Quezon City: University of the Philippines Press, 2008.
Linn, Brian McAllister. *The Philippine War, 1899–1902*. Lawrence: University of Kansas Press, 2000.
Logan, Enid Lynette. "The 1899 Cuban Marriage Law Controversy: Church, State and Empire in the Crucible of Nation." *Journal of Social History* 42, no. 2 (2008): 469–494.
Love, Eric T. *Race over Empire: Racism and U.S. Imperialism, 1865–1900*. Chapel Hill: University of North Carolina Press, 2004.
Lowery, Wesley. "'I Can't Breathe': Five Years after Eric Garner Died in Struggle with New York Police, Resolution Still Elusive." *Washington Post*, June 13, 2019, National sec. Accessed June 25, 2019. https://www.washingtonpost.com.
Lutz, Catherine. 2010. "US Military Bases on Guam in Global Perspective." *Asia-Pacific Journal: Japan Focus* 30, no. 3 (2010): 10.
Maclellan, Nic. "The Nuclear Age in the Pacific Islands." *Contemporary Pacific* 17, no. 2 (2005): 363–372.
Maga, Timorthy P. "Democracy and Defense: The Case of Guam (1918–1941)." *Journal of Pacific History* 20, no. 3 (1985): 156–172.
Maher, Neil M. *Nature's New Deal: The Civilian Conservation Corps and the Roots of the American Environmental Movement*. New York: Oxford University Press, 2009.
Malcolm, George A. *The Government of the Philippine Islands: Its Development and Fundamentals*. Rochester, NY: The Lawyers Co-Operative, 1916.
Maldonado-Torres, Nelson. "On the Coloniality of Being." *Cultural Studies* 21, no. 2 (2007): 247–260.
Mallari, Aaron Abel T. "The Bilibid Prison as an American Colonial Project in the Philippines." *Philippine Sociological Review* 60 (2012): 165–192.
Mancini, J. M. *Art and War in the Pacific World: Making, Breaking, and Taking from Anson's Voyage to the Philippine-American War*. Berkeley: University of California Press, 2018.
———. "The Pacific World and American Art History." In *A Companion to American Art*, by John Davis, Jennifer A. Greenhill, and Jason David LaFountain, 228–245. Malden, MA: Wiley-Blackwell, 2015.
Mardi Gras Grand Bal Masque Given by and for the Benefit of the Kilohana Art League. Honolulu: Hawaiian Gazette Company, 1908.
Marín Román, Héctor. *¡Llego la gringada!: El contexto socio-militar estadounidense en Puerto*

Rico y otros lugares del Caribe hasta 1919. San Juan: Academia Puertorriqueña de la Historia, 2009.
Martinez, Robert. "The Emergence of Imperialist Capitalism and Puerto Rican Emigration, 1879–1901." *Journal of American Ethnic History* 3, no. 2 (Spring 1984): 54–66.
Martínez-Fernández, Luis. "Life in a 'Male City': Native and Foreign Elite Women in Nineteenth-Century Havana." *Cuban Studies* 25 (1995): 27–49.
Maurice, Arthur Bartlett. "The Washington of the Future." *New Country Life* 34, no. 5 (September 1918): 46–54.
McCartney, Paul T. *Power and Progress: American National Identity, the War of 1898, and the Rise of American Imperialism.* Baton Rouge: Louisiana State University Press, 2006.
McCoy, Alfred W., and Francisco A. Scarano, eds. *Colonial Crucible: Empire in the Making of the Modern American State.* Madison: University of Wisconsin Press, 2009.
McCullough, David. *The Path between the Seas: The Creation of the Panama Canal, 1870–1914.* New York: Simon and Schuster, 1977.
McElfresh, Earl B. *Maps and Mapmakers of the Civil War.* New York: Harry N. Abrams, 1999.
Memmott, Paul, and James Davidson. "Exploring a Cross-Cultural Theory of Architecture." *Traditional Dwellings and Settlements Review* 19, no. 2 (2008): 51–68.
Merrill, Dennis. *Negotiating Paradise: U.S. Tourism and Empire in Twentieth-Century Latin America.* Chapel Hill: University of North Carolina Press, 2009.
Mignolo, Walter D. *The Darker Side of the Renaissance: Literacy, Territoriality, and Colonization.* Ann Arbor: University of Michigan Press, 1995.
———. *The Darker Side of Western Modernity: Global Futures, Decolonial Options.* Durham, NC: Duke University Press, 2011.
———. "Delinking: The Rhetoric of Modernity, the Logic of Coloniality, and the Grammar of De-coloniality." *Cultural Studies* 21, no. 2 (2007): 449–514.
Miller, Bonnie. M. *From Liberation to Conquest: The Visual and Popular Cultures of the Spanish-American War of 1898.* Amherst: University of Massachusetts Press, 2011.
Mitchell, W. J. T. "Imperial Landscape." In *The Cultural Geography Reader*, edited by Timothy S. Oakes and Patricia L. Price, 165–169. New York: Routledge, 2006.
Monmonier, Mark. *Maps with the News: The Development of American Journalistic Cartography.* Chicago, IL: University of Chicago Press, 1989.
Monnig, Laurel Anne. "'Proving Chamorro': Indigenous Narratives of Race, Identity, and Decolonization on Guam." PhD diss., University of Illinois, 2007.
Moore, Charles. *Daniel H. Burnham: Architect, Planner of Cities.* 2 vols. Boston, MA: Houghton Mifflin Company, 1921.
———, ed. *The Improvement of the Park System of the District of Columbia.* United States Senate Report no. 166, 57th Congress, 1st Session. Washington, DC: Government Printing Office, 1902.
Moore, Jason W. *Capitalism in the Web of Life: Ecology and the Accumulation of Capital.* London: Verso, 2015.
Morán, Francisco. "José Martí o el convidado de piedra: desenfoques de la identidad nacional." *Arr—idéhistorisk tidsskrift* 1–2 (2013): 1–30.
Moran, Katherine D. "Catholicism and the Making of the U.S. Pacific." *Journal of the Gilded Age and Progressive Era* 12, no. 4 (2013): 434–474.
Morawski, Erica N. "Negotiating the Hotel Nacional de Cuba: Politics, Profits, and Protest." *Journal of the Society of Architectural Historians* 78, no. 1 (March 2019): 90–108.
Moreen, Linda Levin. "Midcentury Planning in San Juan, Puerto Rico: Rexford Guy Tugwell,

Henry Klumb, and Design for 'Modernization.'" Master's thesis, Washington University in St. Louis, 2013.

Morley, Ian. *American Colonisation and the City Beautiful: Filipinos and Planning in the Philippines, 1916–35.* London: Routledge, 2019.

———. *Cities and Nationhood: American Imperialism and Urban Design in the Philippines, 1898–1916.* Honolulu: University of Hawai'i Press, 2018.

Moses, Kelema. "Almost, but Not Quite: Architecture and the Reconstruction of Space in the Territory of Hawaii." In *Colonial Frames, Nationalist Histories: Imperial Legacies, Architecture, and Modernity,* edited by Madhuri Desai and Mrinalini Rajagopalan, 161–184. Burlington, VT: Ashgate, July 2012.

Mundigo, Axel I., and Dora P. Crouch. "The City Planning Ordinances of the Laws of the Indies Revisited. Part 1: Their Philosophy and Implications." *Town Planning Review* 48, no. 3 (1977): 247–268.

Na'puti, Tiara. "Archipelagic Rhetoric: Remapping the Marianas and Challenging Militarization from 'A Stirring Place.'" *Communication and Critical/Cultural Studies* 16, no. 1 (2019): 4–25.

———. "Speaking the Language of Peace: Chamoru Resistance and Rhetoric in Guahan's Self-Determination Movements." *Anthropologica* 56, no. 2 (2014): 301–313.

Na'puti, Tiara R., and Michael Lujan Bevacqua. "Militarization and Resistance from Guåhan: Protecting and Defending Pågat." *American Quarterly* 67, no. 3 (2015): 837–858.

Natividad, Lisalinda, and Gwyn Kirk. "Fortress Guam: Resistance to US Military Mega-Buildup." *Asia-Pacific Journal: Japan Focus* 19, no. 1 (2010): 1–17.

Navarro-Rivera, Pablo. "The Imperial Enterprise and Educational Policies in Colonial Puerto Rico." In *Colonial Crucibles: Empire in the Making of the Modern American State,* edited by Alfred W. McCoy and Francisco A. Scarano, 163–174. Madison: University of Wisconsin Press, 2009.

Negroni, Héctor Andrés. *Historia militar de Puerto Rico.* San Juan: Comisión Puertorriqueña para la Celebración del Quinto Centenario del Descubrimiento de América y Puerto Rico, 1991.

Negrón-Muntaner, Frances (director). *War for Guam.* Documentary film. San Juan: Polymorphous Pictures, 2015. Accessed April 14, 2021. www.warforguam.com.

Nelson, Christopher. *Mapping the Civil War: Featuring Rare Maps from the Library of Congress.* Colorado: Fulcrum, 1992.

Niell, Paul. "El Templete: Classicism and the Dialectics of Colonial Urban Space in Early-Nineteenth Century Havana, Cuba." In *Buen Gusto and Classicism in the Visual Cultures of Latin America, 1780–1910,* edited by Paul B. Niell and Stacie G. Widdifield, 49–71. Albuquerque: University of New Mexico Press, 2013.

———. *Urban Space as Heritage in Late Colonial Cuba: Classicism and Dissonance on the Plaza de Armas of Havana, 1754–1828.* Austin: University of Texas Press, 2015.

Niell, Paul B., and Stacie G. Widdifield, eds. *Buen Gusto and Classicism in the Visual Cultures of Latin America, 1780–1910.* Albuquerque: University of New Mexico Press, 2013.

Nieuwenhuis, Marijn. "A Right to Breathe." *Critical Legal Thinking,* January 19, 2015. Accessed June 1, 2019. http://criticallegalthinking.com.

Nixon, Rob. *Slow Violence and the Environmentalism of the Poor.* Cambridge, MA: Harvard University Press, 2013.

Noble, Safiya Umoja. "Teaching Trayvon: Race, Media, and the Politics of Spectacle." *Black Scholar* 44, no. 1 (2014): 12–29.

Nolan, Ron S., Ron R. McConnaughey, and Charles R. Stearns. "Fishes Inhabiting Two

Small Nuclear Test Craters at Enewetak Atoll, Marshall Islands." *Micronesia* 11, no. 2 (1975): 205–217.
O'Malley, Therese. "'A Public Museum of Trees': Mid-Nineteenth Century Plans for the Mall." In *The Mall in Washington, 1791–1991,* edited by Richard Longstreth, 37–58. Washington, DC: National Gallery of Art, 1991.
Olivares, José de, and William Smith Bryan. *Our Islands and Their People as Seen with Camera and Pencil.* 2 vols. St. Louis, MO: N. D. Thompson, 1899.
Olmsted, Frederick Law. "The Esthetic Value of Tropical Scenery." *Landscape Architecture* 5, no. 3 (April 1915): 124–133.
———. "A Report upon the Landscape Architecture of the Columbian Exposition to the American Institute of Architects." *American Architect and Building News* 41, no. 924 (September 9, 1893): 151–154.
Ortiz Colom, Jorge. "The Puerto Rican Casa Criolla: Identity and Domestic Space." Unpublished conference paper presented at the 2011 Vernacular Architecture Forum annual meeting in Falmouth, Jamaica. https://www.academia.edu.
Owen, Amy. 2010. "Guam Culture, Immigration and the US Military Build-Up." *Asia Pacific Viewpoint* 51, no. 3 2010: 304–318.
Pallasmaa, Juhani. *The Eyes of the Skin: Architecture and the Senses.* New York: Wiley and Sons, 1995.
Pante, Michael. "Mobility and Modernity in the Urban Transport Systems of Colonial Manila and Singapore." *Journal of Social History* 47, no. 4 (2014): 855–877.
Parenti. Christian. *Tropic of Chaos: Climate Change and the New Geography of Violence.* New York: Bold Type Books, 2011.
Parsons, William E. "Burnham as a Pioneer in City Planning." *Architectural Record* 38 (July–December 1915): 13–31.
Peñate, Florencia. "Apuntes sobre la escultura en Centro Habana y su entorno." *Arquitectura y urbanismo* 31, no. 3 (2010): 88–96.
Perez, Cecelia. "A Chamorro Retelling of Liberation." In *Kinalamten Pulitikat-Sinehten I Chamorro/Issues in Guam's Political Development: The Chamorro Perspective,* 70–77. Mangilao, Guam: Guam Political Status Education Coordination Commission, 1996.
Perez, Craig Santos. "Cultures of Commemoration: The Politics of War, Memory, and History in the Mariana Islands by Keith L. Camacho)." Review. *Contemporary Pacific* 25 (2013): 190–192.
Pérez, Louis A., Jr. *Cuba in the American Imagination: Metaphor and the Imperial Ethos.* Chapel Hill: University of North Carolina Press, 2008.
———. *On Becoming Cuban: Identity, Nationality, and Culture.* Chapel Hill: University of North Carolina Press, 2008.
———. *The War of 1898: The United States and Cuba in History and Historiography.* Chapel Hill: University of North Carolina Press, 2000.
Peterson, Jon A. *The Birth of City Planning in the United States, 1840–1917.* Baltimore, MD: John Hopkins University Press, 2003.
———. "The Senate Park Commission Plan for Washington, DC: A New Vision for the Capital and the Nation." In *Designing the Nation's Capital: The 1901 Plan for Washington, DC,* edited by Sue Koehler and Pamela Scott, 1–48. Washington, DC: US Commission of Fine Arts, 2006.
Petrosia-Husa, Carmen. "Traditional Medicine in the Marshall Islands." In *Republic of the*

Marshall Islands Ministry of Internal Affairs Historic Preservation Office, Alele Museum. Majuro Atoll: Republic of the Marshall Islands Alele Museum, 2004.

Phillips, Sarah T. *This Land, This Nation: Conservation, Rural America, and the New Deal.* New York: Cambridge University Press, 2007.

Pickles, John. "Texts, Hermeneutics and Propaganda Maps." In *Writing Worlds: Discourse, Text, and Metaphor in the Representation of Landscape,* edited by Trevor Barnes and James Duncan, 193–230. London: Routledge, 2011.

Pinney, Christopher. "The Parallel Histories of Anthropology and Photography." In *Anthropology and Photography, 1860–1920,* ed. Elizabeth Edwards, 74–95. New Haven, CT: Yale University Press in association with the Royal Anthropological Institute, 1992.

Puar, Jasbir K. "Introduction: The Cost of Getting Better." In *The Right to Maim: Debility, Capacity, Disability,* 11–12. Anima. Durham, NC: Duke University Press, 2017.

Pujols, Rolando, and Teresa García Ortiz. *Guía de El Capitolio.* [Spain]: Com-Relieve, 1998.

Quijano, Ánibal. "Coloniality and Modernity/Rationality." *Cultural Studies,* 21, no. 2 (2010): 168–178.

———. "Coloniality of Power, Eurocentrism, and Latin America." *Nepantla: Views from the South* 1, no. 3 (2000): 533–580.

Quiles Rodríguez, Edwin. *La ciudad de los balcones.* San Juan: Editorial Universidad de Puerto Rico, 2009.

———. *San Juan tras la fachada: Una mirada desde sus espacios ocultos, 1508–1900.* 2nd ed. San Juan: Instituto de Cultura Puertorriqueña, 2014.

Rabasa, José. *Inventing America: Spanish Historiography and the Formation of Eurocentrism.* Norman: University of Oklahoma Press, 1993.

Raeburn, John. *A Staggering Revolution: A Cultural History of Thirties Photography.* Champaign: University of Illinois Press, 2006.

Rafael, Vicente L. *Motherless Tongues: The Insurgency of Language amid Wars of Translation.* Durham, NC: Duke University Press, 2016.

Read-Miller, Cynthia. *Main Street U.S.A., in Early Photographs: 113 Detroit Publishing Co. Views.* New York: Dover, 1988.

Reed, Robert R. *City of Pines: The Origins of Baguio as a Colonial Hill Station and Regional Capital.* 2nd ed. Baguio City, Philippines: A-Seven, 1999.

Reese, Carol McMichael, and Thomas F. Reese. "The Architectural Image of Modern Industry in the Canal Zone: Architect Austin Willard Lord." In *The Panama Canal and Its Architectural Legacy, 1905–1920.* Panama City: Fundación Ciudad del Saber, Autoridad del Canal de Panamá and Fundación Arte y Cultura, 2013.

Reheis, Fritz. *Die Kreativität der Langsamkeit.* Darmstadt, Germany: Primus, 1999.

Reps, John W. *The Making of Urban America: A History of City Planning in the United States.* Princeton, NJ: Princeton University Press, 1965.

Richardson, Claiborne T. "The Filipino-American Phenomenon: The Loving Touch." *Black Perspective in Music* 10, no. 1 (Spring 1982): 3–28.

Ries, John, and Mark Weber. "The Fateful Year 1898: The United States Becomes an Imperial Power. The Greate Debate over American Overseas Expansion." *Institute for Historical Review* 13, no. 4 (1993): 4–13.

Rifkin, Mark. "Indigenous Orientations." In *Beyond Settler Time: Temporal Sovereignty and Indigenous Self-Determination,* 1–48. Durham, NC: Duke University Press, 2017.

Rigau, Jorge. *Puerto Rico 1900: Turn-of-the-Century Architecture in the Hispanic Caribbean, 1890–1930.* New York: Rizzoli, 1992.

Ripoll, Carlos. *José Martí, the United States, and the Marxist Interpretation of Cuban History.* New Brunswick, NJ: Transaction Books, 1984.

Ristow, Walter. *American Maps and Mapmakers: Commercial Cartography in the Nineteenth Century.* Detroit, MI: Wayne University Press, 1985.

Rob, Kitchin, and Martin Dodge. "Rethinking Maps." *Progress in Human Geography* 31, no. 3 (2007): 331–344.

Roberts, Brian Russell, and Michelle Ann Stephens, eds. *Archipelagic American Studies.* Durham, NC: Duke University Press, 2017.

Rogers, Robert F. *Destiny's Landfall: A History of Guam.* Honolulu: University of Hawai'i Press, 1995.

Roig de Leuchsenring, Emilio. *La Habana: Apuntes históricos.* Havana: Municipio de la Habana, 1939.

Rosa, Hartmut. *Social Acceleration: A Theory of Modernity.* New York: Columbia University Press, 2015.

Rosskam, Edwin, and Louise Rosskam. Transcript of an oral history interview conducted August 3, 1965. Smithsonian Archives of American Art, Washington, DC, 2002.

Rouse, Irving. *The Taíno: Rise and Decline of the People Who Greeted Columbus.* New Haven, CT: Yale University Press, 1993.

Rowe, Aimee Carrillo, and Eve Tuck. "Settler Colonialism, and Cultural Studies." *Cultural Studies* 17, no. 1 (2017): 1–13.

Royle, Stephen A. "Conservation and Heritage in the Face of Insular Urbanization: The Marshall Islands and Kiribati." *Built Environment* 25, no. 3 (1999): 212–213.

Ruth, H. Mark, J. B. Jones, and Morris M. Grobins. *Guidebook to the Architecture of Guam.* Taipei, Taiwan: The Institute, 1977.

Rutkow, Eric. *American Canopy: Trees, Forests, and the Making of a Nation.* New York: Scribner, 2012.

Rydell, Robert W. *All the World's a Fair: Visions of Empire at American International Expositions, 1876–1916.* Chicago, IL: University of Chicago Press, 2013.

———. "The World's Columbian Exposition of 1893: Racist Underpinnings of a Utopian Artifact." *Journal of American Culture* 1, no. 2 (1978): 253–275.

Sandoval-Strausz, A. K. *Hotel: An American History.* New Haven, CT: Yale University Press, 2007.

San Nicolas-Rocca, Tonia, and James Parrish. "Capturing and Conveying Cultural Knowledge Using Social Media." *International Journal of Knowledge Management* 9, no. 3 (2013): 1–18.

Santos, Angel. "United States Return Was Re-occupation, Not Liberation." *Pacific Daily News,* July 21, 1991, 21–22.

Santos Perez, Craig. "New Pacific Islander Poetry." *Poetry* 208, no. 4 (2016): 373–377.

Scarano, Francisco A. "Censuses in the Transition to Modern Colonialism: Spain and the United States in Puerto Rico." In *Colonial Crucibles: Empire in the Making of the Modern American State,* edited by Alfred W. McCoy and Francisco A. Scarano, 210–219. Madison: University of Wisconsin Press, 2009.

———. *Puerto Rico: Cinco siglos de historia.* 2nd ed. Mexico: McGraw-Hill, 2000.

Scarpaci, Joseph L., Roberto Segre, and Mario Coyula. *Havana: Two Faces of the Antillean Metropolis.* Chapel Hill: University of North Carolina Press, 2002.

Schmidt-Nowara, Christopher. "From Columbus to Ponce de León: Puerto Rican Commemorations between Empires, 1893–1908." In *Colonial Crucibles: Empire in the Making*

of the Modern American State, edited by Alfred W. McCoy and Francisco A. Scarano, 230–237. Madison: University of Wisconsin Press, 2009.
Schulten, Susan. "The Cartography of Slavery and the Authority of Statistics." *Civil War History* 56, no. 1 (2010): 5–32.
———. *The Geographical Imagination in America, 1880–1950.* Chicago, IL: University of Chicago Press, 2001.
———. "Mapping American History." In *Maps: Finding Our Place in the World,* edited by James R. Akerman and Robert W. Karrow, Jr., 159–205. Chicago, IL: University of Chicago Press, 2007.
———. *Mapping the Nation: History and Cartography in Nineteenth-Century America.* Chicago, IL: University of Chicago Press, 2012.
Schulz, Joy. *Hawaiian by Birth: Missionary Children, Bicultural Identity, and U.S. Colonialism in the Pacific.* Lincoln: University of Nebraska Press, 2017.
Schuyler, David. "Frederick Law Olmsted and the World's Columbian Exposition." *Journal of Planning History* 15, no. 1 (February 2016): 3–28.
Schwartz, Rosalie. *Pleasure Island: Tourism and Temptation in Cuba.* Lincoln: University of Nebraska Press, 1997.
Scobie, Alexander. *Hitler's State Architecture: The Impact of Classical Antiquity.* University Park: Published for College Art Association by the Pennsylvania State University Press, 1990.
Scott, James C. *Seeing Like a State: How Certain Schemes to Improve the Human Condition Have Failed.* New Haven, CT: Yale University Press, 1999.
Scott, Mel. *American City Planning since 1890.* Berkeley: University of California Press, 1969.
Scott, Pamela. "L'Enfant's Washington Described: The City in the Public Press, 1791–1795." *Washington History* 3, no. 1 (Spring / Summer 1991): 96–111.
———. "'This Vast Empire': The Iconography of the Mall, 1791–1848." In *The Mall in Washington, 1791–1991,* edited by Richard Longstreth, 39–40. Washington, DC: National Gallery of Art, 1991.
Segre, Roberto. "Havana, from Tacón to Forestier." In *Planning Latin America's Capital Cities, 1850–1950,* edited by Arturo Almandoz, 193–213. New York: Routledge, 2002.
Sepúlveda Rivera, Ánibal. *Puerto Rico urbano: Atlas histórico de la ciudad puertorriqueña.* San Juan: Carimar, 2004.
Severson, Don, Michael D. Horikawa, and Jennifer Saville. *Finding Paradise: Island Art in Private Collections.* Honolulu: Honolulu Academy of Arts, 2002.
Shaw, Angel Velasco, and Luis Francia. *Vestiges of War: The Philippine-American War and the Aftermath of an Imperial Dream, 1899–1999.* New York: New York University Press, 2002.
Shirley, Steven. *Guided by God: The Legacy of the Catholic Church in Philippine Politics.* Singapore: Marshall Cavendish Academic, 2004.
Short, John Rennie. *Representing the Republic: Mapping the United States, 1600–1900.* London: Reaktion Books, 2001.
Silva, Noenoe K. *Aloha Betrayed: Native Hawaiian Resistance to American Colonialism.* Durham, NC: Duke University Press, 2004.
Simpson, Audra. *Mohawk Interruptus: Political Life across the Borders of Settler States* Durham, NC: Duke University Press, 2014.
Smith-Norris, Martha. *Domination and Resistance: The United States and the Marshall Islands during the Cold War.* Honolulu: University of Hawaiʻi Press, 2016.

Souder-Jaffery, Laura Marie Torres. "Psyche under Siege: Uncle Sam, Look What You've Done to Us." In *Uncle Sam in Micronesia: Social Benefits, Social Costs,* edited by Donald H. Rubinstein and Vivian Dames, 120–124. Guam: Micronesian Area Research Centre, University of Guam Press, 1991.

Stepan, Nancy Leys. *Picturing Tropical Nature.* Ithaca, NY: Cornell University Press, 2001.

Stevens Releford, Jodi, and Will C. McClatchey. "Survivor Rongelap: Health Issues and Use of Traditional Medicine among the Women of Rongelap Atoll." *Ethnobotany Journal* 9 (2011): 287–305.

Taft, William H. *Hearing before Committee on Insular Affairs, Friday, February 21, 1902.* Washington, DC: Government Printing Office, 1902.

Talusan, Mary. "Music, Race, and Imperialism: The Philippine Constabulary Band at the 1904 St. Louis World's Fair." "World's Fair 1904," special issue, *Philippine Studies* 52, no. 4, (2004): 499–526.

Tanji, Miyume. "Chamorro Warriors and Godmothers Meet Uncle Sam." In *Gender, Power, and Military Occupations: Asia Pacific and the Middle East since 1945,* edited by Christine De Matos and Rowena Ward, 98–117. Hoboken, NJ: Taylor and Francis, 2012.

Teaiwa, Teresia K. "Militarism, Tourism and the Native: Articulations in Oceania." PhD diss., University of California, 2001.

Tejeira-Davis, Eduardo. "The Architecture of the Panama Canal: Colonialism, Syncretism and Coming to Terms with the Tropics." In *Tropical Architecture: Critical Regionalism in the Age of Globalization,* edited by Alexander Tzonis, Liane Lefaivre, and Bruno Stagno, 155–158. Chichester, UK: Wiley-Academy, 2001.

———. *Panamá: An Architectural and Landscape Guide.* Seville, Spain: Junta de Andalucía, 2007.

Theroux, Paul. *The Old Patagonian Express: By Train through the Americas.* Boston, MA: Houghton Mifflin, 1979.

Thomas, Nicholas. *Colonialism's Culture: Anthropology, Travel, and Government.* Princeton, NJ: Princeton University Press, 1994.

Thompson, Krista A. *Eye for the Tropics: Tourism, Photography, and Framing the Caribbean Picturesque.* Durham, NC: Duke University Press, 2006.

Thompson, Lanny. *Imperial Archipelago: Representation and Rule in the Insular Territories under US Dominion after 1898.* Honolulu: University of Hawai'i Press, 2010.

———. *Nuestra isla y su gente: La construcción del "otro" puertorriqueño en "Our Islands and Their People."* 2nd ed., rev. and exp. Río Piedras: Universidad de Puerto Rico, Centro de Investigaciones Sociales y Departamento de Historia, 2007.

Thompson, Lanny, and María Dolores Luque. *El viaje cartográphico del teniente William H. Armstrong: Puerto Rico, 1908–1912 / The Cartographic Journey of William H. Armstrong: Puerto Rico, 1908–1912.* 2 vols. San Juan: Centro de Investigaciones Históricas and Fundación Puertorriqueña de Humanidades, 2020.

Thompson, Laura. "Guam's Bombed-Out Capital." *Institute of Pacific Relations* 16, no. 6 (1947): 66–69.

Thrum, Thomas G., ed. *Hawaiian Almanac and Annual for 1896.* Honolulu: T. G. Thrum, 1896.

Thurston, Lorrin A. *Hand-Book on the Annexation of Hawaii.* St. Joseph, MI: A. B. Morse, 1897.

Tinio McKenna, Rebecca. *American Imperial Pastoral: The Architecture of US Colonialism in the Philippines.* Chicago, IL: University of Chicago Press, 2017.

Tió, Teresa. "The Graphic Arts of Puerto Rico." *Puerto Rico: Art and Identity.* San Juan: Universidad de Puerto Rico, 1998.

Tucker, Richard P. *Insatiable Appetite: The United States and the Ecological Degradation of the Tropical World.* Berkeley: University of California Press, 2000.

Tugwell, Rexford. *The Place of Planning in Society.* San Juan: Puerto Rico Planning Board, 1958.

Turner, Frederick Jackson. *The Significance of the Frontier in American History.* Mansfield Centre, CT: Martino, 2014.

Tyler, Elaine. *Homeward Bound: American Families in the Cold War.* New York: Basic Books, 2008.

Upton, Dell. *Another City: Urban Life and Urban Spaces in the New American Republic.* New Haven, CT: Yale University Press, 2008.

US Department of Justice. "Guam Claims Program." Last modified June 12, 2018. Accessed June 13, 2018. https://www.justice.gov.

US Marine Corps Forces Pacific. "Draft Environmental Impact Statement / Overseas Environmental Impact Statement for Commonwealth of the Northern Marianas Islands Joint Military Training." Edited by United States Department of the Navy. Honolulu, HI: Naval Facilities Engineering Command, Pacific, 2015.

Uttal, David H. "Seeing the Big Picture: Map Use and the Development of Spatial Cognition." *Developmental Science* 3 (2000): 247–286.

Vergara, Benito M. *Displaying Filipinos: Photography and Colonialism in Early 20th Century Philippines.* Quezon City: University of the Philippines Press, 1995.

Vernon, Christopher. "Daniel Hudson Burnham and the American City Imperial." *Thesis Eleven* 123, no. 1 (2014): 80–105.

Viernes, James Perez. "Fanhasso i Taotao Sumay: Displacement, Dispossession, and Survival in Guam." Master's thesis, Pacific Islands Studies, University of Hawai'i, 2008.

———. "Won't You Please Come Back to Guam? Media Discource, Military Buildup, and Chamorros in the Space Between." CPIS (Negotiating Culture, Place, and Identity in the Pacific) occasional paper. *Contemporary Pacific* 44 (2007): 103–118.

Villalba Garrido, Evaristo. *Cuba y el turismo.* Havana: Editorial de Ciencias Sociales, 1993.

Vivoni Farage, Enrique. *El Capitolio de Puerto Rico, 1907–1929: Origen y transformación de un ideal puertorriqueño.* San Juan: Puerto Rico: n.p., 1991.

Vlach, John Michael. "The Shotgun House: An African Architectural Legacy." In *Common Places: Readings in American Vernacular Architecture,* edited by Dell Upton and John Michael Vlach, 58–78. Athens: University of Georgia Press, 1986.

Wadsworth, Frank. "The Development of the Forest Land Resources of the Luquillo Mountains, Puerto Rico." PhD diss., University of Michigan, 1949.

Wasserman, Harvey. *Killing Our Own: The Disaster of America's Experience with Atomic Radiation.* New York: Random House, 1982.

Weaver, Peter L. *The Luquillo Mountains: Forest Resources and Their History.* San Juan: International Institute of Tropical Forestry, 2012.

Weiss, Joaquín E. *La arquitectura colonial cubana: Siglos XVI al XIX.* Havana: Instituto Cubano del Libro, Agencia Española de Cooperación International, and Consejería de Obras Públicas y Transportes Junta de Andalucia, 1996.

Whiting, Edward Clark, and William Lyman Phillips. "Frederick Law Olmsted—1870–1957: An Appreciation of the Man and His Achievements." *Landscape Architecture* 48, no. 3 (April 1958): 144–157.

Williams, Riánna M. "Hawaiian *Ali'i* Women in New York Society: The Ena-Coney-Vos-Gould Connection." *Hawaiian Journal of History* 38 (2004): 147–164.
Williams, Walter L. "United States Indian Policy and the Debate over Philippine Annexation: Implications for the Origins of American Imperialism." *Journal of American History* 66, no. 4 (1980): 810–831.
Wilson, Richard Guy. "Imperial American Identity at the Panama Canal." In *Modulus 1980–81: The University of Virginia School of Architecture Review*. Charlottesville: University of Virginia, 1981, 22-29.
Wilson, William H. *The City Beautiful Movement*. Baltimore, MD: John Hopkins University Press, 1989.
Winchester, Simon. *Pacific: Silicon Chips and Surfboards, Coral Reefs and Atom Bombs, Brutal Dictators, Fading Empires, and the Coming Collision of the World's Superpowers*. New York City: HarperCollins, 2015.
Winthrop, Beekman. *Fifth Annual Report of the Governor of Porto Rico Covering the Period from July 1, 1904, to June 30, 1905*. Washington, DC: Government Printing Office, 1905.
Wolfe, Patrick. "Settler Colonialism, and the Elimination of the Native." *Journal of Genocide Research* 8, no. 4 (2006): 387–409.
———. *Settler Colonialism and the Transformation of Anthropology: The Politics and Poetics of an Ethnographic Event*. New York: Cassell, 1999.
Wood, Denis. "Maps and Mapmaking." *Cartographica* 30, no. 1 (Spring 1993): 1–9.
Woodward, David. *The All-American Map: Wax Engraving and Its Influence on Cartography*. Chicago, IL: University of Chicago Press, 1977.
Woodward, Valerie. "'I Guess They Didn't Want Us Asking Too Many Questions': Reading American Empire in Guam." *Contemporary Pacific* 25, no. 1 (2013): 67–91, 218.
Worcester, Dean Conant. "The Non-Christian Peoples of the Philippine Islands." *National Geographic Magazine* 24, no. 11 (November 1913): 1157–1256.
———. *The Philippines Past and Present*. Vol. 2. New York: Macmillan Company, 1914.
Worster, Donald. *Dust Bowl: The Southern Plains in the 1930s*. New York: Oxford University Press, 1979.
———. *Nature's Economy: A History of Ecological Ideas*. London: Cambridge University Press, 1994.
Young, James Rankin. *Reminiscences and Thrilling Stories of the War by Returned Heroes*. Lancaster, PA: H. B. Bixler, 1899.
Zapata, Claudia E. "Walter Horne's 'Triple Execution' Postcards: Death on the Border." *Panhandle-Plains Historical Review* 88 (Fall 2017): 49–63.

Contributors

Alejandro T. Acierto is an artist, musician, and writer broadly concerned with the breath, the voice, and the processes that enable them. He has presented projects domestically and internationally and is coauthor of the artist book *CQDE: A Feminist Manifestx of Code-ing* published by Sybil Press with KT Duffy. His writing also appears in the *Journal for Asian Diasporic Visual Cultures and the Americas*. He was an inaugural artist in residence for critical race studies at Michigan State University and a Mellon Assistant Professor of Digital Art and New Media at Vanderbilt University. He is currently an assistant professor of interdisciplinary arts and performance at Arizona State University, New College.

Chris Balaschak is an associate professor and coordinator of art history at Flagler College in St. Augustine, Florida. Professor Balaschak specializes in histories of photography, modern and contemporary art, and visual culture. His research is focused on visual culture at the intersection of place-based politics, environmentalism, and social planning. Dr. Balaschak's book *The Image of Environmental Harm in American Social Documentary Photography* (Routledge, 2021) considers the ways that American photographers responded to the environmental consequences of federal infrastructure throughout the twentieth century.

Sylvia C. Frain earned her PhD with the National Centre for Peace and Conflict Studies at the University of Otago and currently serves as a research associate with the Micronesian Area Research Center at the University of Guam. She was the inaugural postdoctoral fellow with the Pacific Media Centre at Auckland University of Technology and continues as a member of the Vakatele Pacific Research Network. Along with the National Centre for Peace and Conflict Studies alumni Dr. Monica Carr, she cofounded The Everyday Peace Initiative to bridge peace research and community action for everyday peace builders.

JOSEPH R. HARTMAN is assistant professor of art history and Latinx and Latin American studies at the University of Missouri–Kansas City. Hartman's book *Dictator's Dreamscape: How Architecture and Vision Built Machado's Cuba and Invented Modern Havana* (2019) focuses on the intersections of architecture, visual culture, and politics in Cuba and the United States' insular empire. The Graham Foundation for Advanced Studies in the Fine Arts supported the book's publication. Hartman's articles have appeared in the *Journal of the Society of Architectural Historians*, *Cultural Politics* and *The Latin Americanist*, among others. Hartman is currently conducting research for a book manuscript on the cultural politics and visual history of hurricanes in the modern Caribbean.

STACY L. KAMEHIRO is associate professor of history of art and visual culture at the University of California, Santa Cruz. Her book *The Arts of Kingship: Hawaiian Art and National Culture of the Kalākaua Era* offers a detailed account of Hawaiian public art, architecture, and cultural institutions from 1874 to 1891. She has published on Hawaiian colonial visual and material culture, race images in American trade cards, phrenological casts from Oceania, empire and American art history, world fairs, and civic engagement in public art projects. Kamehiro's current work examines Hawaiian material culture collecting and exhibition practices in the nineteenth century in local and international contexts.

BONNIE M. MILLER is professor of history at the University of Massachusetts Boston. She is the author of *From Liberation to Conquest: The Visual and Popular Cultures of the Spanish American War of 1898* (2011). Other publications include book chapters on the Trans-Mississippi and International Exposition commemorative stamp issue of 1898 and a survey of war and visual culture throughout US history. In food studies Miller has published an essay on the historical evolution of pizza, an analysis of the food exhibits of the San Francisco Panama-Pacific International Exposition, and a history of rice consumption in the United States. Most recently, she was guest editor for a special issue in *Food, Culture & Society* on the cultural history of food at fairs and expositions.

ERICA MORAWSKI is assistant professor in the Department of Art and Design History at Pratt Institute in New York. She earned her PhD at the University of Illinois at Chicago. Her research investigates how design mediates relationships between state and populace through approaches that seek to privilege underrepresented histories. Focusing primarily on the Hispanic Caribbean within a global context, her research is especially engaged with industrial design and architecture. She has published in the *Journal of Design History*,

Journal of the Society of Architectural Historians, and has essays in *The Politics of Furniture: Identity, Diplomacy and Persuasion* and *Design History beyond the Canon*.

IAN MORLEY is an associate professor in the Department of History at the Chinese University of Hong Kong. He has published widely on the design of the American colonial environment in the Philippines. Examples of his work include *Cities and Nationhood: American Imperialism and Urban Design in the Philippines, 1898–1916* (University of Hawai'i Press, 2018) and *American Colonisation and the City Beautiful: Filipinos and City Planning in the Philippines, 1916–35* (Routledge 2019), the latter being joint winner of the 2020 International Planning History Society Bosma Book Prize for Planning History Innovation.

PAUL B. NIELL is associate professor in the Department of Art History at Florida State University. He specializes in the architecture and material culture of the Caribbean with an emphasis on the Spanish-speaking islands in the colonial period. His articles have appeared in *The Art Bulletin*, the *Bulletin of Latin American Research*, and the *Colonial Latin American Review*, among others. He is author of *Urban Space as Heritage in Late Colonial Cuba: Classicism and Dissonance on the Plaza de Armas of Havana, 1754–1828* (University of Texas Press, 2015) and coeditor, with Stacie G. Widdifield, of *Buen Gusto and Classicism in the Visual Cultures of Latin America, 1780–1910* (University of New Mexico Press, 2013).

KRYSTLE STRICKLIN is a PhD candidate in the Department of History of Art and Architecture at the University of Pittsburgh. She was awarded a 2019–2020 Smithsonian American Art Museum Predoctoral Fellowship to complete her research on photography, violence, and death in the American empire. She has been the recipient of numerous grants and awards, including the Ailsa Mellon Bruce Predoctoral Fellowship from the Center for Advanced Study in the Visual Arts, and, most recently, the Joan and Stanford Alexander Award for research on the history of photography from the Museum of Fine Arts, Houston.

LANNY THOMPSON is professor and director of the Department of Sociology and Anthropology at the University of Puerto Rico–Río Piedras. His publications have explored the connections among photographic representations and hegemony, education and disciplinary institutions, and laws and governance in Puerto Rico, Cuba, Hawai'i, Guam, and the Philippines. His articles have appeared in academic journals in Spain, Puerto Rico, the Philippines, and the United States. He is the author of *Imperial Archipelago: Representation and Rule in the Insular Territories under US Dominion after 1898*. Recently he has explored the philosophical and methodological bases of archipelagic thinking.

CHRISTOPHER VERNON is associate professor in the School of Design at the University of Western Australia. He is an award-winning teacher of design and the history and theory of landscape architecture. Vernon is a leading authority on the lives and works of Walter Burley Griffin and Marion Mahony Griffin, designers of Australia's capital city Canberra, widely lecturing and publishing on the subject. More broadly, his research focuses upon architecture and landscape as collective expressions of identity, be it place or nation, especially within the context of designed capitals such as Canberra, New Delhi, and Brasília.

BRENDA S. GARDENOUR WALTER holds a BA in history from the University of New Hampshire and a masters and PhD in medieval history from Boston University. Her research examines the role of Aristotelian discourse, learned medicine, and scholastic theology in the construction of alterity, as well as the continued influence of medieval "otherness" in popular culture. Her most recent publications examine the multivalent relationships between cultural constructions of the body, architectural theory, and the natural world. She is emerita professor of history at the Saint Louis College of Pharmacy.

Index

Page numbers for figures are in **boldface**.

Perspectives on the Global Past

Anand A. Yang and Kieko Matteson
SERIES EDITORS

Interactions: Transregional Perspectives on World History
Edited by Jerry H. Bentley, Renate Bridenthal, and Anand A. Yang

Contact and Exchange in the Ancient World
Edited by Victor H. Mair

Seascapes: Maritime Histories, Littoral Cultures, and Transoceanic Exchanges
Edited by Jerry H. Bentley, Renate Bridenthal, and Kären Wigen

Anthropology's Global Histories: The Ethnographic Frontier in German New Guinea, 1870–1935
Rainer F. Buschmann

Creating the New Man: From Enlightenment Ideals to Socialist Realities
Yinghong Cheng

Glamour in the Pacific: Cultural Internationalism and Race Politics in the Women's Pan-Pacific
Fiona Paisley

The Qing Opening to the Ocean: Chinese Maritime Policies, 1684–1757
Gang Zhao

Navigating the Spanish Lake: The Pacific in the Iberian World, 1521–1898
Rainer F. Buschmann, Edward R. Slack Jr., and James B. Tueller

Nomads as Agents of Cultural Change: The Mongols and Their Eurasian Predecessors
Edited by Reuven Amitai and Michal Biran

Sea Rovers, Silver, and Samurai: Maritime East Asia in Global History, 1550–1700
Edited by Tonio Andrade and Xing Hang

Exile in Colonial Asia: Kings, Convicts, Commemoration
Edited by Ronit Ricci

Burnt by the Sun: The Koreans of the Russian Far East
Jon K. Chang

Shipped but Not Sold: Material Culture and the Social Protocols of Trade during Yemen's Age of Coffee
Nancy Um

Encounters Old and New in World History: Essays Inspired by Jerry H. Bentley
Edited by Alan Karras and Laura J. Mitchell

At the Edge of the Nation: The Southern Kurils and the Search for Russia's National Identity
Paul B. Richardson

Liminality of the Japanese Empire: Border Crossings from Okinawa to Colonial Taiwan
Hiroko Matsuda

Sudden Appearances: The Mongol Turn in Commerce, Belief, and Art
Roxann Prazniak

A Power in the World: The Hawaiian Kingdom in Oceania
Lorenz Gonschor

Transcending Patterns: Silk Road Cultural and Artistic Interactions through Central Asian Textile Images
Mariachiara Gasparini

Spreading Protestant Modernity: Global Perspectives on the Social Work of the YMCA and YWCA, 1870–1970
Edited by Harald Fischer-Tiné, Stefan Huebner, and Ian Tyrrell

Land of Plants in Motion: Japanese Botany and the World
Thomas R. H. Havens

Imperial Islands: Art, Architecture, and Visual Experience in the US Insular Empire after 1898
Edited by Joseph R. Hartman